DAWN & DUSK RAINBOW PRAYER

Traditional Hymns,
Psalms, Canticles, Sayings of Jesu[illegible]
and Readings on the Christian Li[illegible]
for the Liturgical Year

meditation rendering by
Stephen Joseph Wolf

www.idjc.org

Dawn & Dusk Rainbow Prayer

If you need the masculine pronouns for God in traditional translations, you will not like this rendering. For the holy name *YHVH* or Yahweh, the Hebrew word for "My Lord" (***Adonai***) is used, pronounced ***ah-duh-'nigh***, and the Aramaic word ***Abba*** for Father. See page 760 for the other choices made in this meditation rendering.

HOW TO USE THIS BOOK

I take off my shoes, sit up, offer up my still incomplete awareness of the illusions by which I live, and ask God to speak God's name in the center of my soul.

I make the Sign of the Cross with the Psalm 70 verse and the Doxology: ***Glory to the Father and to the Son and to the Holy Spirit, as it was in the beginning, is now, and will be forever.****

I sing one of the Songs.

For each Psalm or Canticle, I recite the Antiphon and then the full poem. If limited by time, I omit the *Psalms* with headings in *italics*, (from the traditional Office of Readings, Daytime, and Night Prayer.)

I choose a Reading, or read a chapter from my Bible using a daily reading plan, and then recite the day's Responsory.

I recite the Gospel Antiphon followed by the Gospel Canticle. (In Morning Prayer instead of the Gsopel Canticle I often use the Gospel Reading of the day from my Bible as indicated with the Antiphon; most people will simply use the Gospel Canticle.) Then come the Doxology ****Glory to***..., and then the Antiphon is repeated.

Petitions and Intercessions are provided, and they conclude with the Lord's Prayer and the Sign of the Cross. - Steve Wolf

ISBN 978-1-937081-74-4 This First Edition

ISBN 978-1-937081-72-0 *Dawn & Dusk Rainbow for Ordinary Time* (does not include Advent, Christmas, Lent & Easter) 525 pp.

ISBN 978-1-937081-73-7 *Rainbow Prayer* (abridged version) 175 pp.

printed and distributed by Ingram Books

published by IDJC Press www.idjc.org

Dawn & Dusk Rainbow Prayer

First Sunday of Advent, Christmas Day, Solemnity of Mary, Epiphany, & Baptism of the Lord – use Sunday of Week One
Easter Sunday, 2nd Sunday of Easter, Ascension, Pentecost, Trinity Sunday, & Corpus Christi – use Sunday of Week One
Holy Family & Palm Sunday – use Sunday of Week Two
Christmas Weekdays – Week One until Jan 1, then Week Two
Ash Wednesday – use Wednesday of Week Two

WEEK I
VIGIL of SUNDAY
(Saturday Evening)

+ *God, come to my assistance;* Psalm 70:2
Lord, make haste to help me!

Glory...

ORDINARY TIME

A **Now thank we all our God**
With heart and hands and voi-ces,
Who won-drous things has done,
In whom this world re-joi-ces;
Who from our mo-thers' arms
Has blessed/ us on our way
With count-less gifts of love,
And still is ours to-day.

All praise and thanks to God
Our Ab-ba now be giv-en,
With Son and Spir-it as
They reign in high-est heav-en:
The one e-ter-nal God,
Whom heav-en and earth a-dore!
For thus it was, is now,
And shall be ev-er-more.

111, see Ecclesiastes 50:22-24
Text: Martin Rinckart, 1636,
translation by Catherine Winkworth, 1858, altered
Music: 67 67 66 66, NUN DANKET; Johann Cruger, 1648

B **We gath-er to-geth-er**
to ask the Lord's bless-ing;
Who chast-ens and hast-ens
the Way to make known.
The wick-ed op-press-ing
now cease/ from dis-tress-ing.
Sing prais-es to the Name\;
God for-gets not God's own.

Be-side us to guide us,
our God with us join-ing,
Or-dain-ing, main-tain-ing
the king-dom div-ine;
So from the be-gin-ning
the fight/ we were win-ning,
You, Lord, were at our side\,
all glo-ry be thine!

We all do ex-tol you,
our Lead-er tri-umph-ant,
And pray that you still our
De-fend-er will be.
Let your con-gre-ga-tion
es-cape the trib-u-la-tion;
Your Name be ev-er praised\!
O Lord, make us free!

132, Text: Dutch:*Wilt heden nu treden*, 1597,
translated by Theodore Baker, 1894, altered
Music: 12 11 12 11 KREMSER; *Nederlandtsche Gedenckclanck*,
by Adrianus Valerius, 1626; arranged and translated
from Dutch to Latin by Edward Kremser, 1877

ADVENT

Cre-a-tor of the stars of night,
Your peo-ple's ev-er-last-ing light,
Re-deem-er Je-sus, save us all,
And hear your ser-vants when we call.

You griev-ing that the an-cient curse
Should doom to death a u-niv-erse,
Find now the med-i-cine of grace,
To save and heal the hu-man race.

See now the Bride-groom of the bride,
As drew the world to eve-ning tide;
Pro-ceed-ing from a vir-gin shrine,
As ful-ly hu-man and div-ine.

This Awe-some Name, ma-jes-tic now,
All knees to bend and hearts to bow;
All things ce-les-tial God does own,
And things ter-res-trial, God a-lone.

To God the Fa-ther, God the Son,
And God the Spir-it, Three in One,
Laud, ho-nor, might, and glo-ry be
From age to age e-ter-nal-ly.

6, Text: 7th Century unknown author;
translated by John M. Neale, 1852, altered
Music: CONDITOR, LM; *Conditor Alme Siderum*, Sarum plainsong, Mode IV

CHRISTMAS

An-gels we have heard on high
Sweet-ly sing-ing o'er the plains,
And the moun-tains in re-ply
E-cho back their joy-ous strains.

Refrain **G**lo__-ri-a in ex-cel-sis De-o!
Glo__-ri-a in ex-cel-sis De\-o!

Shep-herds why this ju-bi-lee?
Why your joy-ous strains pro-long?
Say what may the ti-dings be
Which in-spire your heav'n-ly song.

Refrain

Come to Beth-le-hem and see
Him whose birth the an-gels sing;
Come, a-dore on bend-ed knee
Christ the Lord the new-born King.

Refrain

17, Text: French, 18th C.;
translated from *Crown of Jesus Music, II,* London, 1862.
Music: 77 77 GLORIA with refrain, traditional French carol

LENT

Lord, who through-out these for-ty days
For us did fast and pray,
Teach us with you to mourn our sins
And close by you to stay.

As you with Sa-tan did con-tend,
And did the vic-t'ry win,
O give us strength in you to fight,
In you to con-quer sin.

As you did hun-ger bear, and thirst,
So teach us, gra-cious Lord,
To die to self, and so to live
In your most ho-ly Word.

And through these days of pen-i-tence,
And in your Pas-chal Way,
Yes, ev-er-more through life and death,
Lord Je-sus, with us stay.

A-bide with us, and when this life
With suf-fer-ing has passed
An East-er of un-end-ing joy
May we at-tain at last.

48, Text: Claudia F. Hernaman,
Child's Book of Praise: A Manuel of Devotion, 1873,altered
Music: ST. FLAVIAN, CM, *Day's Psalter* , 1563

EASTER

At the Lamb's high feast we sing,
Praise to our vic-tor-ious King,
Who has washed us in the tide
Flow-ing from his pier-ced side;
Praise we him/, whose love div-ine
Gives his sa-cred blood for wine,
Gives his bod-y for the feast,
Christ the Vic-tim, Christ the Priest.

Where the Pas-chal blood is poured,
Death's dark an-gel sheathes his sword;
Is-rael's hosts tri-um-phant go
Through the wave that drowns the foe.
Praise we Christ/, whose blood was shed,
Pas-chal Vic-tim, Pas-chal Bread;
With sin-cer-i-ty and love
Eat we Man-na from a-bove.

Migh-ty Vic-tim from the sky,
Hell's fierce pow'rs be-neath you lie;
You have o-pened Par-a-dise,
That in you your saints may rise.
Hymns of glo/-ry and of praise,
Fa-ther now to you we raise;
Ris-en Lord, all praise to thee,
Ev-er with the Spir-it be.

64, Text: Author unknown, 6th Century?,
translated by Robert Campbell,1849,altered
Music: 77 77 D, SALZBURG; Jakob Hintze, 1678

PSALM 4

Antiphon *You are witnesses of these things,* Lk 24:46
the Christ to suffer, and rise on the third day.

Advent & Lent My God, be merciful to me
and hear my prayer.

Christmas & Easter Alleluia, alleluia, alleluia.

When I call, answer me, saving God.
From distress you give me relief.
Be merciful to me and hear my prayer.

Until when, human, will you shame the glory?
Until when will you love delusion and seek the lie?
Know that Adonai set apart the faithful for Adonai
and will hear when I call.

When you tremble in awe, do not sin.
Search in your heart and on your bed, and be silent.
Offer sacrifices of goodness, and trust Adonai.

Many are asking, "Who can show us good?
Adonai, let the light of your faces shine upon us."

You put joy in my heart, more joy
than when their grain and new wine abound.
In the peace of God's face I will lie down and sleep,
for you alone, Adonai, make me dwell in safety.

Glory... Antiphon

PSALM 61

Antiphon *Come to me, all who labor and are burdened,*
and I will rest you; my yoke is gentle
and my burden is light. Mt 11:28-30

Advent & Lent God, you are my refuge
and my tower of strength.

Christmas & Easter Alleluia, alleluia, alleluia.

Hear, God, my cry! Listen to my prayer!
From the edge of the earth I call to you
as my heart grows faint.

To the high rock you lead me
for you are my refuge
and tower of strength against adversity.

I would dwell in your tent for forevers
and take refuge in the shelter of your wings.
For you, God, hearing my vows,
gave inheritance to those revering your name.

You increase the days upon days of the royal one,
and the years for generation and generation,
enthroned in God's presences forever,
appointed and protected in God's love and fidelity.

I will sing praise of your name forever
to fulfill my vows day by day.

Glory... Antiphon

PSALM 113

Antiphon *No servant can serve two lords,*
and you cannot serve
God and mammon. Lk 16:13

Advent Rejoice, Jerusalem,
let your joy overflow;
your Savior will come to you,
alleluia.

Christmas The whole world longs to see
the Ruler who is our peace, alleluia.

Epiphany Begotten of God before the daystar
shined or time began, our Savior
has appeared on earth, alleluia.

Lent The Lord says: turn away from sin
and open your heart to the Gospel.

Easter The Lord our God,
high above the heavens,
raises up the lowly from the dust,
alleluia.

Ascension Christ neither left heaven when
coming to us nor withdrew from us
when going again into heaven.
Saint Augustine

Hallelujah!

Praise, you who serve Adonai!
Praise the name Adonai!

Blessed be the name of Adonai
from now and to forevermore.
From the rising of the sun to its setting
praised be the name Adonai.

Exalted over all the nations is Adonai,
the glory above the heavens.
Who is like our God Adonai,
sitting enthroned on high,
stooping to look down
on the heavens and the earth?

Adonai raises the poor from dust
and lifts up the needy from ash heaps
to sit with royals, the royals of the people,
and settles the childless woman in a home,
a happy mother of children.

Hallelujah!

Glory...

Antiphon

---

50 of the psalms are unattributed.
73 of the psalms are attributed to David (about 1,000 BC),
12 each to sons of Asaph & Korah, 2 of Solomon and one (Ps 90) to Moses.

PSALM 116:10-19

Antiphon *As I, the Lord and Teacher,*
washed your feet,
so also are you
to wash the feet of each other. Jn 13:14

Advent I, the Lord, am coming to save you;
already I am near;
soon I will set you free.

Christmas Precious are you
in the eyes of the Lord,
alleluia.

Epiphany Awesome is the Lord our God,
transcending all other "gods,"
alleluia.

Baptism of the Lord As Jesus was baptized,
he came out of the water
and the heavens opened.

Lent I will offer the sacrifice of praise
and call on the name of the Lord.

Easter Lord, you have broken
the chains that held me bound;
I will offer you a sacrifice of praise,
alleluia.

I believed it and so said,
"I am greatly afflicted."
I said when it dismayed me,
"Everyone is a liar."

How can I repay to Adonai
all the goodness to me?
I will lift the cup of salvation
and call on the name of Adonai.

My vows to Adonai I will now fulfill
in the presence of all the people.
Precious in the eyes of Adonai
are the saints to the death.

Adonai, I am your servant,
your servant and child of your servant;
you freed me from the chains.
I will offer the sacrifice of thanksgiving
and call on the name of Adonai.

My vows to Adonai I will now fulfill
in the presence of all the people,
in courts of the house of Adonai,
in your midst, Jerusalem.

Hallelujah!

Glory...

Antiphon

PSALM 141

Antiphon	*Blessed are the merciful,* *for they will receive mercy.* Mt 5:7
Advent	Proclaim the good news among the nations: our God will come to save us.
Christmas	As the smoke of incense, Lord, may my prayer rise to you, alleluia.
Epiphany	The star burned as a flame, pointing the way to God, the Ruler of rulers, alleluia.
Lent 1st 3rd Sundays	Lord God, we ask you to receive us and be pleased with the sacrifice we offer you this day with humble and contrite hearts.
Lent 5th Sun	I will place my law in their hearts; I will be their God, and they will be my people.
Easter	Like the evening offering my hands rise up in prayer to you, O Lord, alleluia.

Adonai, I call to you; be quick to come to me.
Hear my voice when I call to you.
May my prayer be as incense set before you,
lifting my hands in evening sacrifice.

Set guard, Adonai, over my mouth.
Keep watch over the gate of my lips.
Let my heart not be drawn to evil matter,
to join in bad deeds with their doers
or to eat of their delicacies.

Let the just person strike me, a kindness,
and rebuke me, as oil on my head;
my head will not refuse this,
my prayer is ever against bad deeds.

Their rulers will drop over cliff edge;
they will learn that my words were well spoken:
"As a farmer breaks up the earth,
bones were scattered at the mouth of Sheol."

But on you, Lord Adonai, are my eyes,
and in you I take refuge;
do not give my self over to death.

Keep me from the hands of the snares
and from the traps of those doing the bad.
When they fall together into their nets,
keep me in safety.

Glory... Antiphon

PSALM 142

Antiphon *Let the light of you shine before humanity,*
that they may see your good works
and give glory to your Abba in heaven.
Mt 5:16

Advent
Know that the Lord is coming
and with all the saints;
that day will dawn
with a wonderful light, alleluia.

Christmas
You, Lord, are my refuge
in the land of the living,
alleluia.

Epiphany
The magi saw the sign and
brought their gifts in homage, alleluia.

Lent 1st 3rd Sundays
Call upon the Lord who will hear you
and to your cries will answer:
here I am.

Lent 5th 7th Sundays
I count as loss everything
but the surpassing worth
of knowing Christ Jesus my Lord.

Easter
You led me forth from my prison,
that I may give praise to your name,
alleluia.

My voice cries to Adonai;
my voice asks for mercy from Adonai,
before whom I pour out my complaint,
before whom I tell my trouble.
When my spirit grows faint within me
then you know my way.

In the path where I walk they hid a snare for me.
Look right and see: the one with concern for me
has fled away from me for refuge;
there is no one who cares for my life.

I cry to you, Adonai, and say you are my refuge,
my portion in the land of the living.
Listen, El, to my cry, for I am in desperate need.

Rescue me from the strong ones pursuing me;
set my self free from prison to praise your name.
The just ones will gather about me
because you are good to me.

Glory…

Antiphon

—

True
Humility
is the grace of
awareness of how I am
created uniquely in God's
image, seeing myself as neither
better than I am nor less than I am.
Humility is reality; pride is an illusion.
Debasement of the self is also an illusion.

PHILIPPIANS 2:6-11

Antiphon *Do nothing out of selfishness*
or for vainglory,
but humbly deem others
as greater than yourselves. Phil 2:3

Advent 1st Sun The Lord will come with mighty power;
all mortal eyes shall see the Lord.

Advent 3rd Sun Lord, send the Lamb, the ruler of the earth,
from the rock in the desert
to the mountain of the daughter of Zion.

Christmas The eternal Word,
born of God before time began,
emptied the self for our sake
and became human.

Lent 1st Sun Christ died for our sins,
the innocent for the guilty
to bring us back to God,
in the body put to death,
in the spirit raised to life.

Lent 3rd Sun No one takes my life away from me;
I lay it down freely; I shall take it up again.

Lent 5th Sun Although he was the Son of God,
Christ learned obedience through suffering.

Easter Learning obedience through suffering,
the Son of God became for all
the source of eternal salvation,
alleluia.

Christ Jesus, subsisting in the form of God,
did not deem equality with God
something to grab,
but emptied himself,
taking the form of a slave,
becoming in human likeness.

And being found in human fashion,
he humbled himself,
becoming obedient until death,
and death on a cross.

And so God highly exalted him,
and gave to him the name above every name,
that in the name of Jesus
every knee should bend,
of heavenly beings and earthly beings,
and beings under the earth;

And every tongue acknowledge
to the glory of God the Father
that Jesus Christ is Lord.

Glory...

Antiphon

ORDINARY TIME READING **ROMANS 11:30-36**

As you then disobeyed God, but now have received mercy by way of these disobediences, so also others have disobeyed in the same mercy so that they also may now receive mercy. For God locked up all in disobedience so that God may show mercy to all.

O the depth of riches and wisdom and knowledge of God; how inscrutable the judgments and unsearchable the ways, for who has known the mind of the Lord? Or who has been the Lord's counselor? Or who has given anything to the Lord to be repaid?

Because of God, through God, and to God all things are. To God is the doxa-glory for the eons.

RESPONSORY Ps 111:2,4,10

Great are the works of the Lord…
...pondered by all who delight in them.
Praise enduring for deeds of wonder…
...pondered by all who delight in them.
Glory to the Father and to the Son and to the Holy Spirit:
...Great are the works of the Lord,
pondered by all who delight in them.

Life is a mystery to be lived,
not a problem to be solved.
Soren Kierkegaard

ADVENT READING **1 THESSALONIANS 5:19-24**

Do not quench the Spirit. Do not despise prophecies. Prove all things and hold fast to the good. Abstain from every form of bad doings. May the God of peace, God's own self, completely sanctify you and may your entire spirit and soul and body be kept without blame in the presence of our Lord Jesus Christ. The Caller is faithful and will indeed do it.

RESPONSORY Ps 85:7

Lord, show to us…

…your mercy and unfailing love.

And grant us your salvation…

…your mercy and unfailing love.

Glory to the Father and to the Son and to the Holy Spirit:

… Lord, show to us your mercy and unfailing love.

CHRISTMAS **GALATIANS 4:3-7**

And so when we were in youth, having been enslaved under the elements of the cosmos, when the fullness of time had come, God sent forth God's own Son, being born of a woman, becoming under the law, that he might redeem those under the law, that we might receive the full adoption as sons and daughters.

And because we are sons and daughters, God sent forth the Spirit of the Son of God into our hearts, crying, "Abba, Father."

So you are no more a slave, but a son, a daughter, and if a grown child through God also an heir.

RESPONSORY Christmas Eve

Today you will know…
…the Lord is coming.
And in the morning you will see his glory…
…the Lord is coming.
Glory to the Father and to the Son and to the Holy Spirit:
…Today you will know the Lord is coming.

RESPONSORY Christmas Season

The Word became flesh…
…alleluia, alleluia.
And dwelt among us…
…alleluia, alleluia.
Glory to the Father and to the Son and to the Holy Spirit:
…The Word became flesh and dwelt among us, alleluia, alleluia.

LENT READING, Weeks 1 & 3 **2 CORINTHIANS 6:1-4a**

And working together we urge you to not receive for no purpose the grace of God, who says, *In an acceptable time I heard you and in a day of salvation I helped you.*

Behold now an acceptable time; behold now a day of salvation.

Nothing giving cause to stumble, lest the ministry be blamed, in everything we commend ourselves as servants of God.

RESPONSORY

Listen to us, O Lord, and have mercy...
...for we have sinned against you.
Christ Jesus, hear our humble petitions...
...for we have sinned against you.
Glory to the Father and to the Son and to the Holy Spirit:
...Listen to us, O Lord, and have mercy
for we have sinned against you.

LENT READING, Week 5 **1 PETER 1:17-21**

You who call on the one Abba with no partiality as to the work of each, pass your time with the fear of a stranger, knowing that not with corruptible silver or gold were you redeemed from your vain conduct and delivered from that of your ancestors, but by the precious blood of Christ, as of a lamb unblemished and unspotted, chosen from the foundation of the world and shown forth in the last of times for you, believing through him in God who raised him from the dead and gave him glory, so that your faith and hope are in God.

RESPONSORY

We worship you, O Christ...
...and we praise you.
By your cross you have redeemed the world...
...and we praise you.
Glory to the Father and to the Son and to the Holy Spirit:
...We worship you, O Christ, and we praise you.

EASTER READING, Before Ascension **1 PETER 2:9-10**

You are a chosen race, a royal priesthood, a holy nation, a people belonging so you may tell out the doing of your having been called out of darkness into the marvellous light of God. Then you were not a people, but now are people of God; then you saw no mercy, but now are shown mercy.

RESPONSORY, in the Octave of Easter:

This is the day the Lord has made;
let us rejoice and be glad.

RESPONSORY, Weeks 3 to 6:

The disciples rejoiced...
...alleluia, alleluia.
When they saw the risen Lord...
...alleluia, alleluia.
Glory to the Father and to the Son and to the Holy Spirit:
...The disciples rejoiced, alleluia, alleluia.

ASCENSION VIGIL READING **EPHESIANS 2:4-6**

Being rich in mercy and because of loving us with much love even when we were dead in transgressions, God made us alive in Christ (by grace you are and have been saved) and raised us and seated us in the heavens with and in Christ Jesus.

RESPONSORY Ps. 47:6

God ascends to shouts of joy…
…alleluia, alleluia.
The Lord to the blast of trumpets…
…alleluia, alleluia.
Glory to the Father and to the Son and to the Holy Spirit:
…God ascends to shouts of joy, alleluia, alleluia.

PENTECOST VIGIL READING **ROMANS 8:9-11**

You are not in flesh but in Spirit, since the Spirit of God dwells in you. If anyone does not have the Spirit of Christ, this one is not of him. But if Christ is in you, the body is dead because of sin and the spirit is life because of righteousness.

If the Spirit of the one who raised Jesus from the dead dwells in you, the one who raised Christ Jesus from the dead will also give life to your mortal bodies through the indwelling of the Spirit in you.

RESPONSORY

The Holy Spirit is the Paraclete…
…alleluia, alleluia.
Who will teach you all things…
…alleluia, alleluia.
Glory to the Father and to the Son and to the Holy Spirit:
…The Holy Spirit is the Paraclete, alleluia, alleluia.

Gospel Canticle For Evening

Antiphons

Advent Wk 1	See the Lord coming from afar; his splendor fills the earth.
Advent Wk 3	There was no "god" before me and after me there will be none.
Christmas Eve	See the Ruler of rulers coming forth from God like a radiant spouse from the wedding chamber.
Christmas	Blessed is the womb which bore you, Christ, and the breast that nursed you, Lord and Savior of the world, alleluia.
Epiphany	Seeking the star, the magi said: this must signify the birth of some great royal. Let us search and lay our treasures at these feet: gold, frankincense and myrrh.
Baptism of the Lord	Our Savior came to be baptized, that through the cleansing waters of baptism our old self might be restored to new life.
Lent Wk 1	Human beings cannot live on bread alone, but by every word that comes from the mouth of God.

Lent Wk 3	Now that we have been justified by faith, let us be at peace with God through our Lord Jesus Christ.
Lent Wk 5	Unless a grain of wheat falls into the ground and dies, it remains only a single grain; but if it dies, it produces a rich harvest.
Easter Vigil thru 2nd Sun	The Son of Humanity has been glorified and God has been glorified in him.
Easter Wk 3	Stay with us, Lord, for evening draws near and daylight is fading, alleluia.
Easter Wk 5	I am the way, the truth, and the life; all who come to the Abba come through me, alleluia.
Ascension Vigil	Abba, I have shown your name to the ones you have given me, and now I pray for them rather than for the cosmos, for I am coming to you, alleluia.
Pentecost Vigil	Come, Holy Spirit, fill up believing hearts and set them on fire with your love. Though speaking many different languages, you united the nations in professing the same faith, alleluia.
Trinity	Glory and praise for ever! Dan 3
Corpus Christi	Praise the Lord, Jerusalem. Ps 147

Antiphons for Gospel Canticle For Evening, continued

Ordinary Time Antiphons *YEAR A*
Responsorial

Week 3	The Lord is my light and my salvation.	Ps 27
5	The just are a light to the upright.	Ps 112
7	The Lord is kind and merciful.	Ps 103
9	Lord, be my rock of safety.	Ps 31
11	We are the people of God, the sheep of this flock.	Ps 100
13	For ever I will sing the goodness of the Lord.	Ps 89
15	Seed falling on good ground will yield fruit.	Ps 65
17	Lord, I love your commands.	Ps 119
19	Lord, let us see your kindness.	Ps 85
21	Lord, your love is eternal.	Ps 138
23	If today you hear the voice of the Lord, harden not your hearts.	Ps 95
25	The Lord is near to all who call.	Ps 145
27	The Lord's vineyard is the house of Israel.	Ps 80
29	Give the Lord glory and honor.	Ps 96
31	In you, Lord, I have found my peace.	Ps 131
33	Blessed are those who fear the Lord.	Ps 128

CANTICLE of MARY (The Magnificat)
LUKE 1:46-55

+ **My soul** is stretched full with praise of the Lord,
and my spirit, beyond joy in God, my Savior,
who chose to lay eyes on this humble servant.

Behold, now and forward,
each and every age will call me blessed,
for the Mighty One did great things to me.

Holy is the name and the mercy
to generations and generations,
the ones fearing the One,

Who scattered the haughty of mind and heart,
pulled the powerful off their high place,
and lifted with dignity the humble in need.

The hungering are filled with good things,
the rich are sent away empty,
and servant Israel is given relief

with a memory of mercy to remember,
the promise spoken to our ancestors,
to Abraham and his descendants forever.

Glory...

Antiphon

INTERCESSIONS

- Lord, make your Church ever new…
- Watch over our pope and bishops…
- Keep us united in our diversity…
- Inspire leaders with your justice…
- Keep married couples in love…
- For respect for the dignity of the human person…
- For a culture of vocations all over the world…
- For all who have died…

- In gratitude for blessings, Abba thank you…
- For the sins of this day, Lord Jesus have mercy…
- With concerns over tomorrow, Holy Spirit help…

CLOSING PRAYER FOR MORNING AND EVENING

Our Fa-ther, who art in heav-en,
hal-lowed be thy name.
Thy king-dom come,
thy will be done
on earth as it is in heav-en.
Give us this day our dai-ly bread
and for-give us our tres-pass-es,
as we for-give those who tres-pass a-gainst/ us,
and lead us not in-to temp-ta/-tion,
but de-liv-er us from e\-vil.
A-men.

WEEK I
SUNDAY MORNING

\+ *God, come to my assistance;* Psalm 70:2
Lord, make haste to help me!

Glory…

ORDINARY TIME

Come, **Ho-ly Spir-it**, who ev-er One
Are with the Fa\-ther and/ the Son;
Come, Ho-ly Spir-it, our souls pos-sess
With your full flood of\ ho-li-ness;
With your full flood of\ ho-li-ness.

In will and deed, by heart and tongue,
With all our pow-ers, your praise/ be sung;
Light up in love our hu-man frame,
Till others catch the\ liv-ing flame;
Till others catch the\ liv-ing flame.

Fa-ther Al-migh-ty, hear now our cry
Through Je-sus Christ\ our Lord/ most high,
Who with the Ho-ly Spir-it and Thee
Do live and reign e\-ter-nal-ly;
Do live and reign e\-ter-nal-ly.

87, Text: attributed to Ambrose of Milan,
Nunc Sancte nobis Spiritus, d.397;
trans. by John Henry Newman, *Tracts for the Times*, 1836, altered
Music: LAMBILLOTTE, LM; with repeat;
Louis Lambillotte, SJ, 1796-1855
Popular melody for: *Come, Holy Ghost, Creator Blest…*

ADVENT & LENT

On this day, the first of days,
God the Fa-ther's Name we praise;
Who, cre-a-tion's Lord and Spring
Did the world from dark-ness bring.

On this day th'e-ter-nal Son
Ov-er death has tri-umph won;
On this day the Spir-it came
Bring-ing gifts of liv-ing flame.

Fa-ther, who did fash-ion me
Im-age of your-self to be,
Fill me with your love div-ine,
Let my ev'ry thought be thine.

God, the bless-ed Three-in-One,
Dwell with-in my heart a-lone;
As you give your-self to me
May I give my-self to thee.

119, Text: *Le Mans Breviary*, 1748,
Hymns Ancient and Modern, Henry W. Baker, 1861, altered
Music: 77 77 LUBECK, 77 77, *Gesanbuch*
by Johann A. Freylinghausen, 1704

CHRISTMAS

O come, all ye faith-ful,
joy-ful and tri-um-phant,
O come ye, O come/ ye,
to Beth\-le-hem.
Come and be-hold him,
born the King of an\-gels;

Refrain

O *come, let us a-dore him,*
O come, let us a-dore him,
O come, let us a-dore him /,
Christ \ the Lord.

Sing, choirs of an-gels, sing in ex-ul-ta-tion;
O sing, all ye cit-i-zens of heav'n\ a-bove!
Glo-ry to God, all glo-ry in the high\-est;
Refrain

Yea, Lord, we greet thee,
born this hap-py morn-ing;
O Je-sus, to thee/ be/ glo\-ry giv'n;
Word of the Fa-ther,
now in flesh ap-pear\-ing.
Refrain

27, Text: John f. Wade, 1743; translated by Frederick Oakeley, 1841
Music: ADESTE FIDELES, attributed variously to
John Wade, John Reading, or Simon Portogallo

EASTER

The day of Res-ur-rec-tion!
Earth, tell it out a-broad
The Pass-o-ver of glad-ness,
the Pass-o-ver of God.
From death to life e-ter-nal,
From earth un-to the sky,
Our Christ has brought us o-ver,
the vic-t'ry song on high.

Our hearts be free of e-vil, that we may see a-right
The Lord in rays e-ter-nal of res-ur-rec-tion light;
To lis-ten for his ac-cent, may we be calm and plain,
May his own greet-ing hear-ing,
we raise the vic-tor strain.

Now let the heav'ns be joy-ful!
Let earth the song be-gin!
A-round the world keep tri-umph,
and all that is there-in!
Let all things seen and un-seen
their notes in glad-ness blend
For Christ the Lord has ris-en,
our joy that has no end.

70, Text: John of Damascus, d. 749,
translated from Greek by John M. Neale, 1862, altered
Music: 76 76 D, AURELIA, Samuel S. Wesley, 1864
Popular melody for: *The Church's One Foundation*

PSALM 1

Antiphon *Blessed are the poor in spirit,*
for theirs is the reign of heaven. Mt 5:3

Advent, Christmas & Lent See how the cross of the Lord
stands revealed as the tree of life.

Easter The Lord is risen, alleluia.

Blessings are on the human being
who stands not in selfish counsel,
who walks not the way of sinners,
who sits not in the seat of mockers,
but rather delights in the law of Adonai
and meditates on it by day and by night.

This blessed one is like a tree
planted by streams of water
which yields fruit in the season
and its leaf withers not
and prosperity finds what this one does.

Not so those who do the bad,
but rather like the chaff blown in the wind
those who do the bad
will be unable to stand in the judgment
nor sinners in the assembly of the just.

Adonai watches over the way of the just
and bad ways will perish.

Glory… Antiphon

PSALM 2

Antiphon *Wind blows where it will;*
you hear its sound not knowing
from where it comes and goes away;
so with everyone who is born of the Spirit.
Jn 3:8

Advent & Lent
Here is a ruler of my own choosing
who will reign on Mount Zion.

Christmas
The Lord said to the Lord,
you are my son,
this day I am your Abba,
alleluia.

Epiphany
The wise magi opened their treasures
and offered to the Lord gifts
of gold, frankincense and myrrh,
alleluia.

Easter
Alleluia,
woman, for whom are you looking?
Why seek the living among the dead?
Alleluia.

A tree gives glory to God by being a tree.
See *New Seeds of Contemplation* by Thomas Merton

Why do nations rage and peoples plot vanity?
Rulers of the earth make their stand
and rulers gather together
against Adonai and the anointed of Adonai:
"Let us break their chains,
let us throw off their fetters."

The One enthroned in the heavens laughs,
the Lord scoffs and rebukes them.
In anger and in wrath the Lord terrifies them.
"I indeed installed my ruler
on my holy mountain of Zion.

I will proclaim a decree of Adonai who said,
'You are my son, this day I am your father.
Ask of me and nations are your inheritance,
and your possession to the ends of earth.
You will rule them with a scepter of iron
and dash them to pieces of what potters make.'

Rulers, now be wise!
Royals of earth, be warned!
Serve Adonai with fear; rejoice with trembling!
Kiss my son, lest he be angry
and you be destroyed
for in a moment he can flare up in wrath.

Blessings on all who take refuge in God."

Glory...

Antiphon

PSALM 63:1-8

Antiphon *Watch ready, for you know*
neither the day nor the hour. Mt 25:13

Advent On that day
sweet wine will flow from the mountains,
milk and honey from the hills, alleluia.

Christmas Tell us, shepherds, what have you seen?
Who has appeared to you?
We have seen a newborn infant
and a choir of angels praising the Lord,
alleluia.

Lent I will praise you all my life, O Lord;
in your name I will lift up my hands.

Easter thru 2nd Sun The splendor of Christ risen from the dead
has shone on the people redeemed,
alleluia.

Easter 3rd 5th Sun Whoever thirsts will drink freely
of life-giving water, alleluia.

Ascension People of Galilee, why are you looking up
into the sky? Jesus who has been taken up
into heaven will return in the same way,
alleluia.

Pentecost O Lord, how good and gentle
is your Spirit in us, alleluia.

God, you are my God; you I earnestly seek.
My soul, she thirsts for you,
my body, he longs for you,
as in a land with no water, dry and weary.

So in the sanctuary I saw you,
beheld you in your power and glory.
Your love is better than life itself;
my lips will glorify you.

So I will praise you in all the ways I am alive;
calling your name I will lift up my hands.
As with fatness and richness,
my soul will be satisfied;
with singing lips my mouth will sing praise.

When I remember you on my bed,
through night watches I think of you,
you who are my help;
then in the shadow of your wings I sing.
My very self stays close to you;
your right hand upholds me.

Glory…

Antiphon

The contemplative life
provides an area, a space of liberty, of silence, in which
possibilities are allowed to surface and new choices become manifest.

See *The Intimate Merton*, by Thomas Merton

PSALM 93

Antiphon *Do you ask if I am a ruler from yourself*
or have others told you about me? Jn 18:34

Advent The Lord is coming without delay
to reveal things kept hidden
and show himself to all humanity,
alleluia.

Christmas Jerusalem, your light has come;
the glory of the Lore dawns upon you;
humans of every ethnicity will walk
in the splendor of your sunrise,
alleluia.

Baptism of the Lord The servant baptizes the Master,
the waters of the Jordan tremble,
a dove hovers as a sign of witness,
and the voice of God is heard:
you are my beloved Son,
alleluia.

Lent Your statutes, O Lord, stand firm;
your truth is greater
than the sea-thunders.

Easter *Do you believe because you see me?*
Blessed are those not seeing
but believing. Jn 20:29

Adonai reigns, robed in majesty;
robed is Adonai and armed with strength.

The world is firmly established;
she cannot be moved.
Your throne was set up from long ago;
from eternity you are.

The seas lifted up, Adonai,
the seas lifted up their voice;
the seas lifted up their pounding.

More than thunders of great waters
or mighty breakers of the sea,
mighty in the height is Adonai.

Your statutes stand very firm;
your house, Adonai, is adorned in holiness
for length of days.

Glory…

Antiphon

DANIEL 3:57-90

Antiphon *Taking the five loaves and the two fishes,*
looking up to heaven, he blessed, and broke,
and gave them to the disciples
to set before the crowd. Lk 9:16

Advent 1st Sun The mountains and hills will
sing praise to God; all the trees of the forest
will clap their hands, for the Lord coming
is of the reign to last forever.

Advent 3rd Sun Mountains and hills shall be level,
crooked paths straight, rough ways
smooth. Come, Lord, do not delay.

Christmas The angel said to the shepherds:
I proclaim to you a great joy;
the Savior of the world is born for you,
alleluia.

Lent Springs and rainwater, bless the Lord;
exalt and sing praise to forever.

Easter thru 2nd Sun Our Redeemer has risen from the tomb;
let us sing a hymn of praise,
alleluia.

Easter 3rd 5th Sun All creation will be freed;
all peoples will know the glory
and freedom of God's children,
alleluia.

Ascension Give glory to the Ruler of rulers,
sing praise to God,
alleluia.

Pentecost Let streams and rivers
and all creatures that live in the waters
sing praise to God,
alleluia.

Bless the Lord, all you works of the Lord,
exalt and sing praise to forever.
Angels of the Lord, bless the Lord,
You heavens, bless the Lord,
All you waters above the heavens, bless the Lord,
All you powers, bless the Lord,
Sun and moon, bless the Lord,
Stars of heaven, bless the Lord.

All you rain and dew, bless the Lord,
All you winds, bless the Lord,
You fire and heat, bless the Lord,
You ice and cold, bless the Lord,
You dews and falling snows, bless the Lord,
You snows and frosts, bless the Lord,
You nights and days, bless the Lord,
You light and darkness, bless the Lord,
You lightning and clouds, bless the Lord.

Daniel 3:57-90, continued

Let the earth bless the Lord,
exalt and sing praise to forever.
You mountains and hills, bless the Lord,
All things growing in the ground, bless the Lord,
You seas and rivers, bless the Lord,
You springs and rain, bless the Lord,
You sea monsters and swimmers, bless the Lord,
All you birds of the air, bless the Lord,
All you wild beasts and cattle, bless the Lord,
You sons and daughters, bless the Lord.

O Israel, bless the Lord,
exalt and sing praise to forever.
You priests of the Lord, bless the Lord,
You servants of the Lord, bless the Lord,
You spirits and souls of the just, bless the Lord,
You holy and humble in heart, bless the Lord,
Hananiah, Azariah, and Mishael, bless the Lord,
exalt and sing praise to forever…

Give thanks to the Lord, who is good,
whose mercy endures to forever.
Bless the God of "gods"
all you who worship the Lord;
sing praise and give thanks to the One God
whose mercy endures to forever.

(No doxology)

Antiphon *Taking the five loaves and the two fishes,*
looking up to heaven, he blessed, and broke,
and gave them to the disciples
to set before the crowd. Lk 9:16

Advent 1st Sun The mountains and hills will
sing praise to God; all the trees of the forest
will clap their hands, for the Lord coming
is of the reign to last forever.

Advent 3rd Sun Mountains and hills shall be level,
crooked paths straight, rough ways
smooth. Come, Lord, do not delay.

Christmas The angel said to the shepherds:
I proclaim to you a great joy; the Savior
of the world is born for you, alleluia.

Lent Springs and rainwater, bless the Lord;
exalt and sing praise to forever.

Easter thru 2nd Sun Our Redeemer has risen from the tomb;
let us sing a hymn of praise, alleluia.

Easter 3rd 5th Sun All creation will be freed;
all peoples will know the glory
and freedom of God's children, alleluia.

Ascension Give glory to the Ruler of rulers,
sing praise to God, alleluia.

Pentecost Let streams and rivers
and all creatures that live in the waters
sing praise to God, alleluia.

PSALM 148

Antiphon *This I command,*
that you love one another. Jn 15:17

Advent I shall enfold Zion with my salvation
and shed my glory around Jerusalem,
alleluia.

Lent All rulers and peoples of the earth,
give praise to the Lord.

Christmas & Easter The name of the Lord is praised
in heaven and on earth,
alleluia.

Pentecost Breathe forth your Spirit, Lord,
and they are created,
and you renew the faces of earth,
alleluia. Ps 104

Hallelujah!

Give praise from the heavens!
Give praise in the heights.
Give praise all you angels.
Give praise all you hosts.

Give praise sun and moon.
Give praise all stars shining.
Give praise, you heavens of the heavens
and waters above the heavens.

Let them praise the name Adonai,
who commanded and they were created,
who set them in place forever,
to forever the decree Adonai gave,
not to pass away.

Praise Adonai, you earth,
you sea creatures and all in the deep,
lightning and hail, snow and cloud,
wind of the storm, all who do Adonai's bidding,

you mountains and hills,
fruit trees and cedars,
wild animals and all cattle,
small creatures and birds of flight,

you rulers of the earth and the nations,
royals and all people ruling on earth,
young men and young women,
old folks and children:

Let them praise the name Adonai
whose name alone is exalted,
whose splendor is above earth and the heavens,

who raised a horn for the people,
praise of all the saints,
of the sons and daughters of Israel,
of people close to the Lord.

Hallelujah!

Glory... Antiphon

PSALM 149:1-6,9c

Antiphon *John the Baptist told his disciples,*
this joy of mine is full; it is fitting
for the Christ to increase
and for me to decrease. Jn 3:30

Advent A great prophet will come to Jerusalem
making of that people a new creation.

Christmas A little child is born for us;
little and yet called the mighty God,
alleluia.

Lent 1st 3rd Sun Taking delight in the people, the Lord
crowns the humble with salvation.

5th Sun The hour has come
for the Son of Humanity to be glorified.

Easter 1st 2nd Sun Alleluia,
the Lord is risen as promised, alleluia.

3rd 5th Sun The saints will rejoice in glory, alleluia.

Ascension Lifted up as they watched,
a cloud took him from their sight, alleluia.

Pentecost The apostles preached in different tongues
and proclaimed the great works of God,
alleluia.

Hallelujah!

Sing to Adonai a new song,
praise in the assembly of saints.
Let Israel rejoice in their Maker,
let the people of Zion be glad in their ruler.

Let them praise the name
with dance, tambourine and harp.
Let them make music for Adonai
who delights in Adonai's people.

Adonai crowns humble ones with salvation.
Let the saints rejoice in honor,
Let them sing for joy on their beds.
Praises of God be in their mouths
and a two-edged sword in their hands.

Retribution on the nations
and punishment on the peoples
binding royalty in restraint
and nobility in rings of iron:
the judgment decreed for them,
such is the glory of the saints.

Hallelujah!

Glory…

Antiphon

Grace wakes us up when we're ready.

Sr. Helen Prejean, October 28, 2011

ORDINARY TIME READING **REVELATION 7:9-12**

I saw, behold, a crowd too great to number, out of every nation and tribe and people and tongue, standing before the throne and before the Lamb clothed in white robes and with palms in their hands.

They cried out with a loud voice saying,
Salvation to our God sitting on the throne, and to the Lamb.

And all the angels stood around the throne with the elders and the four living creatures, and fell on their faces before the throne and worshipped God, saying *Amen, blessing and glory and wisdom and thanks and honor and power and strength to our God to the eons of the eons. Amen.*

RESPONSORY Lk 18:13, 22:69

Lord Jesus Christ, Son of the living God...
...have mercy on us.
You are seated at the right hand of the Father...
...have mercy on us.
Glory to the Father and to the Son and to the Holy Spirit:
...Lord Jesus Christ, Son of the living God,
have mercy on us.

ADVENT READING **ROMANS 13:11-12**

Know that this is the *kairos* time, the hour for you to be raised out of sleep, for now our salvation is nearer than when we became believers. The night has advanced and the day draws near. So let us cast off the deeds of the darkness, and let us put on the armor of the light. As in the new day, let us walk not in revellings to drunken bouts, not in sex to excesses, not in strife to jealousy, but put on the Lord Jesus Christ, and as for the flesh, give its lust no room to think.

RESPONSORY Lk 18:13, 22:69

Lord Jesus Christ, Son of the living God...
...have mercy on us.
You are seated at the right hand of the Father...
...have mercy on us.
Glory to the Father and to the Son and to the Holy Spirit:
...Lord Jesus Christ, Son of the living God,
have mercy on us.

CHRISTMAS READING **HEBREWS 1:1-4**

Of old, having spoken to the ancestors by the prophets often and in many ways, in these last days God spoke to us in a Son, appointed as heir of all things, and indeed through whom God made the eons.

He is the radiance of the glory, the representation of the reality, and the bearer of all things by the word of the power of God, and having made a cleansing of sins, he has sat at the right hand of the greatness on high. By so much, he has inherited the more excellent name, better even than that of the angels.

RESPONSORY

The Lord has made known... *...alleluia, alleluia.*
The saving power... *...alleluia, alleluia.*
Glory to the Father and to the Son and to the Holy Spirit:
...The Lord has made known the saving power, alleluia.

LENT READING, Weeks 1 & 3 **NEHEMIAH 8:9,10**

Nehemiah the governor and Ezra the priest and scribe and the Levites instructing the people said to all the people, "This day is sacred to Adonai your God. Do not mourn and do not weep," for all the people wept as they listened to the words of the Law. And he said to them, "Go! Eat choice foods! And drink sweet things! And send portions to ones with nothing prepared, for this day is sacred to our Lord, and do not grieve, for the joy of Adonai is your strength."

RESPONSORY Lk 18:13

Lord Jesus Christ, Son of the living God...
...have mercy on us.
You were wounded for our offenses...
...have mercy on us.
Glory to the Father and to the Son and to the Holy Spirit:
...Lord Jesus Christ, Son of the living God,
have mercy on us.

LENT READING, Week 5 **LEVITICUS 23:4-7**

These are feasts of Adonai, sacred assemblies that you must proclaim at their time: in the first month on the fourteenth day, the twilight, the passover to Adonai; and on the fifteenth day of that month the Feast of the Unleavened Breads to Adonai, seven days of unleavened breads you must eat. On the first day must be an assembly of the sacred, for none of you must do any regular work.

RESPONSORY Rev 5:9

Lord, by your own blood…
…you brought us back to God.
From every tribe and tongue and people and nation…
…you brought us back to God.
Glory to the Father and to the Son and to the Holy Spirit:
…Lord, by your own blood you brought us back to God.

EASTER READING **ACTS 10:40-43**

God raised this one on the third day and gave him to be visible not to all the people, but to witnesses chosen by God, to us who ate and drank with him after his rising out of the dead. And he commanded us to proclaim to the people and witness solemnly that he is the one designated by God as judge of the living and the dead. To him all the prophets witness: forgiveness of sins received through his name by everyone believing in him.

RESPONSORY, Easter Sunday & Second Sunday Ps 118:24

This is the day the Lord has made;
let us rejoice and be glad.

RESPONSORY, Weeks 3 to 6 Lk 18:13

Lord Jesus Christ, Son of the living God…
...have mercy on us.
You were wounded for our offenses…
...have mercy on us.
Glory to the Father and to the Son and to the Holy Spirit:
Lord Jesus Christ, Son of the living God, have mercy on us.

ASCENSION READING **HEBREWS 10:11-14**

Every other priest stands daily ministering and offering often the same sacrifices, which can never take away sins. Having offered the single sacrifice for all time, this Christ sat at the right hand of God, waiting since until his enemies are put as a footstool of his feet, for by one offering he has made perfect for all time the ones being made holy.

RESPONSORY

Christ ascended into heaven... *...alleluia, alleluia.*
He led captivity captive... *...alleluia, alleluia.*
Glory to the Father and to the Son and to the Holy Spirit:
...Christ ascended into heaven, alleluia, alleluia.

PENTECOST READING **ACTS 5:30-32**

The God of our ancestors raised Jesus, whom you killed by hanging on a tree. This one is exalted to the right hand of God as ruler and savior to bring conversion to Israel and forgiveness of sins. Of these things, we are witnesses with the Holy Spirit given by God to the obedient.

RESPONSORY

All were filled with the Holy Spirit...
...alleluia, alleluia.
They began to speak...
...alleluia, alleluia.
Glory to the Father and to the Son and to the Holy Spirit:
...All were filled with the Holy Spirit, alleluia, alleluia.

Gospel Canticle For Morning

Antiphons

Advent Wk 1	The Holy Spirit
A. Matt 24:37-44	will come upon you, Mary;
B. Mark 13:33-37	you have no need to be afraid.
C. Lk 21:25-28,34-36	
Advent Wk 3	John sent two of his disciples to ask:
A. Matt 11:2-11	are you the One
B. John 1:6-8,19-28	whose coming was told,
C. Luke 3:10-18	or should we look for another?
Christmas	Glory to God in the highest,
Eve. Matt 1:1-25	and peace on earth
Night. Luke 2:1-14	to the people of God,
Dawn. Luke 2:15-20	alleluia.
Day. John 1:1-18	
Solemnity of	Marvelous is the mystery proclaimed:
Mary ABC	human nature is made new
Luke 2:16-21	as God becomes human.
Epiphany	Christ has washed the spouse
ABC	in Jordan's waters, the Magi hasten
Matt. 2:1-12	with gifts to the royal wedding,
	and the wedding guests rejoice,
	alleluia.
Baptism of	The heavens opened,
the Lord	the Spirit came down as a dove,
A. Matt 3:13-17	and a voice out of the heavens:
B. Mark 1:7-11	you are my beloved Son,
C. Lk 3:15-16,21-22	in you I am well pleased.

Antiphons for Gospel Canticle For Morning, continued

Lent Wk 1 A. Matt 4:1-11 B. Mark 1:12-15 C. Luke 4:1-13	Jesus was led by the Spirit into the desert to be tempted and fasting for forty days and forty nights, was hungry.
Lent Wk 3 A. John 4:5-42 B. John 2:13-25 C. Luke 13:1-9	Destroy this temple and in three days I will rebuild it, he said, speaking of the temple of his body.
Lent Wk 5 A. John 11:1-45 B. John 12:20-33 C. John 8:1-11	Our friend Lazarus has fallen asleep; let us go and wake him.
Easter Sunday A. Matt 28:1-10 B. Mark 16:1-7 C. Luke 24:1-12	Very early on the morning after the Sabbath, when the sun had just risen they came to the tomb, alleluia.
Easter Wk 2 ABC John 20:19-31	With your hand, touch the mark of the nails; doubt no longer, but believe, alleluia.
Easter Wk 3 A. Luke 24:13-35 B. Luke 24:35-48 C. John 21:1-19	It was fitting for Christ to suffer so on the third day to rise from the dead, alleluia.
Easter Wk 5 A. John 14:1-12 B. John 15:1-8 C. Jn 13:31-33a,34-35	One who lives in me and I in that one will yield much fruit, says the Lord, alleluia.

Ascension	I am ascending
A. Matthew 28:16-20	to my Abba and your Abba,
B. Mark 16:15-20	to my God and your God,
C. Luke 24:46-53	alleluia.
Pentecost	Receive the Holy Spirit;
Vigil: John 7:37-39	whose sins you forgive
Day: John 20:19-23	are forgiven them, alleluia.

YEAR B

Ordinary Time Antiphons *Responsorial*

Trinity Sunday
Blessed the people
the Lord has chosen. Ps 33

A- John 3:16-18 B- Mt 28:16-20 C- Jn 16:12-15

Corpus Christi
I will take the cup of salvation,
and call on the name of the Lord. Ps 116

A- John 6:51-58 B- Mk 14:12-16,22-26 C- Lk 9:11b-17

Week

3 Teach me your ways, O Lord. Ps 25

A- Matt 4:12-23 B- Mark 1:14-20 C-Lk1:1-4; 4:14-21

5 Praise the Lord
who heals the brokenhearted. Ps 147

A- Matt 5:13-16 B- Mark 1:29-39 C- Luke 5:1-11

7 Lord heal my soul
for I have sinned against you. Ps 41

A- Matt 5:38-48 B- Mark 2:1-12 C- Luke 6:27-38

9 Sing with joy to God our help. Ps 81

A- Matt 7:21-27 B- Mark 2:23-3:6 C- Luke 7:1-10

11 Lord, it is good to give thanks to you. Ps 92

A- Matt 9:36-10:8 B- Mark 4:26-34 C- Lk 7:36 - 8:3

Antiphons & Gospel Reading for Sundays in Odd Weeks, cont.

Week		
13	I will praise you Lord for you have rescued me.	Ps 30
	A- Matt 10:37-42 **B-** Mark 5:21-43 **C-** Luke 9:51-62	
15	Lord, let us see your kindness, and grant us your salvation.	Ps 85
	A- Matt 13:1-23 **B-** Mark 6:7-13 **C-** Lk 10:25-37	
17	The hand of the Lord feeds us.	Ps 145
	A- Matt 13:44-52 **B-** John 6:1-15 **C-** Luke 11:1-13	
19	Taste and see the goodness of the Lord.	Ps 34
	A- Matt 14:22-33 **B-** John 6:41-51 **C-** Lk 12:32-48	
21	Taste and see the goodness of the Lord.	Ps 34
	A- Matt 16:13-20 **B-** John 6:60-69 **C-** Lk 13:22-30	
23	Praise the Lord, my soul!	Ps 146
	A- Matt 18:15-20 **B-** Mark 7:31-37 **C-** Lk 14:25-33	
25	The Lord upholds my life.	Ps 54
	A- Matt 20:1-16a **B-** Mark 9:30-37 **C-** Luke 16:1-13	
27	May the Lord bless us all the days of our lives.	Ps 128
	A- Matt 21:33-43 **B-** Mark 10:2-16 **C-** Luke 17:5-10	
29	Lord, let your mercy be on us.	Ps 33
	A- Matt 22:15-21 **B-** Mark 10:35-45 **C-** Luke 18:1-8	
31	I love you, Lord, my strength.	Ps 18
	A- Matt 23:1-12 **B-** Mark 12:28b-34 **C-** Luke 19:1-9	
33	You are my inheritance, O Lord!	Ps 16
	A- Matt 25:14-30 **B-** Mark 13:24-43 **C-** Luke 21:5-19	

CANTICLE of ZECHARIAH (The Benedictus)
LUKE 1:68-79

+ **Blessed be** the Lord the God of Israel
who chose a people to visit with redemption,
and raised salvation in the house of David,
saving strength from God's own servant,

speaking from the age of the prophets
through the mouth of the holy prophet:
Salvation out of enmity,
even out of those who hate us,

to show our ancestors how mercy works, -
and to remember the holy promise of the Lord,
the covenant made for our ancestor Abraham,
calming our fear and making us free
to serve with holy justice before God all our days.

And you also child -
will be called a prophet of the Most High
for you will go before the Lord to prepare his way
and give to people a knowledge of salvation
known in accepting forgiveness of their sins.

From the tender mercy of our God,
the sun rising from the height will visit with light
for those who sit in the dark or shadow of death
and to guide our feet into the way of peace.

Glory...

Antiphon

PETITIONS FOR THE CONSECRATION TO GOD
OF THE DAY AND ITS REST

- For the Church and her ministry and apostolates...
- For secular authorities and all serving as stewards...
- For people who are poor or sick or in sorrow...
- For peace and the basic needs of each human being...
- For acceptance of the gift of the infinite love of God...
- For the blessings of faithful Sabbath rest...
- In gratitude for blessings and grace...
- For those who have asked for my prayer...
- For those for whom I have promised to pray...
- For those who weigh on my heart...

CLOSING PRAYER FOR MORNING AND EVENING

Our Fa-ther,
who art in heav-en,
hal-lowed be thy name.
Thy king-dom come,
thy will be done
on earth as it is in heav-en.
Give us this day our dai-ly bread
and for-give us our tres-pass-es,
as we for-give those who tres-pass a-gainst/ us,
and lead us not in-to temp-ta/-tion,
but de-liv-er us from e\-vil.
A-men.

HYMN, TE DEUM

You are God: we praise you;
You are the Lord; we acclaim you;
You are the eternal Father: all creation worships you.

To you all angels, all the powers of heaven,
Cherubim and Seraphim, sing in endless praise:
Holy, holy, holy, Lord, God of power and might,
heaven and earth are full of your glory.

The glorious company of apostles praise you.
The noble assembly of prophets praise you.
The white-robed army of martyrs praise you.

All over the world the holy church acclaims you:
Father, of majesty unbounded,
your true and only Son, worthy of all worship,
and the Holy Spirit, advocate and guide.

You, Christ, are the royal of glory,
the eternal Son of the Father.

When you became human to set us free
you did not spurn the Virgin's womb.

You overcame the sting of death,
and opened the reign of heaven to all believers.

You are seated at God's right hand in glory.
We believe that you will come and be our judge.

Come then, Lord, and help your people,
bought with the price of your own blood,
and bring us with your saints
to glory everlasting. Amen.

WEEK I
SUNDAY EVENING

\+ *God, come to my assistance;* Psalm 70:2
Lord, make haste to help me!

Glory…

A ORDINARY TIME

Praise God, from whom all bless-ings flow;
Praise God, all crea-tures here be-low;
Praise God a-bove, ye heav'n-ly host,
Praise Fa-ther, Son, and Ho-ly Ghost.

For maj-es-ty and migh-ty deeds,
With blast of horn and tam-bou-rine,
With harp and dance and flute and string,
Let ev'-ry hu-man breath now sing.

Give praise to reach the migh-ty dome,
Give praise with cym-bals, crash-ing sound,
Give praise with lyre and bless-ed skill,
Praise God to wake the ho-ly hill.

Praise God, from whom all bless-ings flow;
Raise hands, all crea-tures here be-low;
Praise God, our Fa-ther and the Son
And Ho-ly Spir-it, Three in One.

120, Text: from Psalm 150; verse 1 by Thomas Ken, 1695, altered;
verses 2,3 by Stephen J. Wolf, 2009
Music: OLD HUNDREDTH, LM, Louis Bourgeois,
first published in *Genevan Psalter*, 1551

ORDINARY TIME

B **Ho-ly God\, we praise/ your Name;**
Lord of all\, we bow\ be-fore you!
All on earth\ your scep/-ter claim,
All in heav-en a-bove\ a-dore you;
  In-fin/-ite\ your vast do/-main,
  Ev-er-last\-ing is\ your reign.

Hark! The loud\ cel-es/-tial hymn
An-gel choirs\ a-bove\ are rais-ing,
Cher-u-bim\ and ser/-a-phim,
In un-ceas\-ing chor\-us prais-ing;
  Fill the/ heav-ens with sweet ac/-cord:
  Ho-ly, ho\-ly, ho\-ly Lord.

Ho-ly Fa\-ther, Ho/-ly Son,
Ho-ly Spir\-it, Three\ we name you;
While in ess\-ence on/-ly One,
Un-div-i\-ded God\ we claim you;
  And a/-dor\-ing bend the/ knee,
  While we en-ter the mys\-ter-y.

96, Text: Ignaz Franz, *Grosser Gott*, about 1774,
translated by Clarence Walworth, 1858, altered
Music: 78 78 77 GROSSER GOTT,
Katholisches Gesangbuch, Vienna, 1774

ADVENT

On Jor-dan's bank the Bap-tist's cry
An-nounc-es that the Lord is nigh;
A-wake and heark-en, for he brings
Glad ti-dings of the King of kings.

Then cleansed be ev-'ry soul from sin;
Make straight the way of God with-in,
Pre-pare we in our hearts a home,
Where such a migh-ty guest may come.

For you are our sal-va-tion, Lord,
Our ref-uge and our sure re-ward;
Shine forth, and let your light re-store
Our souls to heav'n-ly grace once more.

All praise, e-ter-nal Son, to thee
Whose ad-vent set your peo-ple free,
Whom with the Fa-ther we a-dore
And Ho-ly Spir-it ev-er-more.

14, Text: Charles Coffin, d.1749;
translated by John Chandler, d.1876, altered
Music: WINCHESTER NEW, CM,
Musikalisches Handbuch, Hamburg, 1690;
adapted by William H. Havergal, d.1870

23, Text: see Luke 2:14; Charles Wesley, 1739
Music: 7777777777 MENDELSSOHN, Felix Mendelssohn, 1840

CHRISTMAS

Hark! the her-ald an-gels sing\,
"Glo-ry to the new-born King;
Peace on earth and mer-cy mild\,
God and sin-ners re-con-ciled!"
Joy-ful, all ye na-tions rise\,
Join the tri-umph of the skies\;
With th'an-gel-ic host pro-claim.
"Christ is/ born in Beth-le-hem!"

REFRAIN *Hark! the her-ald an-gels sing,*
"Glo-ry / to the new-born King!"

Christ, by high-est heav'n a-dored\.
Christ, the ev-er-last-ing Lord,
Late in time be-hold him come\,
Off-spring of the vir-gin's womb.
Veiled in flesh the God-head see\,
Hail th'in-car-nate De-i-ty\!
Pleased as man with us to dwell
Je-sus/, our Em-man-u-el! REFRAIN

Come, De-sire of na-tions, come\,
Fix in us your hum-ble home;
Oh, to all your-self im-part\,
Formed in each be-liev-ing heart!
Hail, the heav'n-ly Prince of Peace\!
Hail, the Sun of Right-eous-ness\!
Light and life to all he brings,
Ris-en with heal-ing in his wings. REFRAIN

LENT

Lord, your al-migh\-ty Word
Cha-os and dark/\-ness heard,
And took their flight;
Hear us we hum-bly pray,
And where the gos-pel day
Sheds not its glo-rious ray, Let there be light!

Sa-vior, you came\ to give
Those who in shad/\-ows live
Heal-ing and sight,
Health to the sick in mind,
Sight to the in-ly blind,
Now to all hu-man-kind Let there be light!

Spir-it of truth\ and love,
Life-giv-ing, ho/\-ly dove,
Speed forth your flight!
Move on the wa-ter's face
Bear-ing the lamp of grace,
And in earth's sad-dest place, Let there be light!

Holy and bless\-ed Three,
Glo/-rious Trin/\-i-ty,
Wis-dom, love, might;
Bound-less as o-cean tide,
Roll-ing in full-est pride,
Thru the world far and wide, Let there be light!

EASTER

Je-sus Christ is ris'n to-day\, Al//\/-le/-lu\-ia!
Our tri-umph-ant ho-ly day\, Al//\/-le/-lu\-ia!
Who did once up-on the cross, Al//\/-le/-lu\-ia!
Suf/-fer\ to re-deem our loss\, Al\/\//-le/-lu\-ia!

Hymns of praise, then, let us sing\, Al_-le-lu-ia!
Un-to Christ, our heav'n-ly King\, Al_-le-lu\-ia!
Who en-dured the cross and grave, Al_-le-lu-ia!
Sin/-ners\ to re-deem and save\, Al_-le-lu-ia!

But the pain which he en-dured\, Al_-le-lu-ia!
Our sal-va-tion has pro-cured\, Al_-le-lu-ia!
Now a-bove the sky he's King, Al_-le-lu-ia!
Where/ the\ an-gels ev-er sing\, Al_-le-lu-ia!

Sing we to our God a-bove\, Al_-le-lu-ia!
Praise e-ter-nal as God's love\, Al_-le-lu-ia!
Praise God, all you heav'n-ly host, Al_-le-lu-ia!
Fa/-ther\, Son, and Ho-ly Ghost\, Al_-le-lu-ia!

68, Text: Bohemian Carol, *Surrexit Christus hodie* , 1372,
translated by John Walsh, 1708,
stanzas 1-3 by John Arnold, 1749,
stanza 4 by Charles Wesley, 1740, altered
Music: 77 77 EASTER HYMN with alleluias, *Lyra Davidica,* 1708

110, Text: Based on Genesis 1:3,
Thou Whose Almighty Word, John Marriott, 1813, altered
Music: 664 6664, ITALIAN HYMN (MOSCOW), Felice de Giardini, 1769

PSALM 91

Antiphon *It has been written,*
"not on bread alone
shall the human live." Lk 4:4

Advent & Lent Have no fear of terror at night;
in the shadow of the Almighty,
find rest.

Christmas A light has shined into the night:
grace, mercy and justice, alleluia.

Easter Alleluia, alleluia, alleluia.

One who dwells in the shelter of Elyon,
in the shadow of Shaddai, will find rest.
I will say of Adonai, my refuge, my fortress:
in my God do I trust.

Surely the Lord will save you
from fowler snare, from deadly pestilence.
With the feather of the Lord you will be covered,
and under those wings you will find refuge,
shield and rampart, the fidelity of the Lord.

You will have no fear of terror at night
nor of arrows flying by day,
of pestilence stalking in the darkness,
nor of plague that destroys at midday.

A thousand may fall at your side,
and ten thousand at your right hand;
near to you they will not come.

Observe with your eyes, simply watch;
punishment of doers of the bad you will see.
Make Adonai, who is my refuge,
make Elyon your dwelling.

Harm will not befall you,
nor will disaster come near your tent.
God's own Angels, the Lord will command
to guard you in all of your ways.

In their hands they will lift you up;
your foot will not strike against the stone.
Upon lion and cobra you will tread,
you will trample the great lion and serpent.

"Because you love me, I will rescue you,
I will protect all who know my Name.
You will call upon me and I will answer.
I am with you in trouble;
I will deliver you and honor you.

In length of days I will satisfy you,
and show you my salvation."

Glory...

Antiphon

Psalm 91 is often used for night prayer

PSALM 64

Antiphon *Abba, forgive them,*
for they know not what they do. Lk 23:34

Advent & Lent: Let the just rejoice
and take refuge in the Lord.

Christmas & Easter: Alleluia, alleluia, alleluia.

—

What is justice? The root of justice is in the awareness that God created an abundance intended as a blessing for all. If anyone is denied their just due of this abundance our God has given for us all, that is injustice. The ancient Hebrew test for whether we live in a just society is to ask how the widows, orphans, and alien strangers in our midst are doing.

Deal with your neighbor with justice; oppress no alien, orphan, or widow; shed no innocent blood; and follow no other "god."
Jeremiah 7:5b,6

Hear my voice, O God, in complaint;
threatened by enmity, you protect my life.
You hide me from conspiracies,
from the noisy crowd of people doing bad things,

who sharpen their tongue like the sword,
aim their arrow of harmful words,
and shoot from ambush the innocent person;
they shoot suddenly and without fear.

They encourage those who plan harm,
and they talk of hidden snares,
saying, "who will see them?"
They plot injustices they call "the perfect plan!"
Surely the human mind and heart are cunning.

But God will shoot sudden arrows
striking down those plans.
Their ruin will be by their own tongues;
all who see them will shake heads at them.

All humanity will fear,
then come to proclaim the work of God,
and ponder the deeds of God.
Let the just rejoice
and take refuge in Adonai;
let all the upright of heart give praise.

Glory...

Antiphon

PSALM 110:1-6a,7

Antiphon *Give them food yourselves.* Lk 9:13a

Advent 1st Sun — Rejoice, daughter of Zion;
shout for joy, daughter of Jerusalem,
alleluia.

Advent 3rd Sun — Our Lord will come to claim the glorious
throne in the assembly of the royals.

Christmas — You have been endowed from your birth
with royal gifts; in eternal splendor,
before the dawn of light on earth,
I have begotten you, alleluia.

Lent 1st Sun — Worship your Lord;
serve only the one God.

Lent 3rd Sun — Lord, all powerful Ruler,
free us for the sake of your name.

Lent 5th Sun — The hour has come
for the Son of Humanity to be glorified.

Easter thru 2nd Sun — Mary Magdalene and the other Mary
came to see the Lord's tomb, alleluia.

Easter 3rd Sun — The Lord has cleansed us, and is seated
on high at God's right hand, alleluia.

Easter 5th Sun — The Lord is risen and is seated
at the right hand of God, alleluia.

Ascension He ascended into heaven and is seated
at the right hand of God, alleluia.

Pentecost Seek the things that are above
where Christ is seated at God's right hand,
alleluia.

Adonai said to my Lord:
"Sit at my right hand
until I make enmity
as a footstool for your feet."

A scepter of your might
Adonai will extend from Zion,
and rule in the midst of enmity!

Your troops are willing on the day of your battle.
In holy majesty from the womb of the dawn,
to you is the dew of your youth.
Adonai pledged in a mind unchanging,
"You are a priest to forever
in the order of Melchizedek."

The Lord is at your right hand
and will crush rulers on the day of wrath,
will judge the nations...
and will drink from a brook on the way
with head lifted up in it all.

Glory...

Antiphon

PSALM 111

Antiphon *Stretching out his hand right away,*
Jesus took hold of Simon, and said,
Little-faith, why did you doubt? Mt 14:31

Advent Let the mountains break out with joy
and the hills answer with gladness,
for the world's true light, the Lord,
comes with power and might.

Christmas The Ruler who is our peace
comes in splendor to reign supreme
over all rulers of the earth,
alleluia.

Baptism of the Lord The voice resounded from heaven;
this is my Son
in whom I take great delight;
listen to what he says to you,
alleluia.

Lent We have been redeemed
by the precious blood of Christ,
the lamb without blemish.

Easter The Lord has redeemed
the people of God,
alleluia.

Hallelujah!

I will extol Adonai with all my heart
in the assembled council of the upright.
Great are the works of Adonai,
pondered by all who delight in them.

Glorious and majestic are the deeds,
and this wise design endures to forever.
Remembered are the deeds of wonder
by gracious and compassionate Adonai,

providing food for ones fearing the One,
remembering the covenant to forever,
and having shown power at work,
giving the people the lands of the nations.

Faithful and just is the handiwork of Adonai,
whose precepts are worthy of trust.
Steadfast are they forever to forever,
done with fidelity and honesty.

Redemption is sent for Adonai's people;
ordained to forever is the covenant.
Holy and awesome is the Name.

The beginning of wisdom is fear of Adonai,
good understanding for all who live by it.
Praise endures to eternity.

Glory...

Antiphon

PSALM 114

Antiphon *I tell you, forgive;*
not seven times,
but to seventy times seven. Mt 18:22

Advent Christ our King will come to us,
the Lamb of God foretold by John.

Christmas In the beginning,
before time began,
the Word was God,
alleluia.

Lent 1st & 3rd Sun This is the time to win God's favor,
a good and acceptable day
to be saved.

Lent 5th Sun The Lord Sabaoth protects us,
sets us free, guides us, and saves us.

Easter thru 2nd Sun Come and see the place
where the Lord was buried,
alleluia.

Easter Season We have been rescued
from the power of darkness
and brought into
the reign of the Son,
alleluia.

When Israel came out from Egypt,
the house of Jacob
free from people of another tongue,
Judah became as God's sanctuary,
and Israel God's dominion.

The sea looked and fled,
the Jordan turned back.
The mountains skipped like rams
and hills like a flock of lambs.

What to you, sea, that you fled?
Jordan, that you turned back?
Mountains, that you skipped like rams?
You hills, like a flock of lambs?

Tremble, earth, at the presences of the Lord!
Tremble at the presences of the God of Jacob,
who turned rock into pools of waters,
hard rock into springs of waters.

Glory...

Antiphon

O God,
your sea is so great
and my boat is so small.

Breton fishing prayer

(*Lent*) 1 PETER 2:21-24

Antiphon *Be ready always for*
everyone asking you for a word
about the hope in you. 1 Ptr 3:15b

Lent 1st Sun Now we must go up to Jerusalem,
where all that has been written
about the Son of Humanity will be fulfilled.

Lent 3rd Sun Ours were the sufferings he bore;
ours the torments he endured.

Lent 5th Sun He was pierced for our offenses
and burdened with our sins;
by his wounds we are healed.

To this you were called,
for indeed Christ suffered on behalf of you,
leaving to you an example to follow in his steps:

He did not sin, nor was guile found in his mouth;
he was reviled and did not revile in return;
suffering he did not threaten,
but delivered himself to the one judging justly.

Our sins he carried in his body up onto the tree,
that dying to sins, we might live for justice.
By his bruises, you are cured.

Glory…

Antiphon

(*All except Lent*) REVELATION 19:1b,2a,5b,6b,7

Antiphon *We are an Easter people*
and **alleluia** *is our song.* St. Augustine

Advent Let us patiently await our blessed hope,
the coming of our Savior.

Christmas The Savior of the world is born, alleluia.

Easter Be not afraid; go and tell my
brothers and sisters to set out for Galilee;
there they will see me, alleluia.

Alleluia!
Salvation and glory and power are to our God,
whose judgments are true and just.

Alleluia!
Praise our God, all you servants of the Lord,
you small and you great, who hold God in awe.

Alleluia!
The Lord is reigning, our God, the Almighty.
Let us rejoice and let us exult,
and we will give the glory to the Lord.

Alleluia!
The day has come
for the marriage of the Lamb,
and the bride has prepared herself.

Glory... Antiphon

ORDINARY TIME READING **2 CORINTHIANS 1:3-7**

Blessed be the God and Father of our Lord Jesus Christ, Father of compassion and God of all comfort (*parakleseos*), comforting us in all our affliction that we may be able to comfort those in every affliction, through the comfort by which we ourselves are comforted by God. As the sufferings of Christ abound in us, so through Christ also abounds our comfort.

Now when we are afflicted, it is on behalf of your comfort and salvation; when we are comforted, it is on behalf of your comfort enduring in the same sufferings which we also suffer. Our hope for you is firm, knowing that as you partake in the sufferings, so also you partake of the comfort.

RESPONSORY Ps 138:5,4

May all creation sing of your ways...
...for great is your glory.
And praise the words of your mouth...
...for great is your glory.
Glory to the Father and to the Son and to the Holy Spirit:
...May all creation sing of your ways,
for great is your glory.

ADVENT READING **PHILIPPIANS 4:4-7**

Rejoice in the Lord always; I say it again, rejoice. Let your kindness be known to all human beings. The Lord is near. Be anxious about nothing, but in everything, by prayer and thanksgiving petition, let your requests be made known to God. And the peace of God which surpasses all understanding will guard your hearts and your minds in Christ Jesus.

RESPONSORY Ps 85:7

Lord, show to us...
...your mercy and unfailing love.
And grant us your salvation...
...your mercy and unfailing love.
Glory to the Father and to the Son and to the Holy Spirit:
... Lord, show to us your mercy and unfailing love.

CHRISTMAS READING **1 JOHN 1:1-3**

What was from the beginning, what we have heard, what we have seen with our eyes, what we have looked at and our hands have touched concerning the Word of Life, and the life has been shown, we have seen and we bear witness and we proclaim to you the life eternal, which was with the Father and has been shown to us. What we have seen and heard, we proclaim also to you that you also may have communion with us. Indeed our communion is with the Father and with the Son, Jesus Christ.

RESPONSORY Jn 1:14

The Word became flesh... *...alleluia, alleluia.*
And dwelt among us... *...alleluia, alleluia.*
Glory to the Father and to the Son and to the Holy Spirit:
...The Word became flesh and dwelt among us;
alleluia, alleluia.

LENT READING, Weeks 1 & 3 **1 CORINTHIANS 9:24-27**

Do you not know that all runners on a racecourse run, but one receives the prize? Run so that you may obtain. Everyone in the struggle exercises self-control in all things, and they in order to receive a corruptible crown. But we, one incorruptible. And so I do not run without clarity nor fight beating the air. But I treat my body in discipline and lead it as a servant, lest having proclaimed to others I myself be disqualified.

RESPONSORY

Listen to us, O Lord, and have mercy...
...for we have sinned against you.
Christ Jesus, hear our humble petitions...
...for we have sinned against you.
Glory to the Father and to the Son and to the Holy Spirit:
...Listen to us, O Lord, and have mercy
for we have sinned against you.

LENT READING, Week 5 **ACTS 13:26-30**

Men and women, brothers and sisters, daughters and sons of Abraham, and those among you fearing God, to us the word of this salvation was sent forth. For the dwellers of Jerusalem and their rulers, knowing neither this man nor the voices of the prophets being read every sabbath, fulfilled them in judging him. And finding no cause for death, they asked Pilate that he be destroyed. And when they finished all the things written concerning him, taking him down from the tree, they laid him in a tomb. But God raised him out of the dead.

RESPONSORY

We worship you, O Christ...
...and we praise you.
By your cross you have redeemed the world...
...and we praise you.
Glory to the Father and to the Son and to the Holy Spirit:
... We worship you, O Christ, and we praise you.

EASTER READING **ROMANS 10:8b-10**

The word is near you, in your mouth and in your heart; this is the word of faith we proclaim.

If you confess with your mouth that Jesus is Lord, and believe in your heart that God raised him from the dead, you will be saved, for with the heart one believes and is justified, and with the mouth one confesses and is saved.

RESPONSORY, in the Octave of Easter

This is the day the Lord has made;
let us rejoice and be glad.

RESPONSORY, Weeks 2 through 7

The Lord is risen from the tomb...
...alleluia, alleluia.
He hung upon the cross for us... *...alleluia, alleluia.*
Glory to the Father and to the Son and to the Holy Spirit:
... The Lord is risen from the tomb; alleluia, alleluia.

ASCENSION READING **1 PETER 3:18,21-22**

Christ died once for sins, a just human for the unjust, put to death in the flesh and made alive in the spirit, that he might bring you to God. Jesus Christ, at the right hand of God, having gone into heaven, subject to him are angels and authorities and powers.

RESPONSORY Jn 20:17

I am ascending to my Father and your Father...
...alleluia alleluia.
To my God and your God... *...alleluia alleluia.*
Glory to the Father and to the Son and to the Holy Spirit:
... I am ascending to my Father and your Father; alleluia alleluia.

PENTECOST READING **EPHESIANS 4:3-6**

Be eager to keep the unity of the Spirit in the bond of peace. There is one body and one Spirit, as also you were called in one hope of your calling, one Lord, one faith, one baptism, one God and Father of all, over all and through all and in all.

RESPONSORY

The Spirit of the Lord has filled the whole world...
...alleluia alleluia.
Sustaining all creation and knowing every word spoken... *...alleluia alleluia.*
Glory to the Father and to the Son and to the Holy Spirit:
... The Spirit of the Lord has filled the whole world; alleluia alleluia.

Gospel Canticle For Evening

Antiphons

Advent Wk 1
Do not be afraid, Mary,
you have found favor with God;
you will conceive
and give birth to a Son, alleluia.

Advent Wk 3
Tell John what you see:
blind see, lame walk,
lepers are cleansed, deaf hear,
dead are raised to life,
and the poor hear the good news.

Christmas
Christ the Lord is born;
the Savior has appeared.
Earth echoes songs of angel choirs.
On earth friends of Christ exult:
Glory to God in the highest,
alleluia.

Solemnity of Mary
Blessed is the womb which bore you,
Christ, and the breast that nursed you,
Lord and Savior of the world, alleluia.

Epiphany
Three mysteries mark this holy day:
the star leads the Magi to the infant Christ;
water is changed into wine for the wedding
feast; Christ wills to be baptized by John
in the river Jordan to bring us salvation.

Antiphons for the Gospel Canticle For Evening, continued

Baptism of the Lord

Christ Jesus loved us, poured out
his blood to wash away our sins,
and made us a realm of royals
and priests for God our Abba.

Lent Wk 1

Watch over us, eternal Savior and
let not the cunning tempter seize us.
All our trust is in your unfailing help.

Lent Wk 3

Whoever drinks
the water that I will give
will never be thirsty again,
says the Lord.

Lent Wk 5

When I am lifted up from the earth,
I will draw all people to myself.

Easter Sunday thru 2nd Sun

On the evening of the first day of
the week, the disciples were gathered
together behind locked doors;
suddenly Jesus stood among them
and said: Peace be with you,
alleluia.

Easter Wk 3

Jesus said to the disciples:
Bring me some of the fish
you have just caught.
Simon Peter jumped to shore,
pulling the net, full of big fish,
alleluia.

Easter Wk 5

I give you a new commandment:
love one another as I have loved you,
says the Lord,
alleluia.

Ascension

O Victor Ruler,
do not leave us orphans
but send us the Abba's promised gift,
the Spirit of truth,
alleluia.

Pentecost

The Holy Spirit
appeared before the apostles
in tongues of fire,
gave them spiritual gifts,
and sent them
to preach to all the cosmos,
alleluia.

Trinity Sunday

O Lord our God,
how wonderful your name. Ps 8

Corpus Christi

How holy this feast
in which Christ is our food;
his passion is recalled;
grace fills our hearts;
and we receive a pledge
of the glory to come,
alleluia. Aquinas

Antiphons for the Gospel Canticle For Evening, continued

Ordinary Time Antiphons Week		*YEAR C Responsorial*
3	Your words, Lord, are Spirit and life.	Ps 19
5	In the sight of the angels I will sing your praises, Lord.	Ps 138
7	The Lord is kind and merciful.	Ps 103
9	Go out to all the world telling the good news.	Ps 117
11	Lord, forgive the wrong I have done.	Ps 32
13	You are my inheritance, O Lord.	Ps 16
15	Turn to the Lord in your need.	Ps 69
17	Lord, I called for help and you answered me.	Ps 138
19	Blessed the people the Lord has chosen.	Ps 33
21	Go out to all the world telling the good news.	Ps 117
23	In every age O Lord you have been our refuge.	Ps 90
25	Praise the Lord who lifts up the poor.	Ps 113
27	If today you hear the voice, harden not your hearts.	Ps 95
29	Our help is from the Lord.	Ps 121
31	I will praise your name forever, my ruler and my God.	Ps 145
33	The Lord comes to rule the earth with justice.	Ps 98

CANTICLE of MARY (The Magnificat)
LUKE 1:46-55

+ **My soul** is stretched full with praise of the Lord,
and my spirit, beyond joy in God, my Savior,
who chose to lay eyes on this humble servant.

Behold, now and forward,
each and every age will call me blessed,
for the Mighty One did great things to me.

Holy is the name and the mercy
to generations and generations,
the ones fearing the One,

Who scattered the haughty of mind and heart,
pulled the powerful off their high place,
and lifted with dignity the humble in need.

The hungering are filled with good things,
the rich are sent away empty,
and servant Israel is given relief

with a memory of mercy to remember,
the promise spoken to our ancestors,
to Abraham and his descendants forever.

Glory…

Antiphon

INTERCESSIONS

- For those who have gone before us marked with the sign of faith…
- In gratitude for blessings…; Abba thank you.
- For the sins of this day…; Lord Jesus have mercy.
- With concerns over tomorrow…; Holy Spirit help.

THE ROAD AHEAD — Thomas Merton

My Lord God,
I have no idea where I am going.
I do not see the road ahead of me.
Nor do I really know myself,
and the fact that I think I am following your will
does not mean that I am actually doing so.
But I believe that the desire to please you
does in fact please you.
And I hope I have that desire in all that I am doing.
I hope that I will never do
anything apart from that desire.
And I know that if I do this
you will lead me by the right road,
though I may know nothing about it.
Therefore I will trust you always though
I may seem to be lost and in the shadow of death.
I will not fear, for you are ever with me,
and you will never leave me to face my perils alone.

OUR FATHER…

WEEK I
MONDAY MORNING

+ *God, come to my assistance;* Psalm 70:2
Lord, make haste to help me!

Glory...

ORDINARY TIME

From all that dwell be/-low the\ skies,
Let the Cre-a-tor's praise a-rise;
Let the Re-deem/-er's/ Name\ be\ sung,
Through ev-'ry land, by ev-'ry tongue.

E-ter-nal are your/ mer-cies\, Lord;
E-ter-nal truth at-tends your Word.
Your praise shall sound/ from/ shore\ to\ shore,
Till suns shall rise and set no more.

In ev-'ry land be/-gin the\ song;
To ev-'ry land the strains be-long;
In cheer-ful sounds/ all/ voi\-ces\ raise,
And fill the world with loud-est praise.

92, see Psalm 117
Text: Isaac Watts, *The Psalms of David,* 1719;
Robert Spence, *Pocket Hymn Book,* 1780, altered
Music: DUKE STREET, LM; John Hatton, 1793

ADVENT

Come, Thou long ex-pect-ed Je-sus
Born to set your peo-ple free;
From our fears and sins re-lease us,
Let us find our rest in thee.

Is-rael's strength and con-so-la-tion,
Hope of all the earth you are;
Dear de-sire of ev-'ry na-tion,
Joy of ev-'ry long-ing heart.

Born your peo-ple to de-liv-er,
Born a child and yet a king,
Born to reign in us for-ev-er,
Now your gra-cious king-dom bring.

By your own e-ter-nal Spir-it
Rule in all our hearts a-lone;
By your all suf-fic-ient mer-it,
Raise us to your glo-rious throne.

4, Text: Charles Wesley,
Hymns for the Nativity of our Lord, 1745, altered
Music: 87 87 D, STUTTGART, Christian F. Witt, 1715;
adapted by Henry J. Gauntlett, d.1876
Alternate Melody: HYFRYDOL, Rowland H. Prichard, 1830,
Love Divine All Love Excelling

CHRISTMAS

The/ God whom\ earth and/ sea and sky
A-dore and laud and mag-ni-fy,
Who o'er their/ three\-fold fab\-ric reigns,
The vir-gin's spot-less womb con-tains.

The/ God whose\ will by/ moon and sun
And all things in due course is done,
Is borne up/-on\ a maid\-en's breast,
By full-est heav'-nly grace pos-sessed.

Blest/ in the\ mes-sage/ Ga-briel brought;
Blest by the work the Spir-it wrought:
The Great De/-sire\ of all\ the earth
Took hu-man flesh and hu-man birth.

All/ ho-nor\, laud, and/ glo-ry be,
To you, O Je-sus, of the Three,
All glo-ry/, as\ you ev\-er meet
Our Fa-ther and the Pa-ra-clete.

36, Text: Venantius Fortunatus, *Quem terra, pontus...,* d.609;
translated by John M. Neale, 1854, altered
Music option: ERHALT UNS HERR, LM;
Klug's *Geistliche Lieder, 1543;*
Popular melody for: *The Glory Of These Forty Days*

LENT

At break of day fill us with wis-dom and love;
Give fa-vor and pros-per the work of our hands.
A thou-sand years hu-man like one day to you,
Our ref-uge through each gen-er-a-tion, re-new.

Be-fore bring-ing forth world-ly moun-tains
and earth,
You are God e-ter-nal with no end or birth.
There is some-where in us made sad when
we learn
That we are dust and to this dust we re-turn.

Though sev-en-ty years is the sum of our days,
Or eigh-ty if we are made strong in your ways.
Like grass that sprouts green in the new
mor-ning air
Years end like a sigh, ebb a-way, this we share.

So wis-en'd with trou-bles, this we com-pre-hend:
You want us to sing a glad song in the land.
At break of day fill us with wis-dom and love;
Give fa-vor and pros-per the work of our hands.

82, Text: Psalm 90, by Stephen J. Wolf, 2007,
tribute to the priesthood of William Nolan
Music: 11 11 11 11, ST. DENIO, Welsh Melody,
John Roberts, *Canaidau y Cyssagr*, 1839
Popular melody for: *Immortal, Invisible, God Only Wise*

EASTER

The strife is o'er, the bat\-tle done;
Now is the vic-tor's tri\-umph won;
Now is the song of praise\ be-gun.
Al-le-lu-ia!
Al-le-lu-ia! Al-le-lu-ia! Al-le-lu-ia!

Death's migh-tiest pow'rs
   have done\ their worst,
And Je-sus has his foes\ dis-persed;
Let shouts of praise and joy\ out-burst.
Al-le-lu-ia!
Al-le-lu-ia! Al-le-lu-ia! Al-le-lu-ia!

On the third morn he rose\ a-gain
Glo-rious in ma-jes-ty\ to reign;
Oh, let us swell the joy\-ful strain!
Al-le-lu-ia!
Al-le-lu-ia! Al-le-lu-ia! Al-le-lu-ia!

72, Text: from Psalm 98:1 by an unknown author, 1695,
translated by Francis Pott, 1859, altered
Music: 888 VICTORY with alleluias, Giovanni P. Da Palestrina, 1591,
adapted by William Monk, d.1889

PSALM 9

Antiphon *Foxes have holes and birds of the sky nests,*
but the Son of Humanity has no place
where his head may lay. Lk 9:58

Christmas & Easter The Lord is a refuge for the oppressed,
a stronghold in times of trouble;
alleluia.

I will praise Adonai with all my heart;
I will tell of all the wonderful things.
I will be glad and rejoice in you,
I will sing praise to your name, Most High.

When enmity turns back
it stumbles before you
for you upheld my right and my cause;
you sat on the throne judging justly.

You rebuked nations, you destroyed bad ways;
their name you blotted out to forever and ever.
Enmity is overtaken by endless ruin;
cities are uprooted and their memories perish.

Adonai reigns to forever,
set up on the throne for judgment
to judge the world in fairness
and to govern peoples with justice.

Adonai is the refuge for the oppressed,
the stronghold in times of trouble.
Those who know your name will trust in you,
for you never forsake seekers of Adonai.

Sing praise to Adonai, enthroned in Zion.
Proclaim the deeds among the nations
for the One who can avenge violence remembers
and does not ignore the cry of the afflicted.

Have mercy on me, Adonai,
and see the persecution of enmity.
Lift me up from the gates of death
that I may declare all of your praises
in the gates of your daughter Zion.
I will rejoice in your salvation.

Nations fell into the pit they dug;
in the net that they hid are their own feet caught.
Adonai is known by justice;
bad ways get snared in their handiwork.

The nations forgetting God return to Sheol,
but the needy will not be forgotten
nor will the hope of the afflicted ever perish.

Arise Adonai; let not the human triumph.
Let the nations be judged in your presences.
Strike the nations, Adonai,
and let them know their humanity.

Glory... Antiphon

PSALM 5

Antiphon *If someone wishes to sue you*
to get your tunic,
let that one take also the cloak. Mt 5:40

Advent & Lent: Lord, you hear my morning voice;
with my morning request before you,
I wait.

Dec 26: The newborn Christ has given
The crown of glory to Stephen.

Christmas & Easter: All those who love your name
will rejoice in you,
alleluia.

Give ear to my words, Adonai;
consider my sighing.
Listen to the sound of my cry for help,
for to you I pray, my Ruler and my God.

Hear, Adonai, my morning voice;
with my morning request before you, I wait.

You are not pleased with doings of the bad,
nor can the doers dwell with you.
The arrogant cannot stand before your eyes.
You hate when wrong is done, you destroy lies,
you abhor bloodshed and deceit.

By the greatness of your mercy, Adonai,
I will come into your house,
In reverence I will bow in your holy temple.

Lead me in your justice, Adonai;
because of enmity
make straight before me your way.

Their mouth is not to be trusted,
their heart is destruction,
their throat an open grave,
and their tongue speaks deceit.

If you, God, declare them guilty
let their fall be by their intrigue;
let them be banished if they have sinned,
if they have rebelled against you.

But let all who take refuge in you be glad;
let them sing for joy forever.
You spread protection over them
that they may rejoice in you and love your name.

You bless the just, Adonai,
surrounding them with favor as a shield.

Glory…

Antiphon

It's letting go of the sense that
the past should have been any different or better.

See *The Tricky Part* by Martin Moran

PSALM 84

Antiphon *Why do you look for me?*
Do you not know that I have to be
in my Abba's house? Lk 2:49

Advent The Lord, the ruler over
the royals of the earth, will come;
blessed are they who are ready
and go and give welcome.

Christmas Tell us, shepherds, what did you see?

Lent Blessed are the ones dwelling
in your house, my Ruler and my God.

Easter My heart and my flesh
rejoice in God alive, alleluia.

How lovely are your dwellings,
Adonai Sabaoth!
My soul she yearns and even faints
for the courts of Adonai;
my heart and my flesh cry out for God alive.

Even the sparrow found a home
and the swallow a nest for her
where she may settle her young ones
near your altar, Adonai Sabaoth,
my Ruler and my God.

Blessed are the dwellers in your house,
ever they praise you.
Blessed are the ones whose strength is in you,
who make a pilgrimage in their hearts.

Passing through the Baca Valley,
springs are found,
pools covered over with autumn rains.
They go from strength to strength
and appear before God in Zion.

Adonai, God Sabaoth, hear my prayer!
Listen, God of Jacob. God, our shield, look!
Look on the face of your anointed one!

Better is one day in your courts
than a thousand elsewhere.
Better to be doorkeeper in my God's house
than to dwell in tents of those who do the bad,

for God Adonai is sun and shield.
Adonai bestows grace and honor,
withholding no goodness
from blameless walkers.

Adonai Sabaoth,
blessed is the one trusting in you.

Glory... Antiphon

Psalm 84 is often used
for the blessing of a new sacred space.

ISAIAH 2:2-5

Antiphon *Blessed are the peacemakers,*
for they will be called
sons and daughters of God. Mt 5:9

Advent Sing a new song to the Lord;
sing praise to the ends of the earth.

Dec 26 Stephen saw the heavens open.

Christmas The angel said to the shepherds:
I proclaim to you a great joy;
the Savior of the world
is born for you,
alleluia.

Lent They will beat their swords into
plowshares and their spears
into pruning hooks.

Easter The house of the Lord
has been raised on high,
where all the nations
will make their way,
alleluia.

I want not the
things you have, but you.

Paul of Tarsus 2 Cor 12:14

In the last of the days
the mountain of Adonai's temple
will be established as chief of the mountains,
raised above the hills.

All the nations will stream to it.
Many peoples will come and say,
"Come, let us go up to the mountain of Adonai,
to the house of the God of Jacob,
who will teach us the ways
so we may walk in the path."

Indeed, from Zion the law will go out
and from Jerusalem the word of Adonai,
who will judge between the nations
and settle disputes for many peoples.

They will beat their swords into plowshares
and their spears into pruning hooks.
Nations will not take up the sword against nations,
and they will train for war no more.

House of Jacob, come!
Let us walk in Adonai's light.

Glory…

Antiphon

1 CHRONICLES 29:10b-13

Antiphon *Every thing we have to give*
is from you, our God. 1Chr 29:14b

Advent & Lent Now, our God,
we praise your name and your glory.

Dec 26 Stephen saw Jesus standing
at the right hand of God.

Christmas & Easter Yours is the reign, Lord,
for you rule over all rulers, alleluia.

Praise be to you, Adonai, God of Israel,
our Abba from everlasting to everlasting.

To you, Adonai, are the greatness and power
and glory and majesty and splendor
for all in the heavens and on the earth.

To you, Adonai, are the reign
and exaltation as head over all,
and wealth and honor from before you.

And you rule over all in your hand,
strength and power in your hand,
to lift up and give strength to all.

Now, our God, we give thanks to you
and praise your name and your glory.

Glory... Antiphon

PSALM 29

Antiphon *A voice out of heaven: this is my Beloved Son in whom I am well pleased.* Mt 3:17

Ascribe to Adonai, you in the heavens,
acknowledge Adonai as glory and strength.
Give to Adonai the glory of the Name.
Worship Adonai in holy splendor.

The voice of Adonai over the waters,
the God of glory thunders.
Adonai over mighty waters,
the voice of Adonai in power and majesty,
the voice of Adonai breaking cedars,

Adonai breaks the cedars of Lebanon
and makes Lebanon leap like a calf
and Sirion like a young bull.

The voice of Adonai strikes flashes of lightning,
the voice of Adonai shakes the desert,
Adonai shakes the desert of Kadesh.

The voice of Adonai makes the deer give birth
and strips the forests bare,
and all in the temple cry, "glory."
Adonai sits over the flood
and Adonai is enthroned as Ruler to forever.

May Adonai give strength to the people;
may Adonai bless the people with peace.

Glory... Antiphon

PSALM 96

Antiphon *Render to Ceasar the things of Ceasar,*
and to God the things of God. Mt 22:21

Advent Will the Son of Humanity coming to
earth find faith in human hearts?

Christmas Christ is born for us;
come and let us adore.

Epiphany My own eyes have seen
the salvation you have prepared
in the sight of every people.

Lent Sing to the Lord
and praise the Name.

Easter Say it among the nations:
the Lord rules,
alleluia.

Sing to Adonai a new song!
Sing to Adonai, all the earth!
Sing to Adonai and praise the name!
Proclaim salvation from day to day!

Declare among the nations the glory of the Lord!
Among all the peoples the marvelous deeds,
for great is Adonai, greatly being praised,
the one to be feared above all so-called "gods."

For all "gods" of the nations
are do-nothing idols,
but Adonai made the heavens,
splendor and majesty and strength and glory
in the holy sanctuary.

Ascribe to Adonai, families of nations!
Acknowledge Adonai as glory and strength!
Give to Adonai the glory of the Name!

Bring offerings and come into the courts!
Worship Adonai in holy splendor!
Tremble in the presence all you earth!

Say among the nations, "Adonai is our ruler!"
Firmly set, the world cannot be moved
and peoples will be judged with equity.

Let the heavens rejoice and the earth be glad.
Let the sea resound and all its fullness.
Let the fields and all that is in them be jubilant
and all the trees of the forests sing for joy

before Adonai who comes,
who comes to judge the earth,
who will judge the world and its peoples
with justice and honesty.

Glory... Antiphon

Praying the psalms continually ponders and proclaims
the action of God in the history of salvation. Pope Paul VI, 1970

ORDINARY TIME READING **2 THESSALONIANS 3:7-13**

You yourselves know how good it is to imitate us. We were not idle among you, nor did we eat bread as a gift from anyone, but by labor and struggle by night and by day working, to not be a burden on any of you, not that we have no authority, but so that we ourselves might give to you an example to imitate.

Even when we were with you, we gave you as a charge that if anyone does not wish to work, neither let that one eat. For we hear of some walking among you idly, not working but walking around the work, and to such we charge and exhort in the Lord Jesus Christ that from your quiet working you may eat bread. And you, brothers and sisters, do not lose heart in doing good.

RESPONSORY Ps 72:18,19

Blessed be the Lord, the God of Israel…
…blessed from now and to forever.
The One alone doing marvelous deeds…
…blessed from now and to forever.
Glory to the Father and to the Son and to the Holy Spirit:
…Blessed be the Lord, the God of Israel;
blessed from now and to forever.

ADVENT READING **ISAIAH 2:3-4**

Come, let us go up to the mountain of Adonai, to the house of the God of Jacob, who will teach us the ways so we may walk in the path. Indeed, from Zion the law will go out and from Jerusalem the word of Adonai, who will judge between the nations and settle disputes for many peoples.

They will beat their swords into plowshares and their spears into pruning hooks. Nations will not take up the sword against nations, and they will train for war no more.

RESPONSORY

Your light will come, Jerusalem...
...the Lord will dawn on you in radiant beauty.
The glory of the Lord you will see within you...
...the Lord will dawn on you in radiant beauty.
Glory to the Father and to the Son and to the Holy Spirit:
...Your light will come, Jerusalem;
the Lord will dawn on you in radiant beauty.

CHRISTMAS READING **ISAIAH 49:8-10**

This says Adonai: "In the time of favor, I will answer you, and in the day of salvation I will help you. I will keep you and I will make you as a covenant of the people, to restore land to reassign desolate inheritances, to say to captives, 'Come out!' and to those in darkness, 'Be free!'

They will feed beside roads, their pasture on every barren hill; they will not hunger, nor will they thirst, nor will the desert heat beat on them, nor the sun. One having compassion on them will guide them and beside springs of waters lead them."

RESPONSORY

The Lord has made known...
...alleluia, alleluia.
The saving power...
...alleluia, alleluia.
Glory to the Father and to the Son and to the Holy Spirit:
...The Lord has made known the saving power, alleluia.

After Epiphany

All the royal powers on earth
...will bow down in worship.
Men and women of every nation...
...will bow down in worship.
Glory to the Father and to the Son and to the Holy Spirit:
...All the royal powers on earth
will bow down in worship.

LENT READING, Weeks 1 & 3 **EXODUS 19:4-6a**

You saw what I did in Egypt, and I carried you on wings of eagles, and I brought you to myself, and now if to obey you obey my voice and you keep my covenant, then you will be my possession from all the nations, although all the earth is mine; and you will be for me a realm of priests, a holy nation.

RESPONSORY Lk 18:13

The Lord God will set me free…
…from the hunter's snare.
From all those who would trap me with lying words,
…and from the hunter's snare.
Glory to the Father and to the Son and to the Holy Spirit:
…The Lord God will set me free from the hunter's snare.

LENT READING, Week 5 **JEREMIAH 11:19-20**

Yet as a trusting lamb is led to slaughter, I did not know that they plotted plots against me to destroy the tree with its fruit and to cut me off from the land of the living so my name would be remembered no more.

But Adonai Sabaoth, just Judge, searcher of mind and heart, let me see your vengeance upon them, for to you I have entrusted my cause.

RESPONSORY Rev. 5:9

Lord, by your own blood…
…you brought us back to God.
From every tribe and tongue and people and nation…
…you brought us back to God.
Glory to the Father and to the Son and to the Holy Spirit:
…Lord, by your own blood you brought us back to God.

EASTER READING **ROMANS 10:8b-10**

The word is near you, in your mouth and in your heart; this is the word of faith we proclaim.

If you confess with your mouth that Jesus is Lord, and believe in your heart that God raised him from the dead, you will be saved, for with the heart one believes and is justified, and with the mouth one confesses and is saved.

RESPONSORY, in the Octave of Easter

This is the day the Lord has made;
let us rejoice and be glad.

RESPONSORY, Weeks 2 through 7

The Lord is risen from the tomb…
…alleluia, alleluia.
He hung upon the cross for us…
…alleluia, alleluia.
Glory to the Father and to the Son and to the Holy Spirit:
…The Lord is risen from the tomb; alleluia, alleluia.

Gospel Canticle For Morning

Antiphons

Advent Wk 1 Matt 8:5-11	Lift up your eyes, Jerusalem, and see the great power of your Ruler; your Savior comes to set you free.
Advent Wk 3 Matt 21:23-27	From heaven comes, the Lord and Ruler, holder of honor and royal authority.
Dec 26	The gates of heaven opened to Stephen, crowned first of martyrs.
Christmas	Helpless, he lay in a manger; glorious, he shined in the heavens; humbled, he lived among humanity; eternal, he dwelt with the Abba.
After Epiphany	The wise came from the East to adore the Lord in Bethlehem. Opening their treasures, they offered the three gifts: gold for the great Ruler, frankincense for the true God, and myrrh for his burial.
Lent Wk 1 Matt 25:31-46	You have been blessed by my Abba; come and receive the dominion prepared for you from the foundation of the world.

Antiphons for Gospel Canticle For Morning, continued

Lent Wk 3 Luke 4:24-30	I tell you for sure, no prophet is accepted in their own country.
Lent Wk 5 John 8:1-11	Whoever follows me does not walk in the dark but will have the light of life.
Easter Wk 1 Mt 28:8-15	Go quickly and tell the disciples: the Lord is risen, alleluia.
Easter Wk 3 John 6:22-29	Work not for food that perishes, but for food that remains to eternal life, alleluia.
Easter Wk 5 John 14:21-26	Whoever loves me is loved by my Abba, and I will love them and show myself to them, alleluia.
Easter Wk 7 John 16:29-33	The world will persecute you but have courage; I have overcome the world, alleluia.
Ordinary Antiphon	*Blessed be the Lord our God.*

Gospel Reading for Monday of

Week **1** Mark 1:14-20	**13** Matt 8:18-22	**25** Luke 8:16-18
3 Mark 3:22-30	**15** Mt 10:34 - 11:1	**27** Lk 10:25-37
5 Mark 6:53-56	**17** Matt 13:31-35	**29** Lk 12:13-21
7 Mark 9:14-29	**19** Matt 17:22-27	**31** Lk 14:12-14
9 Mark 12:1-12	**21** Matt 23:13-22	**33** Lk 18:35-43
11 Matt 5:38-42	**23** Luke 6:6-11	

CANTICLE of ZECHARIAH (The Benedictus)
LUKE 1:68-79

+ **Blessed be** the Lord the God of Israel
who chose a people to visit with redemption,
and raised salvation in the house of David,
saving strength from God's own servant,

speaking from the age of the prophets
through the mouth of the holy prophet:
Salvation out of enmity,
even out of those who hate us,

to show our ancestors how mercy works, -
and to remember the holy promise of the Lord,
the covenant made for our ancestor Abraham,
calming our fear and making us free
to serve with holy justice before God all our days.

And you also child -
will be called a prophet of the Most High
for you will go before the Lord to prepare his way
and give to people a knowledge of salvation
known in accepting forgiveness of their sins.

From the tender mercy of our God,
the sun rising from the height will visit with light
for those who sit in the dark or shadow of death
and to guide our feet into the way of peace.

Glory...

Antiphon

PETITIONS FOR THE CONSECRATION TO GOD OF THE DAY AND ITS WORK

- For the Church and her ministry and apostolates...
- For secular authorities and all serving as stewards...
- For people who are poor or sick or in sorrow...
- For peace and the basic needs of each human being...
- For justice for migrant workers and refugees...
- For starving children awakening our conscience...
- For people living in subhuman conditions...
- For human beings enslaved or unjustly imprisoned...
- For laborers where treated as mere tools for profit...
- For good work for all to do in dignity...
- In gratitude for blessings and grace...

FOR WORKERS IN OFFICES, SHOPS & MARKETS

adapted from the *Book of Blessings*

O God, lead all who plan and conduct business to
wise and honest decisions and give them the grace
to carry them out fairly for the common good.
Like the Carpenter, may all who skillfully transform
the things you have created know their dignity
and be fulfilled in making human lives better.
And may buyers and sellers
embody justice and charity and find joy
in the progress of the whole earthly city.

OUR FATHER...

WEEK I
MONDAY EVENING

\+ *God, come to my assistance;* Psalm 70:2
Lord, make haste to help me!

Glory...

ADVENT

Draw near to your Je-ru-sa-lem, O Lord,
Your faith-ful peo-ple cry with one ac-cord;
Ride on in tri-umph; Lord, be-hold we lay
Our stub-born hearts and proud wills
in your way!
Your road is read-y
and your path made straight;
With long-ing ex-pec-ta-tion is our wait.

Ho-san-na! wel-come to our hearts! for here
You have a temp-le, too, as Zi-on dear;
O en-ter in, dear Lord, un-bar the door;
And in that temp-le dwell for-ev-er-more.
Your road is read-y
and your path made straight;
With long-ing ex-pec-ta-tion is our wait.

8, Text: Jeremy Taylor, *Festival and Penitential Hymns,* 1655;
abridged in *Sarum Hymnal,* 1868, altered
Music: 10 10 10 10 10 10 UNDE ET MEMORES,
William H. Monk, 1823-1899
Popular melody for: *Lord Who At The First Eucharist Did Pray*

ORDINARY TIME & EASTER

For the/ beau-ty of the earth,
For the glo-ry of the skies,
For the/ love which from our birth
O-ver and a-round us lies.
Lord of all, to you we raise
This our song of grate-ful praise.

For the/ beau-ty of each hour,
Of the day and of the night,
Hill and/ val-ley, tree and flow'r,
Sun and moon and stars of light.
Lord of all, to you we raise
This our song of grate-ful praise.

For the/ joy of ear and eye,
For the heart and mind's de-light,
For the/ mys-tic har-mo-ny
Link-ing sense to sound and sight.
Lord of all, to you we raise
This our song of grate-ful praise.

For the/ joy of hu-man love,
Bro-ther, sis-ter, par-ent, child,
Friends on/ earth and friends a-bove,
Sa-cred res-pite from the wild.
Lord of all, to you we raise
This our song of grate-ful praise.

For your/ peo-ple ev-er-more
Lift-ing ho-ly hands a-bove,
Off-'ring/ up on ev-'ry shore
Faith and sac-rif-i-cial love.
Lord of all, to you we raise
This our song of grate-ful praise.

Per-fect/ gift of pres-ence thine
Won-drous gift so free-ly giv'n,
Gra-ces/ hu-man and div-ine,
Peace on earth and joy in heav'n.
Lord of all, to you we raise
This our song of grate-ful praise.

94, Text: Lyra Eucharistica, 1864;
Folliot S. Pierpoint, 1864, altered
Music: 77 77 77, DIX, Conrad Kocher, 1838;
adapted by William H. Monk, 1823-99

When God looks at us God sees Jesus,
and only Jesus, the innocent, guiltless Jesus.

See *Who Told You That You Were Naked?* by John Jacob Raub

CHRISTMAS

O lit-tle town of Beth-le-hem,
How still we/ see you lie!
A-bove a deep and dream-less sleep
The si-lent/ stars go by;
Yet in your dark-ness shi-ning
The ev-er-last-ing Light;
The hopes and fears of all the years
Are met in you to-night.

For Christ is born of Ma\-ry,
And fa-thered/ all a-bove,
While hu-mans sleep, the an-gels keep
Their watch of/ won-d'ring love.
O morn-ing stars, to-geth-er
Pro-claim the ho-ly birth
And prais-es sing to God, the King,
And peace to all on earth.

O ho-ly Child of Beth-le-hem,
Des-cend to/ us, we pray;
Cast out our sin and en-ter in,
Be born in/ us to-day.
We hear the Christ-mas an-gels
The great glad tid-ings tell:
Oh, come to us, a-bide with us,
Our Lord Em-man-u-el!

LENT

At the name of Je/-sus, ev-'ry knee shall bow,
Ev-'ry tongue con-fess/ him King of glo-ry now;
'Tis the Fa/-ther's plea\-sure that we call him Lord,
Who from the be-gin\-ning is the migh-ty Word.

At his voice cre-a/-tion sprang at once to sight,
All the an-gels' fa/-ces, all the hosts of light,
Thrones and dom/-in-a\-tions, stars up-on their way,
All the heav'n-ly or\-ders, in their great ar-ray.

Hum-bled for a sea/-son, to re-ceive a name
From the lips of sin/-ners un-to whom he came,
Faith-ful-ly/ he bore\ it, spot-less to the last,
Carr-ied it vic-tor\-ious when from death he passed.

Bro-thers, Sis-ters, name/ him, with love strong as death
But with awe and won/-der, and with halt-ed breath!
He is God/ our Sa\-vior, he is Christ the Lord,
Ev-er to be wor\-shipped, trust-ed and a-dored.

43, Text: Caroline M. Noel, *The Name of Jesus and Other Verses for the Sick and Lonely*, 1870, altered
Music: 11 11 11 11 ADORO TE DEVOTE,
Benedictine Plainsong, Mode V, 13th Century

30, Text: based on Micah 5:2; Phillips Brooks, 1868, altered
Music: 86 86 76 86 ST.LOUIS, Lewis Henry Redner, 1868
Christmas – O Little Town of Bethlehem

PSALM 7

Antiphon *Why do you see*
the piece of dust in your neighbor's eye
but ignore the wood beam
in your own eye? Lk 6:41

Christmas Mary and Joseph
were filled with wonder
at all that was said of the child.

Easter Alleluia, alleluia, alleluia.

My God, **Adonai**, in you I take refuge;
save me and deliver me from all who pursue me.
Like lions they want to tear me up,
rip my self to pieces with no one to save me.

My God, Adonai, if I deserve this,
if there is guilt on my hands,
if I did wrong to one at peace with me,
or if I robbed without cause from an adversary,

then let that one pursue my self
and overtake my life
and trample my honor to the ground;
let that one put me down in the dust.

Arise, Adonai, rise up in your anger
against the rages of enmity.

Awake, my God, and decree your justice
and let the assembly of peoples gather to you;
rule over us from the height.
Let Adonai be the judge of the peoples.

Judge me, Adonai, as you judge me in justice,
as you judge my integrity, Most High.
May violence end now and the just be secure;
search our minds and hearts, God of justice.

My shield, God Most High,
saves the honest of heart,
and judges each day with justice,
holding the threat of wrath.

If none repent, they will sharpen their sword
and bend their bow with string and make ready
with weapons of death and flaming arrows.
See, trouble is conceived and evil is pregnant,
then comes to birth disillusionment.

They dig holes and scoop them out
but fall into the pits they made.
Their trouble recoils on their heads;
on their heads their violence makes landing.

I give thanks for the justice of Adonai
and sing praise to the name of Most High Adonai.

Glory...

Antiphon

PSALM 71

Antiphon *Amen I tell you*
that no prophet is acceptable
in their native place. Lk 4:24

Advent & Lent: You are my hope,
Lord Adonai,
my confidence since youth.

Christmas & Easter: Alleluia, alleluia, alleluia.

In you, **Adonai**, I take refuge;
to forever, let me not be shamed.
In your justice you rescue and deliver me.
Turn your ear to me and save me!

Be to me as a rock, and a refuge to go to always.
Command that I be saved,
for you are my rock and my fortress.
My God, deliver me
from the hands and from the grasp
of doers of the cruel bad,

for you are my hope, Lord Adonai,
my confidence since my youth.
I have relied on you from birth,
from my mother's womb you brought me forth;
my praise is ever to you.

To many I became like a portent
but you are my strong refuge.
My mouth is filled all the day
with praise of your splendor.
Cast me not away at my time of old age;
forsake me not when my strength is gone.

Enmity speaks against me;
waiting on my life, conspirers together say,
"God has forsaken that one! Pursue to seize,
for no one is coming to the rescue!"

God, be not far from me.
God, come quickly to help me!
May accusations against me perish in shame.
May scorn and disgrace
cover the desire to do harm.

But I will hope always and add praise of you.
My mouth will tell of your just deeds,
all the day of your salvation,
though I know not its measure;

I will come in mighty acts of Lord Adonai;
I will tell of your singular justice.
You taught me, God, since my youth;
to this day I declare your marvelous deeds.

Psalm 71, continued

Even in my old age and gray hair
you do not forsake me, God,
till I delcare your power to this generation,
your might to all yet to come,
and your justice to the heavens,
you, God, who have done great things.
Who, God, is equal to you?

Though you let me see troubles, many and bitter,
you will again let me live.
And from the depths of the earth
you will again raise me up.
You will restore my honor
and you will again comfort me.

With the harp instrument I will praise you
and your faithfulness, my God;
I will sing praise to you with lyre,
Holy One of Israel.

My lips will shout for joy
when I sing praise to you,
even my self whom you redeemed.

Also my tongue will tell
all the day of your justice,
for desires of some to harm me
are in shame and confusion.

Glory...

Psalm 71 is known as a song of the elders.

Antiphon *Amen I tell you*
that no prophet is acceptable
in their native place. Lk 4:24

Advent & Lent: You are my hope,
Lord Adonai,
my confidence since youth.

Christmas & Easter: Alleluia, alleluia, alleluia.

PSALM 11

Antiphon *Blessed are you poor,*
for yours is the reign of God. Lk 6:20b

Christmas & Easter Have courage;
I have overcome the world, alleluia.

In Adonai I take refuge.
How can you say to my self,
"Flee, bird, to your mountain
for look, doers of bad now bend their bow,

they set their arrow on the string
to shoot from the shadow at the upright of heart.
When the foundations are destroyed,
what can the upright do?"

Adonai is in the holy temple,
on Adonai's throne in the heavens
with eyes observing, examining
the sons and daughters of humanity.

Adonai examines the good and the bad,
hating in the soul the love of violence,
and will rain onto bad ways
coal and sulphur on fire
and scorching wind, the lot of their cup,

for Adonai is just, loving justice;
we will see the faces of the Just One.

Glory... Antiphon

PSALM 15

Antiphon *Blessed are the clean of heart,*
for they will see God. Mt 5:8

Christmas & Easter This one will abide in your tent
and live on your holy mountain,
alleluia.

Adonai, who may dwell in your tent sanctuary?
Who may live on your holy mountain?
One walking without blame, one doing the right,
speaking the truth in the heart,

whose tongue does not slander,
who does no wrong to a neighbor,
who casts no slur on a mutual human,
in whose eyes vile acts are despised

while those who fear Adonai are honored,
whose sworn oath is not changed even to pain,
who lends money without usury,
and accepts no bribe against the innocent.

One faithful in these
will be unshaken to forever.

Glory… Antiphon

Humans, you have been told what is
good and what Adonai requires of you; do justice,
love goodness, and walk humbly with your God. Micah 6:8

PSALM 123

Antiphon *Talitha koun;*
little girl, I say to you, arise. Mk 5:41

Advent The Lord, the Ruler over the
rulers of the earth, will come;
blessed are they who are ready
to go and give welcome.

Lent Our eyes are to our God
till the Lord shows to us mercy.

Christmas & Easter The Lord will be your light forever;
your God will be your glory, alleluia.

I lift up my eyes to you, sitting in the heavens.
As eyes of a servant are to the hand of a master,

as the eyes of a maid
are to the hand of a mistress,
see, our eyes are to Adonai
till our God shows to us mercy.

Have mercy on us, Adonai, have mercy on us,
for we have endured much contempt.
Much ridicule of proud ones
and contempt of arrogant ones
have we ourselves endured.

Glory…

Antiphon

PSALM 124

Antiphon *One finding one's own life will lose it,*
and one losing one's own life for my sake
will find it. Mt 10:39

Advent & Christmas Sing a new song to the Lord,
praises to the ends of the earth.

Lent Our help is in the name of the Lord,
the One Maker of heavens and earth.

Easter The snare was broken
and we were set free, alleluia.

If Adonai was not for us, let Israel now say,
if Adonai was not for us
when human beings attacked against us,
then they would have swallowed us alive
when their anger blazed against us.

Then the floods would have engulfed us,
the torrents would have swept over our selfs,
and the raging waters would have swept over us.

Praise be to Adonai,
who did not let us be torn by their teeth.
Our selfs, like a bird,
escaped from the snare of fowlers.

The snare being broken we escaped.
Our help is in the name of Adonai,
the Maker of heavens and earth.

Glory… Antiphon

EPHESIANS 1:3-10

Antiphon *Jesus called to himself the Twelve*
and began to send them out
two by two. Mk 6:7a

Advent & Lent God chose us in Christ
as sons and daughters are adopted.

Dec 17-23 Coming to earth,
will the Son of Humanity,
find faith in human hearts?

Christmas The shepherds went in haste
and found Mary and Joseph,
with the child cradled in a manger.

Easter When I am lifted up from the earth
I will draw all people to myself,
alleluia.

Blessed be the God and Abba
of our Lord Jesus Christ,
who has blessed us in Christ
with every spiritual blessing in the heavens.

God chose us in Christ
before the foundation of the world,
to be holy and free of blemish before him.

In love, God gave us a destiny:
as parents adopt, through Jesus Christ himself,
in accord with the good pleasure of God's will
to the praise of the glory of grace
by which we are favored as God's beloved.

In Christ we have the redemption
through his blood, the forgiveness of sins,
in accord with the riches of his grace
which he made abound to us.

In all wisdom and intelligence
the mystery of God's will is made known to us
in accord with God's good pleasure and purpose:

A stewardship of the fullness of time,
heading up all things in Christ,
the things in the heavens and the things on earth.

Glory…

Antiphon

ORDINARY TIME READING **COLOSSIANS 1:9b-14**

May you be filled with the full knowledge of God's will in all wisdom and spiritual understanding, to walk worthily and all-pleasing to the Lord in every good work bearing fruit, and growing in the full knowledge of God, be empowered with all power as the glory of God is mighty, and endure all long-suffering with joy.

Give thanks to the Father who has made you fit for your part of the lot of the saints in light, who delivered us out of the authority of darkness and transitioned us into the reign of his beloved Son, in whom we have redemption, the forgiveness of our sins.

RESPONSORY Ps 41:5

You, Lord, are the one who can heal me…
…for it is you I have grieved.
Lord, show to me your mercy…
…for it is you I have grieved.
Glory to the Father and to the Son and to the Holy Spirit:
…You, Lord, are the one who can heal me,
for it is you I have grieved.

ADVENT READING **PHILIPPIANS 3:20b-21**

And we await a Savior, the Lord Jesus Christ, who will change the body of our humility, conforming it to the body of his glory, as it is his ability to subject even all things to himself.

RESPONSORY Ps 146:7; 63:3; 67:2

Come and set us free…
…Lord God of power and glory…
Let your face shine upon us
and we will know salvation…
…Lord God of power and glory…
Glory to the Father and to the Son and to the Holy Spirit:
…Come and set us free, Lord God of power and glory.

CHRISTMAS READING **COLOSSIANS 1:13-16**

The Father delivered us out of the authority of darkness, transitioning us into the reign of the beloved Son in whom we have redemption, the forgiveness of our sins. The Son is the image of the invisible God, the firstborn of all creation. In him all things were created, in the heavens and on the earth, the visible and the invisible, whether thrones, lordships, rulers or authorities. All creation has come to be through and for him.

RESPONSORY Jn 1:14

Before Epiphany
The Word became flesh…
…alleluia, alleluia.
And dwelt among us…
…alleluia, alleluia.
Glory to the Father and to the Son and to the Holy Spirit:
…The Word became flesh and dwelt among us,
alleluia, alleluia.

After Epiphany

All people will be blessed in him…
…in every tribe of the human race.
All nations will acclaim his glory…
…in every tribe of the human race.
Glory to the Father and to the Son and to the Holy Spirit:
…All people will be blessed in him,
in every tribe of the human race.

LENT READING, Weeks 1 & 3 **ROMANS 12:1-2**

I appeal to you, brothers and sisters, through the compassion of God, to present your bodies as a living sacrifice, holy and well-pleasing to God, your worship and reasonable service. Be not conformed to this age, but be transformed by the renewal of your mind, that what you do may prove to be the will of God, the good and well-pleasing and perfect.

RESPONSORY Lk 18:13

To you, O Lord…
…I make my prayer for mercy.
Heal my soul, for I have sinned against you…
…I make my prayer for mercy.
Glory to the Father and to the Son and to the Holy Spirit:
…To you, O Lord, I make my prayer for mercy.

LENT READING, Week 5 **ROMANS 5:6-10**

Us being weak, yet in accord with time on behalf of the impious, Christ died. Hardly will anyone die for a just person, though perhaps someone would dare die for a good person. But God commends God's own love for us in that while we were still sinners Christ died for us. Justified now by his blood, by much more through him shall we be saved from the anger. For if being enemies we were reconciled to God through the death of the Son of God, by much more having been reconciled we shall be saved by his life.

RESPONSORY Rev. 5:9

We worship you, O Christ…
…and we praise you.
By your cross you have redeemed the world…
…and we praise you.
Glory to the Father and to the Son and to the Holy Spirit:
…We worship you, O Christ, and we praise you.

EASTER READING, Before Ascension **HEBREWS 8:1b-3a**

We have a high priest, who sat at the right of the throne of the greatness in the heavens, a minister of the holy things and of the true tabernacle, erected by the Lord, not by human beings. Every high priest is appointed to offer both gifts and sacrifices.

RESPONSORY, in the Octave of Easter

This is the day the Lord has made;
let us rejoice and be glad.

RESPONSORY, Weeks 2 to 6

The disciples rejoiced…
…alleluia, alleluia.
When they saw the risen Lord…
…alleluia, alleluia.
Glory to the Father and to the Son and to the Holy Spirit:
…The disciples rejoiced, alleluia, alleluia.

EASTER READING, After Ascension **ROMANS 8:14-17**

As many as are led by the Spirit of God, these are sons and daughters of God. For you did not receive a spirit of slavery, for fear again, but you received a spirit of adoption, by which we cry, "Abba, Father."

That very Spirit gives witness to our spirit that we are children of God. And if children, then also heirs, heirs on one hand of God, joint heirs on the other of Christ, since we suffer with him in order that we may also be glorified with him.

RESPONSORY, After Ascension Jn 14:26

The Holy Spirit is the Paraclete…
…alleluia, alleluia.
Who will teach you all things…
…alleluia, alleluia.
Glory to the Father and to the Son and to the Holy Spirit:
…The Holy Spirit is the Paraclete, alleluia, alleluia.

Gospel Canticle For Evening

Antiphons

Advent Wk 1

The angel of the Lord
brought God's message to Mary,
and she conceived
by the power of the Holy Spirit,
alleluia.

Advent Wk 3

All generations will call me blessed:
the Lord has looked with favor
on every lowly servant.

Christmas

O radiant child!
You brought healing to human life
as you came forth from the womb
of Mary, your mother,
like a new spouse from
the marriage chamber.

After Epiphany

When they saw the star of the Magi
they were filled with great joy;
entering the house,
they offered their gifts to the Lord:
gold, frankincense and myrrh.

Lent Wk 1

Whatever you do for one of these
least of my brothers and sisters,
you do for me.

Lent Wk 3
Jesus walked through the crowd
and went away.

Lent Wk 5
I am my own testimony,
says the Lord,
and my Abba who sent me
also testifies on my behalf.

Easter Wk 1
Jesus met the women
and greeted them;
they came and knelt at his feet,
alleluia.

Easter Wk 3
This is what God asks of you:
trust in the one whom God has sent,
alleluia.

Easter Wk 5
The Holy Spirit, the Paraclete,
whom Abba will send in my name,
will teach you,
and remind you of all that I told you,
alleluia.

Ordinary
Antiphon
My soul is stretched full
with praise of the Lord.

CANTICLE of MARY (The Magnificat)
LUKE 1:46-55

+ **My soul** is stretched full with praise of the Lord,
and my spirit, beyond joy in God, my Savior,
who chose to lay eyes on this humble servant.

Behold, now and forward,
each and every age will call me blessed,
for the Mighty One did great things to me.

Holy is the name and the mercy
to generations and generations,
the ones fearing the One,

Who scattered the haughty of mind and heart,
pulled the powerful off their high place,
and lifted with dignity the humble in need.

The hungering are filled with good things,
the rich are sent away empty,
and servant Israel is given relief

with a memory of mercy to remember,
the promise spoken to our ancestors,
to Abraham and his descendants forever.

Glory…

Antiphon

INTERCESSIONS

- Lord, keep married couples in love…
- Grow our youth in wisdom and grace…
- For respect for the dignity of the human person…
- For all who have died…

- In gratitude for blessings, Abba thank you…
- For the sins of this day, Lord Jesus have mercy…
- With concerns over tomorrow, Holy Spirit help…

PRAYER OF SAINT FRANCIS

Lord, make me an instrument of your peace.
Where there is hatred, let me sow love.
Where there is injury, pardon.
Where there is discord, unity.
Where there is doubt, faith.
Where there is error, truth.
Where there is despair, hope.
Where there is sadness, joy.
Where there is darkness, light.
O Divine Master, grant that I may not so much seek
to be consoled as to console,
to be understood as to understand,
to be loved as to love.
For it is in giving that we receive.
It is in pardoning that we are pardoned.
And it is in dying that we are born to eternal life.

OUR FATHER…

WEEK I
TUESDAY MORNING

+ *God, come to my assistance;* Psalm 70:2
Lord, make haste to help me!

Glory...

ORDINARY TIME

Lord of all be-ing, throned a-far,
Your glo-ry flames from sun and star;
Cen-ter and soul of ev-'ry sphere\\,
And yet to lov-ing hearts how near.

Sun of our life, your liv-ing ray
Sheds on our path the glow of day;
Star of our hope, your gen-tle light\\
Shall ev-er cheer the long-est night.

Lord of all life, be-low, a-bove,
Whose light is truth, whose warmth is love;
Be-fore the bril-liance of your throne\\
We ask no lus-ter of our own.

Give us your grace to make us true,
And kind-ling hearts that burn for you,
Till all your liv-ing al-tars claim\\
One ho-ly light, one heav-'nly flame.

108, Text: Oliver Wendell Holmes, 1809-1894
Music: JESU DULCIS MEMORIA, LM; Model 1
Popular melody for: *O Radiant Light, O Sun Divine*

ADVENT

The ad-vent of our\ King
Our/ thoughts must\ now em-ploy;
Then let us meet him on/ the/ road
With songs of\ ho-ly joy.

The co-e-ter-nal\ Son
A/ maid-en's\ off-spring see;
A ser-vant's form Christ did/ put/ on,
To set his\ peo-ple free.

In glo-ry from his\ throne
A/-gain will\ Christ de-scend,
And sum-mon all who are/ his/ own
To joys that\ nev-er end.

Our joy-ful prais-es\ sing
To/ Christ, who\ set us free;
As trib-ute to the Fa/-ther/ bring,
And Ho-ly\ Ghost, to thee.

15, Text: Charles Coffin, d.1749;
translated by Robert Campbell, d.1868, altered
Music: 66 86 ST. THOMAS (WILLIAMS); Aaron Williams, d.1776

CHRISTMAS

Joy to the world, the Lord is come!
Let earth re-ceive her King;
Let ev\-'ry\ heart\\ pre-pare\ him\ room\\
And heav'n and na-ture/ sing.
And\ heav'n and na-ture/ sing.
And\ hea/v'n, and hea\\v'n and na-ture sing.

Joy to the earth, the Sa-vior reigns!
Let us their songs em-ploy,
While fields\ and\ floods\\,
rocks, hills\, and\ plains\\
Re-peat the sound-ing/ joy.
Re\-peat the sound-ing/ joy.
Re\-peat/, Re-peat\\ the sound-ing joy.

He rules the world with truth and grace
And makes the na-tions prove
The glo\-ries\ of\\ his right\-eous\-ness\\
And won-ders of his/ love.
And\ won-ders of his/ love.
And\ won/-ders, won\\-ders of his love.

26, Text: based on Luke 2:10 and Psalm 98;
Isaac Watts, 1719, altered
Music: ANTIOCH CM, George Frideric Handel, 1742

LENT

For-ty days and for-ty nights
You were fast-ing in the wild;
For-ty days and for-ty nights
Temp-ted, and yet un-de-filed.

Should not we your sor-row share
And from world-ly joys ab-stain,
Fast-ing with un-ceas-ing prayer,
Strong with you to suf-fer pain?

When temp-ta-tions on us press,
Je-sus, Sa-vior, hear our call!
Vic-tor in the wil-der-ness,
Grant we may not faint nor fall!

Keep, O keep us, Sa-vior dear,
Ev-er con-stant by your side;
That with you we may ap-pear
At th'e-ter-nal Eas-ter-tide.

47, Text: George H. Smyttan, *The Penny Post,* 1856, altered
Music: 7 7 7 7 HEINLEIN, Attributed to Martin Herbst, d. 1681

73, Text: see John 20; attrib. to Jean Tisserand, d. 1494;
translated by John M. Neal, 1851, altered
Music: 888, O FILII ET FILIAE; Chant Mode II,
Airs sur les hymnes sacrez, odes et noels, 1623

EASTER

Ye sons and daugh\-ters of\ the King,
With heav'n-ly hosts\ in glo\-ry sing,
To-day the grave\ has lost\ its sting:
Al-le-lu-ia!

On that first morn\-ing of\ the week,
Be-fore the day\ be-gan\ to break,
The Ma-rys went\ their Lord\ to seek:
Al-le-lu-ia!

An an-gel bade\ their sor\-row flee,
By speak-ing thus\ un-to\ the three:
"Your Lord is gone\ to Gal\-i-lee":
Al-le-lu-ia!

That night th'A-pos\-tles met\ in fear,
A-midst them came\ their Lord\ most dear
And said, "Peace be\ un-to\ you here":
Al-le-lu-ia!

Bless-ed are they\ that have\ not seen
And yet whose faith\ has con\-stant been,
In life e-ter\-nal they\ shall reign:
Al-le-lu-ia!

And we with ho\-ly Church\ u-nite,
As ev-er-more\ is just\ and right,
In glo-ry to\ the King\ of light:
Al-le-lu-ia!

Al-le-lu-ia\! Al-le\-lu-ia! Al-le-lu-ia!

PSALM 10

Antiphon *New wine is put*
into fresh wineskins. Mk 2:22

Christmas & Easter The Lord hears
the desire of the afflicted,
defends the orphan,
and frees the oppressed,
alleluia.

Why, Adonai, do you stand distant
and hide in times of the trouble?
In arrogance doers of the bad hunt the weak
and are caught in schemes they devise.

Doers of the bad boast of what their hearts crave,
blessing the greedy and reviling Adonai.
In pride they point their nose away
and seek God in none of their thoughts.

Their haughty ways prosper always,
your laws are kept at a distance,
and they sneer at all who oppose them.

They say to themselves
"I will not be shaken, but happy,
untroubled for generations to come."
Their mouths are full of curses, lies and threats,
trouble and bad things kept under their tongue.

They lie in wait to ambush villages and murder,
their secret eyes on the innocent victim.
They lie in wait to ambush like a lion,
undercover lying in wait to catch the helpless,
they catch and drag the helpless off in their nets.

The victims are crushed and collapse,
falling under their strength.
They say to themselves "El has forgotten,
with faces covered, and sees nothing anymore."

Arise, Adonai! God, lift up your hand!
Do not forget the helpless ones.
For why do those doing bad revile God and say,
to themselves, "God will not call an accounting"?

But you do see trouble and grief,
and consider taking the matter in hand;
to you the victims commit themselves,
to you, the helper of orphans.

Stop the arm of the doer of the bad;
call to account lest bad things be kept secret.
Adonai rules forever and ever;
the nations will vanish from the land.

You hear, Adonai, the desire of the afflicted;
you encourage their heart and open your ear
to defend the orphaned and the oppressed.
May humanity repeat no terror on the earth.

Glory… Antiphon

PSALM 68

Antiphon *When you are invited, take the lowest place;*
one exalting the self will be humbled,
and one humbling the self will be exalted.
Lk 14:10,11

Christmas & Easter Peoples of earth, sing to God;
sing praise to the Lord,
alleluia.

May God arise
and may enmity flee and be scattered.
As smoke is blown, let it blow;
as wax melts before fire
may bad ways perish from before God.

But may just ones be glad
and rejoice before God;
may they be happy with joy.
Sing to God! Sing praise to the name!
Extol the Rider of the Clouds,
and rejoice in the name Adonai,

Abba of the fatherless
and defender of widows,
God dwelling in holiness.
God sets the lonely into a family
and leads prisoners forth with songs,
but ones rebelling live on sun-scorched land.

When you went out before your people, God,
when you marched through the wasteland,
the earth shook and heavens poured rain
before the One God of Sinai,
before God, the God of Israel.

You gave a shower of abundances, God,
on your inheritance;
even the weary you refreshed.
Your people settled in her, God;
you provided for the poor from your bounty.

The Lord announced the word,
a great company of proclaimers.
Rulers and armies flee, they flee,
and in resident camps the plunder is divided.

While you sleep among campfires
wings of dove are sheathed with silver
and her feathers with the shine of gold.
When Shaddai scatters the rulers,
the scattering is like snow on Zalmon.

A majestic mountain, the mountain of Bashan,
a rugged mountain is the mountain of Bashan.
Why gaze in envy, you rugged mountains,
at the mountain God chooses for the reign,
indeed where Adonai will dwell to forever?

Psalm 68, continued

Chariots of God are tens of thousands,
thousands of the multitude
into the Sinai sanctuary.
You ascended to the height and led captive;
you received gifts from human beings,
and even from those rebelling,
to your dwelling, God Adonai.

The Lord is being praised day by day,
bearing our burden is El our Savior.
Our El, the El of salvation,
the Lord Adonai is the escape from death.
Surely God will silence the plans of enmity,
in the crown of their hair where sins go on.

The Lord says, "From Bashan I will bring,
I will bring from depths of the sea,
that you may wash your foot in their defeat
and the tongues of your dogs have their share."

They view your processions, God,
processions into the sanctuary
of my God and my Ruler.
Singers are in front, followed by musicians
among girls playing tambourines.

In great congregations, praise God;
praise Adonai in the assembly of Israel!
There little Benjamin leads the royals of Judah,
their throng the royals of Zebulun and Naphtali.

You, God, summoned your power.
Show strength, God, as you did for us!
Because of your temple at Jerusalem,
to you the rulers will bring gifts.

Rebuke the beast of the reeds,
the herd of bulls among calves of nations;
being humbled with bars of silver,
nations that delight in wars are scattered.
Envoys from Egypt will come;
Ethiopia will submit their hands to God.

Peoples of the earth, sing to God!
Sing praise to the Lord, the Rider in the skies,
the ancient heavens, see!
The voice thunders, the voice of might.

Proclaim the power of God over Israel,
the majesty and power in the skies.
Awesome are you, God, in your sanctuary;
the God of Israel gives power and strengths
to the people praising God.

Glory…

Antiphon *When you are invited, take the lowest place;*
one exalting the self will be humbled,
and one humbling the self will be exalted.
Lk 14:10,11

Christmas & Easter Peoples of earth, sing to God;
sing praise to the Lord, alleluia.

PSALM 24

Antiphon *She will bear a son,*
and you will name him Jesus;
he will save his people from their sins. Mt 1:21

Christmas Come,
let us worship Christ, the Son of God,
who was obedient to Mary and Joseph.

Lent The pure of heart with clean hands
ascend the mountain of the Lord.

Easter The one who came down from heaven
has ascended above all the heavens,
alleluia.

Name of God

Adonai *is Hebrew for "My Lord."* **YHVH** *is usually translated* LORD *in all caps, for most faithful Jews would not speak the name* Yahweh, *but instead would say* Adonai. Yhvh *is the name revealed to Moses at the burning bush, and means 'I am who I am,' or 'I will be who I will be,' or simply 'I am.'* **El** *can mean any god, remembering that nations and cities would have their own gods. The plural for* El *is* **Elohim**, *which can mean many gods, but in the psalms refers to the one* Yhvh *without any sense of being multiple gods.* **El Shaddai** *(God Almighty) is how the Patriarchs spoke of the one God.* **Yhvh Sabaoth** *(Lord of Hosts) refers to God enthroned with an army of angels.*

The earth and everything,
the world and all who are alive are Adonai's,
God who founded the earth on the seas
and established the earth on the waters.

Who may ascend to the mountain of Adonai?
And who may stand in the holy place?
The clean of hand and pure of heart
who do not lift the soul to an idol
and do not swear by falsehood
will receive the blessing from Adonai
and vindication from the God who saves.

Such is the generation of ones who seek,
who seek your faces, God of Jacob.

Lift up your heads, you gates;
lift up, you ancient doors,
that the Crown of glory may enter.

Who is this Crown of glory?
Adonai, strong and mighty,
Adonai, mighty of battle.

Lift up your heads, you gates;
lift up, you ancient doors,
that the Crown of glory may enter.

Who is this Crown of glory?
Adonai Sabaoth is the Crown of glory.

Glory…

Antiphon

PSALM 85

Antiphon *Take courage;*
it is me. Come. Mt 14:27,29

Advent The Lord will come
from the holy place
to save all people.

Christmas Tell us, shepherds,
what have you seen?
Who has appeared to you?
We have seen a newborn infant and
a choir of angels praising the Lord,
alleluia.

Lent Love and Fidelity meet;
Justice and Peace kiss.

Easter You will turn back, O God,
and revive us again;
may your people rejoice in you,
alleluia.

You showed favor, **Adonai**, to your land;
you restored the fortune of Jacob.
You forgave the iniquity of your people;
you pardoned all of their sin.
You set aside all of your wrath;
you turned from your fierce anger.

Restore us, God of our salvation!
And put away your displeasure toward us.
Will you be angry with us to forever?
Will you prolong your anger
to generation and generation?

Will you not revive us again
that your people may rejoice in you?
Show us, Adonai, your unfailing love
and grant us your salvation.

I will listen to what El Adonai will say,
promising peace to the people, even to the saints,
but not letting them return to folly.
Surely near to those in awe is their salvation,
the glory to dwell in our land.

Love and Fidelity meet;
Justice and Peace kiss.
Fidelity springs forth from the earth
and Justice looks down from the heavens.

Indeed Adonai will give the good
and our land will yield her harvest,
Justice going forward to prepare the way
for the steps of the Lord.

Glory…

Antiphon

TOBIT 13:1b-8

Antiphon *Behold,*
I make all things new. Rev 21:5b

Advent & Lent Blessed be God
and the reign forever.

Christmas The angel said to the shepherds:
I proclaim to you a great joy;
the Savior of the world
is born for you,
alleluia.

Easter Keep this day as a festival day
and give praise to the Lord,
alleluia.

Blessed be God who lives forever
and the reign of our God for all ages,
who scourges but then has mercy,
casts down to the deepest grave
and brings up from the great abyss.
No one can escape this hand.

Israelites, acknowledge before the nations
God who has scattered you among them
and even there shown you great mercy.

Let God be exalted by every living being
because our Lord is our God,
our Father and God forever.

Though scourged for your iniquities,
mercy will be on you all;
you will be gathered from all the nations
among whom you have been scattered.

With all your heart and soul
turn with honesty to the Lord
who will turn the face to you
and no longer hide.

See now what has been done for you,
and with full voice praise Adonai.
Bless the Lord of justice
and exalt the Ruler of the ages.

In the land of my exile I acknowledge the Lord
and make known to a sinful nation
this power and majesty:
"Turn, you sinners, and do right before the Lord,
who may look upon you with favor and mercy."

My God, I will exalt you
and rejoice in the Ruler of Heaven.
Let all speak of this majesty
in Jerusalem with exaltation.

Glory...

Antiphon

ISAIAH 26:1b-4,7-9,12

Antiphon *My soul yearns for you in the night;*
within me my spirit longs for you.

Dec 17-23 Throw open the gates of the citadel,
for our God is here among us,
alleluia.

Dec 27 John, apostle and evangelist,
was the disciple Jesus loved
even above the others.

Christmas A little child is born for us;
little and yet called the mighty God,
alleluia.

Easter We have placed all our hope
in the Lord, who has given us peace,
alleluia.

Our city is strong;
salvation makes walls and rampart.
Open gates, so the just nation may enter,
the one keeping faiths.

Your steadfast mind will keep peace,
peace because of trusting.
Trust in Adonai to forever,
for in Yah Adonai is the Rock of eternities…

The path of justice is level;
the Upright One smooths the way of the just.
Yes, in the way of your laws, Adonai, we wait,
for your name and your renown
are the desire of our heart.

My soul yearns for you in the night;
within me my spirit longs for you.
Just as your judgments are on the earth,
so people of the world learn justice…

Adonai, you establish for us peace;
indeed all we have accomplished
you did for us.

Glory…

Antiphon

PSALM 33

Antiphon *Where your treasure is,*
there also will your heart be. Lk 12:34

Dec 27 Dying on the cross,
Christ entrusted his mother to John.

Christmas & Easter The mercy of God fills the earth,
alleluia.

Sing joyfully to Adonai, you just,
for praise is fitting for the upright.

Praise Adonai with a harp,
make music on the lyre of ten.
Sing a new song with skill
and play with a shout of joy.

For true is the word of Adonai
and all the faithful deeds done.
The earth is full of the goodness of Adonai,
who loves justice and integrity.

The heavens were made by the word of Adonai
and all their hosts by the breath of the mouth,
as one gathers in a heap the waters of the sea,
as one puts into the deep of the storehouses.

Let all the earth, let them fear,
let all alive in the world revere Adonai
who spoke and it came to be,
who commanded and it stood firm.

Adonai foils the plans of the nations
and thwarts the designs of peoples.
The plan of Adonai stands firm to forever,
heartfelt thoughts to generation and generation.

Blessed is the nation for whom Adonai is God,
the people chosen for this inheritance.
From the heavens Adonai looks down and sees
all sons and daughters of Adam and Eve,

and from the place of dwelling watches
all those alive on the earth.
The one who formed our heart
knows all our deeds.

No ruler is saved by the size of an army;
no warrior escapes by greatness of strength.
The horse is a vain hope for deliverance;
despite greatness of strength it cannot save.

See the eye of Adonai on those who place
their fear and hope in the unfailing love
that delivers them from death
and keeps them alive in famine.

Our being waits for Adonai,
who is our help and our shield,
in whom our heart rejoices,
the holy name in whom we trust.

Adonai, may you rest on us your unfailing love
even as we hope in you.

Glory... Antiphon

PSALM 67

Antiphon *Woman (of Canaan), great is your faith*
let it be done as you desire. Mt 15:28

Dec 17-23 Lord, make known your will
all over the earth; proclaim your
salvation to every nation.

Christmas & Easter The earth has yielded its harvest;
may the nations be glad
and sing for joy, alleluia.

May God be gracious to us and bless us,
may God's faces shine upon us.
How else can your ways be known on the earth
and your salvation among all the nations?

May the peoples praise you, God,
may the peoples praise you, all of them.

May the nations be glad and sing for joy
for you rule the peoples
and guide nations of the earth into justice.

May the peoples praise you, God,
may the peoples praise you, all of them.

The land will yield her harvest, God will bless us,
and all the ends of the earth will revere our God.

Glory...

Antiphon

ORDINARY TIME READING **ROMANS 13:11-14**

Know that this is the time (the *kairos*), the hour for you to be raised out of sleep, for now our salvation is nearer than when we became believers. The night has advanced and the day draws near. Let us cast off therefore the deeds of the darkness, and let us put on the armor of the light.

As in the new day, let us walk not in revellings to drunken bouts, not in sex to excesses, not in strife to jealousy, but put on the Lord Jesus Christ, and as for the flesh, give its lust no room to think.

RESPONSORY Ps 71:1,5

In you, Lord, I take refuge…
…you, Lord, are my hope.
My trust, O Lord, from my youth,…
…you, Lord, are my hope.
Glory to the Father and to the Son and to the Holy Spirit:
…In you, Lord, I take refuge; you, Lord, are my hope.

ADVENT READING **GENESIS 49:8-10**

You, Judah, will your brothers praise; your hand on the neck of enmity, the sons of your father will bow to you. Judah, lion cub, my son, you return from prey crouching, lying like a lion and like a lioness, whom no one would dare rouse. The scepter will not depart from Judah nor the ruling staff from between his feet until when he comes, the one to whom is due the obedience of the peoples.

RESPONSORY

Your light will come, Jerusalem…
…the Lord will dawn on you in radiant beauty.
The glory of the Lord you will see within you…
…the Lord will dawn on you in radiant beauty.
Glory to the Father and to the Son and to the Holy Spirit:
…Your light will come, Jerusalem;
the Lord will dawn on you in radiant beauty.

CHRISTMAS READING **ISAIAH 62:11-12**

"See," Adonai proclaimed to the end of the earth, "Say to the Daughter of Zion, 'See your salvation coming! See his reward with him, his recompense in his company!' " They will be called the Holy People and the Redeemed of Adonai, and you will be called One-Being-Sought and the City-Not-Deserted.

RESPONSORY

The Lord has made known…
…alleluia, alleluia.
The saving power…
…alleluia, alleluia.
Glory to the Father and to the Son and to the Holy Spirit:
…The Lord has made known the saving power, alleluia.

After Epiphany

All the royal powers on earth
…will bow down in worship.
Men and women of every nation…
…will bow down in worship.

Glory to the Father and to the Son and to the Holy Spirit:
...All the royal powers on earth
will bow down in worship.

LENT READING, Weeks 1 & 3 **JOEL 2:12-13**

Even now, declares Adonai, return to me with all your heart and with fasting and weeping and mourning! Rend now your heart, not your garments, and return to your God Adonai, gracious and compassionate, slow of angers and abundant of love and relenting from the calamity.

RESPONSORY Lk 18:13

The Lord God will set me free...
...from the hunter's snare.
From all those who would trap me with lying words,
...and from the hunter's snare.
Glory to the Father and to the Son and to the Holy Spirit:
...The Lord God will set me free from the hunter's snare.

LENT READING, Week 5 **ZECHARIAH 12:10-11a**

I will pour out on the house of David and on the one living in Jerusalem a spirit of grace and supplications and they will look on me whom they pierced and they will mourn as one mourns for an only child and grieve bitterly as one grieves for the firstborn. On that day the weeping in Jerusalem will be great.

RESPONSORY Rev. 5:9

Lord, by your own blood...
...you brought us back to God.
From every tribe and tongue and people and nation...
...you brought us back to God.
Glory to the Father and to the Son and to the Holy Spirit:
...Lord, by your own blood you brought us back to God.

EASTER READING **ACTS 13:30-33**

God raised out of the dead Jesus, who appeared over many days to the ones who came up with him from Galilee to Jerusalem, who are now his witnesses to the people. And we evangelize to you what was promised to our ancestors, that God has fulfilled to their children this promise, raising up Jesus, as also it is written in the second psalm: *You are my Son; today I have begotten you.*

RESPONSORY, in the Octave of Easter

This is the day the Lord has made;
let us rejoice and be glad.

RESPONSORY, Weeks 2 through 7

The Lord is risen from the tomb...
...alleluia, alleluia.
He hung upon the cross for us...
...alleluia, alleluia.
Glory to the Father and to the Son and to the Holy Spirit:
...The Lord is risen from the tomb, alleluia, alleluia.

Gospel Canticle For Morning

Antiphons

Advent Wk 1
Luke 10:21-24

From the root of Jesse a bud will
blossom, the glory of the Lord
will fill the earth, and all creation
shall see the saving power of God.

Advent Wk 3
Matt 21:28-32

Arise, arise, Jerusalem;
wake from your slumber!
shake the chain from your neck,
captive daughter Zion.

Christmas

The Word became flesh and lived
among us, full of grace and truth;
from this fullness we have all received
gift upon gift of love, alleluia.

After Epiphany
Mark 6:34-44

The wise ones offered gifts
of gold, frankincense, and myrrh
to the Lord, the Son of God
and Ruler Most High, alleluia.

Lent Wk 1
Matt 6:7-15

Lord, teach us to pray
as John taught his disciples.

Lent Wk 3
Matt 18:21-35

The Lord said to Peter,
I do not tell you to forgive
only seven times,
but seventy times seven.

Antiphons for Gospel Canticle for Morning, continued

Lent Wk 5 John 8:21-30	When you have lifted up the Son of Humanity, says the Lord, you will know that I am.
Easter Wk 1 John 20:11-18	Jesus called her by name: Mary. She turned to him and said: Rabboni. Then he said to her: Do not grab me; I have not yet ascended to my Abba, alleluia.
Easter Wk 3 John 6:30-35	Moses did not give you the bread of heaven; my Abba gives you the true bread from heaven, alleluia.
Easter Wk 5 John 14:27-31a	Peace I leave with you, alleluia; my peace is my gift to you, alleluia.
Easter Wk 7 John 17:1-11a	The Lord is risen from the dead as he promised; let all the earth rejoice and be glad for he shall reign forever, alleluia.
Ordinary Antiphon	*God raised salvation in the house of David.*

Gospel Reading for Tuesday of

Week **1**	Mark 1:21-28	**13**	Matt 8:23-27	**25**	Luke 8:19-21
3	Mark 3:31-35	**15**	Matt 11:20-24	**27**	Lk 10:38-42
5	Mark 7:1-13	**17**	Matt 13:36-43	**29**	Lk 12:35-38
7	Mark 9:30-37	**19**	Mt 18:1-5,10,12-14	**31**	Lk 14:15-24
9	Mark 12:13-17	**21**	Matt 23:23-26	**33**	Luke 19:1-10
11	Matt 5:43-48	**23**	Luke 6:12-19		

CANTICLE of ZECHARIAH (The Benedictus)
LUKE 1:68-79

+ **Blessed be** the Lord the God of Israel
who chose a people to visit with redemption,
and raised salvation in the house of David,
saving strength from God's own servant,

speaking from the age of the prophets
through the mouth of the holy prophet:
Salvation out of enmity,
even out of those who hate us,

to show our ancestors how mercy works, -
and to remember the holy promise of the Lord,
the covenant made for our ancestor Abraham,
calming our fear and making us free
to serve with holy justice before God all our days.

And you also child -
will be called a prophet of the Most High
for you will go before the Lord to prepare his way
and give to people a knowledge of salvation
known in accepting forgiveness of their sins.

From the tender mercy of our God,
the sun rising from the height will visit with light
for those who sit in the dark or shadow of death
and to guide our feet into the way of peace.

Glory...

Antiphon

PETITIONS FOR THE CONSECRATION TO GOD OF THE DAY AND ITS WORK

- For the Church and her ministry and apostolates…
- For secular authorities and all serving as stewards…
- For people who are poor or sick or in sorrow…
- For peace and the basic needs of each human being…
- For those who weigh on my heart…

SUSCIPE of MOTHER CATHERINE McAULEY

My God, I am yours for time and eternity.
Teach me to cast myself entirely
into the arms of your loving providence,
with the most lively, unlimited confidence
in your compassionate, tender pity.
Grant me, O most merciful Redeemer,
that whatever you ordain or permit
may be acceptable to me.
Take from my heart all painful anxiety;
suffer nothing to sadden me but sin,
nothing to delight me but the hope of coming
to the possession of you, my God and my all,
in your everlasting reign.

OUR FATHER…

WEEK I
TUESDAY EVENING

\+ *God, come to my assistance;* Psalm 70:2
Lord, make haste to help me!

Glory…

ORDINARY TIME

What a Friend we have in Je-sus,
All our sins and griefs to bear!
What a priv-i-lege to car-ry
Ev-'ry-thing to God in prayer!
Oh, what peace we of-ten for-feit,
Oh, what need-less pain we bear,
All be-cause we do not car-ry
Ev-'ry-thing to God in prayer!

Glo-ry be to God the Fa-ther,
Son, and Spir-it ev-'ry-where.
Glo-ry be as the Be-got-ten
Son of Ab-ba hears our prayer
At the right hand of the Fa-ther,
Lamb of God, our mer-cy home.
Fa-ther, Son and Ho-ly Spir-it,
Glo-ry be to you a-lone.

133, Text: based on Matthew 21:22; Joseph Scriven, 1865;
verse 2 Stephen J. Wolf, 2011
Music: FRIEND; Charles C. Converse, 1868

ADVENT

O God, our help in a-ges past,
Our hope for years to come,
Our shel-ter from the storm-y blast,
And our e-ter-nal home.

Be-neath the shad-ow of your throne
Your saints have dwelt se-cure;
Suf-fic-ient is your arm a-lone,
And our de-fense is sure.

Be-fore the hills in or-der stood,
Or earth re-ceived her frame,
From ev-er-last-ing you are God,
To end-less years the same.

A thou-sand a-ges in your sight
Are like an eve-ning gone;
Short as the watch that ends the night
Be-fore the ri-sing sun.

Time, like an ev-er-flow-ing stream,
Bears all our lives a-way;
They fly, for-got-ten, as a dream
Dies at the op'n-ing day.

O God, our help in a-ges past,
Our hope for years to come,
Be now our guard while trou-bles last,
And our e-ter-nal home.

CHRISTMAS

O come, lit-tle chil-dren;
come one and come all,
O come to the man-ger in Beth-le-hem's stall,
And see what our Fa-ther in heav-en a-bove
Has sent to us all on this earth with his love.

O see, in the man-ger so meek and so mild,
O see in the soft light the heav-en-ly child,
In swad-dling clothes fold-ed,
his beau-ty more sweet
Than an-gels, whose voic-es
his low-ly birth greet.

His bed, lit-tle chil-dren, a man-ger with hay;
His Moth-er and Jo-seph in ec-sta-sy pray,
The shep-herds in won-der
their glad wor-ship bring,
While cho-rus of an-gels
sweet Glo-ri-a's sing.

28, Text: Johann C. von Schmid, d.1854;
translated by Melanie Schute, d.1922, altered
Music: 11 11 11 11 IHR KINDERLEIN KOMMET,
by Johann A. Schulz, d.1800

115, Text: from Psalm 90:1,2,4, Isaac Watts,
The Psalms of David, 1719, altered
Music: C.M., 86 86, ST. ANNE, William Croft, 1708

LENT

The word of God, pro-ceed-ed forth
Yet leav-ing not his Fa-ther's side,
And go-ing to his work on earth
Had reached at length life's eve-ning tide.

Soon by his own false friend be-trayed,
Giv-en to foes, to death he went;
His ve-ry self, in form of bread,
Gi-ven to them, his friends he sent.

The man-ger, Christ their e-qual made;
That up-per room, their soul's re-past;
The cross, their ran-som dear-ly paid,
Heav-en, their high re-ward at last.

All praise and thanks to you as-cend
For ev-er-more, blest one in three.
O grant us life that shall not end
In our true na-tive land to be.

58, Text: Thomas Aquinas, d. 1274;
translated, st. 1 & 4 by John M. Neale, d. 1866,
st. 2 & 3 by Gerard Manley Hopkins, d. 1889, altered
Music: OLD HUNDREDTH, LM, Louis Bourgeois,
first published in Genevan Psalter, 1551
Popular Melody for: *Praise God From Whom All Blessings Flow*
Alternate melody: *From All That Dwells Below The Skies*

EASTER

Sing with all the saints in glo-ry,
Sing the res-ur-rec-tion song!
Death and sor-row, earth's dark sto-ry,
To the for-mer days be-long.
All a-round the clouds are/ break-ing,
Soon the/ storms of time shall cease;
In God's im-age we, a-wa-king,
Know the ev-er-last-ing peace.

O what glo-ry, far ex-ceed-ing
All that eye has yet per-ceived!
Ho-liest hearts, for a-ges plead-ing,
Nev-er that full joy con-ceived.
God has prom-ised, Christ pre/-pares it,
There on/ high our wel-come waits.
Ev-'ry hum-ble spir-it shares it;
Christ has passed th'e-ter-nal gates.

69, Text: William J. Irons, 1873
Music: 8787D, HYMN TO JOY, Ludwig van Beethoven, 1770,
adapted by Edward Hodges, 1827
Popular melody for: *Joyful Joyful We Adore You*

PSALM 14

Antiphon *If we say we have no sin, we deceive ourselves;*
if we confess our sins,
God is faithful and forgiving. 1 John 1:8,9

Christmas & Easter Alleluia, alleluia, alleluia.

The fool says in the heart, "There is no God."
They are corrupt, vile are their deeds;
no one is doing good.

Adonai looks down from the heavens
on sons and daughters of Adam and Eve
to see if even one is wise enough to seek God.

All turned aside together to corruption;
no one is doing good, not even one.

Will doers of the bad never learn?
Devouring my people as they eat bread,
they do not call on Adonai.

There they are, in dread of dread,
for God is in the company of the just.
They frustrate the hopes of the poor,
but in Adonai the poor find refuge.

Who from Zion could bring salvation to Israel?
When Adonai restores the fortune to the people,
let Jacob rejoice, let Israel be glad.

Glory... Antiphon

PSALM 74

Antiphon *The Son of Humanity*
took our infirmities
and bore our diseases. Mt 8:17
Isaiah 53:4

Advent & Lent Remember, O God, your people
you redeemed of old.

Christmas & Easter Alleluia, alleluia, alleluia.

Why, God, do you reject us to forever?
Your anger smolders
against sheep of your pasture.
Remember your people you gathered of old,
your tribe of heirs you redeemed,
Mount Zion where you dwelt.

Lift high your steps through everlasting ruin,
the enmity destruction to the sanctuary.
Enmity roared in your meeting place
and set up their standard signs.

They behaved like ones raising axes
through a thicket of trees,
and now her carved panels
they smashed with axe and hatchet.
They sent your sanctuary to the ground with fire
and defiled the dwelling place of your Name.

Psalm 74, continued

They said in their heart, "We will crush them."
Completely they burned in the land
all the places to worship God.
We see no miraculous signs;
there is no longer a prophet among us.
Until when? No one knows.

Until when, God,
will enmity mock and revile your name?
To forever?
Why do you hold back your hand,
even your right hand
from the fold of your bosom?

But God, my Ruler from of old,
bringing salvation onto the midst of the earth,
you split open the sea by your power,
you break the heads of dragons in the waters.

You crushed the heads of Leviathan,
giving him as food
to people and desert creatures.
You opened up streams and springs
and dried up everflowing rivers.

To you is the day and to you is the night,
and you established the moon and the sun.
You set all the boundaries of the earth;
summer and winter were made by you.

Remember how enmity mocks Adonai,
and foolish people revile your name.
Do not hand over to the wild beast
the life of your dove;
remember to forever
the life of your afflicted ones.

Scary places of the land
are haunted with violence.
So have regard for your covenant.
Let not the oppressed retreat, nor the disgraced;
may the poor and the needy praise your name.

Rise up, God! Defend your cause!
Remember the all-day mockery of fools.
Ignore not the clamor of enmity
nor those in continual uproar.

Glory…

Antiphon *The Son of Humanity*
took our infirmities
and bore our diseases. Mt 8:17
Isaiah 53:4

Advent & Lent Remember, O God, your people
you redeemed of old.

Christmas & Easter Alleluia, alleluia, alleluia.

PSALM 20

Antiphon *The Spirit of the Lord is upon me;*
the Lord anointed me
to evangelize the poor
and sent me
to proclaim release to captives,
sight to the blind,
and freedom to the crushed,
to proclaim a year
of the Lord's acceptance. Lk 4:18
and see Isaiah
61:1-2 & 58:6

Advent & Lent Now I know that the Lord saves
the Lord's own anointed.

Christmas You have been endowed from your birth
with royal gifts; in eternal splendor,
before the dawn of light on earth,
I have begotten you.

Easter Now the reign of our God has begun
and power is given to Christ, the anointed,
alleluia.

May Adonai answer you on the day of distress.
May the name of the God of Jacob protect you,
send you help from the sanctuary,

support you from Zion,
remember all of your sacrifices,
accept your burnt offerings,
give to you as your heart desires,
and make all of your plans succeed.

We will shout for joy at your victory
and lift a banner in the name of our God;
may Adonai grant all your requests.

Now I know
that Adonai saves the chosen anointed
and answers from the holy heavens
with a strong hand of saving powers.

Some trust in the chariot
and others in the horses,
but we in the name of our God Adonai.
They kneel and they fall,
but we rise up and stand firm.

Adonai, save the ruler;
answer us on the day we call.

Glory...

Antiphon

PSALM 21:2-8,14

Antiphon *Jesus and his disciples ate at the house of Levi*
and with them tax collectors and sinners;
many from there followed him. Mk 2:15

Advent, Christmas & Lent Be exalted, Lord, in your strength;
we sing praise of your might.

Easter You have assumed your authority;
you have established your reign, alleluia.

In your strength, Adonai, the crown rejoices,
and in your victory; how great is the joy!
You granted the desire of their heart
and did not withhold the request of their lips.

Indeed, you welcomed them with rich blessings
and placed on their head a crown of pure gold.
They asked from you life
and you gave length of days forever and ever.

Great is the glory through your victory;
on them you bestowed splendor and majesty.
Surely you granted them blessings for eternity
making them glad with joy in your presences,

for the ruler trusting in Adonai will be unshaken
through the unfailing love of the Most High…
Be exalted, Adonai, in your strength!
We will sing and we will praise your might.

Glory… Antiphon

PSALM 125

Antiphon *If you know to give good gifts to your children,*
how much more will the heavenly Abba
give the Holy Spirit to all who ask. Lk 11:13

Advent The Lord will come from the holy place
to save the people of God.

Lent The Lord surrounds the people of God
from now and to forevermore.

Christmas & Easter Peace be with you; Jn 20:19
it is I, do not be afraid; alleluia. Mk 6:50

They who trust in Adonai are like Mount Zion;
not to be shaken, they endure to forever.

As mountains surround around Jerusalem,
so Adonai surrounds around the people
from now and to forevermore.

Indeed the sceptor of bad doings
will not remain over the lot of the just
lest the hands of the just be used for the bad.

Do good, Adonai, to the good,
even to those honest in their hearts!
But those who turn to bad ways
Adonai will banish with doers of the bad.

Peace be upon Israel!

Glory... Antiphon

PSALM 131

Antiphon *Scribes and Pharisees*
preach and do not do it;
they put on human shoulders
heavy burdens bound,
but are unwilling
to lift a finger to move them. Mt 23:3b,4

Advent & Lent Unless you become like a child
by no means may you enter
the reign of God. Mk 10:15

Christmas The Savior of the world is born.

Easter The hope of Israel is the Lord, alleluia.

Adonai, my heart is not proud
and my eyes are not haughty
and I am not busied with the great matters,
with things so wonderful as to be beyond me.

But indeed I have become still
and quiet in my soul
like a child with a mother, being weaned.
Like one being weaned is my soul within me.

Israel, put your hope in Adonai
from now and to forevermore.

Glory... Antiphon

REVELATION 4:8b,11; 5:9,10,12,13b

Antiphon *Holy, Holy, Holy, Lord God Almighty*
who was and is and is to come. Rev 4:8b

Advent, Christmas & Lent
Lord, out of every
tribe and tongue and people and nation,
you made to our God
a realm of royals and priests.

Easter
Let all creation serve you, for all things
came into being at your word, alleluia.

Worthy are you, our Lord and our God,
to receive the glory and honor and power,
for you have created all things,
and by your will all things were created and are.

Worthy are you to receive the scroll and unseal it
for you were sacrificed, and by your blood
ransomed for God those from every
tribe and tongue and people and nation.

You made of them for our God
a realm of royals and priests,
and thus will they reign over the earth.

Worthy is the Lamb, sacrificed to receive
the power and riches and wisdom and strength
and honor and glory and blessing.

Glory...

Antiphon

ORDINARY TIME READING **1 JOHN 3:1-2**

See what manner of love the Father has given to us, that we may be called children of God, and we are. The world does not know us because it did not know him. Beloved, now we are children of God, and what we shall be has not yet been shown. We know that when it is shown, we shall be like him because we shall see him as he is. Everyone who carries this hope is made pure as God is pure.

RESPONSORY Ps 100:5

The love of the Lord endures to forever...
...for God is good.
Faithful love to all generations,...
...for God is good.
Glory to the Father and to the Son and to the Holy Spirit:
...The love of the Lord endures to forever, for God is good.

ADVENT READING **1 CORINTHIANS 1:4-9**

I give thanks to God always concerning you, on the grace of God given to you in Christ Jesus, because in everything you were enriched in him, in all speech and all knowledge, as the testimony of Christ was confirmed in you, that you be lacking in no gift, awaiting the revelation of our Lord Jesus Christ, who will also confirm you to the end, blameless in the day of our Lord Jesus Christ.

Faithful is God, through whom you were called to communion with God's Son Jesus Christ our Lord.

RESPONSORY Ps 146:7; 63:3; 67:2

Come and set us free…
…Lord God of power and glory…
Let your face shine upon us
and we will know salvation…
…Lord God of power and glory…
Glory to the Father and to the Son and to the Holy Spirit:
…Come and set us free, Lord God of power and glory…

CHRISTMAS READING **1 JOHN 1:5b-7**

God is light, and in God there is no darkness, none. If we say we have communion with God and we walk in the dark, we lie and are not doing the truth.

But if we walk in the light as God is in the light, we have communion with each other, and the blood of Jesus the Son cleanses us from all sin.

RESPONSORY Jn 1:14

The Word became flesh…
…alleluia, alleluia.
And dwelt among us…
…alleluia, alleluia.
Glory to the Father and to the Son and to the Holy Spirit:
…The Word became flesh and dwelt among us,
alleluia, alleluia.

After Epiphany

All people will be blessed in him…
…in every tribe of the human race.

All nations will acclaim his glory…
…in every tribe of the human race.
Glory to the Father and to the Son and to the Holy Spirit:
…All people will be blessed in him,
in every tribe of the human race.

LENT READING, Weeks 1 & 3 **JAMES 2:14-18**

What is the profit, my brothers and sisters, if anyone claims to have faith but has not works? Can the faith save that one? If a brother or sister is naked and lacks the daily food, and anyone of you says, "Go in peace, be warm and filled," and not give the necessaries of the body, what is the profit? So indeed faith if it has not works is dead by itself.

But someone will say, "You have faith and I have works." Show me your faith without the works, and I will show you by my works the faith.

RESPONSORY Lk 18:13

To you, O Lord…
…I make my prayer for mercy.
Heal my soul, for I have sinned against you…
…I make my prayer for mercy.
Glory to the Father and to the Son and to the Holy Spirit:
…To you, O Lord, I make my prayer for mercy.

LENT READING, Week 5 **1 CORINTHIANS 1:27b-30**

God chose the weak things of the world to shame the strong things. God chose the base things of the world and the despised things, the things not being, so that God might abolish the things being, so that no flesh might boast before God, of whom you are in Christ Jesus, who became to us wisdom from God, and justice and holiness and redemption.

RESPONSORY Rev. 5:9

We worship you, O Christ…
…and we praise you.
By your cross you have redeemed the world…
…and we praise you.
Glory to the Father and to the Son and to the Holy Spirit:
…We worship you, O Christ, and we praise you.

EASTER READING, Before Ascension **1 PETER 2:4-5**

Approach the Lord, a living stone, rejected by humans, chosen precious by God. And as living stones you are being built, a spiritual house for a holy priesthood, to offer spiritual sacrifices acceptable to God through Jesus Christ.

RESPONSORY, in the Octave of Easter

This is the day the Lord has made;
let us rejoice and be glad.

RESPONSORY, Easter Weeks 2 to 6

The disciples rejoiced…

…alleluia, alleluia.

When they saw the risen Lord…

…alleluia, alleluia.

Glory to the Father and to the Son and to the Holy Spirit:

…The disciples rejoiced, alleluia, alleluia.

EASTER READING, After Ascension **ROMANS 8:26-27**

The Spirit shares in our weakness. For we do not know how to pray as is fitting, but the Spirit prays on our behalf with inexpressible groanings. And the one searching our heart knows what is the mind of the Spirit, because the Spirit intercedes on behalf of the saints according to the will of God.

RESPONSORY, After Ascension Jn 14:26

The Holy Spirit is the Paraclete…

…alleluia, alleluia.

Who will teach you all things…

…alleluia, alleluia.

Glory to the Father and to the Son and to the Holy Spirit:

…The Holy Spirit is the Paraclete, alleluia, alleluia.

Gospel Canticle For Evening

Antiphons

Advent Wk 1

Seek the Lord while he may be found;
call on him while he is near,
alleluia.

Advent Wk 3

Before Mary and Joseph
had come together,
they learned that Mary was with child
by the power of the Holy Spirit,
alleluia.

Christmas

Let us dance with delight in the Lord
and let our hearts
be filled with rejoicing,
for eternal salvation
has appeared on the earth,
alleluia.

After Epiphany

Christ, you are Light from Light;
when you appeared on earth,
the magi offered their gifts to you,
alleluia.

Lent Wk 1

When you wish to pray,
go to your room, shut the door,
and pray to your Father in secret.

Antiphons for Gospel Canticle For Evening, continued

Lent Wk 3

This is how my heavenly Abba
will treat each one of you, unless
you forgive your brothers and sisters
from the heart.

Lent Wk 5

The One who sent me is with me
and has not left me alone.

Easter Wk 1

While I was weeping at the tomb
I saw my Lord,
alleluia.

Easter Wk 3

The bread of God
that comes down from heaven
gives life to the world,
alleluia.

Easter Wk 5

If you loved me,
you would surely be glad
that I am going to the Abba,
alleluia.

Ordinary
Antiphon

My spirit is beyond joy
in God, my Savior

CANTICLE of MARY (The Magnificat)
LUKE 1:46-55

+ **My soul** is stretched full with praise of the Lord,
and my spirit, beyond joy in God, my Savior,
who chose to lay eyes on this humble servant.

Behold, now and forward,
each and every age will call me blessed,
for the Mighty One did great things to me.

Holy is the name and the mercy
to generations and generations,
the ones fearing the One,

Who scattered the haughty of mind and heart,
pulled the powerful off their high place,
and lifted with dignity the humble in need.

The hungering are filled with good things,
the rich are sent away empty,
and servant Israel is given relief

with a memory of mercy to remember,
the promise spoken to our ancestors,
to Abraham and his descendants forever.

Glory...

Antiphon

INTERCESSIONS

- For a culture of vocations all over the world…
- For all who have died…

- In gratitude for blessings…; Abba thank you.
- For the sins of this day…; Lord Jesus have mercy.
- With concerns over tomorrow…; Holy Spirit help.

PRAYER FOR GENEROSITY — Saint Ignatius of Loyola

Lord, teach me to be generous,
to serve you as you deserve,
to give and not to count the cost,
to fight and not to heed the wounds,
to toil and not to seek for rest,
to labor and not to ask reward,
save knowing that I do your will.

OUR FATHER...

It is quite possible for a human
to have none but the purest thoughts
and yet be so distracted mulling over them
that one remains the while far removed from God.

See *Chapters on Prayer* (#55) by Evagrius Ponticus

WEEK I
WEDNESDAY MORNING

\+ *God, come to my assistance;* Psalm 70:2
Lord, make haste to help me!

Glory...

A ORDINARY TIME

A-ma-zing\ Grace! How sweet the sound
That saved a\ wretch like me.
I once\ was\ lost, but now/ am\ found,
Was blind, but\ now I see.

'**T**was grace that\ taught my heart to fear,
And grace my\ fears re-lieved.
How prec\-ious\ did that grace/ ap\-pear
The hour I\ first be-lieved.

Through ma-ny\ dan-gers, toils, and snares,
I have al\-rea-dy come.
'Tis grace\ hath\ brought me safe/ thus\ far,
And grace will\ lead me home.

When we've been\ there ten thou-sand years,
Bright shi-ning\ as the sun,
We've no\ less\ days to sing/ God's\ praise
Than when we'd\ first be-gun.

77, Text: John Newton, 1779
Music: NEW BRITAIN, CM, composer unknown;
Virginia Harmony, 1831

B ORDINARY TIME

As Ab-ba loves you, Je-sus you love us
Tell-ing us to re-main in your love
In your com-mand to love one an-oth-er
As you have loved us, call-ing us friends.

You are the vine and we are your branch-es;
Let Ab-ba prune us so we bear fruit.
Your word re-mem-b'ring, lov-ing each oth-er
As you have loved us, call-ing us friends.

No great-er love has one than to lay down
One's ver-y life for e-ven a friend.
We you have cho-sen, lov-ing each other
As you have loved us, call-ing us friends.

We have been with you from the be-gin-ning;
To tes-ti-fy in Spir-it and truth
In word and ac-tion, lov-ing each oth-er
As you have loved us, call-ing us friends.

81, Text: from John 15, Stephen J. Wolf, 2007, 2016, public domain
tribute to the priesthood of Charley Giacosa
Music: BUNESSAN 5554 D, Scots Gaelic melody
Popular melody for ***Morning Has Broken***

ADVENT

The/ King shall come when/ morn-ing dawns,
And light tri-umph\-ant/ breaks;
When/ beau-ty gilds the east-ern hills,
And/ life/ to joy\ a-wakes.

O/ bright-er than that/ glo-rious morn
Shall this fair morn\-ing/ be,
When/ Christ, our King, in beau-ty comes,
And/ we/ his face\ shall see.

The/ King shall come when/ morn-ing dawns,
And light and beau\-ty/ brings:
Hail/, Christ the Lord! your peo-ple pray,
Come/ quick/-ly, King\ of kings.

16, Text: author unknown;
translated from Greek by John Brownlie,
Hymns of the Russian Church, 1907
Music: MCKEE, CM; African American Spiritual,
arranged by Harry T. Burleigh, 1866-1949
Popular melody for: *In Christ There Is No East or West*

CHRISTMAS

Of the Fa-ther's love be-got\-ten
Ere the worlds be-gan\ to be,
He is Al-pha and O-me\-ga,
He the Source, the End\-ing he,
Of the things that are, that have/\\/ been,
And that fu-ture years shall see
Ev-er-more and ev-er-more\.

This the birth for-ev-er bless\-ed
When the Vir-gin, full\ of grace
By the Ho-ly Ghost con-ceiv\-ing
Bore the Sa-vior of\ our race
And the Babe, the world's Re-deem/\\/-er,
First re-vealed his sa-cred face
Ev-er-more and ev-er-more\.

He of whom the in-spired sing\-ers
Sang of old with one\ ac-cord,
He whom voic-es of the proph\-ets
Prom-ised in their faith\-ful word:
Now he shines, the long-ex-pec/\\/-ted.
Let cre-a-tion praise its Lord
Ev-er-more and ev-er-more\.

31, Text: *Corde natus ex Parentis* by Aurelius C. Prudentius, 413;
translated by John M. Neal, 1854
Music: 87 87 87 7 DIVINUM MYSTERIUM, 12th C. chant, Mode V

LENT

The/ glo-ry\ of these/ for-ty days
We cel-e-brate with songs of praise;
For Christ, by/ whom\ all things\ were made,
Him-self has fast-ed and has prayed.

A/-lone and\ fast-ing/ Mo-ses saw
The lov-ing God who gave the law;
And to E/-li\-jah, fast\-ing, came
The steeds and char-i-ots of flame.

So/ Dan-iel\ trained his/ mys-tic sight,
De-liv-ered from the li-on's might;
And John, the/ Bride\-groom's friend\, be-came
The her-ald of Mes-si-ah's Name.

Then/ grant us\, Lord, like/ them to be
In faith-ful fast and prayer with thee;
Our spir-its/ strength\-en with\ your grace,
And give us joy to see your face.

56, Text: Gregory the Great, 6th Century,
translated by Maurice F. Bell, *The English Hymnal*, 1906, altered
Music option: ERHALT UNS HERR, LM;
Klug's *Geistliche Lieder*, 1543

EASTER

Christ the Lord is ris'n to\\-day,
Al\\\\-le\\-lu-ia!
Daugh-ters, sons and an-gels\\ say,
Al\\\\-le\\-lu-ia.
Raise your joys and tri\\-umphs\\ high,
Al\\/-le-lu-ia!
Sing, ye heav'ns, and earth, re\\-ply,
Al\\\\-le\\-lu-ia!

Lives a-gain our glo-rious\\ King,
Al\\\\-le\\-lu-ia!
Where, O Death, is now your\\ sting,
Al\\\\-le\\-lu-ia!
Once he died our souls\\ to\\ save,
Al\\/-le-lu-ia!
Where your vic-to-ry, O\\ Grave, Al\\\\-le\\-lu-ia!

Hail the Lord of earth and\\ heav'n,
Al\\\\-le\\-lu-ia!
Praise to God by both be\\ giv'n! Al\\\\-le\\-lu-ia!
Chil-dren of the Res-ur-rec\\-tion, Al\\/-le-lu-ia!
Our e-lec-tion has been\\ won! Al\\\\-le\\-lu-ia!

61, Text: Charles Wesley, 1739, altered
Music marked: 77 77 LLANFAIR with alleluias,
Robert Williams, d. 1821
Alternate music: 77 77 EASTER HYMN with alleluias,
Lyra Davidica, 1708

PSALM 18:2-30

Antiphon *You shall love the Lord, your God*
with all your heart and soul and mind,
and your neighbor as yourself. Mt 22:37,39
see also
Dt 6:5 & Lev 19:18

I love you, Adonai, my strength,
my rock Adonai, my fortress and deliverer;
in my God and Rock I take refuge,
my shield and horn, my salvation and stronghold.

I call out praise to Adonai
and am saved from enmity.

They tangled me in cords of death
and overwhelmed me in torrents of destruction.
Cords of Sheol coiled around me
and snares of death confronted me.

In my distress I called "Adonai,"
I cried for help from my God,
who heard from the temple my voice;
my cry went into these ears.

The earth trembled and quaked
and foundations of mountains shook
and trembled because of anger.
Smoke rose from the nostrils
and fire from the mouth consumed blazing coals.

Psalm 18, continued

The heavens parted
and dark clouds came down under the feet.
Mounted on the cherub,
flying and soaring on wings of wind,
a canopy of darkness covered all around,
dark waters in the clouds of the skies.

From the brightness of the presence
the clouds advanced hailstone and lightning bolts.
Adonai thundered from the heavens,
the voice of the Most High resounding
as hailstone and lightning bolts.

Arrows shot, scattering them all;
with great lightning bolts they are routed.
Valleys of waters were exposed
and foundations of earth laid bare
at your rebuke, Adonai,
at the blast of the breath of your nostril.

You reached from on high and took hold of me
and drew me out from the deep waters;
you rescued me from enmity
and from those too strong, too powerful for me.

They confronted me in the day of my disaster
but Adonai was my support,
brought me out to the spacious place,
and rescued me because of delight in me.

Adonai dealt with me as my ways are upright,
rewarded me as my hands are clean,
for I kept to the ways of Adonai.
Indeed all of God's laws are before me
and I did not turn from those decrees.

Blameless before God, on guard against sin,
in the sight of Adonai I am rewarded
as my ways are just and my hands are clean.

To the faithful you show yourself faithful,
to the honest you show yourself honest,
and to the pure you show yourself pure,

but to the crooked you show yourself shrewd,
for you save humble people
but bring low the eyes of the haughty.

Indeed you make my lamp burn;
my God Adonai makes light in my darkness.
Indeed with you I can advance against troops,
with my God I can scale a wall.

Glory…

Antiphon *You shall love the Lord, your God*
with all your heart and soul and mind,
and your neighbor as yourself. Mt 22:37,39
& Dt 6:5, Lev 19:18

Our lives become a parchment; our sufferings and our actions are the ink. The workings of the Holy Spirit are the pen, and with it God writes a living gospel. Jean-Pierre de Caussade, Jesuit

PSALM 89:2-38

Antiphon *One loving father or mother or son or daughter more than me is not worthy of me.* Mt 10:37

Advent & Christmas — Mary treasured all these words
and pondered them in her heart.

Dec 28 — Clothed in white robes, the holy
innocents walk with the Lord.

Easter — Wherever you are, Lord,
there is mercy, there is truth,
alleluia.

Forever will I sing the great love of Adonai;
with my mouth I will make known
your fidelity to generation and generation.
Indeed I will declare forever love standing firm,
your faithfulness established in the heavens.

"I made a covenant with my chosen ones,
sworn to my servant David.
I will establish your line to forever,
and to generation and generation
I will make firm your throne."

The heavens praise your wonder, Adonai,
and your fidelity in the holy assembly.
For who in the sky can compare to Adonai;
who is like Adonai among heavenly beings?

God is greatly feared in the council of holy ones
and is awesome over all who surround around.
Adonai Sabaoth, who is like you?
Mighty Adonai, your fidelity is around you.

You rule over the surging of the sea;
when waves mount up you still them.
You crushed Rahab like the slain
and scattered enmity
with the arm of your strength.

To you are the heavens and to you is the earth;
the world and all her fullness you founded.
North and South you created;
Tabor and Hermon sing for joy at your name.

To you is the arm strong with power;
your hand is exalted, your right hand.
Justice and Judgment
are the foundation of your throne;
Hesed-Love and Fidelity go before your faces.

Blessed are people who learn to acclaim Adonai;
they walk in the light of your presences.
In your name they rejoice all the day
and in your judgment they exult,

for you are the glory of their strength
and by your favor you exalt our horn.
Indeed Adonai is our shield
and the Holy One of Israel is our Ruler.

Psalm 89, continued

Once in a vision you spoke to your faithful ones:
"I bestowed strength on a warrior;
I raised from the people a young man.

I chose David my servant,
I anointed him with my sacred oil,
and my hand will sustain him;
surely my arm will strengthen him.

Enmity will not subject him to tribute
and people doing the bad will not oppress him.
Before him I will crush foes
and strike down adversity,

and my fidelity and my love are with him,
and through my hands will his horn be exalted.
And I will set his hand over the sea
and his right hand over the rivers.

He will call out to me: 'You are my Father,
my God and Rock of my salvation.'
I will also appoint him firstborn
and most exalted among rulers of the earth.

I will maintain my love for him to forever
and my unfailing covenant with him.
I will establish his line to forever
and his throne as days of the heavens.

If his sons and daughters forsake my law
and do not follow my statutes,
if they violate my decrees
and keep not my commands,

then I will punish their sins with the rod
and their iniquity with floggings.
But I will not take my love from them,
nor will I ever betray my fidelity.

I will not violate my covenant
nor will I alter the utterance of my lips.
Once I swore by my holiness;
I will not lie to David:

His line will continue to forever
and his throne like the sun before me.
Like the moon it is established forever,
a faithful witness in the sky."

Glory...

Antiphon *One loving father or mother or son or daughter more than me is not worthy of me.* Mt 10:37

Advent & Christmas Mary treasured all these words
and pondered them in her heart.

Dec 28 Clothed in white robes, the holy
innocents walk with the Lord.

Easter Wherever you are, Lord,
there is mercy, there is truth, alleluia.

PSALM 36

Antiphon *Blessed are your eyes for they see*
and your ears for they hear
what many prophets and just ones
longed to see and hear. Mt 13:16,17a

Advent & Lent Lord, in your light
we see light.

Dec 28 Let us worship the newborn Christ
who crowns with joy the holy
innocents who died in his stead.

Christmas Tell us, shepherds,
what have you seen?
Who has appeared to you?
We have seen a newborn infant
and a choir of angels
praising the Lord,
alleluia.

Easter You, Lord, are the fountain of life,
alleluia.

An oracle of sin in the midst of my heart:
There is no fear of God in the eyes of a sinner,
whose own eyes are full of self-flattery,
who hates to detect sin.

Words of this mouth are bad and deceitful:
Ceasing to be wise or do good,
they plot the bad while still in bed
and commit to a course of the no-good
and reject nothing that is wrong.

Adonai, to the heavens is your love
and your fidelity to the skies.
Your justice is like the mountains,
your judgment, deep and great;
human and beast you preserve, Adonai.

How priceless is your unfailing love.
High ones and humans find refuge
in the shadow of your wings.

They feast on the abundance of your house;
in the river of your delights you give them drink.
With you is the fountain of life,
and in your light we see light.

Continue your love to those who know you
and your just defense of the honest of heart.
Let the foot of pride not come to me
nor the hand of bad ways drive me away.

See, doers of the bad lie fallen;
they are thrown down, unable to rise.

Glory…

Antiphon

JUDITH 16:1,13-15

Antiphon *O Lord, you are great and glorious,*
wonderful in strength, invincible.

Christmas The angel said to the shepherds: I proclaim to you a great joy; the Savior of the world is born for you, alleluia.

Easter You sent forth your Spirit,
and all creatures were created, alleluia.

Begin a song to my God with timbrels;
sing to my Lord with cymbals.
Sing to my Lord a new song;
exalt and acclaim the name.

I will sing to my God a new song;
O Lord, you are great and glorious,
wonderful in strength and unbeatable.

Let your every creature serve you,
for you spoke, and they were made.
You sent forth your spirit,
and they were created;
no one can resist your word.

Mountain foundations are shaken by waters
and rocks melt like wax at your glance.
But to those who fear you, you show mercy.

Glory... Antiphon

ISAIAH 33:13-16

Antiphon *Blessed is the one who works justice*
and speaks honesty.

Christmas A little child is born for us;
little and yet called the mighty God,
alleluia.

Easter Our eyes will see the Ruler
in radiant beauty, alleluia.

Hear what I have done, you who are far away!
And acknowledge my power, you who are near.

Sinners are terrified in Zion
and trembling grips the godless.
Who of us can dwell in fire that consumes?
Who of us can dwell in everlasting burning?

One working justice and speaking honesty,
rejecting the gains of extortion,
waving off acceptance of the bribe,
stopping ears from hearing of bloodshed,
shutting eyes to not gaze on the bad:

That one will dwell on the heights
in a mountain fortress refuge,
supplied with bread and waters never-failing.

Glory…

Antiphon

PSALM 47

Antiphon *Behold, I am with you all the days*
until the completion of the eon. Mt 28:20

Christmas & Easter God rules over all the earth;
make music with all your skill, alleluia.

All you nations, clap your hands!
Shout to God with cries of joy!
How awesome, Most High Adonai.

The great Ruler over all the earth
subdued nations under us
and peoples under our feet,
and chose for us an inheritance,
the pride of Jacob the beloved.

God ascended with shouts of joy,
Adonai amid sound of trumpet.
Sing praises to God, sing praises.
Sing praises to our Ruler, sing praises.

For God, Ruler of all the earth, sing praises.
God reigns over the nations,
God sits on the holy throne.

Nobles of nations assemble
with the people of the God of Abraham.
The shields of the earth belong to God
who is greatly exalted.

Glory... Antiphon

PSALM 98

Antiphon *I will give you a mouth and wisdom that will not be contradicted or withstood.* Lk 21:15

Sing to Adonai a new song
who has done marvelous things,
working salvation at the right hand and holy arm.

Adonai made known salvation,
justice revealed for the eyes of the nations.
Love is remembered
and fidelity to the house of Israel

and all the ends of the earth see
the salvation of our God.
Shout for joy to Adonai, all you earth!
Break into song and sing praise.

Make music to Adonai with harp,
with harp and the sound of singing,
with trumpets and blast of ram horn:
Shout for joy before Adonai, the Ruler.

Let the sea resound, the fullness of the world,
and those living in her.
Let the rivers clap hands,
let the mountains sing together for joy

before Adonai who comes to judge the earth,
who will judge the world with justice
and peoples with equity.

Glory… Antiphon

ORDINARY TIME READING **TOBIT 4:15a,16a,18a,19**

What you yourself dislike do not do to anyone else. Give some of your food to the hungry and some of your clothing to the naked. Seek advice from every wise person. At all times bless and ask the Lord God that your ways may be made straight and that your plans may prosper.

RESPONSORY Ps 25:4

Push and pull my heart...
...as is your will, my Lord.
Keep my feet on your path...
...as is your will, my Lord.
Glory to the Father and to the Son and to the Holy Spirit:
...Push and pull my heart, as is your will, my Lord.

ADVENT READING **ISAIAH 7:10-15**

Adonai spoke again to Ahaz to say, "Ask for a sign from your God Adonai; ask to dig deep or to go high above." But Ahaz said, "I will not ask, I will not test Adonai." So Isaiah said, "Hear now, house of David! Is it not enough for you to try the patience of humans? Will you also try the patience of my God?

And so the Lord will give to you a sign to see: the virgin with child, bearing a son, and she will call his name Immanuel! He will be eating curds and honey when he knows to reject the bad and choose the good."

RESPONSORY

Your light will come, Jerusalem…
…the Lord will dawn on you in radiant beauty.
The glory of the Lord you will see within you…
…the Lord will dawn on you in radiant beauty.
Glory to the Father and to the Son and to the Holy Spirit:
…Your light will come, Jerusalem;
the Lord will dawn on you in radiant beauty.

CHRISTMAS READING **ISAIAH 45:22-25**

"Turn to me and be saved, all you ends of the earth, for I am God and there is no other. By myself I swore integrity out of my mouth, the word that will not be revoked. Indeed, in front of me every knee will bow, and every tongue will swear, and say, 'In my Adonai alone are justice and strength,' to whom will come and be shamed all who have raged otherwise." In Adonai they will find vindication and all the descendants of Israel will exult.

RESPONSORY

The Lord has made known…
…alleluia, alleluia.
The saving power…
…alleluia, alleluia.
Glory to the Father and to the Son and to the Holy Spirit:
…The Lord has made known the saving power, alleluia.

After Epiphany

All the royal powers on earth
…will bow down in worship.
Men and women of every nation…
…will bow down in worship.
Glory to the Father and to the Son and to the Holy Spirit:
…All the royal powers on earth
will bow down in worship.

LENT READING, Weeks 1 & 3 **DEUTERONOMY 7:6b,8-9**

Your God Adonai chose you to be the people treasured from all the peoples on the faces of the earth. Because of Adonai's love for you and to keep the oath sworn to your ancestors, Adonai brought you out with a mighty hand and redeemed you from the house of slaveries from the hand of Pharaoh, king of Egypt, so you know that your God Adonai is the God, the faithful God keeping the covenant and the love to a thousand generations of those loving God and keeping God's commands.

RESPONSORY Lk 18:13

The Lord God will set me free…
…from the hunter's snare.
From all those who would trap me with lying words,
…and from the hunter's snare.
Glory to the Father and to the Son and to the Holy Spirit:
…The Lord God will set me free from the hunter's snare.

LENT READING, Week 5 **ISAIAH 50:4b-7**

Sovereign Adonai wakens my ear to hear as one taught and opens my ear, and I did not rebel nor draw back. I offered my back to beaters and my cheeks to beard pullers and did not hide my faces from mockings and spittings because Sovereign Adonai helps me. For this I will not be disgraced. For this I set my faces like the flint and I know that I will not be shamed.

RESPONSORY Rev. 5:9

Lord, by your own blood…
…you brought us back to God.
From every tribe and tongue and people and nation...
…you brought us back to God.
Glory to the Father and to the Son and to the Holy Spirit:
…Lord, by your own blood you brought us back to God.

EASTER READING **ROMANS 6:8-11**

If we died with Christ, we believe that we shall also live with him, knowing that Christ raised from the dead dies no more. Death lords it over him no more, for in that he died to sin he died once. But in that he is alive, he is alive to God. So also you reckon yourselves dead indeed to sin, but alive to God in Christ Jesus.

RESPONSORY, in the Octave of Easter

This is the day the Lord has made;
let us rejoice and be glad.

RESPONSORY, Weeks 2 through 7

The Lord is risen from the tomb…
…alleluia, alleluia.
He hung upon the cross for us…
…alleluia, alleluia.
Glory to the Father and to the Son and to the Holy Spirit:
…The Lord is risen from the tomb, alleluia, alleluia.

Gospel Canticle For Morning

Antiphons

Advent Wk 1
Matt 15:29-37

The One who is coming after me
is greater than I; I am not worthy
to untie the strap of his sandals.

Advent Wk 3
Luke 7:18b-23

Be comforted, my people, be comforted,
says the Lord your God.

Dec 28

The powers-that-be put children to death
in place of Christ, all now in heaven.

Christmas

Christ our God, in whom
the fullness of the Godhead dwells,
took on our wounded nature and
became the first new human, alleluia.

After Epiphany
Mark 6:45-52

We have seen the star in the East
and have come with gifts
to worship the Lord.

Lent Wk 1
Lk 11:29-32

This faithless generation asks for a sign,
but no sign will be given it
except the sign of the prophet Jonah.

Lent Wk 3
Matt 5:17-19

The Lord said:
do not think that I have come
to abolish the law and the prophets;
I have come not to abolish
but to fulfill them.

Antiphons for Gospel Canticle For Morning, continued

Lent Wk 5 John 8:31-42	If you are faithful to my teaching, says the Lord, you will indeed be my disciples. You will know the truth and the truth will make you free.
Easter Wk 1 Luke 24:13-35	Beginning with Moses and the prophets, Jesus broke open for them all that had been written of him in the Scriptures, alleluia.
Easter Wk 3 John 6:35-40	Who sees the Son and believes in him will live forever, and I will raise up on the last day, alleluia.
Easter Wk 5 John 15:1-8	I am the true vine, alleluia; you are the branches, alleluia.
Easter Wk 7 Jn 17:11b-19	Thanks be to God who has given us the victory through our Lord Jesus Christ, alleluia.
Ordinary Antiphon	*Show us, Lord, how mercy works,* *and remember your holy covenant.*

Gospel Reading for Wednesday of

Week **1**	Mark 1:29-39	**13**	Matt 8:28-34	**25**	Luke 9:1-6
3	Mark 4:1-20	**15**	Matt 11:25-27	**27**	Luke 11:1-4
5	Mark 7:14-23	**17**	Matt 13:44-46	**29**	Lk 12:39-48
7	Mark 9:38-40	**19**	Matt 18:15-20	**31**	Lk 14:25-33
9	Mark 12:18-27	**21**	Matt 23:27-32	**33**	Lk 19:11-28
11	Matt 6:1-6,16-18	**23**	Luke 6:20-26		

CANTICLE of ZECHARIAH (The Benedictus)
LUKE 1:68-79

+ **Blessed be** the Lord the God of Israel
who chose a people to visit with redemption,
and raised salvation in the house of David,
saving strength from God's own servant,

speaking from the age of the prophets
through the mouth of the holy prophet:
Salvation out of enmity,
even out of those who hate us,

to show our ancestors how mercy works, -
and to remember the holy promise of the Lord,
the covenant made for our ancestor Abraham,
calming our fear and making us free
to serve with holy justice before God all our days.

And you also child -
will be called a prophet of the Most High
for you will go before the Lord to prepare his way
and give to people a knowledge of salvation
known in accepting forgiveness of their sins.

From the tender mercy of our God,
the sun rising from the height will visit with light
for those who sit in the dark or shadow of death
and to guide our feet into the way of peace.

Glory...

Antiphon

PETITIONS FOR THE CONSECRATION TO GOD OF THE DAY AND ITS WORK

- For the Church and her ministry and apostolates…
- For secular authorities and all serving as stewards…
- For people who are poor or sick or in sorrow…
- For peace and the basic needs of each human being…

COME HOLY SPIRIT — Cursillo

Come, Holy Spirit, fill the hearts of your faithful,
And kindle in us the fire of your love.

Send forth your Spirit and we shall be created,
And you shall renew the face of the earth.

Let us pray:

O God, who by the light of the Holy Spirit
did instruct the hearts of the faithful, grant,
that by the same Holy Spirit
we may be truly wise
and ever rejoice in her consolations,
through Christ our Lord.

OUR FATHER…

84, Text: Ephesians 1:3-14, Stephen J. Wolf, 2008,
with gratitude to the Institute for Priestly Formation
Music: 8787D, HYMN TO JOY, Ludwig van Beethoven, d. 1827;
adapted by Edward Hodges, 1824
Popular melody for: *Joyful, Joyful, We Adore Thee*

WEEK I
WEDNESDAY EVENING

\+ *God, come to my assistance;* Psalm 70:2
Lord, make haste to help me!
Glory...

Bles-sed be the God and Fa-ther
Of our Lord/ Je-sus Christ,
Who has blessed us in the Christ\,
bless-ings in their Spir-it breath.
As God chose us in the Mes-si-ah
be-fore/ found-ing sky or earth,
To be ho-ly, clean of blem-ish,
in God's eye: a-dop-tion worth.

In the Son we have re-demp-tion,
God's for-give-ness of our sin,
By the rich-es of his grace\
lav-ished on us gath-ered in.
Giv-ing wis-dom, know-ledge/, vis-ion,
mys-t'ry/ of the Fa-ther's will,
Sum-ming up all things in Je-sus,
fa-vored in the full-ness sent.

In our hear-ing of the gos-pel
word of our sal-va\-tion,
One by one we too were cho-sen,
joined as part-ners with the Son.
By the prom-is'd Ho-ly/ Spir-it,
signed and/ sealed as heirs of God,
God's pos-ses-sion, God's re-demp-tion,
God's be-lov-ed, Ab-ba's own.

ADVENT

Com-fort, com-fort, O my peo-ple,
Speak of peace, thus says our God;
Com-fort those who sit in dark-ness,
Mourn-ing un-der sor-row's load;
Speak un-to Je-ru-sa-lem
Of the peace that waits for them;
Tell her all her sins I cov-er,
And that war-fare now is o-ver.

For the her-ald's voice is cry-ing
In the des-ert far and near,
Call-ing peo-ple to re-pen-tance
Since the king-dom now is here.
Now that warn-ing cry o-bey!
Now pre-pare for God a way!
Let the val-leys rise to meet him,
And the hills bow down to greet him.

Make now straight what long was crook-ed,
Make the rough-er pla-ces plain;
Let our hearts be true and hum-ble,
As be-fits the ho-ly reign.
For the glo-ry of the Lord
O-ver earth is shed a-broad.
Hu-man be-ings, see the to-ken
That God's word is ne-ver bro-ken.

15, Text: based on Isaiah 40:1-8 for the Feast of John the Baptist,
Johann G. Olearius, 1611-1684,
trans. by Catherine Winkworth, 1827-1878, alt.
Music: 87 87 77 88, GENEVA 42, Claude Goudimel, *Geneva Psalter*, 1551

CHRISTMAS

God rest ye mer-ry, gen-tle folk,
let noth-ing you dis-may,
Re-mem-ber Christ our Sa\-vior
was born on Christ-mas day;
To save us from the e-vil pow'r
when we had gone a-stray.

Refrain **O/ ti-dings of com\-fort and joy,**
com-fort and joy;
O/ ti/-dings of com\-fort and joy.

From God our heav'n-ly Fa\-ther
a bless-ed an-gel came;
And un-to cer-tain shep\-herds
brought ti-dings of the same;
How that in Beth-le-hem was born
the Son of God by name... *Refrain*

"**S**o, have no fear," the an-gel said,
"but find the vir-gin maid.
Of her is born the Sa\-vior,
so do not be a-fraid.
Now free are all who trus-ted their
re-demp-tion would be paid"... *Refrain*

21, Text: traditional English Carol, 18th C., altered
Music: 86 86 86 with refrain
GOD REST YOU MERRY GENTLEMEN,
Little Book of Christmas Carols, 1846

LENT & EASTER

There's a wide/-ness in God's mer\-cy
Like the wide-ness of\ the sea;
There's a kind/-ness in God's jus\-tice
Which is more than lib\-er-ty.
There is plen\-ti-ful re-demp\-tion
In the blood/ that has\ been shed;
There\ is joy\ for all\ the mem//\-bers
In the sor\-rows of the Head.

For the love/ of God is broad\-er
Than the meas-ures of\ our mind,
And the heart/ of the E-ter\-nal
Be-yond won-der-ful\ and kind.
If our love\ were but more simp\-le
We might take/ him at\ his word,
And\ our lives\ would be\ thanks-giv//\-ing
For the good\-ness of the Lord.

Troub-led souls/, why will you scat\-ter
Like a crowd of fright\-ened sheep?
Fool-ish hearts/, why will you wan\-der
From a love so true\ and deep?
There is wel\-come for the sin\-ner
And more gra/-ces for\ the good;
There\ is mer\-cy with\ the Sa//\-vior,
There is heal\-ing in his food.

114, Text: Frederick W. Fabor, 1814, 1863, altered
Music: 87 87 D, HYFRYDOL; Rowland Prichard, 1811-1887
Popular melody for: *Love Divine, All Love Excelling*

PSALM 70

Antiphon *You have heard it said,*
an eye for an eye and a tooth for a tooth;
but I say to you, do not resist a doer of bad;
when someone strikes you on the right cheek,
give the other as well. Mt 5:38,39

Christmas & Easter Alleluia, alleluia, alleluia.

God, come to save me;
Adonai, make haste to help me!
May plans to seek my life
be shamed and confused;

may the desire for my ruin
be turned back in disgrace
and ones saying "aha!, aha!"
turn back in shame.

May all who seek you
rejoice in you and be glad
and may lovers of salvation say always,
"Let God be exalted."

Yet I am poor and needy, God,
come quickly to me and do not delay,
Adonai, my help and deliverer.

Glory... Antiphon

PSALM 17

Antiphon *The Lord is God of the living.* Lk 20:38

Advent & Lent Lord, hold my steps to your path.

Christmas Now, Master, you set free your servant
according to your word in peace;
my eyes have seen the salvation,
which you have prepared
before the face of all the peoples,
a light for revelation to the nations
and glory for your people, Israel.

Lk 2:29-32
Canticle of Simeon

Easter Alleluia, alleluia, alleluia.

Hear, Adonai, a just plea; listen to my cry.
Give ear to my prayer, from lips without deceit.
May my vindication come from you;
may my eyes see right things.

You probe and examine my heart in the night,
you test me and find nothing wrong.
By resolve my mouth will not sin.

By the word of your lips
my human deeds are kept from violent ways.
Holding my steps to your paths
my feet did not slip.

I call on you, El, for you will answer me.
Give ear to me and hear my prayer.
Show the wonder of your great saving love;
at your right hand are refugees from adversity.

Keep me as the apple daughter of your eye.
You hide me in the shade of your wings
from those who assail me in enmity,
surrounding around my life.
They close their callous hearts,
they speak their arrogant mouth.

Now they surround our tracks;
their eyes are alert, ready to throw to the ground.
They are like a lion, hungry to tear prey,
like a great lion crouching to ambush.

Rise up, Adonai!
Confront and bring down their ways.
Rescue my self by your sword, Adonai,
by your hand from humans,
humans of the world whose reward is this life.

As for those who are cherished by you,
their belly is full, sons and daughters are plenty,
and they store up their wealth for their children.

May justice let me see your faces
and be satisfied waking up to your likeness.

Glory...

Antiphon

PSALM 27

Antiphon *Come after me, and I will make you*
fishers of human beings. Mt 4:19

Christmas & Easter God has raised the Christ
as ruler and savior, alleluia.

Adonai is my light and my salvation.
Whom shall I fear?
Adonai is the stronghold of my life.
Of whom shall I be afraid?

When people doing the bad
advance against me to devour my flesh,
when enmity and adversity go against me,
they will stumble and fall.

Though an army encamp against me,
my heart will not fear.
Though war break out against me,
in this I will be confident.

One thing I ask of Adonai:
to seek and to dwell in Adonai's house,
to gaze on Adonai's beauty
all the days of my life as a seeker in the temple.

I will be kept safely dwelling,
hidden in the shelter of the tabernacle,
on the day of trouble set high upon rock.

Then will my head be lifted above enmity,
and I will sacrifice at the tabernacle
the sacrifice of shouts of joy.

I will sing and make music to Adonai.
Hear, Adonai, my voice calling;
be merciful; answer me.
To you my heart says, "My face seeks you."

Your faces, Adonai, I will seek.
Hide not your faces from me;
turn not away from your servant in anger.

You are my help;
neither reject nor forsake me,
God of my salvation.
Even if my father and my mother forsake me,
you, Adonai, will take me in.

Teach me your way, Adonai,
and lead me through oppression to level paths.
Do not give me over to the desires
of enmity rising with false witnesses
and breathers of violence.

Still I am confident: I will see
the goodness of Adonai in the land of the living.
Wait for Adonai!
Take courage and strengthen your heart.
And wait for Adonai!

Glory... Antiphon

PSALM 28:1-3,6-9

Antiphon *Pray for all, even for those in authority,*
that our living may include quiet and dignity.
1 Tim 2:2

Christmas & Easter Alleluia, alleluia, alleluia.

To you I call, my Rock Adonai,
turn not to me a deaf ear.
For if you remain silent, away from me,
then I will be like one going into the pit.

Hear the sound of my cries for mercy
calling to you for help as I lift my hands
toward the Holy Place of your Holiness.

Drag me not away with those who do the bad,
who speak cordiality with their neighbors
but with malice in their heart.

Praised be Adonai,
who heard the sound of my cries for mercy.
Adonai, my strength and my shield,
in whom my heart trusts,
I am helped and my heart leaps for joy
and in my song I will give thanks.

Adonai is the strength
and the saving refuge of the anointed.
Save your people! Bless your inheritance!
Be their shepherd and carry them to forever!

Glory... Antiphon

PSALM 126

Antiphon *What do you wish me to do for you?*
...Go, your faith has healed you. Mk 10:51,52

Advent & Lent Those who sow in tears
will reap a song of joy.

Christmas & Easter Your weeping will be turned into joy,
alleluia.

When Adonai restored Zion out of captivity
we felt like people in a dream.
Then our mouth was filled with laughter,
and our tongue with a song of joy.

Then they said among the nations
"Their Adonai did great things for them."
Adonai did great things for us;
we were full of joy.

Restore our good fortune, Adonai,
like streams in the Negev desert.
Sowers are now in tears;
they will reap with a song of joy.

Going out, the sower goes out weeping,
carrying seeds for the sowing.
Returning, the sower will return
carrying sheaves with a song of joy.

Glory...

Antiphon

PSALM 127

Antiphon *Look at the birds of heaven and see:*
they do not sow or reap or gather into barns
and your heavenly Abba feeds them. Mt 6:26

Advent & Lent Lord, build the house;
Lord, watch over the city.

Christmas You have been endowed from your birth
with royal gifts.

Easter Whether we live or die, we are the Lord's,
alleluia.

If Adonai does not build the house,
the builders labor in vanity.
If Adonai does not watch over the city,
the watcher stands guard in vain.

It is vanity to rise early or stay up late,
or to eat the bread of hard toil;
the Lord provides as the beloved get their sleep.

See, heritage of Adonai!
Sons are a reward, and daughters of the womb.
Like arrows in the hand of a warrior,
so are children of one's youth.

Blessed are they whose quivers are full of them;
they will not be shamed
when they speak with enmity at the gate.

Glory… Antiphon

COLOSSIANS 1:12-20

Antiphon *Who follows me will have the light of life.* Jn 8:12c

Give joyful thanks to the Abba who made you fit
for your part of the lot of the saints in light,

who delivered us out of the authority of darkness,
transitioning us into the realm of the beloved Son
in whom we have redemption,
the forgiveness of our sins.

The Son is the image of the invisible God,
the firstborn of all creation.
In him all things were created,
in the heavens and on the earth,
the visible and the invisible,
whether thrones, lordships, rulers or authorities.

All creation has come to be through and for him.
He is before all things,
and in him all things hold together.

He is the head of the body, the church,
and the beginning, the firstborn from the dead,
so that in all things he may hold the first place.

In him all the fullness was well pleased to dwell,
and through him reconciliation to himself
of all things on earth and things in the heavens,
making peace through the blood of his cross.

Glory… Antiphon

ORDINARY TIME READING **JAMES 1:19-27**

Know, my beloved brothers and sisters; let every human be swift to hear, slow to speak, and slow to be angry, for human anger does not work toward God's righteous ways. So put away all filthiness and unnecessary waste and receive in meekness the word planted in you that is able to save your souls.

Become doers of the word (the *logos*) and not hearers only misleading yourselves. The hearer of the word who is not a doer is like a human seeing in a mirror one's face of birth, and seeing oneself, goes away right away and forgets what sort he or she is.

But the one who looks into the perfect law of freedom and remains, becoming not a forgetful hearer but a doer of the work, blessed in the doing will this one be. Any who think themselves religious and do not bridle their tongue but deceive their heart, vain is their religion.

This is religion clean and undefiled before the God and Father: to visit orphans and widows in their affliction, and to keep oneself unspotted by the world.

RESPONSORY Ps 26:11,9

Redeem me, my Lord and my God,…
…and in your grace have mercy.
Sweep me not with those doing badness…
…and in your grace have mercy.
Glory to the Father and to the Son and to the Holy Spirit:
…Redeem me, my Lord and my God,
and in your grace have mercy.

ADVENT READING **1 CORINTHIANS 4:5**

Judge not anything before the time, until the coming of the Lord, who will shed light on our dark and hidden things and will show forth what goes on in human hearts. Then will be the praise to each one from God.

RESPONSORY Ps 146:7; 63:3; 67:2

Come and set us free…
…Lord God of power and glory…
Let your face shine upon us
and we will know salvation…
…Lord God of power and glory…
Glory to the Father and to the Son and to the Holy Spirit:
…Come and set us free, Lord God of power and glory…

CHRISTMAS READING **ROMANS 8:1-5**

Now there is no condemnation for the ones in Christ Jesus. For the law of the Spirit of life in Christ Jesus freed you from the law of sin and death. For the thing impossible by the law, weak through the flesh, God did, sending God's own Son in the likeness of sinful flesh condemning sin in the flesh, that the ordering of the law might be fulfilled in us, walking not in accord with the flesh but in accord with the Spirit.

RESPONSORY Jn 1:14

Before Epiphany
The Word became flesh… *…alleluia, alleluia.*
And dwelt among us… *…alleluia, alleluia.*

Glory to the Father and to the Son and to the Holy Spirit:
...The Word became flesh and dwelt among us,
alleluia, alleluia.

After Epiphany

All people will be blessed in him...
...in every tribe of the human race.
All nations will acclaim his glory...
...in every tribe of the human race.
Glory to the Father and to the Son and to the Holy Spirit:
...All people will be blessed in him,
in every tribe of the human race.

LENT READING, Weeks 1 &3 **PHILIPPIANS 2:12b-16**

My beloved, with fear and trembling you work out your salvation, for God is the one working in you both to will and to work on behalf of God's good will.

Do what you do without murmurings or disputes, blameless and harmless, children of God faultless in the midst of a crooked and perverse generation. Shine as luminaries in the world, holding up a word of life, a boast to me in the day of Christ, that not in vain did I run nor in vain labor.

RESPONSORY Lk 18:13

To you, O Lord...
...I make my prayer for mercy.
Heal my soul, for I have sinned against you...
...I make my prayer for mercy.
Glory to the Father and to the Son and to the Holy Spirit:
...To you, O Lord, I make my prayer for mercy.

LENT READING, Week 5 **EPHESIANS 4:32-5:2**

Be kind to one another, tenderhearted, and forgive yourselves as also God in Christ has forgiven you. Be therefore imitators of God, as beloved children, and walk in love.

Christ has loved you and gave up himself on our behalf, an offering and a sacrifice to God for an odor of sweetness.

RESPONSORY Rev. 5:9

We worship you, O Christ…
…and we praise you.
By your cross you have redeemed the world…
…and we praise you.
Glory to the Father and to the Son and to the Holy Spirit:
…We worship you, O Christ, and we praise you.

EASTER READING, Before Ascension **HEBREWS 7:24-27**

Jesus, because he remains unto the eons, has the priestly office without end. And so he is able to save entirely those approaching to God through him, always alive to intercede for them. To us indeed was suitable such a high priest, holy, harmless, undefiled, set apart from sinners, becoming higher than the heavens. He does not have the daily need of the high priests to offer up sacrifices first for their own sins and then for the sins of the people. For he did this once for all, offering up his very self.

RESPONSORY, in the Octave of Easter:

This is the day the Lord has made;
let us rejoice and be glad.

RESPONSORY, Easter Weeks 2 to 6

The disciples rejoiced...
...alleluia, alleluia.
When they saw the risen Lord...
...alleluia, alleluia.
Glory to the Father and to the Son and to the Holy Spirit:
...The disciples rejoiced; alleluia, alleluia.

EASTER READING, After Ascension **1 COR 2:9b-10**

Things which eye has not seen and ear has not heard
and have not come upon the human heart,
how many are prepared for those loving God.

This has been revealed to us by God through the Spirit. For the Spirit searches all things, even the deep things of God.

RESPONSORY, After Ascension Jn 14:26

The Holy Spirit is the Paraclete...
...alleluia, alleluia.
Who will teach you all things...
...alleluia, alleluia.
Glory to the Father and to the Son and to the Holy Spirit:
...The Holy Spirit is the Paraclete, alleluia, alleluia.

Gospel Canticle For Evening

Antiphons

Advent Wk 1	The law will go forth from Zion; the word of the Lord from Jerusalem.
Advent Wk 3	You, O Lord, are the One whose coming was foretold: we long for you to come and set your people free.
Dec 28	Let us adore the Lord who comes to save us.
Christmas	I have come forth from God into the world; I have not come of myself, but the Abba has sent me.
After Epiphany	Herod questioned the Magi: What is this sign of which you speak, this sign of a newborn ruler? We saw a brilliant star in the heavens; its splendor filled the world.
Lent Wk 1	As Jonah was three days and three nights in the belly of the big fish, so will the Son of Humanity spend three days and three nights in the earth.

Antiphons for Gospel Canticle for Evening, continued

Lent Wk 3	The one who obeys God's law and teaches others to do so will be great in the reign of heaven.
Lent Wk 5	Why are you set on killing me when I have told you the truth?
Easter Wk 1	Jesus went in with them, and while they were at table he took bread and said the blessing; he broke the bread and gave it to them, alleluia.
Easter Wk 3	All that the Abba gives me will come to me, and whoever comes to me I shall not turn away, alleluia.
Easter Wk 5	If you live in me and my words live in you, all you ask for will be yours, alleluia.
Easter Wk 7	The Christ will baptize you with fire and the Holy Spirit, alleluia.
Ordinary Antiphon	*The Mighty One has done* *great things for me.*

CANTICLE of MARY (The Magnificat)
LUKE 1:46-55

+ **My soul** is stretched full with praise of the Lord,
and my spirit, beyond joy in God, my Savior,
who chose to lay eyes on this humble servant.

Behold, now and forward,
each and every age will call me blessed,
for the Mighty One did great things to me.

Holy is the name and the mercy
to generations and generations,
the ones fearing the One,

Who scattered the haughty of mind and heart,
pulled the powerful off their high place,
and lifted with dignity the humble in need.

The hungering are filled with good things,
the rich are sent away empty,
and servant Israel is given relief

with a memory of mercy to remember,
the promise spoken to our ancestors,
to Abraham and his descendants forever.

Glory…

Antiphon

INTERCESSIONS

- For all who have had a hard day at work…
- For all who have died…

- In gratitude for blessings…; Abba thank you.
- For the sins of this day…; Lord Jesus have mercy.
- With concerns over tomorrow…; Holy Spirit help.

A PRAYER in a CULTURE of ADDICTION

God of mercy,
your Son ministered to all who came to him.
Give strength to your sons and daughters
who have lost their health and freedom
in the slavery of addiction.
Give them your grace in the work of recovery
and bring them to the freedom of sobriety.
To those who care for them,
grant wisdom to know when to help
and the patient love that perseveres.
Amen.

OUR FATHER…

117, Text: Psalm 23, Henry W. Baker, 1868, altered
Music: ST. COLUMBA, CM; Gaelic Folk Melody
Popular melody for: *O Breathe On Me, O Breath Of God*

WEEK I
THURSDAY MORNING

+ *God, come to my assistance;* Psalm 70:2
Lord, make haste to help me!

Glory...

ORDINARY TIME

The/ King of Love my/ Shep-herd is,
Whose/ good-ness fails me// nev-er;
I noth-ing lack if I am his
And he is mine for-ev-er.

Where/ streams of liv-ing/ wat-er flow,
Our/ ran-somed souls he// leads us,
And where the ver-dant pas-tures grow,
with food cel-es-tial feeds us.

Per/-verse and fool-ish/, do I stray,
But/ yet in love he// seeks me
To on his shoul-der gent-ly lay
And home, re-joic-ing, bring me.

You/ spread a ta-ble/ in our sight
Your/ unc-tion grace be//-stow-ing;
And, oh! the tran-sport of de-light
With our cup ov-er-flow-ing.

And/ so through all the/ length of days
Your/ good-ness fails us// nev-er.
Good Shep-herd, may we sing your praise
With-in your house for-ev-er!

ADVENT

Come, Re-deem-er of our race,
Choic-est Gift of heav'n-ly grace!
Be the bless-ed vir-gin's Son;
Join your race on earth be-gun.

Both of hu-man blood and birth
And of God he comes to earth
Ho-ly Spir-it breath con-ceived.
God and hu-man, we be-lieve.

Wond-rous, this ex-pect-ed Child
Of the vir-gin un-de-filed!
By the world he'll be dis-owned,
Still to be in heav'n en-throned.

Bright-ly will your man-ger shine!
Glo-rious in its light div-ine:
Let our sin not cloud this light;
Keep our gift of faith thus bright.

3, Text: *Veni Redemptor gentium,*
ascribed to Ambrose of Milan, d. 397;
translated by Charles Wesley?
Music: 7 7 7 7 HEINLEIN, attributed to Martin Herbst, d. 1681
Popular melody for: *Forty Days and Forty Nights*

CHRISTMAS

E-ter-nal, in-vis-i-ble, God on-ly wise.
In light in-ac-ces-si-ble hid from our eyes,
Most bless-ed, most glo-rious,
the An-cient of Days,
Your Son and your Spirit,
your great name we praise.

Un-rest-ing, un-hast-ing, and si-lent as light,
Nor want-ing, nor wast-ing, you rule day and night;
Your jus-tice like moun-tains
high soar-ing a-bove
Your clouds which are foun-tains
of bless-ing and love.

Great Fa-ther of glo-ry, Cre-a-tor of light,
Your an-gels a-dor-ing and saints in your sight;
Of all your rich gra-ces this grace, Lord, im-part:
Un-cov-er our fa-ces and make clean our heart.

All prais-es we ren-der; Lord help us to see
The splen-dor of light that is hid-den in thee,
And so let your glo-ry, Al-migh-ty, your art
Be told in the sto-ry of Christ to the heart.

83, Text: based on 1 Timothy 1:17
Walter C. Smith, *Hymns of Christ and the Christian Life*, 1876, altered
Music: 11 11 11 11, ST. DENIO, Welsh Melody, John Roberts,
Canaidau y Cyssagr, 1839
Original Lyrics: *Immortal Invisible God Only Wise*

LENT

Some-bo-dy's knock-in' at your door,
Some-bo-dy's knock-in' at your door,
O/ sin-ner, why don't you an-swer?
Some-bo-dy's knock-in' at your door.

Knocks like Je-sus,
Some-bo-dy's knock-in' at your door,
Knocks like\ Je-sus,

Refrain **Some-bo-dy's knock-in' at your door,**
O/ sin-ner, why don't you an-swer?
Some-bo-dy's knock-in' at your door,

Can't you hear him?
Some-bo-dy's knock-in' at your door,
Can't you\ hear him?
Refrain

An-swer Je-sus,
Some-bo-dy's knock-in' at your door,
An-swer\ Je-sus,
Refrain

54, Text & Music: Traditional African-American

60, Text: William C. Dix;
Altar Songs, Verses on the Holy Eucharist, 1867, altered
Music: 87 87 D, HYFRYDOL, Rowland H. Prichard, 1811-1887

EASTER

Al-le-lu/-ia! sing to Je-\sus!
his the scep-ter, his\ the throne!
Al-le-lu/-ia! his the tri\-umph,
his the vic-to-ry\ a-lone.
Hark! the songs\ of peace-ful Zi\-on
thun-der like/ a migh\-ty flood.
Je\-sus out\ of ev\-'ry na//\-tion
has re-deemed\ us by his blood.

Al-le-lu/-ia! not as or\-phans
are we left in sor\-row now;
Al-le-lu/-ia! he is near\ us,
faith be-lieves, nor ques\-tions how;
Though the cloud\ from sight re-ceived\ him
when the for/-ty days\ were o'er.
Shall\ our hearts\ for-get\ his pro//\-mise:
"I am with\ you ev-er-more?"

Al-le-lu/-ia! King e-ter\-nal,
you the Lord we know as our own;
Al-le-lu/-ia! Son of Ma\-ry,
earth your foot-stool, heav'n\ your throne:
In-ter-ces\-sor, Friend of sin\-ners,
robed in flesh/ our great\ High Priest;
You\ on earth\ both priest\ and vic//\-tim
in the Eu\-cha-ris-tic feast.

PSALM 18:31-51

Antiphon *Hear, Israel,*
the Lord our God is One. Mk 12:29

Christmas & Easter Adonai is alive; may our Rock be exalted,
the God of our salvation,
alleluia.

The ways of God are perfect,
the word of Adonai is flawless,
a shield for all who need refuge.
For who is God besides Adonai?
And who is the Rock except our God?

God arms me with strength,
makes my way good,
makes my feet like the deer
and makes me to stand at full height,
training my hands for the battle;
my arms can bend a bow of bronze.

You give to me your shield of victory,
your right hand sustains me,
stooping to make me great.
You broaden my path beneath me
so my ankles do not turn.

I pursued and overtook enmity
and did not turn back until its defeat…
They fell beneath my feet.

You armed me with strength for the battle
and made the adversity bow at my feet.
You turned back enmity and brought its defeat.

They cried for help, but no one saved them.
Adonai did not answer them.
I beat them as dust in the wind;
like mud in the streets I poured them out.

You delivered me from attacks of people,
you made me as a head of nations;
people I knew not became subject to me.
Hearing me in their ear they obey.

Foreigners cringe before me, losing heart,
trembling out of strongholds.

Adonai is alive and praised;
may my Rock be exalted, my saving God.
God gives victory to me
and subdues nations under me,

saving me from enmity,
and rescuing me from violence.
I praise you, Adonai, among the nations,
and to your name I will sing praise.

You make great victories of your king
with unfailing kindness to David, your anointed,
and his descendants to forever.

Glory…

Antiphon

PSALM 89:39-53

Antiphon *Who does not take their cross*
and follow after me
is not worthy of me. Mt 10:38

Christmas & Easter I am the root and stock of David;
I am the morning star,
alleluia.

Lord, you have rejected and spurned,
you were angry with your anointed one.
You renounced the covenant of your servant,
the crown you defiled in the dust.

You broke through all of the walls
and reduced the strongholds to ruin.
Those passing on the way plundered
and the neighbors were full of scorn.

You exalted the right hand of adversity
and made enmity rejoice.
You turned back the edge of our sword
and did not support us in the battle.

You put an end to the splendor
and cast the throne to the ground.
You cut short the days of youth
and covered us over with shame.

Until when, Adonai?
Will you hide yourself to forever?
Will your wrath burn like fire?
Remember how fleeting am I!

For what futility you created the human race,
sons and daughters of Adam and Eve!
What human can live and not see death,
or save the self from the power of Sheol?

Where, Lord, are your former great loves,
your fidelity sworn to David?
Remember, Lord,
the mockery of your servants!

I bear this in my heart
from many nations, Adonai:
the mockery of enmity,
the mockery of the steps of your anointed one.

Blessed be Adonai to forever.
Amen and amen.

Glory…

Antiphon

Part of the faith journey
is to figure out what my cross is.
Hint: everyone carries a core wound.
Then I can run away from it, try to give
it to someone else, pretend to know nothing
about it, try to bury it, or take it up and follow Jesus.

PSALM 57

Antiphon *This is my comandment,*
that you love one another
as I have loved you. Jn 15:12

Advent & Lent Awake, my soul;
awake the harp and lyre;
I will awaken dawn.

Christmas Tell us, shepherds,
what have you seen?
Who has appeared to you?
We have seen a newborn infant
and a choir of angels
praising the Lord, alleluia.

Easter Be exalted, O God,
above the heavens,
alleluia.

Have mercy on me, God, have mercy on me,
for in you my soul takes refuge
and in the shade of your wings I take refuge
until disasters pass.

I cry out to God Most High,
to El who fulfills me,
who sends from the heavens and saves me
and rebukes the one pursuing me.

God sends love and fidelity to my self;
in the midst of ravenous lions I lie,
in the midst of human beings
with teeth and spear and arrows and tongues,
their sharp swords.

Be exalted, God, above the heavens,
your glory over all the earth.

For my feet they spread a net
and my self was bowed down.
Before me they dug a pit
and fell inside it themselves.

My heart is steadfast, Elohim,
my heart is steadfast;
I will sing and make music.

Awake, my soul!
Wake up the harp and the lyre;
I will wake up the dawn.

I will praise you among the nations, Lord;
I will sing of you among the peoples,
for great to the heavens is your love
and to the skies is your fidelity.

Be exalted above the heavens, God,
your glory over all the earth.

Glory...

Antiphon

PSALM 87

Antiphon *The Abba and I are one.* Jn 10:30

Christmas & Easter
City of God,
you are the source of our life;
with music and dance
we shall rejoice in you,
alleluia.

On the holy mountain
is the foundation of Adonai,
who loves the gates of Zion
more than all of Jacob's dwellings.
Glorious things are being said of you, city of God.

"I will record Rahab and Babylon
among those who know me;
see Philistia and Tyre with Ethiopia:
this one was born there!"

But of Zion it will be said,
"One and another were born in her,
and the Most High will establish her."

Adonai will write when registering peoples,
"This one was born there."
And making music they will sing,
"All of my fountains are in you."

Glory...

Antiphon

JEREMIAH 31:10-14

Antiphon *They will be my people and I will be their God*
for they will return to me with all their heart.
Jer 24:7b

Hear, nations, the word of Adonai;
proclaim it to distant coastlands and say:
"The One who scattered Israel
will gather them and watch them
as one who is shepherd to a flock."

For Adonai will ransom and redeem Jacob
from the hand of those with more strength.

They will come and they will shout
up on the height of Zion
and they will rejoice in the bounty of Adonai,
the grain and new wine and oil,
and younglings of the flock and herd;
and they themselves like a well-watered garden
will sorrow no more, not again.

Then the maiden will be glad in dance,
and young men together with the old.
I will turn their mourning into gladness;
I will comfort them, replacing sorrow with joy.
I will satisfy with abundance the self of the priests
and my people will be filled with my bounty,
declares Adonai.

Glory... Antiphon

ISAIAH 40:10-17

Antiphon *A voice of one cried out in the desert:*
prepare the way of the Lord. Mk 1:3

Christmas The angel said to the shepherds:
I proclaim to you a great joy;
the Savior of the world
is born for you, alleluia.

Easter Like a shepherd
he will gather the Lambs in his arms
and carry them close to his heart,
alleluia.

See! Sovereign Adonai comes with power,
and with a ruling arm.
See! And with reward
accompanied with recompense.

Like a shepherd tending the flock
and gathering lambs in the arms,
carrying them in the heart
and leading gently those with young.

Who can measure the waters in a hand's hollow?
Or mark off the heavens with handbreadths?
Or hold the dust of the earth in a basket?
Or weigh mountains on a scale
or hills in a balance?

Who has understood the mind of Adonai?
What human has given counsel or instruction,
or whom was consulted for enlightenment
and teaching about what is right
and teaching knowledge?
Who can show the path of understanding?

Surely nations are like drops in a bucket
and are regarded as dust on a scale.
Surely islands are weighed like fine dust.

Even Lebanon is not sufficient to make fire,
nor their animals sufficient for burnt-offering.
Before God, all the nations are as nothing,
regarded as worthless and less than nothing.

Glory...

Antiphon

PSALM 48

Antiphon *Take nothing on the way*
except a staff, sandals,
and a single tunic. Mk 6:8

Christmas A little child is born for us;
little and yet called
the mighty God, alleluia.

Easter This is our God,
our guide to forever, alleluia.

Great is Adonai, greatly being praised
in the city of our God, on the holy mountain,
beautiful height, the joy of all the earth,

Mount Zion, the upmost heights,
sacred mountain, the city of the Great Ruler.
God in the citadels is shown as a fortress when,
see, the rulers join forces and invade together.

They saw, were astounded, and fled in terror;
trembling seized them, pain
like a woman in labor.
By the east wind you destroyed
ships of Tarshish;

just as we heard, so we saw in the city
of Adonai Sabaoth, in the city of our God.
God makes her secure to forever.

In your temple we meditate
on your unfailing love.
Like your name, God, so your praise
goes to the ends of the earth;

your right hand is filled with justice.
Mount Zion rejoices
because of your judgments;
the villages of Judah are glad.

Walk about Zion! Go all around!
Count her towers!
Consider at heart her ramparts!
View her citadels!
So that you may tell to the next generation:
This God, our God, forever and ever
will guide us to the always.

Glory...

Antiphon

---

*Emperor Constantine's Edict of Milan in 313 AD
diminished the general risk of being a martyr, which
had been seen by many as the highest form of Christian life.
And so some sought to pattern their lives after Jesus' 40 days of
temptation in the desert, but in desert caves in Egypt and Syria
praying primarily the psalms. Over time others began to live in
nearby caves seeking spiritual direction from the one they would
treat as a kind of father or abba, such as Saint Anthony of Egypt.*

PSALM 99

Antiphon *Were not ten lepers cleansed?*
And this one foreigner alone
gives glory to God? Lk 17:17

Advent & Lent
Exalt the Lord, our God;
and worship at the mountain
of the Lord's holiness.

Christmas & Easter
Great is the Lord in Zion,
and exalted over all the nations,
alleluia.

Adonai reigns; let the nations tremble.
The One sits enthroned on the cherubim;
let the earth shake.

Great in Zion is Adonai,
and exalted over all of the nations.
Let them praise your great and awesome name,
"Holy are you, and mighty."

The Ruler of justice loves you
and establishes equity and justice,
having done what is right in Jacob.

Exalt Adonai, our God!
And worship at the feet on the footstool,
"Holy are you, and mighty."

Moses and Aaron were among the priests,
and Samuel among those calling the name,
calling on El Adonai, who answered them,
who spoke to them from the pillar of cloud.
They kept the statutes and decrees given to them.

Adonai, our God, you answered them.
You were the one Forgiving El to them,
though punishing their misdeeds.

Exalt Adonai our God!
And worship at the holy mountain,
for holy is our God Adonai!

Glory...

Antiphon

ORDINARY TIME READING **ISAIAH 66:1-2**

This Adonai says, "The heavens are my throne and the earth is the footstool of my feet. Where is this house that you will build for me? Where is to be the place for my resting? Even all these my hand made, so all these came into being," declares Adonai.

"This I esteem: the one humble and contrite spirit, who trembles at my word."

RESPONSORY Ps 130:1

Out of the depths I cry to you...
...Lord, hear my voice!
My desire is to do your desire...
...Lord, hear my voice!
Glory to the Father and to the Son and to the Holy Spirit:
...Out of the depths I cry to you, Lord, hear my voice!

ADVENT READING **ISAIAH 45:5-8**

I am Adonai and there is no other; apart from me there is no God. I will strengthen you though you do not know me so that they may know there is none besides me, from the rising of the sun to its setting place.

I am Adonai and there is no other, forming light and creating darkness, bringing prosperity and allowing disaster; I Adonai am the one doing all of these. Heavens at above, let them rain; and let clouds shower justice; let the earth open and let salvation spring up and with justice; let them grow together, as I Adonai have created.

RESPONSORY

Your light will come, Jerusalem…
…the Lord will dawn on you in radiant beauty.
The glory of the Lord you will see within you…
…the Lord will dawn on you in radiant beauty.
Glory to the Father and to the Son and to the Holy Spirit:
…Your light will come, Jerusalem;
the Lord will dawn on you in radiant beauty.

CHRISTMAS READING **WISDOM 7:26-30**

Lady Wisdom Sophia is the shining of eternal light, a spotless mirror of the working of God, an image of God's goodness. But one, she can do all things; while perduring, she renews all things. From age to age she passes into holy souls and makes of them friends of God and prophets.

God's love is as great for nothing as for the one who lives with wisdom. Her beauty is greater than the sun, and every constellation of the stars. She is superior to light itself, taken over by the night, for the bad cannot prevail against wisdom.

RESPONSORY

The Lord has made known...
...alleluia, alleluia.
The saving power...
...alleluia, alleluia.
Glory to the Father and to the Son and to the Holy Spirit:
...The Lord has made known the saving power, alleluia.

After Epiphany

All the royal powers on earth
...will bow down in worship.
Men and women of every nation...
...will bow down in worship.
Glory to the Father and to the Son and to the Holy Spirit:
...All the royal powers on earth
will bow down in worship.

LENT READING, Weeks 1 &3 **1 KINGS 8:51-53a**

For your people and your inheritance whom you brought from Egypt, from the midst of the iron furnace, let your eyes be open to the plea of your servant and to the plea of your people Israel, to listen to them in all their cries to you, for you singled them out from all nations of the earth as an inheritance for you.

RESPONSORY Lk 18:13

The Lord God will set me free…
…from the hunter's snare.
From all those who would trap me with lying words,
…and from the hunter's snare.
Glory to the Father and to the Son and to the Holy Spirit:
…The Lord God will set me free
from the hunter's snare.

LENT READING, Week 5 **HEBREWS 2:9-10**

We see Jesus, who was made for a little while less than the angels for the suffering of death, now crowned with glory and honor, that by the grace of God he might taste of death on behalf of every human.

It was fitting for the One for whom and through whom all things exist, leading many sons and daughters to glory, that the leader of their salvation be perfect through sufferings.

RESPONSORY Rev. 5:9

Lord, by your own blood…
…you brought us back to God.
From every tribe and tongue and people and nation...
…you brought us back to God.
Glory to the Father and to the Son and to the Holy Spirit:
…Lord, by your own blood you brought us back to God.

EASTER READING **ROMANS 8:9-11**

You are not in flesh but in Spirit, since the Spirit of God dwells in you. If anyone does not have the Spirit of Christ, this one is not of him. But if Christ is in you, the body is dead because of sin and the spirit is alive because of vindication.

If the Spirit of the one who raised Jesus from the dead dwells in you, the one who raised Christ Jesus from the dead will also give life to your mortal bodies through the indwelling of the Spirit in you.

RESPONSORY, in the Octave of Easter

This is the day the Lord has made;
let us rejoice and be glad.

RESPONSORY, Weeks 2 through 7

The Lord is risen from the tomb…
…alleluia, alleluia.
He hung upon the cross for us…
…alleluia, alleluia.
Glory to the Father and to the Son and to the Holy Spirit:
…The Lord is risen from the tomb, alleluia, alleluia.

Gospel Canticle For Morning

Antiphons

Advent Wk 1 Matt 7:21,24-27	I shall wait for my Lord and Savior and point him out when he is near, alleluia.
Advent Wk 3 Luke 7:24-30	Arise, arise, Lord; show us your power and might.
Dec 29	The shepherds went to Bethlehem to see for themselves.
Christmas	The Lord our God has come to the people to set us free, alleluia.
After Epiphany Lk 4:14-22	All peoples, bearing gifts, will come from afar, alleluia.
Lent Wk 1 Mt 7:7-12	If you, bad as you are, know how to give your children what is good, how much more will your Abba in heaven pour out his gifts on all who pray.
Lent Wk 3 Lk 11:14-23	It is by the power of God that I throw out demons, says the Lord; the reign of God has come already.
Lent Wk 5 Jn 8:51-59	Jesus said to the authorities: whoever comes from God hears the word of God; you will not listen because you do not come from God.

Antiphons for Gospel Canticle For Morning, continued

Easter Wk 1 Luke 24:35-48	Jesus stood in the midst of the disciples, showed them his wounds, and said: peace be with you, alleluia.
Easter Wk 3 John 6:44-51	Amen, amen, I say to you: whoever believes in me will live forever, alleluia.
Easter Wk 5 John 15:9-11	If you keep my commandments, you will live in my love, alleluia.
Easter Wk 7 John 17:20-26	Go into the cosmos, teach the nations, and baptize them in the name of the Father and of the Son and of the Holy Spirit, alleluia.

Ordinary
Antiphon *Lord, give us knowledge of salvation*
known in the forgiveness of our sins.

Gospel Reading for Thursday of

Week	**1** Mark 1:40-45	**13** Matt 9:1-8	**25** Luke 9:7-9
	3 Mark 4:21-25	**15** Matt 11:28-30	**27** Luke 11:5-13
	5 Mark 7:24-30	**17** Matt 13:47-53	**29** Lk 12:49-53
	7 Mark 9:41-50	**19** Matt 18:21-19:1	**31** Luke 15:1-10
	9 Mark 12:28-34	**21** Matt 24:42-51	**33** Lk 19:41-44
	11 Matt 6:7-15	**23** Luke 6:27-38	

CANTICLE of ZECHARIAH (The Benedictus)
LUKE 1:68-79

+ **Blessed be** the Lord the God of Israel
who chose a people to visit with redemption,
and raised salvation in the house of David,
saving strength from God's own servant,

speaking from the age of the prophets
through the mouth of the holy prophet:
Salvation out of enmity,
even out of those who hate us,

to show our ancestors how mercy works, -
and to remember the holy promise of the Lord,
the covenant made for our ancestor Abraham,
calming our fear and making us free
to serve with holy justice before God all our days.

And you also child -
will be called a prophet of the Most High
for you will go before the Lord to prepare his way
and give to people a knowledge of salvation
known in accepting forgiveness of their sins.

From the tender mercy of our God,
the sun rising from the height will visit with light
for those who sit in the dark or shadow of death
and to guide our feet into the way of peace.

Glory...

Antiphon

PETITIONS FOR THE CONSECRATION TO GOD OF THE DAY AND ITS WORK

- For the Church and her ministry and apostolates…
- For secular authorities and all serving as stewards…
- For people who are poor or sick or in sorrow…
- For peace and the basic needs of each human being…
- For a culture of vocations all over the world…

TAKE LORD RECEIVE — Saint Ignatius of Loyola

Take, Lord, receive
all my liberty, my memory, my understanding,
and all my will, all I have and possess.
You have given all this to me;
to you, Lord, I return;
all is yours;
dispose of it wholly as you will.
Give me your love and your grace;
for me this is enough.

OUR FATHER...

Principles Toward
Harmony of Tensions:
1. Time is greater than space.
2. Unity prevails over conflict.
3. Realities are greater than ideas.
4. The whole is greater than the part.
See *The Joy of the Gospel* by Pope Francis

WEEK I
THURSDAY EVENING

+ *God, come to my assistance;* Psalm 70:2
Lord, make haste to help me!

Glory...

ORDINARY TIME

Beau-ti-ful Sa\-vior, King of Cre-a\-tion,
Son of\ Ma-ry\, Son of God!
Tru-ly I love\ you, Tru-ly I'll serve\ you,
Light of my soul, my Joy, my Crown.

Fair are the mea\-dows, Fair are the wood\-lands,
Robed in\ flow-ers of bloom-ing spring;
Je-sus is fair\-er, Je-sus is pur\-er;
He makes our sad-dest spir-it sing.

Fair is the sun\-shine, Fair is the moon\-light,
Bright are the spark-ling\ stars on high;
Je-sus shines bright\-er, Je-sus shines pur\-er,
Than all the an-gels in the sky.

Beau-ti-ful Sa\-vior, Lord of the na\-tions,
Full-y\ hu-man\, full-y God!
Praise, a-do-ra\-tion, Glo-ry and ho\-nor,
Now and for-ev-er-more, our Lord!

86, Text: based on Psalm 45:3; author unknown, 1677;
translated by Joseph A. Seiss, 1873, altered
Music: ST. ELIZABETH; Hoffman and Richter's
Schleisische Volkslieder, 1842

ADVENT

Faith of our an-ces-tors, liv\-ing still,
In spite of dun-geon, fire\ and sword;
O how our hearts\ beat high\ with joy
When-'er we hear that glo/-rious Word!
Faith of our an-ces-tors, ho-ly faith!
We will be true to you till death.

Faith of our **fa**\-**thers**, we\ will strive
A-mong all peo-ples, as is our call;
That through the truth\ that comes\ from God,
True free-dom may be found/ by all.
Faith of our an-ces-tors, ho-ly faith!
We will be true to you till death.

Faith of our **mo**\-**thers**, we\ will love
Both friend and foe in all\ our strife;
Liv-ing and preach-ing as love\ knows how
By kind-ly words and vir/-tuous life.
Faith of our an-ces-tors, ho-ly faith!
We will be true to you till death.

7, Text: Frederick W. Faber, Jesus and Mary, 1849;
refrain by James G. Walton, 1874; altered
Music: ST. CATHERINE, LM with refrain; Henry F. Hemy, 1864;
adapted by James G. Walton, 1874

CHRISTMAS

Glad-ly/ ma-gi from of old
Did the guid-ing star be-hold;
And with/ joy they hailed its light,
Lead-ing on-ward, beam-ing bright,
So, most gra-cious Lord, may we
Ev-er-more your glo-ry see!

As with/ joy-ful steps they sped,
Sa-vior, to your hum-ble bed,
There to/ bend the knee be-fore
You whom heav'n and earth a-dore,
So may we with will-ing feet
Ev-er seek your mer-cy seat!

Ma-gi/ of-fered gifts most rare
At your cra-dle, crude and bare,
So may/ we with ho-ly joy,
Pure and free from sin's al-loy,
All our cost-liest trea-sures bring,
Christ, to you, our heav'n-ly King!

19, Text: from Matthew 2:1-11, William C. Dix,
As With Gladness Men of Old, 1860, altered
Music: 77 77 77 DIX, Konrad Kocher, 1838
Popular melody for: *For The Beauty Of The Earth*

LENT

O Sa-cred Head, now wound-ed
With grief and shame\ weighed down,
Now scorn-ful-ly sur-round-ed
With thorns, your on\-ly crown.
They mock\ and taunt and jeer you,
Your no-ble coun-ten-ance,
Though migh/-ty worlds shall fear you
And flee be-fore your glance.

My bur-den in your pas-sion,
Lord, you have borne\ for me.
For it was my trans-gres-sion
Which brought this woe\ on thee.
I cast\ me down be-fore you,
Wrath were my right-ful lot;
Have mer/-cy, I im-plore you;
Re-deem-er, spurn me not!

What lang-uage shall I bor-row
To thank you, dear\-est friend,
For this your dy-ing sor-row,
Your pit-y with\-out end?
O make\ me yours for-ev-er,
And should I faint-ing be,
Lord, let/ me nev-er, nev-er
Out-live my love to thee.

EASTER

Let us break bread to-geth-er on our knees;
Let us break bread to-geth-er on our knees;
When I fall on my knees,
With my face to the ris-ing sun,
O/ Lord, have mer-cy on_ me.

Let us drink wine to-geth-er on our knees;
Let us drink wine to-geth-er on our knees;
When I fall on my knees,
With my face to the ris-ing sun,
O/ Lord, have mer-cy on_ me.

Let us praise God to-geth-er on our knees;
Let us praise God to-geth-er on our knees;
When I fall on my knees,
With my face to the ris-ing sun,
O/ Lord, have mer-cy on_ me.

143, Text: Spiritual
Music: 10 10 with refrain
LET US BREAK BREAD, Spiritual

50, Text: possibly Bernard of Clairvaux, 1153;
translated to English by James W. Alexander, 1830, altered
Music: 76 76 D PASSION CHORALE, Hans L. Hassler, 1601

PSALM 25

Antiphon *The time is full*
and the reign of God has drawn near;
repent and believe in the gospel. Mk 1:15

Christmas Mary and Joseph were filled with wonder
at all that was said of the child.

Easter Alleluia, alleluia, alleluia.

To you, **Adonai**, I lift up my soul;
in you, my God, I trust; let me not be shamed
and let enmity not triumph over me.
Indeed all who hope in you will not be shamed;
shamed will be those doing wanton treachery.

Show me your ways, Adonai; teach me your paths.
Guide me in your truth and teach me,
for you are my saving God;
you are my hope all the day.

Remember your mercies, Adonai,
and your loves, for they are from of old.
The sins of my youth and rebellious ways
you do not remember, as you are loving.

You do remember me, for you are good, Adonai.
Good and upright is Adonai,
who instructs sinners in the way,
guides humble ones in the right,
and teaches the way to the humble.

All the ways of Adonai are loving and faithful
for those who keep the covenant demands.
For the sake of your name, Adonai,
now you forgive my iniquity, great as it is.

Who is the human who fears Adonai?
The one being instructed in the Lord's chosen way,
whose life will be days spent in prosperity,
whose descendants will inherit the land,
the confidence of Adonai is with those thus fearing;
the covenant is made known to them.

My eyes are ever on Adonai,
who will free my feet from the snare.
Turn to me! Be gracious to me!
For I am lonely and afflicted.

Troubles of my heart have multiplied;
free me from my anguish!
Look upon my affliction and distress!
Take away all of my sins!

See the enmity, the increase of fierce hate!
Guard my life! Rescue me!
Let me not be shamed, for I take refuge in you.
May integrity and honesty protect me
because I hope in you.

Redeem Israel, God, from all our troubles.

Glory…

Antiphon

PSALM 79:1-5,9-11,13

Antiphon *If you only knew*
what makes for peace. Lk 19:42a

Advent & Lent Help us, God of our salvation;
deliver us and atone for our sins
for the sake of your name.

Christmas & Easter Alleluia, alleluia, alleluia.

God, the nations invaded into your inheritance,
they defiled your holy temple,
they reduced Jerusalem to rubbles.
They gave the bodies of your servants
as food to birds of the air,
the flesh of your saints to beasts of earth.

They poured out their blood
like the waters around Jerusalem
and no one is left to bury.
We are a reproach to our neighbors,
scorn and derision to those around us.
Until when, Adonai, will you be angry?
Will the fire of your jealousy burn to forever?...

Help us, God of our salvation,
for the glory of your name,
and deliver us and forgive our sins
for the sake of your name.

Why should the nations say,
"Where is their God?"
Let vengeance be known among the nations
before our eyes for your servants,
for their blood being poured out.

May the groan of prisoners come before you;
and by your strong arm
preserve the condemned...

We your people, the sheep of your pasture,
will praise you to forever.
Generation to generation
will recount your praise.

Glory...

Antiphon

Some of the Fathers and Mothers of the Desert recited all 150 psalms daily. Saint Benedict (d. 547 AD) in his monastic Rule laid out a pattern of praying all the psalms over each week. Different religious orders used different versions, including Saint Francis of Assisi who developed a shorter breviary of psalm fragments designed to be easy to carry and Saint Ignatius of Loyola who wanted the Jesuits to be more free when working with the poor. The Roman Breviary promulgated in 1568 had many revisions. The Second Vatican Council led to a four-week cycle, which is again being updated as this work is concluded.

PSALM 86

Antiphon *Leave both the weed and the wheat*
to grow together until the harvest. Mt 13:30

Advent & Lent: Bring joy to me, your servant,
for to you, Lord, I lift up my soul.

Christmas & Easter: People of all nations will come
and worship before you, O Lord,
alleluia.

Hear in your ear, Adonai;
answer me for I am poor and needy.
Guard my life for I am devoted;
save your servant, my God,
the one trusting in you.

Have mercy on me, Lord,
for to you I call all the day.
Bring joy to your servant,
for to you, Lord, I lift up my soul.

Indeed, Lord, you are kind and forgiving
and abundant in love for all who call to you.
Hear my prayer, Adonai;
listen to the sound of my cries for mercy.

In the day of my trouble I will call to you
for you will answer me.
There is none like you among so-called "gods"
and there are no deeds like yours, Lord.

All the nations you made will come
and they will worship before you, Lord,
and they will bring glory to your name
for you are great and do marvelous deeds,
you, God, you yourself.

Teach me, Adonai, your way
and I will walk in your truth.
Undivide my heart
that I may fear your name.

I will praise you, Lord my God, with all my heart
and I will glorify your name to forever
for great is your love of me
and you deliver my soul from the depth of Sheol.

Arrogant ones attack against me, God;
a band of ruthless people seek my life
and do not regard you before them.

But you, Lord El, Compassionate and Gracious,
are slow of anger and abundant in love and fidelity.
Turn to me! And have mercy on me!

Grant your strength to your servant
and save the child of your handservant!
Give to me a sign of goodness
that enmity may see and find shame,
for you, Adonai, help me and comfort me.

Glory…

Antiphon

PSALM 30

Antiphon *Who touched my garments?* Mk 5:30

Advent & Lent: When through the night weeping abides,
joy can rejoice in the morning.

Christmas: You have been endowed from your birth
with royal gifts; in eternal splendor,
before the dawn of light on earth,
I have begotten you, alleluia.

Easter: You have turned my mourning into joy,
alleluia.

I will exalt you, Adonai, for you lifted me
and did not let enmity gloat over me.

Adonai, my God, I cried to you for help
and you healed me.
Adonai, you brought my self up from Sheol;
you spared me from going into the pit.

Sing to Adonai, you saints!
Sing praise to the holy name!
One moment in anger,
lifetimes in the Lord's favor;
when through the night weeping abides,
joy can rejoice in the morning. *

* *weeping spends the night*
See *Being There* by Peter Keese

I said in complacent security,
I will be unshaken to forever.
In your favor, Adonai,
you made me stand firm as a mountain;
you hid your faces and I was dismayed.

To you, Adonai, I called
and to you, Lord, I cried for mercy.
What would be the gain in my destruction?
What is gained if I go into the pit?

Will the dust praise you?
Will the dust proclaim your fidelity?
Hear, Adonai! Be merciful to me!
Be my one helper, Adonai!

You turned my wailing into dancing;
you removed my sackcloth and clothed me in joy
so that my heart may sing to you,
and not be silent.
My God Adonai, I will thank you to forever.

Glory... Antiphon

Principle & Foundation:
Life is mostly about learning to live with God so to love as God loves. Things are God-gifts for knowing and loving God; things clung to my center lose this God-given purpose. In a balanced life every blessing and woe can help me say a deeper 'Yes' to God. May my one desire remain to choose each choice that leads to me becoming God's mercy alive.

See *The Spiritual Exercises* (#23) of St. Ignatius of Loyola, d. 1556

PSALM 32

Antiphon *Do you see this woman?*
Her many sins have been forgiven,
and so she has loved much. Lk 7:44,47

Advent & Lent Blessed are human beings
whose sin the Lord does not count,
where transgressions are forgiven.

Christmas In the beginning,
before time began,
the Word was God,
alleluia.

Easter We have been reconciled to God
by the death and resurrection
of the Son, alleluia.

Blessed is the one forgiven of faults,
no longer covered with sin.
Blessed is the human
against whom Adonai does not count sin,
and in whose spirit there is no deceit.

When I kept silent, my bones wasted away
through my groaning all day.
For by day and night
your hand was heavy upon me;
my strength withered as in dry summer heat.

I acknowledged my sin to you,
and did not cover up my iniquity;
I said I will confess my faults to Adonai
and you forgave the guilt of my sin.

For this let every godly one pray to you
at the time to find you.
Surely the rising of mighty waters
will not reach this one.
You are the hiding place for me;
you will protect me from trouble
and surround me with deliverance song.

I will instruct you and I will teach you
and counsel you in the way you should go,
keeping an eye on you.

Do not be like a horse
or like your mule with no understanding;
by bit and bridle and harness they are controlled
or else they will not even come to you.

Many woes have doers of the bad,
but the truster in Adonai
is surrounded in unfailing love.

Rejoice in Adonai!
Just ones, be glad!
And sing, all you upright of heart!

Glory...

Antiphon

PSALM 132

Antiphon *To the one who has, more will be given;*
from the one who has not, even
what that one has will be taken away. Mk 4:25

Advent & Lent Let us go to dwellings of the Lord;
may your saints sing for joy.

Christmas & Easter The Lord has given him the throne
of his ancestor David, alleluia.

Adonai, remember David
and all the hardships he endured,
the oath he swore to Adonai,
the vow he made to the Mighty One of Jacob.

I will not enter into the structure of my house;
I will not go to the mats of my bed;
I will not allow my eyes to sleep
nor let slumber come to my eyelids,
till I find a place for Adonai,
a dwelling for the Mighty One of Jacob.

See, we heard her in Ephrathah;
we came upon her in fields of Jaar.
"Let us go to the dwellings;
let us worship at the feet on the footstool."

Arise, Adonai, to your rest,
you and the ark of your might.
May your priests be clothed with justice
and may your saints sing for joy.

For the sake of your servant David
reject not the face of your anointed one.

Adonai swore an oath to David,
sure and not to be revoked.
"From the descendants of your body
I will place on your throne.

If your sons and daughters keep my covenant
and my statutes that I teach them
then their children to forever
will sit on your throne."

For Adonai chose Zion
and desired her as a dwelling:
"This is my resting place to forever;
here I will sit, for I desired her.

To bless I will bless her provisions;
her poor ones I will satisfy with food,
her priests I will clothe in salvation,
and her saints will sing; they will sing for joy.

Here I will sprout a horn for David;
I will set up a lamp for my anointed one.
Enmity will be clothed with shame.
The crown on David will be resplendent."

Glory... Antiphon

God has given us all these wonderful toys;
ought we not to play with them? Sister Wendy Beckett

REVELATION 11:17-18, 12:10-12a

Antiphon *I am the Alpha and the Omega, says the Lord God, the one who is and who was and who is to come, the Almighty.* Rev 1:8

Christmas The Savior of the world is born, alleluia.

We thank you, Lord God Almighty,
the One who is and who was;
you have taken your great power and reign.

The nations raged and your anger came,
and the time to judge the dead
and to reward your servants and prophets,
the saints, and those fearing your name,
the small and the great…

Now have come the salvation and power
and reign of our God and the authority of Christ.
The accuser of our brothers and sisters was cast,
accusing them before our God day and night.

Their victory was because of the blood of the Lamb
and by the word of their witness.
They loved their life into their death,
and so be glad, you heavens,
and all you dwelling in them.

Glory…

Antiphon

ORDINARY TIME READING **1 PETER 1:3-9**

Blessed be the God and Father of our Lord Jesus Christ, in whose great mercy we are given rebirth to living hope through the resurrection of Jesus Christ from the dead, to the inheritance that is incorruptible, undefiled, and unfading, kept in heaven for you by the power of God, guarded through faith to a salvation ready to be revealed at the end time.

You exult in this, while yet you grieve if necessary for a little while by even many trials, for the proving of your faith, much more precious than gold that perishes even after being refined by fire, that you may be found giving praise and glory and honor at the revelation of Christ.

Without seeing him, you love him; still without seeing him you believe and exult with indescribable joy; and having been glorified, you are receiving the goal of your faith: the salvation of your souls.

RESPONSORY Ps 81:16b

The Lord our God feeds us…

…and with finest of wheat.

Honey out of rock to satisfaction…

…and with finest of wheat.

Glory to the Father and to the Son and to the Holy Spirit:

…The Lord our God feeds us, and with finest of wheat.

ADVENT READING **JAMES 5:7-11**

And so be patient, brothers and sisters, until the parousia of the Lord. Behold, the farmer awaits the precious fruit of the earth, being patient over it until receiving early and late rains. You also be patient and build up your hearts, because the parousia of the Lord has drawn near. Do not murmur, brothers and sisters, about one another lest you be judged. Behold, the judge stands before the doors.

Brothers and sisters, take as an example of suffering and patience the prophets, who spoke in the name of the Lord. Behold we count blessed the ones enduring. You have heard of the endurance of Job, and you have seen the purpose of the Lord, that the Lord is full of compassion and mercy.

RESPONSORY Ps 146:7; 63:3; 67:2

Come and set us free…
…Lord God of power and glory…
Let your face shine upon us
and we will know salvation…
…Lord God of power and glory…
Glory to the Father and to the Son and to the Holy Spirit:
…Come and set us free, Lord God of power and glory…

CHRISTMAS READING **1 JOHN 5:20**

We know that the Son of God has come and has given to us discernment that we might know the true One. And we are in the true One in God's Son Jesus Christ. This is the true God and eternal life.

RESPONSORY Jn 1:14

The Word became flesh…
…alleluia, alleluia.
And dwelt among us…
…alleluia, alleluia.
Glory to the Father and to the Son and to the Holy Spirit:
…The Word became flesh and dwelt among us,
alleluia, alleluia.

After Epiphany

All people will be blessed in him…
…in every tribe of the human race.
All nations will acclaim his glory…
…in every tribe of the human race.
Glory to the Father and to the Son and to the Holy Spirit:
…All people will be blessed in him,
in every tribe of the human race.

LENT READING, Weeks 1 &3 **JAMES 4:7-10**

Be subject to God, but oppose the diabolo who will flee from you. Draw near to God, who will draw near to you. Cleanse your hands, sinners; and purify your hearts, you two-souled. Be distressed and mourn and weep; let your laughter be turned to mourning and your joy to dejection. Be humbled before the Lord, who will exalt you.

RESPONSORY Lk 18:13

To you, O Lord…
…I make my prayer for mercy.
Heal my soul, for I have sinned against you…
…I make my prayer for mercy.
Glory to the Father and to the Son and to the Holy Spirit:
…To you, O Lord, I make my prayer for mercy.

LENT READING, Week 5 **HEBREWS 13:11-15**

Of the blood of animals concerning sins brought into the holies through the high priest, the bodies are burned outside the camp. Indeed that he might sanctify the people through his own blood, Jesus suffered outside the gate. So let us go forth outside the camp to him bearing his reproach, for we have here no continuing city, but seek the one coming. And so through him let us offer up always a sacrifice of praise to God. This is the fruit of lips confessing his name.

RESPONSORY Rev. 5:9

We worship you, O Christ...
...and we praise you.
By your cross you have redeemed the world...
...and we praise you.
Glory to the Father and to the Son and to the Holy Spirit:
...We worship you, O Christ, and we praise you.

EASTER READING, Before Ascension **1 PETER 3:18,21b-22**

Christ died once for sins, a just human for the unjust, put to death in the flesh and made alive in the spirit, that he might bring you to God. Jesus Christ, at the right hand of God, having gone into heaven, subject to him are angels and authorities and powers.

RESPONSORY, in the Octave of Easter

This is the day the Lord has made;
let us rejoice and be glad.

RESPONSORY, Weeks 2 to 6

The disciples rejoiced...
...alleluia, alleluia.
When they saw the risen Lord...
...alleluia, alleluia.
Glory to the Father and to the Son and to the Holy Spirit:
...The disciples rejoiced, alleluia, alleluia.

EASTER READING, After Ascension **1 COR 6:19-20**

Do you not know that your body is a temple of the Holy Spirit in you, which you have from God, and that you are not of yourself? For you were bought of a price. So, glorify God in your body.

RESPONSORY, After Ascension Jn 14:26

The Holy Spirit is the Paraclete…
…alleluia, alleluia.
Who will teach you all things…
…alleluia, alleluia.
Glory to the Father and to the Son and to the Holy Spirit:
…The Holy Spirit is the Paraclete, alleluia, alleluia.

In the name
of the Abba and
of the Son and of
their Holy Breath

Gospel Canticle For Evening

Antiphons

Advent Wk 1 — Blessed are you among women,
and blessed is the fruit of your womb.

Advent Wk 3 — All you who love Jerusalem,
rejoice with her forever.

Christmas — We have found Jesus of Nazareth,
the son of Joseph, the one of whom
Moses and the prophets wrote.

After Epiphany — The people of Seba shall come
bringing gold, frankincense
and myrrh, alleluia.

Lent Wk 1 — Ask and you will receive,
seek and you will find,
knock and the door will be
opened to you.

Lent Wk 3 — A woman in the crowd called out:
how happy your mother must be;
she bore you
and fed you at her breast.
Jesus answered: happier still
are those who hear the word of God
and live by it.

Antiphons for Gospel Canticle For Evening, continued

Lent Wk 5

You are not yet fifty years old;
how can you have seen Abraham?
Amen amen I tell you,
before Abraham was, I am.

Easter Wk 1

See my hands and my feet
and know I am here among you,
alleluia.

Easter Wk 3

I am the living bread
come down from heaven;
anyone who eats this bread
will live forever;
the bread that I will give
is my flesh for the life of the cosmos,
alleluia.

Easter Wk 5

I have said these things to you
so that my joy may be in you
and your joy may be complete,
alleluia.

Easter Wk 7

The Spirit of truth will come
and teach you all truth
and proclaim to you
the things to come,
alleluia.

Ordinary
Antiphon

God has exalted with dignity
the humble in need.

CANTICLE of MARY (The Magnificat)
LUKE 1:46-55

+ **My soul** is stretched full with praise of the Lord,
and my spirit, beyond joy in God, my Savior,
who chose to lay eyes on this humble servant.

Behold, now and forward,
each and every age will call me blessed,
for the Mighty One did great things to me.

Holy is the name and the mercy
to generations and generations,
the ones fearing the One,

Who scattered the haughty of mind and heart,
pulled the powerful off their high place,
and lifted with dignity the humble in need.

The hungering are filled with good things,
the rich are sent away empty,
and servant Israel is given relief

with a memory of mercy to remember,
the promise spoken to our ancestors,
to Abraham and his descendants forever.

Glory...

Antiphon

INTERCESSIONS

- For learning and teaching what makes for peace…
- For all who have died…

- In gratitude for blessings…; Abba thank you.
- For the sins of this day…; Lord Jesus have mercy.
- With concerns over tomorrow…; Holy Spirit help.

VINCENTIAN MISSION PRAYER St John Gabriel Perboyre, C.M.

Divine Savior,
transform me into yourself.
May my hands be your hands.
May my tongue be your tongue.
Grant that every faculty of my body
may serve only to glorify you.
Above all, transform my soul and all its powers,
that my memory, my will and my affections may be
the memory the will and the affections of you.
I pray you destroy in me all that is not of you.
Grant that I may live
but in you, and by you, and for you,
and that I may truly say with St. Paul,
I live now, not I, but Christ lives in me.

OUR FATHER...

SHANTI, by Marty Haugen,
© GIA Publications, 1984,
is the current familiar tune

WEEK I
FRIDAY MORNING

\+ *God, come to my assistance;* Psalm 70:2
Lord, make haste to help me!

Glory…

ORDINARY TIME & EASTER

We walk by faith, and not by sight;
No gra-cious words we hear
From him who spoke as none e'er spoke;
But we be-lieve him near.

We may not touch his hands and side,
Nor fol-low where he trod;
But in his prom-ise we re-joice,
And cry, "My Lord and God!"

Help then, O Lord, our un-be-lief;
And may our faith a-bound,
To call on you when you are near
And seek where you are found.

That, when our life of faith is done,
In realms of clear-er light
We may be-hold you as you are,
With full and end-less sight.

125, Text: CM, based on 2 Cor. 5:7 and John 20:24-29; Henry Alford, 1844, altered. Music: ST. AGNES, CM; John B. Dykes, 1866
Popular melody for: *Shepherd of Souls*

ADVENT

O come, div-ine Mes-si-ah;
The world in si-lence waits\ the day
When hope shall sing its tri-umph
And sad-ness flee\ a-way…

Refrain **D**ear Sav-ior haste! Come, come to earth.
Dis-pel the night and show your face,
And bid us hail the dawn of grace.

O Christ, whom na-tions sigh for,
Whom priest and proph-et long\ fore-told,
Come, break the cap-tive fet-ters,
Re-deem the long\-lost fold… *Refrain*

You come in peace and meek-ness
And low-ly will your cra\-dle be;
All clothed in hu-man weak-ness
Shall we your God\-head see… *Refrain*

O come, div-ine Mes-si-ah;
The world in si-lence waits\ the day
When hope shall sing its tri-umph
And sad-ness flee\ a-way.

11, Text: Abbe Simon-Joseph Pellegrin, d. 1745;
translated by S. Mary of St. Philip, 1877, altered
Music: 78 76 VENEZ DIVIN MESSIE, Traditional French Carol, 16th C.

CHRISTMAS

Rise Up Shepherd and Follow

There's a star in the East on/ Christ-mas morn,
Rise up, shep-herd, and fol-low.
It will lead to the place
where the Christ was born\\,
Rise up, shep-herd, and fol-low.

Refrain Fol/-low, fol\-low,
Rise up, shep-herd, and fol-low.
Fol-low the Star of Beth-le-hem\\,
Rise up, shep-herd, and fol-low.

If you take good\ heed to the an-gel's words,
Rise up, shep-herd, and fol-low.
You'll for-get your\ flocks,
you'll for-get your herds\\\,
Rise up, shep-herd, and fol-low. *Refrain*

32, Text: African-American spiritual
Music: 10 7 11 7 with refrain

LENT

"**Take/ up your\ cross**," the/ Sa-vior said,
"If you would my dis-ci-ple be;
De-ny your/-self\, the world\ for-sake,
And hum-bly fol-low af-ter me."

Take/ up your\ cross, let/ not its weight
Fill your weak spir-it with a-larm;
His strength shall/ bear\ your spir\-it up,
And brace your heart and nerve your arm.

Take/ up your\ cross and/ fol-low Christ,
Nor think til death to lay it down;
In faith-ful/ bear\-ing of\ our cross
We hope to wear his glo-rious crown.

To/ you, great\ Lord, the/ One in Three,
All praise for-ev-er-more as-cend:
O grant us/ in\ our home\ to see
The heav'n-ly life that knows no end.

57, Text: Charles W. Everest,
Visions of Death and Other Poems, 1833, altered
Music option: ERHALT UNS HERR, LM;
Klug's *Geistliche Lieder, 1543;*
Popular melody for: *The Glory Of These Forty Days*

If fear must be my primary or
only motivator, then let my fear be only
of God, whose Son has told us to 'be not afraid.'

PSALM 69:2-22,30-37

Antiphon *Be not afraid of ones who can kill the body*
but are unable to kill the soul;
fear only the One able to destroy
both soul and body in gehenna. Mt 10:28

Save me, Adonai,
for waters have come to my neck.

I sink into the deep mire; there is no foothold.
I have come into deep waters; floods engulf me.

I am worn out from calling out;
my throat is parched and my eyes fail,
looking for my God.

Those hating me for no reason
are more numerous than the hairs of my head.
Many are the ones destroying me
in enmity for no reason.

What I did not steal, must I now restore?
You, God, you know my folly
and my guilts are not hidden from you.

May those who hope in you, God of Israel,
not be disgraced because of me.
For your sake I endure scorn
and shame covers my face.

Psalm 69, continued

I am a stranger to my brothers and sisters,
an alien to the children of my mother.
Zeal for your house consumes me
and insults of your insulters fall on me.

When I weep and fast, my self is a scorn to me.
When I put on my clothing of sackcloth
then I am as sport to them.
Those sitting at the gate mock at me
and drinkers of strong drink in their songs.

But I pray to you, Adonai, in the time of favor;
in the greatness of your love, God,
answer me with your sure salvation.

Rescue me from the mire and let me not sink;
let me be delivered from those who hate
and from the depths of the waters.
Let not the flood of waters engulf me,
nor the deep swallow me
nor the pit close its mouth over me.

Answer me, Adonai, for good is your love!
In your great mercies, turn to me!
Hide not your faces from your servant;
to my trouble, be quick! Answer me!
Come near because of the adversity;
rescue my self and redeem me!

You know my scorn and shame and disgrace;
all in enmity stand before you.
Scorn broke my heart and I became helpless
and I looked for compassion but there was none,
and for comforters, but found none.

They put gall in my food
and for my thirst gave me vinegar to drink…
I am in pain and suffering;
may your salvation protect me, God.

I will praise God's name in song and glory
with a thanksgiving more pleasing to Adonai
than ox or bull with horn and hoof.

The poor ones will see and be glad;
may your hearts now live, you seekers of God,
for Adonai hears the needy ones
and despises not the captives.

Let heaven and earth give praise
with the seas and all moving in them.
For God will save Zion
and rebuild the cities of Judah;

then they will settle there and be her steward
and the children of the servants will inherit her
and lovers of the Name will dwell in her.

Glory…

Antiphon *Be not afraid of ones who can kill the body but*
Mt 10:28 *are unable to kill the soul; fear only the One*
able to destroy both soul and body in gehenna.

PSALM 35:1-2c,3c,9-19,22-23,27-28

Antiphon *The tax collector standing far off*
would not lift his eyes to heaven,
but beat his breast saying,
'God, be merciful to me, a sinner.' Lk 18:13

Christmas & Easter Awake, and rise to my defense;
my God and Lord, contend for me,
alleluia.

Contend, **Adonai**, with my contenders!
Restrain those who would attack!
Take up shield and buckler and arise to my aid!...
Say to my soul, "I am your salvation."...

Then my soul will rejoice in Adonai
and take delight in salvation.
All of my bones will exclaim, "Adonai!
Who, like you, rescues the poor from the strong?
or the poor and the needy from robbers?"

Ruthless witnesses come forward;
on things I do not know they question me.
They repay me bad for the good; forlorn is my soul.

Yet when they were ill I clothed myself in sackcloth
and humbled myself with fasting when
my prayer had returned to my breast unanswered.
As a friend and a sibling I went about weeping,
bowing down like a grieving mother.

But at my stumbling they took glee
and gathered and gathered attackers
and did not cease to slander me unaware,
an ungodly circle of mockers
gnashing their teeth against me.

Until when, Lord? How long will you look on?
Rescue my life from the ravages,
my precious life from the lions.
I will give you thanks in the great assembly;
among people thronging I will praise you.

Let enmity neither gloat without cause or reason
nor wink the eye at me...

You have seen, Adonai; be not silent.
Be not far from me, Lord.
Awake!, my God and Lord,
and rise to my defense.
Vindicate me, Adonai, in your justice...

May those who delight in my vindication
shout and be glad and always say,
"May Adonai be exalted,
who delights in the well being of a servant."
My tongue will tell of your justice
and speak praise of you all the day.

Glory... Antiphon

Luke 18:13 is the source of the popular Jesus Prayer.

PSALM 51

Antiphon *If anyone serves me,*
that one the Abba will honor. Jn 12:26b

Advent & Lent Restore to me, Lord, your saving joy
and sustain in me a willing spirit.

Christmas Tell us, shepherds, what did you see?

Easter Remember me, Lord,
when you come into your realm, alleluia.

Have mercy on me, God,
in accord with your unfailing love;
in accord with your great compassion
blot out my transgressions.

Wash me of my many iniquities
and cleanse me from my sin,
for I know my transgressions
and my sin is before me always.

Against you yourself I sinned,
doing what is bad in your eyes.
You are proven right when you speak
and justified when you judge.
Surely we are sinners from birth,
from conception in a mother's womb.

Surely you desire truth in our inner parts;
in my inmost place you teach me wisdom.
You cleanse me with hyssop and I will be clean;
you wash me and I will be whiter than snow…

You let me hear joy and gladness;
let the bones you let be crushed now rejoice.
Hide your faces from my sins
and blot out all my iniquities.

A clean heart create in me, God!
Renew inside me a spirit to be steadfast.
Do not cast me from your presences,
nor take from me your Holy Spirit.

Restore to me the joy of your salvation
and sustain in me a willing spirit.
I will teach transgressors your ways
and sinners will turn back to you.

Save me from bloodguilt, God,
God of my salvation;
my tongue will sing of your justice.
Lord, open my lips
and my mouth will proclaim your praise.

Sacrifices give you no delight;
I could bring a burnt offering,
but it would give you no pleasure.
The sacrifices, God, you will not despise
are a broken spirit and a contrite heart.

Make Zion prosper in your pleasure,
and build up the walls of Jerusalem.
Then you will delight in the sacrifice of the just,
burnt offerings and whole offerings,
bulls offered on your altar.

Glory... Antiphon

ISAIAH 45:15-25

Antiphon *The reign of God is justice and peace*
and joy in the Holy Spirit. Rom 14:17

Advent & Lent
God fashioned and made
and formed the earth,
creating it to be not an empty waste,
but to be inhabited.

Christmas & Easter
Are you hidden,
God of Israel?

Truly, **God**, you hide yourself,
Saving God of Israel.
Makers of idols will know shame and disgrace,
all going off together in disgrace.

Israel will be saved by Adonai,
salvation everlasting.
You will not know shame or disgrace to the ages.

For this says Adonai, creating the heavens,
who fashioned and made and formed the earth,
creating it to be not an empty waste,
but formed to be inhabited,

"I am Adonai, and there is no other.
Not in secret did I speak,
from some place in a dark land,
saying to descendants of Jacob, 'seek me in vain.'
I, Adonai, speak truth and delare right things.

Gather together and come!
Assemble together, fugitives of the nations.
Those who carry idols of wood do not know:
they are praying to no-gods that cannot save.

Declare and present! Let them counsel together!
Who foretold this from long ago?
Who declared this from the distant past?
Not I, Adonai? There is no god apart from me,
God just and Saving; there is none but me.

Turn to me and be saved,
all you ends of the earth,
for I am God and there is no other.

By myself I swore integrity out of my mouth,
the word that will not be revoked.

Indeed, in front of me every knee will bow,
and every tongue will swear, and say,
'In Adonai alone are justice and strength,'

to whom will come and be shamed
all who have raged otherwise."
In Adonai they will be found just
and all the descendants of Israel will exult.

Glory...

Antiphon

---

*If someone is gay and searches for the Lord and has good will,
who am I to judge?* Pope Francis, July 29, 2013

JEREMIAH 14:17b-22

Antiphon *Before I formed you in the womb*
I knew you. Jer 1:5

Advent Wait for the Lord
who will come with saving power.

Christmas The angel said to the shepherds:
I proclaim to you a great joy;
the Savior of the world
is born for you,
alleluia.

Lent Lord, we admit our no-good ways;
indeed we sin against you.

Easter Christ bore our sins in his own body
as he hung upon the cross,
alleluia.

On sin,
a pondering:
Lord, when I examine
my conscience, every day
I am aware of sin, and it seems
always to be that in that moment of
sinning I was not aware of your love for
me. Why do I forget that you love me? How
can I stay aware of your love? Is it even possible?

Let my eyes overflow with tears
by night, by day, without cease,
for the grievous wounds suffered
by the virgin daughter of my people,
a very crushing blow.

If I go out in the country, see: ones slain by sword!
If I go in the city, see: the ravages of famine!
Indeed, both prophet and priest
have gone to a land they do not know.

To reject you rejected Judah?
Is Zion despised by your self?
Why have you afflicted us so we have no healing?

Our hope is for peace, but no good happens;
for a time of healing, but see: the terror!
We are aware, Adonai, of our no-good ways
and the guilt of our ancestors;
indeed we ourselves sin against you.

For the sake of your Name, neither despise us
nor dishonor the throne of your glory.
Remember, and break not your covenant with us!

Is there one among the worthless nations
that can bring rain or send showers from the skies?
Is that One not you, our God Adonai?
And so we hope in you, for you do all these things.

Glory...

Antiphon

PSALM 95

Antiphon *Where two or three*
are gathered in my name,
there am I in the midst of them. Mt 18:20

Christmas & Easter Come into the Lord's presence
singing for joy,
alleluia.

Come, let us sing to Adonai;
let us shout to our saving Rock.
Let us come before the faces with gratitude
and make a joyful noise with song.

Adonai is the great El,
the great Ruler above all those little "g" gods,
holding in hand the depths of earth
and peaks of mountains,
the sea and dry land formed by the hand.

Come, let us worship and bow and kneel
before Adonai who made us.
For God is our God, and we are the people
of the pasture and flock and care of our God.

"If today you hear this voice
do not harden your heart,
as at Meribah and the desert day at Massah
where your ancestors tested me;
they tried me though they saw my work.

For forty years was my anger on that generation,
the people straying in their heart;
and so they did not know my ways,
and so were unable to enter my rest."

Glory... Antiphon

PSALM 100

Antiphon *Go to the lost sheep*
of the house of Israel. Mt 10:6

Christmas A little child is born for us, alleluia.

Easter Serve the Lord with gladness, alleluia.

Shout for joy to Adonai, all you earth!
Serve Adonai with gladness!
Come into the presence with joyful song.

Know that Adonai is God, who made us,
whose people we are,
in whose pasture we are the sheep.

Enter the gates with thanksgiving,
go into the courts with praise!
Give thanks and give praise to the Name!

Good is Adonai, and loving to forever,
and faithful through generations and generation.

Glory... Antiphon

ORDINARY TIME READING **EPHESIANS 4:25-32**

Put off the lie, and speak the truth to each neighbor, for we are members of one another.

If you become angry, do not sin; do not let the sun set on provocation, and do not give a place for the diabolo.

Let the thief steal no more, but rather let the former stealer labor working with his or her own hands, the good thing, to share with the one who has need.

Keep every corrupt word from coming out of your mouth, but let the word be heard that gives grace to the hearer who needs building up.

And do not grieve the Holy Spirit of God, by whom you were sealed for the day of redemption.

Let all bitterness and rage and anger and fighting and blasphemy be removed from you with all evil.

Be kind to one another, tenderhearted, and forgive yourselves as also God in Christ has forgiven you.

RESPONSORY Ps 143:8

Bring word at break of day...

...in your unfailing love.

Show the way for me to go...

...in your unfailing love.

Glory to the Father and to the Son and to the Holy Spirit:

...Bring word at break of day in your unfailing love.

ADVENT READING **JEREMIAH 30:21,22**

This Adonai says: "Their leader will be from them and will arise from among them, and I will bring their ruler near, who will come close to me.

...So you will be my people, and I will be your God."

RESPONSORY

Your light will come, Jerusalem…
…the Lord will dawn on you in radiant beauty.
The glory of the Lord you will see within you…
…the Lord will dawn on you in radiant beauty.
Glory to the Father and to the Son and to the Holy Spirit:
…Your light will come, Jerusalem,
the Lord will dawn on you in radiant beauty.

A Consciousness Examen in Three Minutes (*an aware prayer*)

1st – *Replay your day. Pick out a high point in it – a good thing you did, like going out of your way to help someone… Give God thanks for the opportunity.*

2nd – *Replay your day again. This time pick out a low point – a bad thing you did, like putting down someone who really needs to be lifted up… Ask Jesus for forgiveness.*

3rd – *Look ahead to tomorrow to a critical point – a hard thing you must do, like dealing with a personal problem… Ask the Holy Spirit for help with it.*

See *Challenge 2000: A Daily Meditation Program based on the Spiritual Exercises of Saint Ignatius* by Mark Link, Jesuit

CHRISTMAS READING **ISAIAH 61:1-2a,10-11**

The Spirit of Sovereign Adonai is on me, because Adonai anointed me to preach good news to poor ones and sent me to bind up ones broken of heart, to proclaim freedom for ones being captive, and release for ones being imprisoned, to proclaim a year of favor of Adonai…

To delight, I delight in Adonai, my soul rejoices in my God, who clothed me in garments of salvation and arrayed me in a robe of justice, as a bridegroom dresses his head like a priest and a bride adorns herself with her jewels, for as the soil makes the sprout to come up and as a garden makes seeds to grow so will Sovereign Adonai make justice spring up and praise before all the nations.

RESPONSORY

The Lord has made known… *…alleluia, alleluia.*
The saving power… *…alleluia, alleluia.*
Glory to the Father and to the Son and to the Holy Spirit:
…The Lord has made known the saving power, alleluia.

After Epiphany

All the royal powers on earth
…will bow down in worship.
Men and women of every nation…
…will bow down in worship.
Glory to the Father and to the Son and to the Holy Spirit:
…All the royal powers on earth
will bow down in worship.

LENT READING, Weeks 1 &3 **ISAIAH 53:11b-12**

After the suffering of the soul my servant will justify the many and bear their iniquities. And so I will give him a portion among the many and a division of the spoil among the numerous because he poured out his life to the death, was numbered with the transgressors, bore the sins of the many, and interceded for the transgressors.

RESPONSORY Lk 18:13

The Lord God will set me free…
…from the hunter's snare.
From all those who would trap me with lying words,
…and from the hunter's snare.
Glory to the Father and to the Son and to the Holy Spirit:
…The Lord God will set me free from the hunter's snare.

LENT READING, Week 5 **ISAIAH 52:13-15**

See, my servant will act wisely and be raised and lifted up and highly exalted!

Just as many were appalled at him, so disfigured beyond human appearance and his form beyond that of a human being, so will he startle many nations.

Because of him rulers will shut their mouth, for what was not told to them they will see, and what they did not hear they will understand.

RESPONSORY Rev. 5:9

Lord, by your own blood…
…you brought us back to God.
From every tribe and tongue and people and nation...
…you brought us back to God.
Glory to the Father and to the Son and to the Holy Spirit:
…Lord, by your own blood you brought us back to God.

EASTER READING **ACTS 5:30-32**

The God of our ancestors raised Jesus, whom you killed by hanging on a tree. This one is exalted to the right hand of God as ruler and savior to bring conversion to Israel and forgiveness of sins.

Of these things, we are witnesses with the Holy Spirit given by God to the obedient.

RESPONSORY, in the Octave of Easter

This is the day the Lord has made;
let us rejoice and be glad.

RESPONSORY, Weeks 2 through 7

The Lord is risen from the tomb…
…alleluia, alleluia.
He hung upon the cross for us…
…alleluia, alleluia.
Glory to the Father and to the Son and to the Holy Spirit:
…The Lord is risen from the tomb, alleluia, alleluia.

Gospel Canticle For Morning

Antiphons

Advent Wk 1 Matt 9:27-31	Our God comes, born a human in David's line, enthroned as ruler forever, alleluia.
Advent Wk 3 John 5:33-36	Guard what is good and cherish what is true, for our salvation is at hand.
Christmas	Jesus Christ our Lord came through blood and water.
After Epiphany Luke 5:12-16	All who once reviled you will come and bow down in worship before your very footprints.
Lent Wk 1 Matt 5:20-26	If your integrity does not surpass that of the scribes and pharisees, you will not enter the reign of heaven.
Lent Wk 3 Mark 12:28-34	Teacher, what is the greatest commandment in the law? and Jesus said: you shall love the Lord your God with your whole heart.
Lent Wk 5 John 10:31-42	For which of the many acts of kindness I have done for you do you want to kill me?

Antiphons for Gospel Canticle For Morning, continued

Easter Wk 1 John 21:1-14	This was the third time Jesus showed himself to the disciples after he had risen from the dead, alleluia.
Easter Wk 3 John 6:52-59	Whoever eats my flesh and drinks my blood shall live in me and I in them, alleluia.
Easter Wk 5 John 15:12-17	My commandment is this: love one another as I have loved you, alleluia.
Easter Wk 7 John 21:15-19	Jesus Christ died and is risen from the dead. Now he lives forever at the right hand of God where he intercedes for us, alleluia.
Ordinary Antiphon	*God chose to visit God's people and brought redemption.*

Gospel Reading for Friday of

Week **1** Mark 2:1-12	**13** Matt 9:9-13	**25** Luke 9:18-22
3 Mark 4:26-34	**15** Matt 12:1-8	**27** Lk 11:15-26
5 Mark 7:31-37	**17** Matt 13:54-58	**29** Lk 12:54-59
7 Mark 10:1-12	**19** Matt 19:3-12	**31** Luke 16:1-8
9 Mark 12:35-37	**21** Matt 25:1-13	**33** Lk 19:45-48
11 Matt 6:19-23	**23** Luke 6:39-42	

CANTICLE of ZECHARIAH (The Benedictus)
LUKE 1:68-79

+ **Blessed be** the Lord the God of Israel
who chose a people to visit with redemption,
and raised salvation in the house of David,
saving strength from God's own servant,

speaking from the age of the prophets
through the mouth of the holy prophet:
Salvation out of enmity,
even out of those who hate us,

to show our ancestors how mercy works, -
and to remember the holy promise of the Lord,
the covenant made for our ancestor Abraham,
calming our fear and making us free
to serve with holy justice before God all our days.

And you also child -
will be called a prophet of the Most High
for you will go before the Lord to prepare his way
and give to people a knowledge of salvation
known in accepting forgiveness of their sins.

From the tender mercy of our God,
the sun rising from the height will visit with light
for those who sit in the dark or shadow of death
and to guide our feet into the way of peace.

Glory...

Antiphon

PETITIONS FOR THE CONSECRATION TO GOD OF THE DAY AND ITS WORK

- For the Church and her ministry and apostolates…
- For secular authorities and all serving as stewards…
- For people who are poor or sick or in sorrow…
- For peace and the basic needs of each human being…
- For guardian angel intercession for those considering use of violence…
- For any elders or children who feel abandoned…
- In gratitude for blessings and grace…

MORNING OFFERING — Apostleship of Prayer*

God, our Father, I offer you my day.
I offer you my prayers, thoughts, words, actions,
joys, and sufferings in union with the Heart of Jesus,
who continues to offer himself in the Eucharist
for the salvation of the world.
May the Holy Spirit, who guided Jesus,
be my guide and my strength today
so that I may witness to your love.
With Mary, the mother of our Lord and the church,
I pray for all Apostles of Prayer
and for the prayer intentions
proposed by the Pope this month.

OUR FATHER…

* https://popesprayerusa.net/

WEEK I
FRIDAY EVENING

\+ *God, come to my assistance;* Psalm 70:2
Lord, make haste to help me!

Glory...

ORDINARY TIME & LENT

When I sur-vey the/ won-drous\ cross
On which the Prince of\ glo-ry/ died,
My rich-est gain I/ count as\ loss,
And pour con-tempt on all my\ pride.

For-bid it, Lord, that/ I should\ boast,
Save in the death of\ Christ my/ God!
May all vain things that/ charm me\ most,
Be sac-ri-ficed as with his\ blood.

Were the whole realm of/ na-ture\ mine,
That trea-sure would be\ far too/ small;
Love so a-ma-zing/, so div\-ine,
Claims my_ soul, my life, my\ all.

55, Text: Isaac Watts, *Hymns and Spiritual Songs*, 1707, altered
Music: HAMBURG, Lowel Mason, 1824;
The Boston Handel and Haydn Society Collection of Church Music, 1825

ADVENT

O God, grant me ser-en-i-ty
to'ac-cept the things I can-not change,
The cour'ge to change the things I can,
And wisd'm to know the diff-er-ence.

Take, Lord, re-ceive my lib-er-ty,
My will en-tire and mem-o-ry,
My un-der-stand-ing, ev-'ry-thing,
Pos-ses-sions all, my off-er-ing.

The giv'n by you I do re-turn;
Con-form my life as is your will.
Suf-fic-ient now, no more to own:
E-nough are love and grace a-lone.

Lord A-do-nai, give love and grace,
Suf-fic-ient these in time and space,
Your love and grace, un-earned and free,
This true a-bun-dance may we see.

Love show-ing more in deed than word,
Love sha-ring in the com-mon good,
I pon-der with a-ffec-tion great
What God has done and does of late.

130, Text: Verse 1: *The Serenity Prayer,*
attributed to Reinhold Niebuhr, d. 1971
Text: Suscipe from *The Spiritual Exercises,* St. IgnatiusLoyola,#234,d.1556,
inspired by *Veneremur,* Jesuit Spirituality Center, Grand Coteau, LA, 1957
Music: TALLIS CANON, LM, Thomas Tallis, d. 1585
An alternate melody: *Praise God From Whom All Blessings Flow*

CHRISTMAS

My life flows on in end-less song
A-bove earth's lam-en-ta-tion.
I hear that near and far-off hymn,
It hails a new cre-a-tion:
Thru all the tu-mult and the strife
I hear that mu-sic ring-ing;
It finds an ech-o\ in my soul;
How can I keep from sing-ing?

What though my joys and com-forts fade
The Lord my Sa-vior liv-eth;
What though the shad-ows gath-er round
Songs in the night he giv-eth:
No storm can shake my in-most calm,
While to that ref-uge cling-ing;
Since Christ is Lord of\ heav'n and earth,
How can I keep from sing-ing?

I lift my eyes; the clouds grow thin;
I see the blue a-bove it;
And day by day clears way the path
Since first I learned to love it:
The peace of Christ makes fresh my heart,
A foun-tain ev-er spring-ing;
All things are mine since\ I am his;
How can I keep from sing-ing?

98, Text: Robert Lowry, 1860, altered
Music: 87 87, ENDLESS SONG, Quaker Hymn; Robert Lowry, 1860

EASTER

All glo-ry, laud, and hon-or,
to you, re-deem-er, King,
To whom the lips of chil-dren
make sweet ho-san-nas ring.
The King you are of Is-ra-el,
and Da-vid's roy-al Son,
Be-lov-ed of the Fa\-ther,
our Roy-al Bless-ed One.

The com-pa-ny of an-gels
are prais-ing you on high,
With hu-man be-ings too all
cre-a-tion makes re-ply.
The Cho-sen of the Cov-e-nant
with psalms be-fore you went;
So too our praise and an\-thems
be-fore you we pre-sent.

To you, be-fore your pass-ion,
a-pos-tles sang your praise;
To you, now high ex-al-ted,
our mel-o-dy we raise.
Ac-cep-ta-ble their voi\-ces;
hear too the praise we bring:
De-light in your be-lov\-ed,
our Sa-vior and our King.

42, Text: St. Theodulph of Orleans, c. 821, for Palm Sunday;
translated by John M. Neal, 1854, altered
Music: 76 76 D, ST. THEODULPH, Melchior Teschner, 1613

PSALM 22

Antiphon *I am the true vine*
and my Abba is the vinegrower. Jn 15:1

My God, my God, why have you forsaken me?
Far from my salvation are the words of my groan.
My God, I cry out by day, but you do not answer,
and at night with no relief.

Yet you Holy One are enthroned, praises Israel.
In you our ancestors trusted and were delivered.
To you they cried and they were saved.
In you they trusted and were not disappointed.

But I am a worm and a no-human,
the scorn of humanity and despised by people.
All those seeing me mock at me;
they shake their heads in insult:
"In the one you trust, let your Adonai rescue you;
let the one who 'delights' in you deliver you!"

You brought me out from the womb,
to trust in you at the breasts of my mother.
From the womb I was cast upon you;
from the womb of my mother, you are my God.
Be not far from me,
for trouble is near with no one to help.

Psalm 22, continued

Many bulls surround me;
the strong of Bashan encircle me.
They open wide their mouths against me,
lions tearing up prey and roaring.

Like the waters I am poured out
and my bones are all out of joint.
My heart like wax melts away within my insides.

Like a broken clay pot, my strength is dried up,
and my tongue is stuck in the roof of my mouth;
you lay me in the dust of death.
Dogs indeed surround around me,
a band of doers of the bad encircles me as a lion
ready to tear into my hands and my feet.

I can count all of my bones;
they stare and they gloat over me.
They divide my garments among them
and for my clothing they cast lots.

But you, Adonai, be not far off;
come quickly to help me, my Strength!
Deliver my precious life from the sword
and from the power of the dog.
Rescue me from the mouth of the lion
and from the horns of wild oxen.

I will declare your name to my siblings
and praise you within the assembly.

You fearing Adonai, give praise!
All you descendants of Jacob, give honor!
All you descendants of Israel, give reverence
before Adonai, who despised not, nor disdained,
nor hid the holy face from those suffering affliction,
but heard their cry for help.

From you comes my praise in the great assembly;
my vows will I fulfill before those who fear you.
The poor ones will eat to satisfaction,
and the seekers will praise Adonai;
may your heart live to forever.

All the ends of the earth
will remember and turn to Adonai,
and all the families of nations will bow down,
for to Adonai is the dominion, ruling over nations.
All those rich on the earth will feast and worship
and kneel, all will go down to the dust,
all who cannot keep their own self alive.

Those to come will be served by being told,
and in the same way serve generations to come.
They will come and they will proclaim
the deeds of the fidelity of the Lord,
the story, to people yet to be born.

Glory…

Antiphon *I am the true vine*
and my Abba is the vinegrower. Jn 15:1

PSALM 26

Antiphon *The tax collectors and prostitutes*
are going into the reign of God
before you. Mt 21:31

Christmas
& Easter Alleluia, alleluia, alleluia.

Vindicate me, Adonai,
for I have walked blameless in my life
and in Adonai I trusted without waver.

Test me, Adonai! And try me!
Examine my heart and my mind!
For your love is before my eyes
and I walk in your truth.

I do not sit with humans of deceit
nor consort with hypocrites.
I abhor the assembly of those who do the bad,
and do not sit with them.

I wash my hands in innocence
and go about your altar, Adonai,
to proclaim a voice of praise
and to tell of all your wonderful deeds.

Adonai, I love the living place of your house,
the dwelling place of your glory.

Take not my soul away with sinners
nor my life with people doing bloody things,
those who scheme in their hands
with their right hand full of bribes.

But I walk blameless in my life.
Redeem me! Be merciful to me!
My foot stands on level ground;
in great assemblies I will praise Adonai.

Glory...

Antiphon

As the psalms
serve well for private
prayer, they are even more
a prayer for the people of God
and for the whole world. But when a
psalm seems to not apply to my life today,
I can simply step in another's shoes and pray in
the stead of someone who is feeling so strongly these
very emotions that they cannot bring themselves to pray.

PSALM 88

Antiphon *Leave the dead to bury their own dead;*
you go proclaim the reign of God. Lk 9:60

Advent & Lent Day and night I cry out;
may my prayer come before you.

Christmas & Easter Alleluia, alleluia, alleluia.

Adonai, **Elohay**, my Savior,
I cry out day and night before you.
May my prayer come before you;
turn your ear to my cry.

My soul is full of troubles
and my life draws near to Sheol.
I am counted among those
going down to the pit,
like a human with no strength,

set apart with the dead ones
like slain ones lying in the grave,
whom you no longer remember,
whom are cut off from your care.

You put me in the pit of the lowest,
in the darkest deep.
Your anger lies heavy upon me
and all your waves overwhelm.

You took friends away from me
and made me repulsive to them;
in confinement I cannot escape.
My eye is dim from grief;
I call to you, Adonai,
and in every day spread my hands to you.

Is it to the dead ones you show wonder?
Do the dead rise up and praise you?
Is your love declared in the grave
or your fidelity in the no-more?
Is your wonder known in the darkness
or your righteous deeds in the land of oblivion?

But to you, Adonai, I cry for help;
in the morning my prayer comes before you.
Why do you reject my self, Adonai?
Why hide your faces from me?

Afflicted and coming close to death
and despairing from youth,
I have suffered your terrors.
Your anger has swept over me
and your terrors destroy me.

They surround me all the day like the floods,
engulfing over me completely.
You took far away my loving companion;
my one friend is darkness.

Glory… Antiphon

PSALM 41

Antiphon *Is it easier to say to the paralytic,*
your sins are forgiven,
or to say, rise and walk?
That you may know
that the Son of Humanity
has authority to forgive sins on earth,
to you paralyzed I say,
'rise; take your mat
and go to your house.' Mk 2:9-11

Advent & Lent
Lord, have mercy on me
and heal my being.

Christmas & Easter
Christ became poor for our sake
that we might become rich,
alleluia.

Blessed are they
who give regard to the weak.
In the time of trouble Adonai will deliver.
Adonai will protect their life,
preserve it blessed in the land,
and give no surrender to the desire of enmity.
Adonai will sustain on the sickbed,
and restore on the bed from all illness.

Adonai, have mercy on me!
Heal my self for I have sinned against you!
Enmity asks in malice:
"When will that one die and be forgotten?"
When they come to see me,
they speak with false hearts, gather slander,
and then go out to the outside to speak.

Together against me they whisper,
imagining the worst for me:
"A vile disease has set in;
that one will not recover."
Even my close friend
has lifted the heel against me,
the human being I trusted,
who ate of my own bread.

But you, Adonai, have mercy on me
and raise me up that I may repay them.
In this I know that you are pleased with me,
for enmity does not triumph over me;
in my integrity you hold me up
and set me in your presences to forever.

Blessed be Adonai, God of Israel,
from everlasting to the everlasting.
Amen and amen.

Glory...

Antiphon

PSALM 46

Antiphon *Do you want to be whole?* Jn 5:6

Advent & Lent
The Lord of hosts is with us,
the God of Jacob a fortress to us.

Christmas
In the beginning,
before time began,
the Word was God,
alleluia.

Easter
River streams make glad
the city of God, alleluia.

God is our refuge and strength,
our help in troubles, ever present.
And so we will not fear,
even if earth were to give way,
even if mountains were to fall
into the heart of the sea,
even if sea waters foam
or mountains quake with their surging.

River streams make glad the city of God,
the holy dwelling place of the Most High.
God is inside her and she will not fall.
God will help her at break of day.
Nations are in uproar and realms fall;
the earth melts at the voice of God.

Adonai Sabaoth is with us;
the God of Jacob is our fortress.

Come and see the works of Adonai,
the desolations brought on the earth:
making wars to cease to the ends of the earth,
breaking the bow and shattering the spear
and burning with fire the chariot and shield.

"Be still! And know that I am God.
I will be exalted among the nations;
I will be exalted on the earth."

Adonai Sabaoth is with us;
the God of Jacob is our fortress.

Glory…

Antiphon

---

be still and know that I am God
be still and know that I am
be still and know
be still
be

PSALM 135

Antiphon *What is the profit for a human to gain*
the whole world but lose their life? Mt 16:26

Advent & Lent: I know that our God is great,
greater than all "gods."

Christmas & Easter: I, the Lord, am your savior
and redeemer, alleluia.

Hallelujah! Praise the name of Adonai!
Servants of Adonai, give praise!
You who minister in the house of Adonai,
in the courts of the house of our God,

praise Adonai, for good is Adonai!
Sing praise to the Name, for it is pleasant!
Adonai has chosen Jacob, Israel the chosen treasure.

For I know that great is our Lord;
greater than all the "gods" is Adonai,
who does as Adonai pleases
in the heavens and on earth and in the deep sea,

making clouds rise from the ends of the earth,
sending lightning with the rain,
and bringing wind from the storehouses,

who struck down the firstborn of Egypt,
from human to animals,
sending signs and wonders to the midst of Egypt
against Pharaoh and against all of his servants,

having struck down
many nations and mighty rulers:
Sihon, ruler of the Amorites, and Og of Bashan,
and all the rulers of Canaan,
who gave their land as an inheritance,
an inheritance to Israel, the people of Adonai.

Your name, Adonai, is to forever,
your renown to generation and generation,
for you, Adonai, will vindicate your people
and will have compassion on your servants.

Idols of the nations are silver and gold,
the work of human hands.
A mouth to them but they cannot speak.
Eyes to them but they cannot see.

Ears to them but they cannot hear,
and there is no breath in their mouth.
Like them will be their makers
and all who trust in them.

House of Israel, praise Adonai!
House of Aaron, praise Adonai!
House of Levi, praise Adonai!
You who fear Adonai, praise Adonai!

Praised be Adonai from Zion,
dwelling in Jerusalem.
Hallelujah!

Glory... Antiphon

REVELATION 15:3b-4

Antiphon *They sang the song of Moses,*
the servant of God,
and the song of the Lamb. Rev 15:3a

Advent & Lent All the nations will come
and worship before you,
Lord God Almighty.

Christmas The Savior of the world
is born, alleluia.

Easter Let us sing to the Lord,
glorious in triumph, alleluia.

Great and wonderful are your works,
Lord God Almighty.
Just and true are your ways,
Ruler of the nations.

Who will not fear, O Lord,
or glorify your name?

Only you are holy.
All the nations will come
and worship before you;
your ordinances are shown to all.

Glory…

Antiphon

ORDINARY TIME READING **ROMAINS 15:1-6**

We who are strong ought to bear the weaknesses of those who are not strong, and not to please ourselves. Let each one of us please his or her neighbor for good and for building up, for even Christ pleased not himself. As it has been written, *The reproaches of those reproaching you fell on me.* What was written for our teaching was written that through patience and through the comfort of the writings we may have hope. May the God of patience and comfort give to you the same mind among yourselves in accord with Christ Jesus.

RESPONSORY Rev 1:5,6

Loving us, Christ washed away our sins...
...in his own blood;
Making us to our God a realm of royals and priests...
...in his own blood;
Glory to the Father and to the Son and to the Holy Spirit:
...Loving us, Christ washed away our sins
in his own blood;

Behold God
beholding you
.......and smiling.

Anthony de Mello, Jesuit

ADVENT READING **2 PETER 3:8b-10**

One day with the Lord is as a thousand years and a thousand years as day one. The Lord is not slow on the promise, as some deem slowness, but is patient with you, not for the purpose that any perish but that all people might come to repentance.

But the day of the Lord will come as a thief, in which the heavens will pass away with rushing sound and the elements burning will be dissolved and the earth and its works will be uncovered.

RESPONSORY Ps 146:7; 63:3; 67:2

Come and set us free…
…Lord God of power and glory…
Let your face shine upon us
and we will know salvation…
…Lord God of power and glory…
Glory to the Father and to the Son and to the Holy Spirit:
…Come and set us free, Lord God of power and glory…

CHRISTMAS READING **ACTS 10:36-39b**

Peter said, "You know the thing having become throughout all Judea, beginning from Galilee after the baptism which John proclaimed: Jesus the one from Nazareth, how God anointed him with the Holy Spirit and power. He went about doing good and curing all those oppressed by the diabolo. God was with him. And we are witnesses of all things he did, both in the country of the Judeans and in Jerusalem..."

RESPONSORY Jn 1:14

The Word became flesh...
...alleluia, alleluia.
And dwelt among us...
...alleluia, alleluia.
Glory to the Father and to the Son and to the Holy Spirit:
...The Word became flesh and dwelt among us,
alleluia, alleluia.

After Epiphany

All people will be blessed in him...
...in every tribe of the human race.
All nations will acclaim his glory...
...in every tribe of the human race.
Glory to the Father and to the Son and to the Holy Spirit:
...All people will be blessed in him,
in every tribe of the human race.

LENT READING, Weeks 1 &3 **JAMES 5:16,19-20**

And so confess your sins to one another, and pray on behalf of one another, that you may be healed. A prayer of a just person made effective is very strong. Brothers and sisters, if one among you errs from the truth and is turned by someone, know that the one turning a sinner out of an error way will save that soul out of death and will cover a multitude of sins.

RESPONSORY Lk 18:13

To you, O Lord…
…I make my prayer for mercy.
Heal my soul, for I have sinned against you…
…I make my prayer for mercy.
Glory to the Father and to the Son and to the Holy Spirit:
…To you, O Lord, I make my prayer for mercy.

LENT READING, Week 5 **1 PETER 2:21-24**

To this you were called, because indeed Christ suffered on your behalf, leaving you an example to follow in the steps of him who was found neither in sin nor with guile in his mouth, who being reviled reviled not in return, who in suffering threatened not, but delivered himself to the one judging justly and carried up our sins in his body onto the tree, that dying to sins we might live to genuine justice, by whose wounds you are healed.

RESPONSORY Rev. 5:9

We worship you, O Christ...
...and we praise you.
By your cross you have redeemed the world...
...and we praise you.
Glory to the Father and to the Son and to the Holy Spirit:
...We worship you, O Christ, and we praise you.

EASTER READING, Before Ascension **HEBREWS 5:8-10**

Though being a Son, he learned obedience from things he suffered, and being perfected he became the source of eternal salvation to all those obeying him, designated by God a high priest in the order of Melchizedek.

RESPONSORY, in the Octave of Easter

This is the day the Lord has made;
let us rejoice and be glad.

RESPONSORY, Weeks 2 to 6

The disciples rejoiced...
...alleluia, alleluia.
When they saw the risen Lord...
...alleluia, alleluia.
Glory to the Father and to the Son and to the Holy Spirit:
...The disciples rejoiced, alleluia, alleluia.

EASTER READING, After Ascension **GAL 5:16,22-23,25**

Walk in the spirit and you will not act on the desires of the flesh. The fruit of the spirit is love, joy, peace, patience, kindness, goodness, faith, meekness, and self-control. Against such things there is no law. We live in the spirit; in the Spirit also let us walk.

RESPONSORY, After Ascension Jn 14:26

The Holy Spirit is the Paraclete…
…alleluia, alleluia.
Who will teach you all things…
…alleluia, alleluia.
Glory to the Father and to the Son and to the Holy Spirit:
…The Holy Spirit is the Paraclete, alleluia, alleluia.

---

love
joy
peace
patience
kindness
goodness
faith
meekness
self-control

fruits of the holy spirit (see above)

Gospel Canticle For Evening

Antiphons

Advent Wk 1
Out of Egypt I have called my Son
to come and save the people.

Advent Wk 3
John the Baptizer said:
this is the one coming after me
who existed before me.

Christmas
The voice proclaimed from heaven:
you are my Son, my beloved,
in whom I take delight.

After Epiphany
An angel warned the magi in a dream
to return to their country
by a different route.

Lent Wk 1
If you are bringing your gift
to the altar, and there you remember
that your brother or sister
has something against you,
leave your gift in front of the altar;
go at once and make peace,
and then come back and
offer your gift.

Lent Wk 3
It is far more important
to love your neighbor as yourself
than to offer sacrifice.

Antiphons for Gospel Canticle For Evening, continued

Lent Wk 5 — Even if you have no faith in my words
at least believe the evidence
of the works I do in God's name.

Easter Wk 1 — The disciple whom Jesus loved said:
it is the Lord,
alleluia.

Easter Wk 3 — Our crucified and risen Lord
has redeemed us,
alleluia.

Easter Wk 5 — To lay down your life for your friends,
there is no greater love;
alleluia.

Easter Wk 7 — Together they persevered in prayer
with Mary, the mother of Jesus,
alleluia.

Ordinary
Antiphon — *God has given relief to servant Israel*
with a memory of mercy to remember.

CANTICLE of MARY (The Magnificat)
LUKE 1:46-55

+ **My soul** is stretched full with praise of the Lord,
and my spirit, beyond joy in God, my Savior,
who chose to lay eyes on this humble servant.

Behold, now and forward,
each and every age will call me blessed,
for the Mighty One did great things to me.

Holy is the name and the mercy
to generations and generations,
the ones fearing the One,

Who scattered the haughty of mind and heart,
pulled the powerful off their high place,
and lifted with dignity the humble in need.

The hungering are filled with good things,
the rich are sent away empty,
and servant Israel is given relief

with a memory of mercy to remember,
the promise spoken to our ancestors,
to Abraham and his descendants forever.

Glory...

Antiphon

INTERCESSIONS

- For all who have died…

- In gratitude for blessings…; Abba thank you.
- For the sins of this day…; Lord Jesus have mercy.
- With concerns over tomorrow…; Holy Spirit help.

SERENITY PRAYER attributed to Reinhold Niebuhr

God, grant me serenity
to accept the things I cannot change,
courage to change the things I can,
and wisdom to know the difference,
living one day at a time,
enjoying one moment at a time,
accepting hardships as a pathway to peace,
taking as Jesus did
this sinful world as it is, not as I would have it,
trusting that you will make all things right
if I surrender to your will,
that I may be reasonably happy in this life
and supremely happy with you forever in the next.

OUR FATHER…

We call God 'Father' (Abba,
Papa, Daddy) because Jesus asks us to,
and in asking us to call his Abba Our Father,
he is asking us to know ourselves as his siblings.

WEEK I
SATURDAY MORNING

\+ *God, come to my assistance;* Psalm 70:2
Lord, make haste to help me!

Glory…

ORDINARY TIME

O sanc-tis-si-ma/, O pi-is-si-ma/,
Dul-cis vir-go Ma-ri\-a!
Ma/-ter a-ma/-ta, In/ te-me-ra/-ta,
O\-ra\, O\-ra\ pro-no\-bis.

Ho-ly, ho-ly Ma-ry,
Strong and hum-ble Ma-ry,
Sweet-ness, vir-gin Ma-ri\-a!
Moth-er of our Sa/-vior,
In your fi-at "yes" and more,
O\-ra\, O\-ra\, pray\ for us.

138, Text: *Stimmen der Volker in Liedern,* 1807
Music: 55 7 55 7, O DU FROLICHE;
Tattersall's *Improved Psalmody,* 1704

Jesus is not half-God and half-
human, but fully God and fully human.
As Mary is the mother of Jesus, and Jesus is God,
we rightly call Mary the Mother of God or God-bearer,
in Greek Theotokos. *We think of her as the First Disciple.*

ADVENT

The an-gel Ga-bri-el from heav-en came,
With wings as drift-ed snow and eyes as flame;
"All hail," the an-gel said, "O low-ly place,
Most high-ly fa-vored maid-en, full of grace."
Of her would come the Christ Em-man-u-el;
With all the an-gels, "Glo-ri-a!" we tell.

"For know a bless-ed Moth-er you shall be,
All gen-er-a-tions' praise e-ter-nal-ly;
Your Son shall be Em-man-u-el, fore-told,
Most high-ly fa-vored la-dy, from of old."
Of her would come the Christ Em-man-u-el;
With all the an-gels, "Glo-ri-a!" we tell.

Then gen-tle Ma-ry meek-ly bowed her head;
"To me be as it pleas-es God!" she said.
"My soul shall laud and mag-ni-fy the Name."
Most high-ly fa-vored la-dy, liv-ing flame.
Of her would come the Christ Em-man-u-el;
With all the an-gels, "Glo-ri-a!" we tell.

9, Text: from *Birjina gaztettobat zegoen,* traditional Basque Carol;
translated by Sabine Baring-Gould, d.1924,
altered significantly for a different melody
Music: 10 10 10 10 10 10 UNDE ET MEMORES, William Monk, d.1899
Popular melody for: *Lord Who At The First Eucharist Did Pray*

40, Text: William C. Dix, *The Manger Throne,* 1865
Music: 87 87 GREENSLEEVES with refrain, English Melody, 16th C.

CHRISTMAS

What child is this/ who, laid to rest/
On Ma-ry's lap\ is sleep\-ing?
Whom an-gels greet/ with an-thems sweet/,
While shep\-herds watch\ are keep-ing?
This, this\ is Christ the King/,
Whom shep-herds guard\ and an-gels sing;
Haste, haste\, to bring him laud/,
The Babe\, the Son\ of Ma-ry.

Why lies he in/ such mean e-state/,
Where ox and ass\ are feed\-ing?
Good Christ-ians, fear/, for sin-ners here/
The si\-lent Word\ is plead-ing.
Nails, spear\ shall pierce him through/,
The cross be borne\ for me, for you.
Hail, hail\ the Word made flesh/,
The Babe\, the Son\ of Ma-ry.

So bring him in/-cense, gold and myrrh/,
Come peas-ant, king\ to greet\ him;
The King of kings/ sal-va-tion brings/,
Let lov\-ing hearts\ en-throne him.
Raise, raise\ a song on high/,
The vir-gin sings\ her lul-la-by.
Joy, joy\ for Christ is born/,
The Babe\, the Son\ of Ma-ry.

LENT

At the cross, her sta-tion keep-ing,
Stood the mourn-ful moth-er weep-ing,
Where he hung, the dy-ing Lord.

Saw him then from judge-ment ta-ken,
And in death by all for-sa-ken,
Till his Spir-it he re-signed.

Sit with her this Sab-bath Ho-ly
Let our time with her be whole-ly
Bless-ed in our grief to share.

Je-sus, may her deep de-vo-tion
Stir in me the same e-mo-tion,
Heart to heart ac-cep-tance find.

59, Text: Jacopone da Todi, *Stabat Mater dolorosa,* d. 1306,
translated by Edward Caswell, altered
Verse 3 by Stephen J. Wolf, 2011
Music: 88 7 STABAT MATER, *Mainz Gesanbbuch,* 1661

EASTER

Com-fort, com-fort, O my peo-ple,
Speak of peace, thus says our God;
Com-fort those who sit in dark-ness,
Mourn-ing un-der sor-row's load;
Speak un-to Je-ru-sa-lem
Of the peace that waits for them;
Tell her all her sins I cov-er,
And that war-fare now is o-ver.

Yes, all sins our God will par-don,
Blot-ting each con-fessed mis-deed;
All that well de-served the an-ger
God will no more see nor heed.
We have suf-fered ma-ny days,
Now our grief has passed a-way;
God will change our hea-vy sad-ness
In-to ev-er spring-ing glad-ness.

88, Text: based on Isaiah 40:1-8, for the Feast of John the Baptist, Johann G. Olearius, d.1684, trans. by Catherine Winkworth, d.1878, altered
Music: 87 87 77 88, GENEVA 42, Claude Goudimel, Geneva Psalter, 1551

PSALM 105

Antiphon *Simeon sang in the temple*
of seeing salvation,
a light for revelation to the nations. Lk 2:29-32

Christmas & Easter The Lord is true to the sacred promises
and leads us to freedom and joy,
alleluia.

Give thanks to Adonai; call on the Name.
Make known among the nations the Lord's deeds!

Glory be to the holy Name;
let the heart of the seeker of Adonai rejoice.
Look to Adonai, to the strength;
seek always the faces of the Lord.

Remember the deeds of wonder done,
the miracles and the judgments mouthed,
you descendants and servants of Abraham,
you chosen ones of Jacob.

Adonai is our God, judge in all the earth,
remembering the covenant to forever
commanded for a thousand generations,
the word made with Abraham,
the oath to Isaac,

confirmed to Jacob as a decree,
to Israel as an everlasting covenant:
"I will give to you land of Canaan,
a portion of your inheritance."

When they were few, few in numbers,
with strangers in their midst,
then they wandered from nation to nation,
from one people to another.

No one was allowed to oppress them
and for their sake rulers were rebuked:
"Do not touch my anointed ones;
do no harm to my prophets."

Famine was allowed onto the land
and the ruler's food supply was destroyed.
A man Joseph was sent before them,
sold as a slave;
they bruised his foot with the shackle

and his neck entered the irons
till the time foretold of him came to pass.
The word of Adonai proved him true.
The ruler sent for him and released him;

the ruler of the peoples set him free
and made him master of his household
and ruler over all his possessions
to instruct the royals as was his pleasure
and to teach the elders.

Psalm 105, continued

Then Israel entered Egypt;
Jacob lived as an alien in the land of Ham.

This people became very numerous,
more fruitful than others.
The hearts of the rulers were turned to hate
and conspired against this servant people.

Moses was sent as servant of the Lord
and Aaron as chosen of the Lord.
They performed the deeds of the Lord,
signs and wonders in the land of Ham.

The Lord sent darkness and it was dark;
for they rebelled against the word.
Their waters were turned into blood
which caused their fish to die.

Their land was teemed with frogs,
even the bedrooms of their rulers.
Swarms of flies were sent at a word,
gnats through all of their country.

Their rains were turned into hail
and lightning flamed through their land.
Their vine and fig tree were struck down
and the trees of their country were shattered.

Locusts came at the word
and grasshoppers without number.
Every green thing in their land was eaten up,
eaten up with the produce of their soil.

Then their firstborn were struck down, all of them,
the firstfruit of their humanity in all of their land.

The Lord brought them out with silver and gold
and no one faltered among the tribes.
Egypt was glad when they left, glad with dread.

A cloud as a cover was spread out
and fire to give them light at night.
They asked for quail and the Lord brought it
and satisfied them with bread from heaven.

The rock was opened and waters gushed out
flowing in the desert as a river,
for the holy promise was remembered,
the promise made to servant Abraham,
and the people were brought out rejoicing,
the chosen ones with shouts of joy.

They received the lands of nations
and inherited the toil of peoples
so that they might keep the precepts
and observe the laws of the Lord.

Hallelujah!

Glory…

Antiphon *Simeon sang in the temple of seeing salvation,*
a light for revelation to the nations. Lk 2:29-32

Christmas & Easter The Lord is true to the sacred promises
and leads us to freedom and joy, alleluia.

PSALM 107

Antiphon *In awe, the disciples asked,*
who then is this, whom
both the wind and the sea obey? Mk 4:41

"**Give thanks** to Adonai, who is good,
whose love is to forever."

Let this be said by the redeemed of Adonai,
who redeemed them from the hand of enmity
and gathered them from the lands,
from east and west, from north and the south sea.

Some wandered in the desert wasteland,
finding no way to a city for settling.
Hungry and thirsty,
their life ebbed away in them.

Then they cried out to Adonai in their trouble,
who delivered them from their distresses
and led them by a direct way
to go to a city for settling.

Let them give thanks to Adonai for unfailing love,
for deeds of wonder done
for sons and daughters of Adam and Eve,
for satisfying the throats of the thirsty
and filling the hungry with good things.

Some sit in the dark and deep gloom,
prisoners of suffering and iron,
for they rebelled against the word of El
and despised the counsel of the Most High
who subjected their heart to the bitter labor,
and no one was there to help.

Then they cried in their trouble to Adonai,
who saved them from their distresses,
brought them out from the dark and deep gloom,
and broke away their chains.

Let them give thanks to Adonai for unfailing love,
for deeds of wonder done
for sons and daughters of Adam and Eve,
for breaking down gates of bronze
and cutting through bars of iron.

Some were fools through their rebellious ways,
afflicted because of their iniquities.
Loathing all food, they drew themselves
near to the gates of death.

Then they cried in their trouble to Adonai,
who saved them from their distresses,
sending forth the word to heal them
and rescue them from their graves.

Psalm 107, continued

Let them give thanks to Adonai for unfailing love,
for deeds of wonder done
for sons and daughters of Adam and Eve,
and let them sacrifice offerings of thanksgiving
and tell of the works with songs of joy.

Some went to the sea in ships
to do trade on the mighty waters.
They saw the works in the deep,
the wonderful deeds of Adonai,
who spoke and stirred up the tempest wind
and lifted up the waves.

They mounted up to the heavens
and went down to the deep;
in peril their courage melted away.
They reeled and staggered like drunkards,
all of them at their wits end.

Then they cried in their trouble to Adonai,
who brought them out from their distresses,
stilling the storm to a whisper
and hushing the waves.
They were glad when it grew calm
and they were guided to the haven they desired.

Let them give thanks to Adonai for unfailing love,
for deeds of wonder done
for sons and daughters of Adam and Eve,
and let them exalt in the assembly of the people,
and in the council of elders give praise.

Adonai turned rivers into desert,
springs of waters into thirsty ground,
and land of fruit into a salt waste
because of bad ways of those living there.

Adonai then turned desert into pools of waters,
parched ground into springs of waters,
and brought hungry ones to live there.

They founded and settled a city,
sowed fields and planted vineyards,
and yielded the fruit of harvest.
They were blessed and they increased greatly,
and their herds were not allowed to diminish.

Then they decreased and were humbled
by oppression, calamity and sorrow.
With contempt poured on them,
nobles were made to wander in a trackless waste.

But the needy were lifted from affliction
and their families increased like a flock.
The upright see this and rejoice,
but doers of the bad shut their mouth.

Whoever is wise, heed these things
and ponder the unfailing love of Adonai.

Glory…

Antiphon *In awe, the disciples asked,*
who then is this, whom
both the wind and the sea obey? Mk 4:41

EXODUS 15:1b-4,8-13,17-18

Antiphon *By faith they passed*
through the Red Sea
as if it were dry land. Heb 11:29a

Christmas Tell us, shepherds, what have you seen?
Who has appeared to you?
We have seen a newborn infant
and a choir of angels praising the Lord,
alleluia.

Easter Those who were victorious sang
the hymn of Moses, the servant of God,
and the hymn of the Lamb,
alleluia.

I will sing to Adonai, exalting exaltation,
who hurled horse and rider into the sea.

My strength and my song,
Yah has become to me salvation.
I will praise my God
and exalt the God of my ancestors.

Adonai the warrior, named Adonai,
hurled Pharaoh's army of chariots into the sea...
By the blast of your nostrils the waters piled up;
like a wall they stood firm in the heart of the sea,
raging deep waters congealed.

The enemy boasted, "I will pursue and overtake,
divide the spoils and gorge on them myself;
I will draw my sword;
my hand will destroy them."

You blew with your breath
and the sea covered them;
they sank like lead in the mighty waters.
Who is like you among "gods," Adonai?

Who like you is majestic and holy,
awesome in glory and working wonders?
You stretched your right hand
and the earth swallowed them.

You will lead in your love
the people you redeemed.
You will guide them in strength
to your holy dwelling...

You will bring them in and you will plant them
on the mountain of your inheritance,
the dwelling place you made, Adonai,
the sanctuary, Lord, that your hands established.
Adonai will reign forever and ever.

Glory...

Antiphon

WISDOM 9:1-6,9-11

Antiphon *And Jesus advanced*
in wisdom and age and favor
before God and humans. Lk 2:52

Advent & Lent May the Holy One from heaven
come down like gentle rain;
may the earth burst into blossom
and bear the tender Savior.

Christmas The angel said to the shepherds:
I proclaim to you a great joy;
the Savior of the world
is born for you,
alleluia.

Easter Lord, you have built
your temple and altar
on your holy mountain,
alleluia.

God of my ancestors, Lord of mercy,
who made all things by your word
and through your wisdom framed humanity
to be master of the creatures you have created,
and to govern the world in holiness and justice
and judge justly and with an upright heart,

* *Sophia, Lady Wisdom*

give me Wisdom, your companion at your throne,
and do not reject me from among your children,
for I am your servant, born of your handmaid,
a feeble human with a short life
and a weak understanding of justice and laws.

Though a human be
ever so perfect in human eyes,
without your Wisdom that same one
will be of no account...

With you is Wisdom,* who knows your works
and was present when you created the world,
who knows what is pleasing in your eyes
and what is right in accord with your ordinances.

Send her forth from the holy heavens
and dispatch her from your majestic throne,
that she may labor beside me
and I may learn what pleases you.

For she knows and understands all things
and will guide me to prudence in my actions
and guard me in her magnificence.

Glory...

Antiphon

Sometime when you are in the presence of
what Thomas Merton called 'children in a moment
when they are really children,' ponder that there was a day
when God was exactly that tall and weighed exactly that much.

PSALM 119:145-152

Antiphon *Ask and it will be given you,*
seek and you will find,
knock and it will be opened to you. Lk 11:9

Christmas & Easter *The words I have spoken to you*
are spirit and life,
alleluia. Jn 6:63b

I call with all my heart: answer me, Adonai;
your decrees I will obey.
I call to you: save me,
and I will keep your statutes.

I rise before dawn and I cry for help;
in your word I put my hope.
My eyes stay open in the night watch
to meditate on your promise.

Hear my voice, as you are loving, Adonai,
as your law makes me alive.
Scheming devisers are near,
but they are far from your law.

You are near, Adonai,
and all your commands are true.
I learned long ago from your statutes
that you established them to forever.

Glory... Antiphon

PSALM 117

Antiphon *As the centurion responded:*
I am not worthy
for you to enter under my roof,
but only say the word
and let your servant be healed. Lk 7:6,7

Advent Israel, prepare yourself
to meet the Lord, who is coming.

Christmas A little child is born for us;
little and yet called the mighty God,
alleluia.

Lent The fidelity of the Lord is to forever.

Easter I am the way, the truth and the life,
alleluia. Jn 14:6

Praise Adonai, all you nations;
and give glory, all you peoples.

Great is this steadfast love toward us;
the fidelity of Adonai to forever.

Hallelujah!

Glory...

Antiphon

ORDINARY TIME READING **2 PETER 1:3-11**

The divine power has given us all things that go with life and piety through the full knowledge of the one who called us to this glory and virtue, through which the precious things and the very great promises have been given to us, so that through these you might come to share in the divine nature and escape from the corruption of worldly desire. Also for this very thing bring all your diligence to supply your faith with virtue, virtue with knowledge, knowledge with self-control, self-control with endurance, endurance with piety, piety with filial friendship (*philadelphia*), and filial friendship with love (*agape*).

If these things abound in you, this will keep you from being barren and unfruitful in full knowledge of our Lord Jesus Christ. Blind and short-sighted is the one who lacks these things, and forgetful of how his or her sins were cleansed.

And so, brothers and sisters, be diligent in your call and firm in your choice, and you will not fail in what you do. Richly supplied will be your entry into the eternal kingdom of our Lord and Savior Jesus Christ.

RESPONSORY Ps 142:6,7a

I cry to you, my Lord,…
…you are my refuge.
My portion in the land of the living,…
…you are my refuge.
Glory to the Father and to the Son and to the Holy Spirit:
…I cry to you, my Lord, you are my refuge.

ADVENT READING **ISAIAH 11:1-9**

A shoot will sprout from the stump of Jesse, and a branch from the roots will bear fruit. The Spirit of Adonai she will rest on him, the Spirit of wisdom and understanding, the Spirit of counsel and power, the Spirit of knowledge and fear of Adonai, and for delight the fear of Adonai.

He will judge, not by seeing with eyes nor by hearing with ears, but he will judge the needy with integrity and decide with justice for poor ones of the earth, and strike the earth with the rod of his mouth and stop bad doings with the breath of his lips.

Justice will be the belt around his loins and fidelity a sash on his hips. The wolf will be a guest of the lamb, and the leopard will lie down with the young goat; the calf and the young lion will be together with a little child leading them. The cow and the bear will graze, and together their young will lie down; the lion like the ox will eat straw. The baby will play by the cobra's den, and the child lay a hand into the viper's nest. There will be no harm or destruction on all my holy mountain, for the earth will be full of knowledge of Adonai, as the waters that cover the sea.

RESPONSORY

Your light will come, Jerusalem…

…the Lord will dawn on you in radiant beauty.

The glory of the Lord you will see within you…

…the Lord will dawn on you in radiant beauty.

Glory to the Father and to the Son and to the Holy Spirit:

...Your light will come, Jerusalem;
the Lord will dawn on you in radiant beauty.

CHRISTMAS READING **ISAIAH 9:1a,5-6**

The people walking in the dark have seen a great light... For a child is born to us, a son is given to us, and the ruling will be on his shoulders. And his name will be Wonder Counselor, God Hero, Father Everlasting, Prince of Peace.

No end to the expanse of ruling and of peace, the throne of David is established over the realm to be upheld with judgment and justice from now and to forever. The zeal of Adonai Sabaoth will do this.

RESPONSORY

The Lord has made known...
...alleluia, alleluia.
The saving power...
...alleluia, alleluia.
Glory to the Father and to the Son and to the Holy Spirit:
...The Lord has made known the saving power, alleluia.

After Epiphany

All the royal powers on earth
...will bow down in worship.
Men and women of every nation...
...will bow down in worship.
Glory to the Father and to the Son and to the Holy Spirit:
...All the royal powers on earth
will bow down in worship.

LENT READING, Weeks 1 & 3 **ISAIAH 1:16-18**

Wash! Make yourselves clean! Take your bad deeds from before my eyes! Stop doing wrong! Learn to do right! Seek justice! Encourage the oppressed! Defend orphans! Plead the case for the widow!

Come! Let us come to an understanding, says Adonai. Though your sins are like the scarlets they shall be white as the snow; though they are red as the crimson they shall be like the wool.

RESPONSORY Lk 18:13

The Lord God will set me free…
…from the hunter's snare.
From all those who would trap me with lying words,
…and from the hunter's snare.
Glory to the Father and to the Son and to the Holy Spirit:
…The Lord God will set me free
from the hunter's snare.

LENT READING, Week 5 **ISAIAH 65:1-3a**

I revealed myself to those who did not ask. I was found by those who did not seek me. I said to a nation not called by my name, "Here am I! Here am I!" I held out my hands all the day to people obstinate, walkers after their imaginings of the no-good way, the people provoking me continually to my faces.

RESPONSORY Rev. 5:9

Lord, by your own blood...
...you brought us back to God.
From every tribe and tongue and people and nation...
...you brought us back to God.
Glory to the Father and to the Son and to the Holy Spirit:
...Lord, by your own blood you brought us back to God.

EASTER READING **ROMANS 14:7-9**

None of us lives to the self, and no one dies for the self. While alive, we live to the Lord; if we die, we die to the Lord. And so whether we live or we die, we are of the Lord. For this Christ died and lived again, that of both the dead and of the living he might be Lord.

RESPONSORY, in the Octave of Easter

This is the day the Lord has made;
let us rejoice and be glad.

RESPONSORY, Weeks 2 through 7

The Lord is risen from the tomb...
...alleluia, alleluia.
He hung upon the cross for us...
...alleluia, alleluia.
Glory to the Father and to the Son and to the Holy Spirit:
...The Lord is risen from the tomb, alleluia, alleluia.

Gospel Canticle For Morning

Antiphons

Advent Wk 1 Mt 9:35-10:1,5a,6-8	Banish your fears, O people of Zion; God, your own God, is coming to you.
Advent Wk 3 (see pg 759)	The reign of God is at hand.
Christmas (see pg 759)	He is the one of whom it has been written: Christ is born in Israel, his reign will last forever.
After Epiphany John 3:22-30	At Cana in Galilee Jesus worked the first of the signs showing his glory.
Lent Wk 1 Matt 5:43-48	Be a true child of God: pray for those who persecute you and speak the bad against you, says the Lord.
Lent Wk 3 Luke 18:9-14	The tax collector stood far away and would not raise his eyes to heaven, but beat his breast and prayed: God, have mercy on me, a sinner.
Lent Wk 5 John 11:45-56	Jesus died to gather into one family all the scattered children of God.

Antiphons for Gospel Canticle For Morning, continued

Easter Wk 1 Mark 16:9-15	When Jesus had risen from the dead on the morning after the sabbath, he appeared first to Mary Magdalene, alleluia.
Easter Wk 3 John 6:60-69	Simon Peter said: Lord, to whom shall we go? You have the words of eternal life; and we believe and are convinced that you are the Christ, the Son of God, alleluia.
Easter Wk 5 John 15:18-21	Christ died and rose from the dead, the Lord of the living and the dead; alleluia.
Easter Wk 7 John 21:20-25	Know that I am with you always, even to the end of the world, alleluia.
Ordinary Antiphon	*Lord, shine on those hidden in the shadows.*

Gospel Reading for Saturday of

Week **1**	Mark 2:13-17	**13**	Matt 9:14-17	**25**	Lk 9:43b-45
3	Mark 4:35-41	**15**	Matt 12:14-21	**27**	Lk 11:27-28
5	Mark 8:1-10	**17**	Matt 14:1-12	**29**	Luke 13:1-9
7	Mark 10:13-16	**19**	Matt 19:13-15	**31**	Luke 16:9-15
9	Mark 12:38-44	**21**	Matt 25:14-30	**33**	Lk 20:27-40
11	Matt 6:24-34	**23**	Luke 6:43-49		

CANTICLE of ZECHARIAH (The Benedictus)
LUKE 1:68-79

+ **Blessed be** the Lord the God of Israel
who chose a people to visit with redemption,
and raised salvation in the house of David,
saving strength from God's own servant,

speaking from the age of the prophets
through the mouth of the holy prophet:
Salvation out of enmity,
even out of those who hate us,

to show our ancestors how mercy works, -
and to remember the holy promise of the Lord,
the covenant made for our ancestor Abraham,
calming our fear and making us free
to serve with holy justice before God all our days.

And you also child -
will be called a prophet of the Most High
for you will go before the Lord to prepare his way
and give to people a knowledge of salvation
known in accepting forgiveness of their sins.

From the tender mercy of our God,
the sun rising from the height will visit with light
for those who sit in the dark or shadow of death
and to guide our feet into the way of peace.

Glory...

Antiphon

PETITIONS FOR THE CONSECRATION TO GOD
OF THE DAY AND ITS WORK

- For the Church and her ministry and apostolates…
- For secular authorities and all serving as stewards…
- For people who are poor or sick or in sorrow…
- For the basic needs of each human being…
- For awareness of being created in the image of God…
- For discovery and discernment of our charisms…
- For consensus on both rights and responsibilities…
- For loving respect for folks who think differently…
- For God's healing of the core wounds of enemies…
- For the world peace that only God can give…
- For elders who feel abandoned…
- For just treatment of migrant workers and refugees…
- For the starving child awakening our conscience…
- For those suffering physical and mental torture…
- For people living in subhuman conditions…
- For human beings enslaved or unjustly imprisoned…
- For workers in degrading or unsafe conditions…
- For laborers where treated as mere tools for profit…
- For rejection of judging the inner guilt of others…
- For a culture of vocations all over the world…
- For those who have asked for my prayer…
- For those for whom I have promised to pray…
- For those who weigh on my heart…

OUR FATHER…

WEEK II
VIGIL of SUNDAY
(Saturday Evening)

+ *God, come to my assistance;* Psalm 70:2
Lord, make haste to help me!

Glory…

CHRISTMAS

Si/-lent night! Ho/-ly night!
All is calm, all is bright,
Round yon Vir\-gin Moth-er and Child.
Ho-ly In-fant, so ten-der and mild,
Sleep in heav-en-ly peace/,
Sleep\ in heav-en-ly peace.

Si/-lent night! Ho/-ly night!
Shep-herds quake at the sight;
Glo-ries stream\ from heav-en a-far,
Heav'n-ly hosts\ sing, Al-le-lu-ia.
Christ, the Sa-vior is born/!
Christ\, the Sa-vior is born!

Si/-lent night! Ho/-ly night!
Son of God, love's pure light
Ra-diant beams\ form your ho-ly face,
With the dawn of re-deem/-ing grace,
Je-sus, Lord at your birth/,
Je\-sus, Lord at your birth.

33, Text: Joseph Mohr, 1818; translator unknown, altered
Music: STILLE NACHT, Franz Guber, 1818

ADVENT

O come, O come, Em-man/\-u-el,
And ran-som cap-tive Is\\-ra-el,
That mourns in lone-ly ex\-ile here
Un-til the Son of God/\ ap-pear.

Re-joice! Re-joice! Em-man /\ -u-el
Shall come to you, O Is \\ -ra-el.

(17th)

O come now Wis-dom of our God Most High,
With love and ten-der strength, Cre-a-tor Guide;
To us the path of true know-ledge show,
And teach us in her sa-ving Way to go.
Re-joice!...

(18th)

O come great Lord of an-cient Is-ra-el,
Who in the fire to Mos-es showed your-self,
And gave the Law up-on Si-nai height;
Stretch out your hand and
free us by your might.
Re-joice!...

(19th)

O come raise up, deep Root of Jes-se's tree,
A sign for peo-ple seek-ing to be free,
Be-fore whom na-tions' rul-ers will bow,
Come save with-out de-lay to keep your vow.
Re-joice!...

(20th)

O come , O Key of Da-vid, Roy-al Pow'r,
And o-pen gates to end our cap-tive hour;
For all be-hind a dark pris-on wall
Re-move the fear that blocks your sac-red call.
Re-joice!

(21st)

O come , O Ra-diant Dawn, e-ter-nal light,
Come shine and put the fear of death to flight.
In splen-dor o-ver dwell-ings of shade
The sun of Jus-tice has our full debt paid.
Re-joice!...

(22nd)

O come, O King of na-tions, migh-ty arc,
Au-then-tic joy of ev-'ry hu-man heart;
O Key-stone, true foun-da-tion to trust,
Come save us whom you fash-ion from the dust.
Re-joice!...

(23rd)

O come, de-sire of all the na-tions, bind
In one the hearts and souls of hu-man-kind;
Come make our sad di-vis-ions to cease,
And be, Em-man-u-el, our King of Peace.
Re-joice!...

12, Text: From Evening Prayer "O Antiphons"
of late Advent, 12th Century?;
translated by John M. Neale, 1851, altered
Music: VENI EMMANUEL, LM with refrain; 15th C.;
adapted by Thomas Helmore, 1856

ORDINARY TIME

Praise to the Lord, the Al-migh-ty,
the King of cre-a-tion! O my soul, praise the Lord,
who is our health and sal-va-tion!
Join the full throng;
Wake, harp and psal-ter and song;
Sound forth in glad ad-o-ra-tion!

Praise to the Lord, the on-ly One,
the Ma-ker of heav-en,
It is the Lord who made the earth,
the seas and all in them.
Can we yet see How our de-sire\ and need
Meet in our Lord's will and un-ion.

Praise to the Lord, who brings our work
to pros-per be-fore us; Who from the heav-ens
sent the mer-cy riv-er in-to us.
Pon-der a-new What the Al-migh-ty can do,
Who in div-ine love be-friends us.

Praise to the Lord,
oh let all that is in us sing prais-ing!
All that has life and breath,
come forth and with us sing prais-ing!
Let the A-men Sound from all peo-ple a-gain;
Glad-ly sing wor-ship and prais-ing!

123, Text: from Nehemiah 9:6, Joachim Neander, 1679;
translated by Catherine Winkworth, 1863, altered;
verse 2 by Stephen J. Wolf, 2009 Music: 14 14 4 7 8
LOBE DEN HERREN; Straslund Gesangbuch, 1665

LENT & EASTER

Je-ru-sa-lem/, **my hap-py home**\,
When shall I come/ to thee?
When shall my sor/-rows have an end\?
Your joys when shall\ I see?

The saints are crowned/ with glo-ry great\;
They see God face/ to face;
They tri-umph still/, they still re-joice\,
No grief or wor-ry their case.

King Da-vid stands/, his harp in hand\
As lea-der of/ the choir:
Ten thou-sand times/ that we be blessed\,
That we his mu\-sic hear.

Our La-dy sings/ Mag-ni-fi-cat\
With tune sur-pass/-ing sweet,
And all the vir/-gins bear their part\,
While sit-ting at\ her feet.

And Mag-da-len/ has left her grief\,
With cheer-ful joy/ does sing
And bless-ed saints/, their har-mo-ny\
To ev-'ry room\ they bring.

Je-ru-sa-lem/, Je-ru-sa-lem\,
God grant that I/ may see
Your end-less joy/, and of the same\
Par-ta-ker al\-ways be.

103, Text: F.B.P., London, around 1583, altered
Music: C.M., 86 86, LAND OF REST, traditional American melody

PSALM 34

Antiphon *The bread that I will give*
is my flesh for the life of the cosmos. Jn 6:51b

Advent Taste and see that the Lord is good.

Lent Avoid the bad and do the good.

Christmas & Easter Alleluia, alleluia, alleluia.

I will extol Adonai at all times,
praise always on my lips.
My soul she will boast in Adonai,
let afflicted ones hear and let them rejoice.

Glorify Adonai with me!
Let us exalt the name together.
I sought Adonai, who answered me
and delivered me from all my fears.

They look to the Name and are radiant;
their faces are never covered with shame.
Adonai heard this poor human call
and saved me from all the troubles.

An angel encamps around
and delivers all who fear Adonai.
Taste and see that Adonai is good!
Blessed is the one who takes this refuge.

Fear Adonai, you saints;
for those who do so there is no lack.
Lions may grow weak and may grow hungry,
but seekers of Adonai lack no good thing.

Come, children! Listen to me!
I will teach you the fear of Adonai.
Who is the human who loves living?
Who desires days to see the good?

Keep your tongue from evil
and your lips from speaking the lie.
Turn from the bad and do the good.
Seek and pursue peace.

The eyes of Adonai are on the just
with ears open to their cry.
The faces of Adonai turn from doers of the bad
to cut off from the earth their memory.

They cry and Adonai hears
and delivers them from all their troubles.
Close is Adonai to the brokenhearted,
saving those whose spirit is crushed.

Many are the troubles of the just
but Adonai delivers them from all of them,
protecting all of their bones;
not one of them will be broken.

The bad will slay the bad
and condemned will be those who hate the just.
The servants of Adonai are being redeemed
and the lives of any who take refuge in God
will not be condemned.

Glory...

Antiphon

PSALM 134

Antiphon *Be not afraid.* Mt 10:26, 14:27, 17:17, 28:10,...; Mk 6:50,...; Lk 5:10, 12:4,...; Jn 6:20,...

See Adonai and give praise,
all you servants of Adonai,
and ministers at night in the house of Adonai.

Lift up your hands in the sanctuary
and praise Adonai!

May Adonai bless you from Zion,
the One Maker of heavens and the earth.

Glory...

Antiphon

PSALM 119:105-112

Antiphon *Every scribe discipled to the reign of heaven*
is like a head of a household
who puts forth from the treasure
things both new and old. Mt 13:52

Advent Let your heart sing for joy.

Christmas The Word is my light
and my salvation.

Lent Jesus took Peter, James, and John
and led them up a high mountain
and was transfigured before them.

Palm Sun Day after day I sat teaching you in the
Temple and you did not lay hands on me.

Easter The human of truth welcomes the light,
alleluia.

Your word is the lamp to my foot
and the light for my path.
I have made an oath and confirmation
to follow your just laws.

I have suffered much, Adonai;
make me alive as is your word.
Accept the willing praise of my mouth!
And now, Adonai, teach me your laws!

My life is constantly in my hand,
but I will not forget your law.
Doers of the bad set a snare for me,
but I did not stray from your precepts.

I have your statutes as a heritage to forever,
they are indeed the joy of my heart.
I set my heart to keep your decrees
to forever, the very end.

Glory…

Antiphon

PSALM 16

Antiphon *Heaven and earth will pass away,*
but my words will not pass away. Mt 13:31

Advent Have courage,
all of you lost and fearful;
take heart and say:
our God will come to save us,
alleluia.

Christmas Show me, Lord, the path of life
for I have no good apart from you,
alleluia.

Lent His face was radiant as the sun
and his clothing white as snow.

Palm Sunday The Lord God is my help;
no shame can harm me.

Easter God freed Jesus from death
and raised him up to life,
alleluia.

The glory of God is
the human person fully alive.

Saint Irenaeus, d. 202

Keep me safe, El, for I take refuge in you.
I said to Adonai, "You are my Lord;
I have no good apart from you."

Worthless are the false gods in the land,
even though some delight in them.
Those who run after other gods
will increase their sorrows;
I will not pour out their blood libations,
nor let their names pass my lips.

Adonai, you assign my portion and my cup;
you make my lot secure.
Boundary lines fall for me in the pleasant places;
surely this inheritance is my delight.

I will praise Adonai who counsels me,
even in the night instructing my heart.
With Adonai before me, always by my side,
I will not be shaken.

And so my heart is glad and my tongue rejoices.
My body will rest in security
because you will not abandon my self to Sheol;
you will not let your faithful one see decay.

You will show me the path of living,
fullness of joy in your presences,
eternal pleasures at your right hand.

Glory…

Antiphon

PSALM 122

Antiphon *Amen, you will be with me in paradise.* Lk 23:43

Advent Comes the desire of all human hearts.

Lent Let us go rejoicing to the house of God.

Christmas & Easter May the peace of Christ
fill our hearts with joy, alleluia.

I rejoiced with those saying to me,
"Let us go to the house of Adonai."
Our feet stand in your gates, Jerusalem.

Jerusalem is built like a city
formed together, a compact.
There the tribes go up, the tribes of Adonai.

Make it in Israel a statute
to praise the name of Adonai,
for there stand the thrones of justice,
the thrones of the house of David.

Pray for the peace of Jerusalem!
May those who love you be secure.
May peace be within your walls,
security within your citadels.

For the sake of my sisters and brothers and friends
I will say, "Now, peace be within you."
For the sake of the house of our God Adonai
I will seek your prosperity.

Glory... Antiphon

PSALM 130

Antiphon *Whoever does the will of God*
is my brother and sister and mother. Mk 3:35

Advent, Christmas & Lent With the Lord there is mercy
and fullness of redemption.

Easter Awake, sleeper, rise from the dead,
and Christ will give you light. Eph 5:14b

Out of the depths I cry to you, Adonai.
Lord, hear my voice.
Let your ears be attentive to my cries for mercy.

If you kept a record of sins, Adonai,
Lord, who could stand?
But with you is the forgiveness,
and so you are revered in awe.

I wait, my soul waits for Adonai,
in whose word I put hope.
My soul waits for the Lord
more than watchers for the morning,
even watchers for the morning.

Put hope, Israel, in Adonai!
For unfailing love is from Adonai,
in whom is full redemption,
who will redeem Israel from all their sins.

Glory… Antiphon

PHILIPPIANS 2:6-11

Antiphon *Do nothing out of selfishness*
or for vainglory,
but humbly deem others
as greater than yourselves. Phil 2:3

Advent 2nd Sun The law was given to Moses,
but grace and truth come
through Jesus Christ.

Advent 4th Sun The fullness of time has come upon us:
God sends the Son into the world.

Christmas The eternal Word,
born of God before time began,
emptied of the self for our sake
and became human.

Lent 2nd Sun Moses and Elijah were speaking to him
of the death he would endure in Jerusalem.

Lent 4th Sun So great was God's love for us that
when we were dead in sin
God brought us to life in Christ Jesus.

Palm Sun The Lord Jesus humbled the self
by showing obedience
even when this meant death on the cross.

Easter Was it not necessary for Christ to suffer
and so enter into glory?
Alleluia.

Christ Jesus, subsisting in the form of God,
did not deem equality with God
something to grab,
but emptied himself,
taking the form of a slave,
becoming in human likeness.

And being found in human fashion,
he humbled himself,
becoming obedient until death,
and death on a cross.

And so God highly exalted him,
and gave to him the name above every name,
that in the name of Jesus
every knee should bend,
of heavenly beings and earthly beings,
and beings under the earth;

And every tongue acknowledge
to the glory of God the Father
that Jesus Christ is Lord.

Glory...

Antiphon

ORDINARY TIME READING **COLOSSIANS 1:3-6**

We give thanks always to God the Father of our Lord Jesus Christ praying concerning you, having heard of your faith in Christ Jesus and the love you have toward all the saints because of the hope being laid up for you in the heavens, which you heard previously in the word of the truth of the gospel coming to you, as it is also bearing fruit and growing in all the world as also in you, from the day you heard and fully knew in truth the grace of God.

RESPONSORY Ps 113:3,4

From the rising of the sun to its setting…
…praised be the name of the Lord.
The glory above the heavens,...
…praised be the name of the Lord.
Glory to the Father and to the Son and to the Holy Spirit:
…From the rising of the sun to its setting,
praised be the name of the Lord.

ADVENT READING **1 THESSALONIANS 5:19-24**

Do not quench the Spirit.

Do not despise prophecies.

Prove all things and hold fast to the good.

Abstain from every form of bad doings.

May the God of peace, God's own self, completely sanctify you and may your entire spirit and soul and body be kept without blame in the presence of our Lord Jesus Christ.

The Caller is faithful and will indeed do it.

RESPONSORY Ps 85:7

Lord, show to us…

…your mercy and unfailing love.

And grant us your salvation…

…your mercy and unfailing love.

Glory to the Father and to the Son and to the Holy Spirit:

… Lord, show to us your mercy and unfailing love.

–

The
primary
addiction is
addiction to self,
plain old selfishness.

Fr Phillip Breen

CHRISTMAS **GALATIANS 4:3-7**

And so when we were in youth, having been enslaved under the elements of the cosmos, when the fullness of time had come, God sent forth God's own Son, becoming of a woman, becoming under the law, that he might redeem those under the law, that we might receive the full adoption as sons and daughters.

And because we are sons and daughters, God sent forth the Spirit of the Son of God into our hearts, crying, "Abba, Father."

So you are no more a slave, but a son, a daughter, and if a grown child through God also an heir.

RESPONSORY

The Word became flesh...
...alleluia, alleluia.
And dwelt among us...
...alleluia, alleluia.
Glory to the Father and to the Son and to the Holy Spirit:
...The Word became flesh and dwelt among us,
alleluia, alleluia.

LENT READING, Weeks 2 & 4 **2 CORINTHIANS 6:1-4a**

And working together we urge you to not receive for no purpose the grace of God, who says, *In an acceptable time I heard you and in a day of salvation I helped you.*

Behold now an acceptable time; behold now a day of salvation. Nothing giving cause to stumble, lest the ministry be blamed, in everything we commend ourselves as servants of God.

RESPONSORY

Listen to us, O Lord, and have mercy…
…for we have sinned against you.
Christ Jesus, hear our humble petitions…
…for we have sinned against you.
Glory to the Father and to the Son and to the Holy Spirit:
…Listen to us, O Lord, and have mercy,
for we have sinned against you.

LENT READING, Palm Sunday **1 PETER 1:17-21**

You who call on the one Abba with no partiality as to the work of each, pass your time with the fear of a stranger, knowing that you were redeemed from your vain conduct and delivered from that of your ancestors not with corruptible silver or gold, but by the precious blood of Christ, as of a lamb unblemished and unspotted, chosen from the foundation of the world and shown forth in the last of times for you, believing through him in God who raised him from the dead and gave him glory, so that your faith and hope are in God.

RESPONSORY

We worship you, O Christ…
…and we praise you.
By your cross you have redeemed the world…
…and we praise you.
Glory to the Father and to the Son and to the Holy Spirit:
…We worship you, O Christ, and we praise you.

EASTER READING **1 PETER 2:9-10**

You are a chosen race, a royal priesthood, a holy nation, a people belonging so you may tell out the doing of your having been called out of darkness into the marvellous light of God. Then you were not a people, but now are people of God; then you saw no mercy, but now are shown mercy.

RESPONSORY

The disciples rejoiced…
…alleluia, alleluia.
When they saw the risen Lord…
…alleluia, alleluia.
Glory to the Father and to the Son and to the Holy Spirit:
…The disciples rejoiced,alleluia, alleluia.

Gospel Canticle For Evening

Antiphons

Advent Wk 2	See the Lord coming from afar, and splendor fills the earth.
Advent Wk 4 17th	O wisdom, O holy Word of God, come and show us the way.
Christmas	See the Ruler of rulers coming forth from God like a radiant spouse from the wedding chamber.
Lent Wk 2	Human beings cannot live on bread alone, but by every word that comes from the mouth of God.
Lent Wk 4	Now that we have been justified by faith, let us be at peace with God through our Lord Jesus Christ.
Palm Sunday	Unless a grain of wheat falls into the ground and dies, it remains only a single grain; but if it dies, it produces a rich harvest.
Easter Wk 4	Stay with us, Lord, for evening draws near and daylight is fading, alleluia.
Easter Wk 6	I am the way, the truth, and the life; all who come to the Abba come through me, alleluia.

Ordinary Time Antiphons		YEAR A Responsorial
Wk 2	Here am I, Lord; I come to do your will.	Ps 40
4	Blessed are the poor in spirit.	Ps 146
6	Blessed are they who follow the law of the Lord!	Ps 119
8	Rest in God alone, my soul.	Ps 62
10	The upright will see God's saving power.	Ps 50
12	Lord, in your great love, answer me.	Ps 69
14	I will praise your name forever, my God.	Ps 145
16	Lord, you are good and forgiving.	Ps 86
18	The hand of the Lord feeds us.	Ps 145
20	O God, let all the nations praise you!	Ps 67
22	My soul is thirsting for you, O Lord my God.	Ps 63
24	The Lord is kind and merciful.	Ps 103
26	Remember your mercies, O Lord.	Ps 25
28	I shall live in the house of the Lord.	Ps 23
30	I love you, Lord, my strength.	Ps 18
32	My soul is thirsting for you O Lord my God.	Ps 63
34	The Lord is my shepherd; there is nothing I shall want.	Ps 23

CANTICLE of MARY (The Magnificat)
LUKE 1:46-55

+ **My soul** is stretched full with praise of the Lord,
and my spirit, beyond joy in God, my Savior,
who chose to lay eyes on this humble servant.

Behold, now and forward,
each and every age will call me blessed,
for the Mighty One did great things to me.

Holy is the name and the mercy
to generations and generations,
the ones fearing the One,

Who scattered the haughty of mind and heart,
pulled the powerful off their high place,
and lifted with dignity the humble in need.

The hungering are filled with good things,
the rich are sent away empty,
and servant Israel is given relief

with a memory of mercy to remember,
the promise spoken to our ancestors,
to Abraham and his descendants forever.

Glory…

Antiphon

INTERCESSIONS

- Lord, make your Church ever new…
- Watch over our pope and bishops…
- Keep us united in our diversity…
- Inspire leaders with your justice…
- Keep married couples in love…
- For respect for the dignity of the human person…
- For a culture of vocations all over the world…
- For all who have died…

- In gratitude for blessings, Abba thank you…
- For the sins of this day, Lord Jesus have mercy…
- With concerns over tomorrow, Holy Spirit help…

CLOSING PRAYER FOR MORNING AND EVENING

Our Fa-ther, who art in heav-en,
hal-lowed be thy name.
Thy king-dom come,
thy will be done
on earth as it is in heav-en.
Give us this day our dai-ly bread
and for-give us our tres-pass-es,
as we for-give those who tres-pass a-gainst/ us,
and lead us not in-to temp-ta/-tion,
but de-liv-er us from e\-vil.
A-men.

WEEK II
SUNDAY MORNING

\+ *God, come to my assistance;* Psalm 70:2
Lord, make haste to help me!

Glory...

ORDINARY TIME

Ho-ly, ho-ly, ho-ly, Lord God Al-migh-ty!
Ear-ly in the morn-ing our song shall rise to thee;
Ho-ly, ho-ly, ho-ly, mer-ci-ful and migh-ty!
God in Three Per-sons, bless-ed Trin-i-ty!

Ho-ly, ho-ly, ho-ly! All the saints a-dore thee,
Cast-ing down their gold-en crowns
a-round the glass-y sea;
Cher-u-bim and ser-a-phim fall-ing down be-fore thee,
Who was, and is, and ev-er-more shall be.

Ho-ly, ho-ly, ho-ly! Though con-fu-sion hide you,
Glo-ry shin-ing through the blurr
of cloud-ed hu-man view;
Ho-ly a-lone are you; there is none be-side you:
Per-fect and pure, your love in all you do.

Ho-ly, ho-ly, ho-ly! Lord God Al-migh-ty!
All cre-a-tion praise your name in earth & sky & sea.
Ho-ly, ho-ly, ho-ly, mer-ci-ful and migh-ty!
God in Three Persons, bless-ed Trin-i-ty!

97, Text: From Revelation 4:8; by Reginald Heber, 1827, altered
Music: 11 12 12 10, NICAEA; John B. Dykes, 1861

ADVENT

Im-mac-u-late Ma-ry,
your prais-es we\ sing.
You reign now in heav-en
with Je-sus our\ King.
A-ve, A-ve, A-ve, Ma-ri-a!
A-ve, A-ve, Ma-ri/\-a!

In heav-en the bless-ed
your glo-ry pro\-claim;
On earth we your chil-dren
in-voke your fair\ name.
A-ve, A-ve, A-ve, Ma-ri-a!
A-ve, A-ve, Ma-ri/\-a!

We pray for our Mo-ther,
the Church up-on\ earth,
And bless, Ho-ly Ma-ry,
the land of our\ birth.
A-ve, A-ve, A-ve, Ma-ri-a!
A-ve, A-ve, Ma-ri/\-a!

10, Text: anonymous in *Parochial Hymn Book;* Boston, 1897;
revision of *Hail Virgin,* by Jeremiah Cummings, altered
Music: 11 11 LOURDES HYMN with refrain, trad. Pyrenean Melody,
pub. Grenoble, 1882; altered by Augustus Edmonds Tozer, d.1910

39, Text: from Matthew 2:1-11, John H. Hopkins, Jr., 1857, altered
Music: 88 44 6 KINGS OF ORIENT w/ refrain, John Hopkins, Jr., 1857

CHRISTMAS

We three kings of O-ri-ent are;
Bear-ing gifts we tra-verse a-far,
Field and foun-tain, moor and moun\-tain,
Fol-low-ing yon-der star.

Refrain **O** / star of won-der, star of night,
Star with roy-al beau-ty bright,
West-ward lead-ing, still pro-ceed-ing,
Guide us to your per-fect Light.

Born a King on Beth-le-hem's plain
Gold I bring to crown him a-gain,
King for-ev-er, ceas-ing nev\-er,
O-ver us all to reign. *Refrain*

Frank-in-cense to of-fer have I;
In-cense owns a De-i-ty nigh;
Prayer and prais-ing, voic-es rais\-ing,
Wor-ship-ping God on high. *Refrain*

Myrrh is mine, its bit-ter per-fume
Breathes a life of gath-er-ing gloom;
Sorr'w-ing, sigh-ing, bleed-ing, dy\-ing,
Sealed in the stone cold tomb. *Refrain*

Glo-rious now be-hold him a-rise;
King and God and sac/-ri-fice;
Al-le-lu-ia! Al-le-lu\-ia!
Sounds through the earth and skies. *Refrain*

LENT

Praise\ to the Ho-liest in the height,
And/ from the depth\ come praise;
The\ words of God most won-der-ful,
Most/ sure are all\ God's ways.
O/ lov-ing wis\-dom of our God!
When/ all was\ sin and shame,
A\ sec-ond A-dam to the fight
And/ to the res\-cue came.

And\ in the gar-den se-cret-ly,
And/ from the Cross\ on high,
Should\ teach dis-cip-les, and in-spire
To/ suf-fer and\ to die.
And/ that a high\-er gift than grace
Should/ flesh and\ blood re-fine,
God's\ Pres-ence and God's ve-ry Self,
And/ Es-sence all di-vine.

52, Text: from Psalm 148:1, John Henry Newman,
The Dream of Gerontius, 1865,altered
Music: KINGSFOLD, CMD, traditional English melody,
adapted by Ralph Vaughan Williams, 1906
Popular melody for: *I Heard the Voice of Jesus Say*

EASTER

Let glo-ry be to God/\ on high:
And peace be on the earth as in the sky;
Good will to all! We bow\ the knee,
We praise, we bless, we wor/\-ship thee;
We give you thanks, your Name/\ we sing,
Al-migh-ty Father! Hea\\-v'nly King!

O Lord, the sole be-got/\-ten Son,
Who bore the crimes the hu-man race had done;
The Fa-ther's Son, the Liv\-ing Word
Who takes a-way the sins/ of the world;
O Lamb of God, whose ve-ry blood was spilt
For all the world, and all\\ its guilt.

Have mer-cy on us, through/\ your blood;
Re-ceive our prayer, O Lamb\\ of God!
For you are ho-ly, you\ a-lone,
At God's right hand, up-on/\ the throne.
O Trin-i-ty, now be/\ a-dored,
With you, O Ho-ly Spir-it, One\ Lord.

105, Text: *Gloria in excelsis Deo,* 8th manuscript of the Liturgy of St. James; translator unknown, 1858, altered
Music: VENI EMMANUEL, LM with refrain; 15th C.; adapted by Thomas Helmore, 1856
Popular melody for: *O Come, O Come Emmanuel*

PSALM 104

Antiphon *Peace to you;*
as the Abba has sent me, so I send you;
receive the Holy Spirit. Jn 20:21

Advent, Christmas, & Lent
The Lord brings forth
bread from the earth,
and wine to warm human hearts.

Easter
Alleluia, the stone was rolled back
from the entrance to the tomb,
alleluia.

Soul of me, praise Adonai!
My God, Adonai, you are beyond measure.
Splendor and majesty clothe you,
wrapped in light as a garment,

stretching out over the heavens like a tent,
laying beams on the waters of the upper chambers.
You make a chariot of the clouds,
riding on wings of wind,
making messengers of the winds
and servants of flaming fire.

You have set foundations on earth,
unmoveable for ever and ever.
Deep is your garment, covering the earth;
above the mountains the waters stood.

At your rebuke, they then fled;
at the sound of your thunder they took flight.
They flowed over mountains
and went down into valleys
to the places you assigned for them.
You set a boundary they are not to cross;
never again are they to cover the earth.

You make springs of water pour into ravines;
between the mountains they flow.
They give drink to all beasts of the field;
they quench the thirst of donkeys.
Birds of the air nest in branches beside them;
they give you their song.

You water mountains from your upper chambers;
by the fruit of your works the earth is satisfied.
You make grass grow for the cattle
and plants for human beings to cultivate

to bring forth food from the earth,
wine to make glad the human heart,
oil to make faces shine,
and bread to sustain the human heart.

They are all Adonai's well watered trees,
cedars of Lebanon planted
where birds make their nests,
and the pine tree where the stork makes a home,
mountains, the high ones, for wild goats,
and crags, a refuge for rock badgers.

Psalm 104, continued

You made the moon to mark off seasons
and the sun that knows when to set.
You bring darkness
and all beasts of the forest prowl in the night.
The lions roar for prey
seeking their food from God.

The sun rises, they steal away,
and into their dens they lie down.
Human beings go out to do their work
and labor until the evening.

How varied are your works, Adonai!
All of them in wisdom you made.
The earth is full of your creatures.

There is the sea, vast and spacious;
living creatures countless there,
small ones and large ones.
There ships go about
and leviathan which you formed for frolic.

All of them look to you
to give them food at their time.
You give to them and they gather,
you open your hands
and they are goodly satisfied.

Peoples, make heard the praise of our God
who preserves our life among the living,
and lets not our feet to slip.

God, you tested us, refined us as silver is refined.
You let us be brought into prison,
you let burdens be put on our backs,
you let human beings set foot on our neck.

We went through the fire and through the waters
and you brought us to a spacious place.

I will come to your temple with burnt offerings,
I will fulfill to you my vows, promised on my lips,
spoken in a time of trouble.

Sacrifices of fat animals I will sacrifice to you;
with offerings of rams I will offer bull and goats.

Come! Listen! Let me tell all who fear God
what God has done for my very self.
To God my mouth cried out
with praise on my tongue.

If I cherished sin in my heart
the Lord would not have listened.
Surely God listened and heard my voice of prayer.

God, be praised, who rejected not my prayer
nor took from within me
the Lord's own *hesed* love.

Glory... Antiphon

PSALM 118

Antiphon *I am the good shepherd,*
and I know mine and mine know me. Jn 10:14

Advent 2nd Sun Zion is our mighty citadel,
our saving Lord its wall and its defense;
throw open the gates,
for our God is here among us, alleluia.

Advent 4th Sun The day of the Lord is near,
coming to save us, alleluia.

Christmas John saw the Spirit coming from heaven
like a dove and resting on him.

Lent 2nd Sun The right hand of the Lord
has raised me up.

Lent 4th Sun O God, my God, I give you thanks;
you are my God.

Palm Sun The great crowd gathered for the feast
cry out: Hosanna in the highest.

Easter 4th Sun I will not die; I will live
and proclaim the deeds of the Lord,
alleluia.

Easter 6th Sun This is the day the Lord has made,
alleluia.

Give thanks to Adonai who is good,
whose love is to forever.

Let Israel now declare:
the love of the Lord to forever.
Let the house of Aaron declare:
the love of the Lord to forever.
Let those who fear Adonai declare:
the love of the Lord to forever.

In anguish I cried to Adonai
who answered me with freedom.
Adonai is with me, I will not be afraid.
What can any human do to me?
Before enmity I keep this in mind:
Adonai is with me, ready to help me.

Better to take refuge in Adonai
than to trust in the human;
Better to take refuge in Adonai
than to trust in a prince.

All of the nations surrounded me,
indeed did they surround me;
in the name of Adonai indeed I cut them.
They swarmed around me like bees,
they crackled like thorns in a fire;
in the name of Adonai indeed I cut them.

To push back they pushed me back to fall
but Adonai came to my help.
Adonai became my strength and my song
and became to me salvation.
Shout joy and victory in your tents, you just.

Psalm 118, continued

Adonai's right hand does a mighty thing,
Adonai's right hand lifted high.
Adonai's right hand does a mighty thing.
I will not die; I will live
and proclaim these deeds indeed.
To chasten, Adonai let me be chastened,
but did not give me to death.

Open for me the gates of the just;
I will enter through them
and give thanks to Adonai.
This is Adonai's gate,
where just ones may enter.
I will give thanks to you for you answered me
and you became to me salvation.

The stone the builders rejected
became the cornerstone.
With Adonai this happened
and it is marvelous in our eyes.
This is the day Adonai has made;
let us rejoice and be glad in it.

Adonai, save us now!
Adonai, grant success now!
Blessed is the one coming in the name of Adonai;
We bless you from the house of Adonai.
Our El Adonai has shined light onto us.

Join with leaf branches in the festal procession
up to the horns of the altar.
To you, my God, I will give thanks.
You, my God, I will give glory.
Give thanks to Adonai who is good,
whose love is to forever.

Glory…

Antiphon *I am the good shepherd,*
and I know mine and mine know me. Jn 10:14

Advent 2nd Sun Zion is our mighty citadel, our saving Lord
its wall and its defense; throw open the gates,
for our God is here among us, alleluia.

Advent 4th Sun The day of the Lord is near;
coming to save us, alleluia.

Christmas John saw the Spirit coming from heaven
like a dove and resting on him.

Lent 2nd Sun The right hand of the Lord
has raised me up.

Lent 4th Sun O God, my God, I give you thanks;
you are my God.

Palm Sun The great crowd gathered for the feast
cry out: Hosanna in the highest.

Easter 4th Sun I will not die; I will live and proclaim
the deeds of the Lord, alleluia.

Easter 6th Sun This is the day the Lord has made,
alleluia.

DANIEL 3:52-57

Antiphon *God sent the Son into the cosmos*
not to condemn, but that the cosmos
might be saved through him. Jn 3:17

Advent 2nd Sun Come to the waters, all you who thirst;
seek while the Lord can be found,
alleluia.

Advent 4th Sun Go out to meet the Lord who is here:
great is the birth, eternal is the reign,
strong is God, Ruler of all, Prince of Peace,
alleluia.

Christmas The angel said to the shepherds:
I proclaim to you a great joy;
the Savior of the world is born for you,
alleluia.

Lent 2nd Sun Let us sing the hymn of the three youths
which they sang in the fiery furnace,
giving praise to God.

Lent 4th Sun God of might, deliver us;
free us from the power of enmity.

Palm Sun God grant that we may be faithful
with angels and children singing to the
conquerer of death: Hosanna in the highest.

Easter 4th Sun Blessed be, O Lord,
your holy and glorious name,
alleluia.

Easter 6th Sun Blessed are you, Lord our God,
in the dome of heaven,
worthy of praise forever,
alleluia.

Blessed are you, **O Lord**, God of our ancestors,
praiseworthy and exalted above all forever.

Blessed is your glorious and holy name,
praiseworthy and exalted above all forever.

Blessed are you in the temple of your sacred glory,
praiseworthy and exalted above all forever.

Blessed are you who sit high on the cherubim
and look into the depths,
praiseworthy and exalted above all forever.

Blessed are you on your royal throne,
praiseworthy and exalted above all forever.

Blessed are you in the dome of heaven,
to be hymned and glorified forever.

Bless the Lord, all you works of the Lord,
sing praise and high exaltation forever.

Glory…

Antiphon

PSALM 150

Antiphon	*Be merciful* *as your Abba is merciful.* Lk 6:36
Advent 2nd Sun	God will come to enlighten the eyes of the servants of God, alleluia.
Advent 4th Sun	Your all-powerful Word, O Lord, will come to earth from the throne of glory, alleluia.
Christmas	Let everything with breath praise the Lord, alleluia,
Lent 2nd Sun	Praise the Lord in the heavenly power.
Lent 4th Sun	Give praise for God's mighty deeds.
Palm Sun	Blessed is the one who comes in the name of the Lord; peace in heaven and glory in the highest.
Easter 4th Sun	Give honor and praise to our God, whose deeds are perfect and ways are true, alleluia.
Easter 6th Sun	Sing to God in praise: Amen, alleluia.

Hallelujah!

To El in the sanctuary, give praise.
In the mighty heavens, give praise.
For the works of power, give praise.
For surpassing greatness, give praise.

With sounding of trumpet, give praise.
With harp and lyre, give praise.
With tambourine and dance, give praise.
With flute and string, give praise.

With cymbals clashing, give praise.
With cymbals resounding, give praise.
Let all that has breath praise Adonai!

Hallelujah!

Glory…

Antiphon

Hallelujah!
It means, "Praise God"!
Can you now and then raise your
hands in the air and say, even quietly,
"God, I praise you"? It's OK that some of us
must go to our inner room and close the door to do this.

When you pray, enter your room and close your door
and pray to your Abba in secret. Mt 6:6

ORDINARY TIME READING **EZEKIEL 36:22-26**

Say to the house of Israel: Sovereign Adonai says that not for your sake do I act, house of Israel, but rather for my holy name which you profaned among the nations where you went. And I will show my great holy name, profaned by you among the nations. Then the nations will know that I am Adonai, declares Sovereign Adonai, when through you I show my holy self before their eyes.

For I will take you out of the nations and I will gather you from all of the countries, and I will bring you back into your land. I will sprinkle on you clean waters, and you will be clean from all of your impurities, and from all of your idols I will cleanse you. I will give to you a new heart and I will put inside of you a new spirit, and I will remove the heart of stone from your flesh and I will give to you a heart of flesh.

RESPONSORY Is 12:4,5

We give thanks to you, Adonai,...
...calling on your name.
We proclaim and make known your deeds...
...calling on your name.
Glory to the Father and to the Son and to the Holy Spirit:
...We give thanks to you, Adonai, calling on your name.

ADVENT READING **ROMANS 13:11-12**

Know that this is the *kairos* time, the hour for you to be raised out of sleep, for now our salvation is nearer than when we became believers. The night has advanced and the day draws near.

So let us cast off the deeds of the darkness, and let us put on the armor of the light.

As in the new day, let us walk not in revellings to drunken bouts, not in sex to excesses, not in strife to jealousy, but put on the Lord Jesus Christ, and as for the flesh, give its lust no room to think.

RESPONSORY Lk 18:13, 22:69

Lord Jesus Christ, Son of the living God…
...have mercy on us.
You are seated at the right hand of the Father…
...have mercy on us.
Glory to the Father and to the Son and to the Holy Spirit:
...Lord Jesus Christ, Son of the living God,
have mercy on us.

CHRISTMAS READING **HEBREWS 1:1-4**

Of old, having spoken to the ancestors through the prophets often and in many ways, in these last days God spoke to us in a Son, appointed as heir of all things, and indeed through whom God made the eons.

He is the radiance of the glory, the representation of the reality, and the bearer of all things by the word of the power of God, and having made a cleansing of sins, he has sat at the right hand of the greatness on high. By so much, he has inherited the more excellent name, better even than that of the angels.

RESPONSORY

The Lord has made known...
...alleluia, alleluia.
The saving power...
...alleluia, alleluia.
Glory to the Father and to the Son and to the Holy Spirit:
...The Lord has made known the saving power, alleluia.

The setting of the Christmas
story is *the whole world being at peace,**
but it is a peace enforced with violence.
The paradox is that he-who-is-our-peace
brings the real peace that only God can give.

*See the *Christmas Proclamation* of Mass in the Night

LENT READING, Weeks 2 & 4 **NEHEMIAH 8:9,10**

Nehemiah the governor and Ezra the priest and scribe and the Levites instructing the people said to all the people, "This day is sacred to Adonai your God. Do not mourn and do not weep," for all the people wept as they listened to the words of the Law.

And he said to them, "Go! Eat choice foods! And drink sweet things! And send portions to ones with nothing prepared, for this day is sacred to our Lord, and do not grieve, for the joy of Adonai is your strength."

RESPONSORY Lk 18:13

Lord Jesus Christ, Son of the living God...
...have mercy on us.
You were wounded for our offenses...
...have mercy on us.
Glory to the Father and to the Son and to the Holy Spirit:
...Lord Jesus Christ, Son of the living God,
have mercy on us.

No peace without justice;
no justice without forgiveness.

Saint Pope John Paul II for *World Day of Peace* after 9-11

LENT READING, Palm Sunday **LEVITICUS 23:4-7**

These are feasts of Adonai, sacred assemblies that you must proclaim at their time: in the first month on the fourteenth day, the twilight, the passover to Adonai; and on the fifteenth day of that month the Feast of the Unleavened Breads to Adonai, seven days of unleavened breads you must eat. On the first day must be an assembly of the sacred, for none of you must do any regular work.

RESPONSORY Rev 5:9

Lord, by your own blood…
…you brought us back to God.
From every tribe and tongue and people and nation…
…you brought us back to God.
Glory to the Father and to the Son and to the Holy Spirit:
…Lord, by your own blood you brought us back to God.

EASTER READING **ACTS 10:40-43**

God raised this one on the third day and gave him to be visible not to all the people, but to witnesses chosen by God, to us who ate and drank with him after his rising out of the dead. And he commanded us to proclaim to the people and witness solemnly that he is the one designated by God as judge of the living and the dead. To him all the prophets witness: forgiveness of sins received through his name by everyone believing in him.

RESPONSORY Lk 18:13

Lord Jesus Christ, Son of the living God…
...have mercy on us.
You were wounded for our offenses…
...have mercy on us.
Glory to the Father and to the Son and to the Holy Spirit:
...Lord Jesus Christ, Son of the living God,
have mercy on us.

If you want peace, go to sleep.
But if you want to be alive, go to prayer.

Geshe Sopa, asked if prayer was how to find peace.

Gospel Canticle For Morning

Advent Wk 2 A. Matthew 3:1-12 B. Mark 1:1-8 C. Luke 3:1-6	I am sending my angel before me to prepare the way for my coming.
Advent Wk 4 A. Mt 1:18-24 B. Luke 1:26-38 C. Luke 1:39-45	Let everything within you watch and wait, for the Lord our God draws near.
Christmas & Feast of the Holy Family A. Matt 2:13-15,19-23 B. Luke 2:22-40 C. Luke 2:41-52	Glory to God in the highest, and peace on earth to the people of God, alleluia.
Lent Wk 2 A. Matt 17:1-9 B. Mark 9:2-10 C. Luke 9:28b-36	Our Lord Jesus Christ abolished death and through the Gospel revealed eternal life.
Lent Wk 4 A. John 9:1-41 B. John 3:14-21 C. Lk 15:1-3,11-32	It was unheard of for anyone to open the eyes of a human born blind until the coming of Christ, the Son of God.
Palm Sunday A. Mt 26:14-27:66 B. Mk 14:1-15:47 C. Lk 22:14-23:56	With palms we run to welcome the Lord who comes, and meet him with songs and hymns and joy and worship and blessing.

Easter Wk 4	I am the shepherd of the sheep;
A. John 10:1-10	I know my sheep,
B. John 10:11-18	and my sheep know me,
C. John 10:27-30	alleluia.
Easter Wk 6	As the Abba has loved me
A. John 14:15-21	so I have loved you;
B. John 15:9-17	live on in my love,
C. John 14:23-29	alleluia.

YEAR B

Ordinary Time Antiphons — Responsorial

Wk 2 Here am I, Lord; I come to do your will. Ps 40
A- John 1:29-34 B- John 1:35-42 C- John 2:1-11

4 If today you hear the voice,
harden not your hearts. Ps 95
A- Matt 5:1-12a B- Mark 1:21-28 C- Luke 4:21-30

6 I turn to you, Lord, in time of trouble. Ps 32
A- Matt 5:17-37 B- Mark 1:40-45 C- Lk 6:17,20-26

8 The Lord is kind and merciful. Ps 103
A- Matt 6:24-34 B- Mark 2:18-22 C- Luke 6:39-45

10 With the Lord there is mercy. Ps 130
A- Matt 9:9-13 B- Mark 3:20-35 C- Luke 7:11-17

12 The love of the Lord is everlasting. Ps 107
A- Matt 10:26-33 B- Mark 4:35-41 C- Luke 9:18-24

14 Our eyes are fixed on the Lord. Ps 123
A- Matt 11:25-30 B- Mark 6:1-6 C- Lk 10:1-12,17-20

Antiphon for Gospel Canticle For Morning, continued

YEAR B

Ordinary Time Antiphons — Responsorial

16 The Lord is my shepherd. Ps 23

A- Matt 13:24-43 **B-** Mark 6:30-34 **C-** Lk 10:38-42

18 The Lord gave them bread from heaven. Ps 78

A- Matt 14:13-21 **B-** John 6:24-35 **C-** Lk 12:13-21

20 Taste and see the goodness of the Lord. Ps 34

A- Matt 15:21-28 **B-** John 6:51-58 **C-** Lk 12:49-53

22 One who does justice lives in
the presence of the Lord. Ps 15

A- Matt 16:21-27 **B-** Mk 7:1-8,14-15,21-23 **C-** Lk 14:1,7-14

24 I will walk before the Lord. Ps 116

A- Matt 18:21-35 **B-** Mark 8:27-35 **C-** Luke 15:1-32

26 The precepts of the Lord
give joy to the heart. Ps 19

A- Matt 21:28-32 **B-** Mk 9:38-43,45,47-48 **C-** Lk 16:19-31

28 Fill us with your love, O Lord. Ps 90

A- Matt 22:1-14 **B-** Mark 10:17-30 **C-** Lk 17:11-19

30 The Lord has done great things for us,
we are filled with joy! Ps 126

A- Matt 22:34-40 **B-** Mark 10:46-52 **C-** Luke 18:9-14

32 Praise the Lord, my soul! Ps 146

A- Matt 25:1-13 **B-** Mark 12:38-44 **C-** Lk 20:27-38

34 The Lord our ruler is robed in majesty. Ps 93

A- Matt 25:31-46 **B-** John 18:33b-37 **C-** Lk 23:35-43

CANTICLE of ZECHARIAH (The Benedictus)
LUKE 1:68-79

+ **Blessed be** the Lord the God of Israel
who chose a people to visit with redemption,
and raised salvation in the house of David,
saving strength from God's own servant,

speaking from the age of the prophets
through the mouth of the holy prophet:
Salvation out of enmity,
even out of those who hate us,

to show our ancestors how mercy works, -
and to remember the holy promise of the Lord,
the covenant made for our ancestor Abraham,
calming our fear and making us free
to serve with holy justice before God all our days.

And you also child -
will be called a prophet of the Most High
for you will go before the Lord to prepare his way
and give to people a knowledge of salvation
known in accepting forgiveness of their sins.

From the tender mercy of our God,
the sun rising from the height will visit with light
for those who sit in the dark or shadow of death
and to guide our feet into the way of peace.

Glory...

Antiphon

PETITIONS FOR THE CONSECRATION TO GOD
OF THE DAY AND ITS REST

- For the Church and her ministry and apostolates…
- For secular authorities and all serving as stewards…
- For people who are poor or sick or in sorrow…
- For peace and the basic needs of each human being…
- For acceptance of the gift of the infinite love of God…
- For the blessings of faithful Sabbath rest…
- In gratitude for blessings and grace…
- For those who have asked for my prayer…
- For those for whom I have promised to pray…
- For those who weigh on my heart…

CLOSING PRAYER FOR MORNING AND EVENING

Our Fa-ther,
who art in heav-en,
hal-lowed be thy name.
Thy king-dom come,
thy will be done
on earth as it is in heav-en.
Give us this day our dai-ly bread
and for-give us our tres-pass-es,
as we for-give those who tres-pass a-gainst/ us,
and lead us not in-to temp-ta/-tion,
but de-liv-er us from e\-vil.
A-men.

HYMN, TE DEUM

You are God: we praise you;
You are the Lord; we acclaim you;
You are the eternal Father: all creation worships you.

To you all angels, all the powers of heaven,
Cherubim and Seraphim, sing in endless praise:
Holy, holy, holy, Lord, God of power and might,
heaven and earth are full of your glory.

The glorious company of apostles praise you.
The noble assembly of prophets praise you.
The white-robed army of martyrs praise you.

All over the world the holy church acclaims you:
Father, of majesty unbounded,
your true and only Son, worthy of all worship,
and the Holy Spirit, advocate and guide.

You, Christ, are the royal of glory,
the eternal Son of the Father.

When you became human to set us free
you did not spurn the Virgin's womb.

You overcame the sting of death,
and opened the reign of heaven to all believers.

You are seated at God's right hand in glory.
We believe that you will come and be our judge.

Come then, Lord, and help your people,
bought with the price of your own blood,
and bring us with your saints
to glory everlasting. Amen.

WEEK II
SUNDAY EVENING

\+ *God, come to my assistance;* Psalm 70:2
Lord, make haste to help me!

Glory...

ORDINARY TIME & ADVENT

Joy-ful, joy-ful, we a-dore you,
God of glo-ry, Lord of love;
Hearts un-fold like flow'rs be-fore you,
Op'n-ing to the sun a-bove.
Melt the clouds of sin and/ sad-ness;
Drive the/ dark of doubt a-way;
Giv-er of e-ter-nal glad-ness,
Fill us with the light of day.

You are giv-ing and for-giv-ing,
Ev-er bless-ing, ev-er blest,
Well-spring of the joy of liv-ing,
O-cean depth of hap-py rest!
You our Fa-ther, Christ our/ bro-ther,
All who/ live in love are thine;
Teach us how to love each oth-er,
Ho-ly Spir-it, joy div-ine.

85, Text: Henry Van Dyke, 1907, altered
Music: 8787D, HYMN TO JOY, Ludwig van Beethoven,d.1827;
ad.by Edward Hodges,1824

ORDINARY TIME

Love Div-ine/, all love ex-cell\-ing,
Joy of heav'n, to earth\ come down,
Fix in us/ your hum-ble dwell-ing,
All your faith-ful mer\-cies crown.
Je-sus, you\ are true com-pass\-ion,
Pure, un-bound/-ed love\ you are;
Vis\-it us\ with your\ sal-va//\-tion,
En-ter-ing\ the tremb-ling heart.

Breathe, oh breathe/, your lov-ing Spir\-it
In-to ev-'ry troub\-led breast;
Let us all/ in you in-her\-it,
Let us find the prom\-ised rest.
Take a-way\ the love of sin\-ning;
Al-pha and/ O-me\-ga be;
End\ of faith\ as its be-gin//\-ning,
Set our hearts\ at lib-er-ty.

Fin-ish, then/, your new cre-a\-tion;
Pure and spot-less let\ us be.
Let us see/ your great sal-va\-tion
Per-fect-ly re-stored\ and free,
Changed from glo\-ry into glo\-ry,
Till in heav'n/ we find\ our place,
Till\ we cast\ our cares\ be-fore//\ you,
Lost in won\-der, love, and grace.

112, Text: from Psalm 106:4; by Charles Wesley, 1747, altered
Music: 87 87 D, HYFRYDOL, Rowland H. Prichard, 1811-1887

CHRISTMAS

O ho-ly night, the stars are bright-ly shi-ning;
It is the night of the dear Sa-vior's birth!
Long lay the world in sin and err-or pi-ning,
Till he ap-peared and the soul felt its worth.
A thrill of hope, the wea-ry soul re-joic-es,
For yon-der breaks a new and glo-rious morn.
Fall on your knees, O hear the an-gel voi-ces!
O night\ div-ine, O\ night
when Christ was born!
O night, O ho-ly night \ \ \, O night div-ine!

Tru-ly he taught us to love one an-oth-er;
His law is love and his Gos-pel is peace.
Chains shall he break
for the slave is our broth-er
And in his Name all op-pres-sion shall cease.
The King of kings lay thus in hum-ble man-ger,
In all our tri-als born to be our Friend!
He knows our need,
to our weak-ness is no stran-ger.
Be-hold\ your King; Son of Ma-ry, Son of God!
Give glo-ry to God:
Fa-ther and Son and Spir-it blest!

29, Text: Placide Cappeau, 1847;
translated from French by John S. Dwight, d. 1893, altered
Music: 11 10 11 10 11 10 11 10 10, Adolphe C. Adam, d. 1856
Said to have been the first music broadcast by radio.

LENT

O sav-ing Vic-tim, o-pen wide
The gate of heav'n to us\ be-low;
Our foes press on/ from ev-'ry side;
Your aid sup-ply\; your strength be-stow.

To your great Name be end-less praise;
Im-mort-al God-head, One\ in Three;
Grant us for end/-less length of days,
In our true na\-tive land to be.

O sa-lu-ta-ris Ho-sti-a,
Quae cae-li pan-dis o\-sti-um:
Bel-la pre-munt/ ho-sti-li-a,
Da ro-bur fer\ au-xi-li-um.

A-men.

49, Text: Thomas Aquinas, 1227-74;
Translated by Edward Caswall, 1849, altered
Music: O SALUTARIS HOSTIA, Abbe Duguet, about 1767

EASTER

For all the saints who from their la-bors rest,
Who you by faith be-fore the world con-fess
Your name, O Je-sus, be for-ev\-er\ blest,
Al/-le\-lu-ia! Al//-le-lu-ia!

You were their rock, their for-tress and their might;
You, Lord, their cap-tain in the well-fought fight;
You, in the dark of night, their one\ true\ light.
Al/-le\-lu-ia! Al//-le-lu-ia!

O blest com-mu-nion, ho-ly and div-ine,
While yet we strug-gle, they in glo-ry shine;
Yet all are one in you, for all\ are\ thine.
Al/-le\-lu-ia! Al//-le-lu-ia!

So when there breaks a yet more glo-rious day,
The saints tri-umph-ant rise in bright ar-ray;
The King of Glo-ry pass-es on\ the\ Way.
Al/-le\-lu-ia! Al//-le-lu-ia!

From earth's wide bounds,
from o-cean's farth-est coast,
Thru gates of pearl stream in the count-less host,
Sing to the Fa-ther, Son, and Ho\-ly\ Ghost:
Al/-le\-lu-ia! Al//-le-lu-ia!

141, Text: William H. How, 1864, altered
Music: 10 10 10 SINE NOMINE with alleluias, by Ralph Vaughan Williams, 1906

PSALM 23

Antiphon *For I was hungry and you gave me to eat,*
thirsty and you gave me drink,
a stranger and you welcomed me,
naked and you clothed me,
ill and you cared for me,
in prison and you visited me. Mt 25:35,36

Adonai is my shepherd; nothing do I lack.
My Lord lays me down in green pastures
and leads me beside still quiet waters,
restoring my soul and guiding me
in paths of justice for the Lord's own namesake.

So when I walk in the deep dark valley
I will not fear for you are with me,
your rod and staff a comfort to me.

A table you prepare before me
in the presence even of enmity.
My head you anoint with oil
and my cup is overflowing.

Surely goodness and love will follow me
all the days of my life
and I will dwell in the Lord's own house
for length of days.

Glory...

Antiphon

PSALM 76

Antiphon *The Son of Humanity*
is Lord also of the sabbath. Mk 2:28

Advent & Lent Giver of light,
you are more majestic
than mountains of game.

Christmas Let all the neighbors of God
bring their gifts.

Easter Alleluia, alleluia, alleluia.

God is known in Judah;
great in Israel is the Name.
In Salem is God's tent,
in Zion the dwelling place.
There flashes broke the arrow,
shield and sword, and weapons of war.

Giver of Light, you are,
more majestic than mountains of game.
Human beings of valiant heart lie plundered;
they sleep their sleep
and warriors can no more lift up their hands.
At your rebuke, God of Jacob,
both chariot and horse lie still.

You are feared, you.
Who can stand before you when you are angry?
From the heavens you pronounced judgment;
the land feared and she was quiet
when you rose, God, for the judgment
to save all the afflicted of the land.

Even the angry humans come to praise you,
and you hold close the survivor of anger.
Make vows! Fulfill vows to your God Adonai!
Let all the neighbors of God bring their gift
to the One rightly feared,
who breaks the spirit of rulers,
the One rightly feared by kings and queens.

Glory...

Antiphon

Four Ways to Pray Deeper:

↓ Talking at God, using memorized prayers to simply pray, or throwing up on God today's urgency;

↓ Talking to God, sharing joys that are lifting my heart and sorrows that are weighing me down;

↓ Listening to God, willing to be surprised by God who is always saying, *I made you, I know you, I love you;*

↓ Being with God, contemplation, beatific vision, we can choose to do the first three, but this is always a gift.

See *Armchair Mystic* by Mark E. Thibodeaux, S.J.

PSALM 112

Antiphon *Blessed are those hungering*
and thirsting for justice;
they will be satisfied. Mt 5:6

Advent Crooked paths will be straightened
and rough ways made smooth;
come, O Lord, do not delay,
alleluia.

Christmas Light dawns out of the dark,
alleluia.

Lent Happy are they who show mercy
for the Lord's sake;
they will stand firm forever.

Easter Out of darkness comes the dawn,
a light for the honest of heart,
alleluia.

Hallelujah!

Blessed are the ones who fear Adonai,
and delight greatly in the commandments.
Mighty in the land will they be,
blessed with generations of upright children,

wealth and riches in their houses,
and justice enduring to forever.
Light dawns in the darkness
for the upright, gracious,
compassionate and just.

The good human, generous and lending,
conducts affairs with justice.
Surely to forever the good one will not be shaken;
remembered forever will the just one be.

The good will have no fear of bad news,
being steadfast of heart and trusting Adonai
with heart secure, no fear to the end,
when face to face with enmity.

The good one scatters, giving to the poor,
with justice enduring to forever;
the dignity of the good one will be lifted in honor.

Doers of the bad will see this and be vexed
with gnashing of teeth and a wasting away,
longings for the bad coming to nothing.

Glory...

Antiphon

Evangelization
is one beggar telling
another beggar where to
find bread. D.T. Niles

PSALM 115

Antiphon *Anyone who loves me will keep my word;*
my Abba will love that one,
within whom we will come
and make our dwelling. Jn 14:23

Advent If there seems a delay, keep watch,
for the Lord will surely come, alleluia.

Lent We worship the one true God
who made heaven and earth.

Palm Sunday The sacrifice of Christ washes away sin
and makes us worthy to serve God.

Christmas & Easter You have been turned from your idols
and to faith in the living God, alleluia.

Not to us, Adonai, not to us,
but to your name give glory
because of your love, because of your fidelity.
Why say the nations, "Where now is their God?"

Our God now is in the heavens
and does all that God pleases.
Their idols are silver and gold,
made of human hands.

Made with a mouth, they cannot speak;
made with eyes, they cannot see;
made with ears, they cannot hear;
made with a nose, they cannot smell;

made with hands, they cannot feel;
made with feet, they cannot walk,
and they make not a sound in their throat.
Like them will become those who make them,
and all who trust in them.

Israel, trust Adonai, your help and your shield.
Aaron, trust Adonai, your help and your shield.
You who fear Adonai, trust Adonai,
your help and your shield.

Adonai remembers us and will bless us,
will bless the house of Israel,
will bless the house of Aaron,
will bless ones who fear Adonai,
the small ones with the great ones.

May Adonai make an increase to you,
to you and to your children.
May you be blessed by Adonai,
Maker of heavens and earth.

All the heavens are the heavens of Adonai,
but earth is given to humanity.
The dead ones do not praise Adonai,
and not all those who go down in silence.

But we, we give glory to Adonai,
from now and to forevermore.
Hallelujah!

Glory... Antiphon

(*Lent*) 1 PETER 2:21-24

Antiphon *Be ready always for everyone*
asking you for a word
about the hope in you. 1 Ptr 3:15b

Lent 2nd Sun God did not spare God's own Son
but gave him up for us all.

Lent 4th Sun Those things have been fulfilled
which God foretold through the prophets
concerning the sufferings
that Christ would endure.

Palm Sun Christ bore our sins in his own body
on the cross so that we might die to sin
and be alive to all that is good.

To this you were called,
for indeed Christ suffered on behalf of you,
leaving to you an example to follow in his steps:

He did not sin, nor was guile found in his mouth;
he was reviled and did not revile in return;
suffering he did not threaten,
but delivered himself to the one judging justly.

Our sins he carried in his body up onto the tree,
that dying to sins, we might live for justice.
By his wounds, you are cured.

Glory… Antiphon

(*All except Lent*) REVELATION 19:1b,2a,5b,6b,7

Antiphon *We are an Easter people*
and **alleluia** *is our song.* St. Augustine

Advent & Christmas Ever wider will the reign spread,
eternally at peace,
alleluia.

Easter Alleluia, salvation and glory and power
are to our God, alleluia.

Alleluia!
Salvation and glory and power are to our God,
whose judgments are true and just.

Alleluia!
Praise our God, all you servants of the Lord,
you small and you great, who hold God in awe.

Alleluia!
The Lord is reigning, our God, the Almighty.
Let us rejoice and let us exult,
and we will give the glory to the Lord.

Alleluia!
The day has come
for the marriage of the Lamb,
and the bride has prepared herself.

Glory…

Antiphon

ORDINARY TIME READING **2 THESS 2:13-17**

We ought to thank God always concerning you, brothers and sisters loved by the Lord, because God chose you as the firstfruit to salvation by sanctification of spirit and faith in the truth, and called you through our gospel to obtain the glory of our Lord Jesus Christ.

So then, brothers and sisters, stand and hold the traditions which you were taught either through speech or through our letter.

And may our Lord Jesus Christ and God our Father, the one who has loved us and given us eternal comfort and a good hope by grace, comfort your hearts and confirm every good work and word.

RESPONSORY Ps 147:5

Great is our Lord…

…and mighty in power.

Unlimited in understanding…

…and mighty in power.

Glory to the Father and to the Son and to the Holy Spirit:

…Great is our Lord, and mighty in power.

ADVENT READING **PHILIPPIANS 4:4-7**

Rejoice in the Lord always; I say it again, rejoice. Let your kindness be known to all human beings. The Lord is near. Be anxious about nothing, but in everything, by prayer and thanksgiving petition, let your requests be made known to God.

And the peace of God which surpasses all understanding will guard your hearts and your minds in Christ Jesus.

RESPONSORY Ps 85:7

Lord, show to us…

…your mercy and unfailing love.

And grant us your salvation…

…your mercy and unfailing love.

Glory to the Father and to the Son and to the Holy Spirit:

… Lord, show to us your mercy and unfailing love.

CHRISTMAS READING **1 JOHN 1:1-3**

What was from the beginning, what we have heard, what we have seen with our eyes, what we have looked at and our hands have touched concerning the Word of Life, and the life has been shown, we have seen and we bear witness and we proclaim to you the life eternal, which was with the Father and has been shown to us.

What we have seen and heard, we proclaim also to you that you also may have communion with us. Indeed our communion is with the Father and with the Son, Jesus Christ.

RESPONSORY Jn 1:14

The Word became flesh...
...alleluia, alleluia.
And dwelt among us...
...alleluia, alleluia.
Glory to the Father and to the Son and to the Holy Spirit:
...The Word became flesh and dwelt among us;
alleluia, alleluia.

LENT READING, Weeks 2 & 4 **1 CORINTHIANS 9:24-27**

Do you not know that all runners on a racecourse run, but one receives the prize? Run so that you may obtain. Everyone in the struggle exercises self-control in all things, and they in order to receive a corruptible crown. But we, one incorruptible. And so I do not run without clarity nor fight beating the air. But I treat my body in discipline and lead it as a servant, lest having proclaimed to others I myself be disqualified.

RESPONSORY

Listen to us, O Lord, and have mercy…
…for we have sinned against you.
Christ Jesus, hear our humble petitions…
…for we have sinned against you.
Glory to the Father and to the Son and to the Holy Spirit:
…Listen to us, O Lord, and have mercy
for we have sinned against you.

LENT READING, Palm Sunday **ACTS 13:26-30**

Men and women, brothers and sisters, daughters and sons of Abraham, and those among you fearing God, to us the word of this salvation was sent forth. For the dwellers of Jerusalem and their rulers, knowing neither this man nor the voices of the prophets being read every sabbath, fulfilled them in judging him. And finding no cause for death, they asked Pilate that he be destroyed.

And when they finished all the things written concerning him, taking him down from the tree, they laid him in a tomb. But God raised him out of the dead.

RESPONSORY

We worship you, O Christ…

…and we praise you.

By your cross you have redeemed the world…

…and we praise you.

Glory to the Father and to the Son and to the Holy Spirit:

… We worship you, O Christ, and we praise you.

EASTER READING **ROMANS 10:8b-10**

The word is near you, in your mouth and in your heart; this is the word of faith we proclaim.

If you confess with your mouth that Jesus is Lord, and believe in your heart that God raised him from the dead, you will be saved, for with the heart one believes and is justified, and with the mouth one confesses and is saved.

RESPONSORY

The Lord is risen from the tomb…

…alleluia, alleluia.

He hung upon the cross for us…

…alleluia, alleluia.

Glory to the Father and to the Son and to the Holy Spirit:

…The Lord is risen from the tomb; alleluia, alleluia.

Gospel Canticle For Evening

Antiphons

Advent Wk 2	Blessed are you, O Virgin Mary, for great is your faith.
Advent Wk 4 18th	O Sacred Lord, who showed yourself to Moses in the burning bush, come and set us free.
Christmas	Christ is born; the Savior has appeared. Glory to God in the highest, alleluia.
Lent Wk 2	Tell no one what you have seen until the Son of Humanity rises from the dead.
Lent Wk 4	My son, you are with me always and all I have is yours. But we have to feast and rejoice, for your brother was dead and has come to life again; he was lost to us and now has been found.
Palm Sunday	Strike the shepherd and his flock shall be scattered. But when I have risen, I will go before you into Galilee. There you shall see me, says the Lord.
Easter Wk 4	My sheep will hear my voice and I will know them, alleluia.
Easter Wk 6	One who loves me will keep my word, alleluia.

Antiphons for Gospel Canticle For Evening, continued

Ordinary Time Antiphons — YEAR C

Responsorial

Wk 2	Proclaim the marvelous deeds of the Lord.	Ps 96
4	I will sing of your salvation.	Ps 71
6	Blessed are they who hope in the Lord.	Ps 1
8	Lord, it is good to give thanks to you.	Ps 92
10	I will praise you, Lord, who rescued me.	Ps30
12	My soul is thirsting for you, O Lord my God.	Ps63
14	Let all the earth cry out to God with joy.	Ps 66
16	One who does justice will live in the presence of the Lord.	Ps 15
18	If today you hear God's voice harden not your hearts.	Ps 90
20	Lord, come to my aid!	Ps 40
22	God, in your goodness, you have made a home for the poor.	Ps 68
24	I will rise and go to my Father. (Lk 15:18)	Ps 51
26	Praise the Lord, my soul!	Ps 146
28	The Lord has revealed to the nations the saving power of God.	Ps 98
30	The Lord hears the cry of the poor.	Ps 34
32	Lord when your glory appears my joy will be full.	Ps 17
34	Let us go rejoicing to the house of the Lord.	Ps 122

CANTICLE of MARY (The Magnificat)
LUKE 1:46-55

+ **My soul** is stretched full with praise of the Lord,
and my spirit, beyond joy in God, my Savior,
who chose to lay eyes on this humble servant.

Behold, now and forward,
each and every age will call me blessed,
for the Mighty One did great things to me.

Holy is the name and the mercy
to generations and generations,
the ones fearing the One,

Who scattered the haughty of mind and heart,
pulled the powerful off their high place,
and lifted with dignity the humble in need.

The hungering are filled with good things,
the rich are sent away empty,
and servant Israel is given relief

with a memory of mercy to remember,
the promise spoken to our ancestors,
to Abraham and his descendants forever.

Glory...

Antiphon

INTERCESSIONS

- For respect for conscience and religious freedom…
- For all who are not yet ready for this week…
- For those who have gone before us marked with the sign of faith…
- In gratitude for blessings…; Abba thank you.
- For the sins of this day…; Lord Jesus have mercy.
- With concerns over tomorrow…; Holy Spirit help.

AN EASTER PRAYER for VOCATIONS

Come, Holy Spirit,
fill the hearts of your faithful;
set fire in us your confirming love.
Give us wisdom to seek the face of God,
understanding of our baptism in Christ, and
right judgment to discern his call in freedom.
Give us courage to say yes to our vocations,
knowledge of what Jesus teaches,
and reverence for the ways of the Father.
Give us wonder and awe in your presence,
that the witness we give
to the resurrection of the Son
may be pleasing to the Father
and help you, Holy Spirit,
renew the face of the earth.

OUR FATHER…

WEEK II
MONDAY MORNING

\+ *God, come to my assistance;* Psalm 70:2
Lord, make haste to help me!

Glory…

ORDINARY TIME

A **I know that my Re/-deem-er\ lives;**
What com-fort this sweet sen-tence gives!
Liv-ing\ Proph/-et/, Priest\, and\ King;
Liv-ing and as he lives I'll sing.

He lives/ hun-gry/ souls to\ feed,
Liv-ing to help in time of need.
Liv-ing to grant/ us/ rich\ sup\-ply,
Liv-ing to guide us with his eye.

He lives/ qui-et/ing our\ fears,
Liv-ing to wipe a-way our tears,
Liv-ing to calm/ our/ troubl\-ed\ heart,
Liv-ing all bless-ings to im-part.

He lives/, glo-ry/ to his\ Name!
Liv-ing, my Je-sus, still the same.
Oh, sweet the joy/ this/ sen\-tence\ gives:
"I know that my Re-deem-er lives!"

93, Text: from Job 19:25-27, Samuel Medley, 1775, altered
Music: DUKE STREET, LM, John Hatton, 1793
Popular melody for: *From All That Dwells Below The Skies*

ORDINARY TIME

B **Our Fa-ther, all cre-a-ting,**
Whose wis-dom, love, and pow'r
First bound two lives to-geth-er
In E-den's pri-mal hour,
To all this day in marr-iage
Those ear-ly gifts re-new:
In homes by you made hap-py
In love by you kept true.

Lord, as with wine at Ca-na,
The wed-ding feast you blessed,
Let spouses know the pres-ence
Of you, their dear-est guest.
Their store of earth-ly glad-ness
Trans-form to heav'n-ly wine,
And teach them in their trust-ing
To know the gift div-ine.

O Spir-it of the Fa-ther
And Son, give them your breath,
And strength of heart in pa-tience,
Your ten-der love their wealth,
That, guard-ed by your pres-ence
And kept from strife with-in,
Their hearts may sense your guid-ance
And know you dwell with them.

ADVENT & LENT

A migh-ty for/-tress is\ our God,
The bul-wark nev-er fail\ \-ing;
Our help-er, God/, a-mid\ the flood
Of mor-tal ills pre-vail\ \-ing:
For still/ our an-cient\ foe
Does seek to work us woe;
His craft and pow'r are great,
And armed with cru-el hate,
On earth is not his e\ \-qual.

Do we in our/ own strength\ con-fide?
Our stri-ving would be los\ \-ing,
Were not the Sa/-vior on\ our side,
The Son of God's own choos\ \-ing:
You ask/ who that may\ be?
Christ Je-sus, it is he;
Lord Sab-a-oth, his name,
From age to age the same,
And he must win the bat\ \-tle.

76, Text: based on Ps. 46; Martin Luther, 1529;
translated by Frederick H. Hedge, d.1890, altered
Music: 87 87 66 66 7 EIN' FESTE BURG; Martin Luther, 1529

127, Text: John Ellerton, 1826-1893, altered significantly
Music: 76 76 D, AURELIA, Samuel S. Wesley, 1864
Popular melody for: *The Church's One Foundation*

CHRISTMAS

In his tem-ple come be-hold him,
See the long ex-pect-ed Lord;
An-cient proph-ets had fore-told him;
God has now ful-filled this word,
Now, to praise him, Al-le-lu-ia!
Break we forth with one ac-cord.

See him in the arms of Sim-eon,
Hear the grate-ful An-na's cry;
While these a-ged saints a-dore him,
See him with the vir-gin lie.
Al-le-lu-ia! Al-le-lu-ia!
Lo, th'in-car-nate God most high.

Je-sus, who in pres-en-ta-tion
Bless-ings giv-en by your poor,
Prince and au-thor of sal-va-tion,
Seal us with your prom-ise sure,
And pre-sent us in the Spir-it
To your Fa-ther cleansed and pure.

24, Text: based on Luke 2:22, the Presentation of the Lord;
Henry J. Pye, d.1903, and William Cooke, d.1894, altered
Music: 87 87 87 ST. THOMAS (TANTUM ERGO)
John F. Wade, d.1786
Popular melody for: *Down In Adoration Falling*

EASTER

Full East-er joy, the day was bright,
Sun shin-ing out/ with fair-er light,
When to their long-ing eyes re-stored,
His glad a-pos-tles saw their Lord.

He bade them see his hands, his side,
Where yet the glo/-rious wounds a-bide;
The to-kens true which made it plain
Their Lord in-deed was ris'n a-gain.

The Christ, the King of gen-tle-ness,
Now you, your-self/, our hearts pos-sess
That we may give you all our days
The trib-ute of our grate-ful praise.

63, Text: *Claro paschali gaudio,* 5th century unknown author,
tranlated by John M. Neale, 1851, 1861, altered
Music: PUER NOBIS NASCITUR, LM,
Trier manuscript 15th C., Michael Praetorius, 1609

Alternate Music: CONDITOR, LM; *Conditor Alme Siderum,*
Sarum plainsong, Mode IV
Popular melody for: *Creator of the Stars of Night*

PSALM 31:1-17,20-25

Antiphon *Everyone who hears my words and does them*
will be like a wise human
who built the house on rock. Mt 7:24

Christmas & Ester Lord, shine your faces on your servant, alleluia.

In you, Adonai, I take refuge;
let me never be shamed.
Deliver me in your justice.
Quickly turn to me your ear! Rescue me!

Be for me a rock of refuge,
a fortress house to save me.
Since you are my rock and my fortress,
for the sake of your name
you lead me and guide me.

You free me from the trap they set for me,
for you are my refuge.
Into your hands I commend my spirit;
you redeem me, Adonai God of truth.

I hate when humans cling to worthless idols,
and I trust in Adonai.
I will rejoice in your love and be glad
for you saw my affliction;
you knew the anguishes of my soul.

You do not put me into hands of enmity;
you set my feet in the spacious place.

Be merciful to me, Adonai, in my distress;
my eyes and my soul and my body
grow weak with sorrow.

My life is consumed by anguish
and my years with groaning.
My strength fails because of my guilt
and my bones grow weak.

Because of enmity I am
the utter contempt of even my neighbors
and a dread to my friends
who see me on the street and flee.

I am forgotten as though dead;
my heart became like broken pottery,
for I hear the slander of many
and terror on every side
when they conspire together against me
and plot to take my life.

But I trust in you, Adonai;
I say you are my God;
my times are in your hand.
Deliver me from the hands
of enmity and pursuers.

Shine your faces on your servant!
Save me in your unfailing love!...

Psalm 31, continued

How great is the goodness
you store up for ones who fear you
and bestow on those taking refuge in you
in the sight of the children of humanity.

You hide them in the shelter of your presence;
from human intrigues you keep them
in a dwelling safe from the strife of tongues.

Adonai is praised for showing wonderful love
to me in the city besieged, and I said in my alarm,
"I am cut off from before your eyes."
Yet you heard the sound of my cries for mercy
when I called to you for help.

Love Adonai, all you saints,
Adonai faithful and preserving,
but paying back in full the arrogant.

Be strong and strengthen your heart,
all you hoping in Adonai!

Glory...

Antiphon *Everyone who hears my words and does them*
will be like a wise human
who built the house on rock. Mt 7:24

Christmas & Ester Lord, shine your faces on your servant,
alleluia.

PSALM 73

Antiphon *Any of you who do not detach*
from all your possessions
cannot be my disciple. Lk 14:33

Christmas & Easter Surely, the God of Israel
is good to the pure of heart, alleluia.

Surely good to Israel is El,
to those pure of heart.
But my feet almost slipped,
as nearly lost were my footholds,
for I envied the arrogant
and the prosperity of doers of the bad.

None of them struggle with death
and healthy are their bodies.
Human burdens are not theirs,
nor human plagues.

And so pride wraps them as a necklace
clothing violence on them.
Their eyes bulge with fat;
their conceits pass the limits of the mind.

They scoff and they speak with malice
and threaten arrogant oppression.
Their mouths lay claim to the heavens,
and their tongues to possession of the earth.

Psalm 73, continued

And so people turn to them for themselves
as they drink all the waters of abundance.
They say, "How does El know?"
and, "Does the Most High know about this?"
See these doers of the bad:
even carefree of Always they increase their wealth.

Surely in vain have I kept my heart clean
and washed my hands in innocence.
But I am plagued all the day
and punished in the mornings.

If I said that I would speak as they do,
see the generation of your children I would betray!

My efforts to understand this
are oppressive to my eyes.
Until! I entered into sanctuaries of God
and understood about their final destiny.

Surely you place them on slippery ground
and cast them down to ruins.
How sudden is their destruction,
swept away complete by terrors.
As with a dream when waking up, Lord,
their fantasy you will despise when you arise.

When my heart was grieved,
and my spirits bitter
and senseless and unknowing,
I was but a brute beast before you.

Yet I am always with you;
you hold me by my right hand.
With your counsel you guide me
and will take me after the glory.

Who in the heavens is to me?
And with you, nothing on earth do I desire.
My flesh and my heart may fail,
but Elohim is the strength of my heart
and my portion to forever.

For see! Those far from you will perish...
But the nearness of Elohim is my good.
I have made you my refuge, Lord Adonai,
to tell of all your deeds.

Glory...

Antiphon *Any of you who do not detach*
from all your possessions
cannot be my disciple. Lk 14:33

Christmas & Easter Surely, the God of Israel
is good to the pure of heart,
alleluia.

If we had any
possessions, we
should need weapons
and laws to defend them.
Saint Francis of Assisi, d. 1221

PSALM 42

Antiphon *When the shepherd sends them forth*
and goes before them, the sheep follow
because they know this voice. Jn 10:4

Advent & Lent When can I go
and meet the face of God?

Holy Week Jesus said: deeply grieved is my soul;
stay and keep watch with me.

Christmas & Easter As a deer pines for flowing water
so my soul longs for you, my God,
alleluia.

As a deer breathes heavy for streams of water,
so my soul throbs for you, God.

My soul she thirsts for God, the living God.
When can I go and meet the faces of God?

My tears were food for me by day and by night,
while all day they said to me,
"Where is your God?"

These things I remember
as my soul pours out before me:
how I would go with the multitude
to lead them to the house of God
sounding shouts of joy and thanksgiving,
a festive throng!

Why are you downcast, my soul?
Why are you disturbed within me?
Put hope in God, whom I will yet praise,
the saving help and presence.

My God, within me my soul she is downcast.
For this I will remember you
from the land of Jordan and heights of Hermon,
from the Mount of Mizar:

Deep calls to deep in the roar of your waterfalls.
All your waves and breakers are swept over me.

By day Adonai directs love
and at night the song within me
is a prayer to the God of my life.

I say to El my Rock, "why do you forget me?
Why must I go about mourning,
oppressed by enmity?"

With mortal agony in my bones,
taunted by adversity,
while all day they say to me,
"Where is your God?"

Why are you downcast, my soul?
Why are you disturbed within me?
Put hope in God, whom I will yet praise,
my saving help and God.

Glory... Antiphon

SIRACH 36:1-6,13-22

Antiphon *The Lord hears the cry of the poor;*
blessed be the Lord. Ps 34

Advent & Lent: Show mercy, Lord,
to the people called by your name.

Christmas: All will know to the ends of the earth
that you, God, are eternal.

Holy Week: The principalities of this world
will be driven out.

Easter: Fill Zion with your praises, Lord,
and let your wonders be proclaimed,
alleluia.

Come to our aid, God of all;
let all the nations be in fear of you.
Raise your hand to the foreign nations,
that they may see your might.

As you have used us to show them your holiness,
so now use them to show us your glory.
They will know as we know
that there is no God but you.

Give new signs and work new wonders;
show the splendor of your right hand and arm…

Gather all the tribes of Jacob,
that they may inherit the land as at the beginning.
Show mercy to the people called by your name:
Israel, whom you named your firstborn.

Have pity on your holy city, Jerusalem,
the foundation for your throne.
Fill Zion with your majesty,
and your temple with your glory.

Give witness of your deeds of old;
fulfill the prophecies spoken in your name.
Reward those who have hoped in you,
and let your prophets be proven true.

Hear the prayers of your servants,
as you are good to your people.
Thus all will know to the ends of the earth
that you are God eternal.

Glory…

Antiphon

Perhaps
the basic sin in
the psalms is idolatry,
letting anything have priority
over God. Perhaps the clearest sign
that I am serving a lifeless idol is when
I am no longer able to hear the cry of the poor.

ISAIAH 42:10-16

Antiphon *I, your Lord,*
have called you for justice. Is 42:6a

Advent Sing a new song to the Lord,
praises to the ends of the earth.

Christmas Arise and sing for joy.

Lent Praise the Lord
from the ends of the earth.

Easter I will turn darkness into light
before them, alleluia.

Sing to Adonai a new song,
praise from the ends of the earth!

Ones going down to the sea and all in it,
and the islands, the ones living in them,
and the desert and its towns
and settlements where Kedar lives,
let them arise, let them sing for joy,

and the people of Sela
let them shout from the top of mountains.
Let them give to Adonai the glory
and proclaim praise in the islands.

Adonai will march out like the mighty human
and stir up zeal like a warrior,
and shouting and raising a cry
will triumph over enmity.

I was silent for a long time
and held back in quiet;
like a woman bearing a child,
I cry out and gasp and pant.

I will lay waste mountains and hills
letting all their vegetation dry up;
I will turn rivers into islands
and dry up pools.

I will lead blind ones by ways they did not know;
along paths they did not know I will guide them.
I will turn what is dark before them into light
and rough places into smooth.

These things I will do
and I will not forsake them.

Glory...

Antiphon

PSALM 19

Antiphon *The Samaritan did mercy to the beaten man;*
you go and do likewise. Lk 10:37

Christmas God has pitched a tent in our midst.

Holy Week Jesus endured the cross,
heedless of the shame, and is seated
at the right hand of the throne of God.

Easter The glory of God illumines the city
and the Lamb of God is its light, alleluia.

The heavens declare the glory of God,
and the sky proclaims the work of God's hands.
Day after day, speech pouring forth,
knowledge is on display night after night.

There is no speech, there is no language,
and no sound is heard.
Yet into all the earth their line goes out
and their words to the ends of the world.

There God has pitched a tent for the sun,
and like a bridegroom coming forth,
and like an athlete running the course, rejoices.

At the end of the heavens is the rising,
to their furthest ends is the circuit,
and nothing is hidden from its heat.

The law of Adonai is perfect, reviving the soul;
statutes of Adonai are trustworthy,
making wise of the simple;
precepts of Adonai are right ones,
giving joy of heart;

the command of Adonai is radiant,
giving light to eyes;
the fear of Adonai is pure, enduring to forever;
ordinances of Adonai are sure and altogether just;

more precious than gold,
much more than pure gold,
sweeter than honey,
the honey of honeycombs.

Your servant is warned by them;
to keep them is a great reward.
Who can discern errors?
From those hidden from me, forgive me!

And keep your servant from willful sins!
May they not control me;
then will I be blameless
and innocent of great transgression.

May the words of my mouth be as pleasing
and the meditation of my heart be as pleasing
before you, Adonai,
my Rock and my Redeemer.

Glory... Antiphon

PSALM 90

Antiphon *Be wary and on guard against all greed*
for life is not about possessions. Lk 12:15

Advent The Lord will come to rule over
the rulers of the earth;
blessed are they who are ready
to go and give welcome.

Lent Each morning, Lord,
you fill us with your kindness.

Christmas & Easter Let the splendor of the Lord our God
be upon us, alleluia.

You, Lord, you have been our refuge
from generation to generation.
Before the mountains were born,
before you brought forth earth,
from eternity to eternity, you are God.

You turn humans back to dust and say,
"Return, sons and daughters of humanity."
A thousand years in your eyes
are like the day yesterday that went by,
like one watch of the night.

You sweep humans into the sleep
like new grass in the morning that sprouts:
in the morning it springs up and sprouts
and then by the evening is withered and dry.

Indeed we can be consumed in your anger
and terrified by your indignation.
You set our iniquities before you,
our secrets in the light of your presences.

Indeed all our days pass away under your anger;
we finish our years like a sigh.
Our days last for seventy years
or eighty if given the strength.

The best part of them are trouble and sorrow,
passing quickly, and we fly away.
Who knows the power of your anger,
who fears your wrath?

Number our days aright;
teach, that we may gain hearts of wisdom.
How long, Adonai, until you relent?
Have compassion on your servants.

Satisfy our morning hunger
with your unfailing love
that we may sing for joy and be glad all our days.
Make us glad, equal to our affliction,
the years of trouble we have seen.

May your deeds be shown to your servants
and your splendor to their children.
May the favor of the Lord our God rest upon us
and the work of our hands be made good;
yes, make good the work of our hands.

Glory... Antiphon

ORDINARY TIME READING **JEREMIAH 15:16**

Your words came and I ate them, and your word was my joy and the delight of my heart, for your name, Adonai God Sabaoth, called to me.

RESPONSORY Ps 147:2

How good to sing praise to our God,...
...and give God the praise that is fitting.
How pleasant to sing a new song,...
...and give God the praise that is fitting.
Glory to the Father and to the Son and to the Holy Spirit:
...How good to sing praise to our God
and give God the praise that is fitting.

My Beloved,

I have made you in my image, one and unique,
not like anyone ever has been or ever will be made in my image.

Having made you, I know you,
all the great things your ego wants everyone to know,
those things you do not want anyone to know,
and everything you do not yet know yourself.

And in knowing you, I love you,
neither because of your strengths nor in spite of your weaknesses;
there is nothing you can do that will make me love you,
and there is nothing you can do that will keep me from loving you.

Remember this always: that I love you just is.
- God

See *A Jesus Breviary* and *31 Days of God's Love-Call*
by Stephen Joseph Wolf

ADVENT READING **ISAIAH 2:3-4**

Come, let us go up to the mountain of Adonai, to the house of the God of Jacob, who will teach us the ways so we may walk in the path. Indeed, from Zion the law will go out and from Jerusalem the word of Adonai, who will judge between the nations and settle disputes for many peoples.

They will beat their swords into plowshares and their spears into pruning hooks. Nations will not take up the sword against nations, and they will train for war no more.

RESPONSORY

Your light will come, Jerusalem…
…the Lord will dawn on you in radiant beauty.
The glory of the Lord you will see within you…
…the Lord will dawn on you in radiant beauty.
Glory to the Father and to the Son and to the Holy Spirit:
…Your light will come, Jerusalem;
the Lord will dawn on you in radiant beauty.

CHRISTMAS READING **ISAIAH 49:8-10**

This says Adonai: "In time of favor, I will answer you, and in the day of salvation I will help you. I will keep you and I will make you as a covenant of people to restore land to reassign desolate inheritances, to say to captives, 'Come out!' and to those in darkness, 'Be free!' They will feed beside roads, their pasture on every barren hill; they will not hunger, nor will they thirst, nor will the desert heat beat on them, nor the sun. One having compassion on them will guide them and beside springs of waters lead them."

RESPONSORY

The Lord has made known…
…alleluia, alleluia.
The saving power…
…alleluia, alleluia.
Glory to the Father and to the Son and to the Holy Spirit:
…The Lord has made known the saving power, alleluia.

After Epiphany

All the royal powers on earth
…will bow down in worship.
Men and women of every nation…
…will bow down in worship.
Glory to the Father and to the Son and to the Holy Spirit:
…All the royal powers on earth
will bow down in worship.

LENT READING, Weeks 2 & 4 **EXODUS 19:4-6a**

You saw what I did in Egypt, and I carried you on wings of eagles, and I brought you to myself, and now if to obey you obey my voice and you keep my covenant, then you will be my possession from all the nations, although all the earth is mine; and you will be for me a realm of priests, a holy nation.

RESPONSORY Lk 18:13

The Lord God will set me free…
…from the hunter's snare.
From all those who would trap me with lying words,
…and from the hunter's snare.
Glory to the Father and to the Son and to the Holy Spirit:
…The Lord God will set me free from the hunter's snare.

LENT READING, Holy Week **JEREMIAH 11:19-20**

Yet as a trusting lamb is led to slaughter, I did not know that they plotted plots against me to destroy the tree with its fruit and to cut me off from the land of the living so my name would be remembered no more.

But Adonai Sabaoth, just Judge, searcher of mind and heart, let me see your vengeance upon them, for to you I have entrusted my cause.

RESPONSORY Rev. 5:9

Lord, by your own blood…
…you brought us back to God.
From every tribe and tongue and people and nation...
…you brought us back to God.
Glory to the Father and to the Son and to the Holy Spirit:
…Lord, by your own blood you brought us back to God.

EASTER READING **ROMANS 10:8b-10**

The word is near you, in your mouth and in your heart; this is the word of faith we proclaim.

If you confess with your mouth that Jesus is Lord, and believe in your heart that God raised him from the dead, you will be saved, for with the heart one believes and is justified, and with the mouth one confesses and is saved.

RESPONSORY

The Lord is risen from the tomb…
…alleluia, alleluia.
He hung upon the cross for us…
…alleluia, alleluia.
Glory to the Father and to the Son and to the Holy Spirit:
…The Lord is risen from the tomb; alleluia, alleluia.

Gospel Canticle For Morning

Antiphons

Advent Wk 2 Luke 5:17-26	I am sending my angel before me to prepare the way for my coming.
Advent Wk 4 (see pg 759)	Like the sun in the morning sky, the Savior of the world will dawn, alleluia.
Christmas (see pg 759)	Helpless, he lay in a manger; glorious, he shined in the heavens. Humbled, he lived among humanity; eternal, he dwelt with the Abba.
After Epiphany Mt 4:12-17,23-25	The wise came from the East to adore the Lord in Bethlehem. Opening their treasures, they offered him three precious gifts: gold for the great Ruler, frankincense for the true God, and myrrh for his burial.
Lent Wk 2 Luke 6:36-38	Be compassionate and forgiving as your Abba is, says the Lord.
Lent Wk 4 John 4:43-54	A royal official, hearing that Jesus had come to Galilee, begged him to heal his son who lay ill in Capernaum.

Antiphons for Gospel Canticle For Morning, canticle

Holy Week John 12:1-11	Righteous Abba, the cosmos does not know you but I know you, for you are the One who sent me.
Easter Wk 2 John 3:1-8	Truly I tell you, unless you are born again, you cannot see the reign of God, alleluia.
Easter Wk 4 John 10:1-18	I am the Good Shepherd; I pasture my sheep and I lay down my life for them, alleluia.
Easter Wk 6 Jn 15:26-16:4a	Raising Jesus Christ from the dead God has given us a new birth to a living hope in the promise of an inheritance that will last forever, alleluia.
Ordinary Antiphon	*Blessed be the Lord our God.*

Gospel Reading for Monday of

Week	**2** Mark 2:18-22	**14** Matt 9:18-26	**26** Luke 9:46-50
	4 Mark 5:1-20	**16** Matt 12:38-42	**28** Lk 11:29-32
	6 Mark 8:11-13	**18** Matt 14:22-36	**30** Lk 13:10-17
	8 Mark 10:17-27	**20** Matt 19:16-22	**32** Luke 17:1-6
	10 Matt 5:1-12	**22** Luke 4:16-30	**34** Luke 21:1-4
	12 Matt 7:1-5	**24** Luke 7:1-10	

CANTICLE of ZECHARIAH (The Benedictus)
LUKE 1:68-79

+ **Blessed be** the Lord the God of Israel
who chose a people to visit with redemption,
and raised salvation in the house of David,
saving strength from God's own servant,

speaking from the age of the prophets
through the mouth of the holy prophet:
Salvation out of enmity,
even out of those who hate us,

to show our ancestors how mercy works, -
and to remember the holy promise of the Lord,
the covenant made for our ancestor Abraham,
calming our fear and making us free
to serve with holy justice before God all our days.

And you also child -
will be called a prophet of the Most High
for you will go before the Lord to prepare his way
and give to people a knowledge of salvation
known in accepting forgiveness of their sins.

From the tender mercy of our God,
the sun rising from the height will visit with light
for those who sit in the dark or shadow of death
and to guide our feet into the way of peace.

Glory...

Antiphon

PETITIONS FOR THE CONSECRATION TO GOD OF THE DAY AND ITS WORK

- For the Church and her ministry and apostolates…
- For secular authorities and all serving as stewards…
- For people who are poor or sick or in sorrow…
- For peace and the basic needs of each human being…
- For justice for migrant workers and refugees…
- For starving children awakening our conscience…
- For people living in subhuman conditions…
- For human beings enslaved or unjustly imprisoned…
- For laborers where treated as mere tools for profit…
- For good work for all to do in dignity…
- In gratitude for blessings and grace…
- For those who have asked for my prayer…
- For those for whom I have promised to pray…
- For those who weigh on my heart…

LORD TAKE ME — Mychal Judge, OFM

Lord, take me where you want me to go;
let me meet who you want me to meet;
tell me what you want me to say;
and keep me out of your way.

OUR FATHER…

WEEK II
MONDAY EVENING

\+ *God, come to my assistance;* Psalm 70:2
Lord, make haste to help me!

Glory…

EASTER

Ho-ly Feast, you ho-ly day!
To be hal-lowed ev-er-more,
Day when Christ our Lord was raised,
Break-ing down the reign of death.
Praise the Giv/-er of all good!
Con-cord Au-thor of all love,
Pour your balm on all our days;
To your peace guide all our ways.

Lo, fair beau-ty of the earth,
From the death of win-ter, rise!
With its Mas-ter now re-turns
Ev'-ry good gift of the year.
Ris-en from/ the grave, now Lord,
Au-thor of cre-a-ted life,
Tread-ing through the path of death,
New life to us all you give.

65, Text: Venantius Fortunatus, d. 609;
translated by Maurice F. Bell,
Hail Thee Festival Day , 1906, altered
Music: 77 77 D, SALZBURG; Jakob Hintze, 1678
Popular melody for: *Songs of Thankfulness and Praise*

ORDINARY TIME

I sing the\ migh-ty pow'r of God,
that made/ the moun-tains rise,
That spread the\ flow-ing seas a-broad,
and built/ the loft-y skies.
I/ sing the wis-dom that or/-dained
the/ sun to rule the day;
The moon shines\ full at God's com-mand,
and all/ the stars o-bey.

I sing the\ good-ness of the Lord,
who filled/ the earth with food,
Who formed the\ crea-tures through the Word,
and then/ pro-nounced them good.
Lord/, how your won-ders are dis/-played,
wher/-e'er I turn my eye,
If I sur\-vey the ground or tread,
or gaze/ up-on the sky.

There's not a\ plant or flow'r be-low,
but makes/ your glo-ries known,
And clouds a\-rise, and temp-ests blow,
by or/-der of your throne;
While/ all that bor-rows life from/ you
is/ ev-er in your care;
And ev-'ry\-where that we can be,
you, God/, are pres-ent there.

101, Text: Isaac Watts, *Divine and Moral Songs for Children,* 1715
Music: 76 76 D, ELLACOMBE; *Gesangbuch der Herzogl,* Wirtemberg, 1784

ADVENT & CHRISTMAS

Ho-ly\ Jo-seph/, you sa-lut-ing
Here we\ meet, with/ hearts sin-cere;
Bless-ed\ Jos-eph/, all u-nite and
Call on\ you to/ hear our prayer.

Refrain **Hap-py\ saint** in hea-ven a-dor-ing
Je-sus\, Sa-vior of the\ race,
Hear your\ fost-er/ sons and daugh-ters,
May we\ find with/ you our place.

You who\ faith-ful/-ly at-tend-ed
Him whom\ heav'n and/ earth a-dore;
Who with\ ten-der/ care de-fend-ed
Mar-y\, Vir-gin/ ev-er pure.
May our\ trust-ing voic-es\ lift-ing
Move you\ for our souls to\ pray;
May your\ smile of/ peace des-cend-ing,
Be-ne\-dic-tions/ on us lay.

Through this\ life, give/ watch a-round us!
Thank our\ Lord for/ ev-'ry breath,
And, when\ part-ing/ fear sur-rounds us,
Guide us\ e-ven/ through our death.

Refrain

137, Text: anonymous, altered significantly
Music: 87 87 D, PLEADING SAVIOR,
Joshua Leavitt, *Christian Lyre*, 1830
Popular melody for: *Sing of Mary, Pure and Lowly*

LENT

The Church's one foun-da-tion
Is Je-sus Christ, her Lord;
She is his new cre-a-tion
By wa-ter and the Word.
From heav'n he came and sought her
To be his ho-ly bride;
By blood re-deem-ing bought her,
And for her life he died.

E-lect from ev-'ry na-tion,
Yet one o'er all the earth,
Her char-ter of sal-va-tion
One Lord, one faith, one birth.
One ho-ly name she bless-es,
Par-takes one ho-ly food,
And to one hope she press-es,
With ev-'ry grace en-dued.

Though with a scorn-ful won-der
Some see her sore op-pressed,
By schis-ms rent a-sun-der,
By her-e-sies dis-tressed,
Yet saints their watch are keep-ing;
Their cry goes up, "How long?"
And soon the night of weep-ing
Shall be the morn of song.

126, Text: see Ephesians 2:20; Samuel J. Stone, 1866, altered
Music: 76 76 D, AURELIA, Samuel S. Wesley, 1864

PSALM 12

Antiphon *A cloud came overshadowing them*
and a voice came out of the cloud:
this is my Beloved Son; hear him. Mk 9:7

Christmas & Easter Alleluia, alleluia, alleluia.

Help, Adonai, for the godly are no more;
the faithful vanish from humanity's children.
They speak the lie to each of their neighbors,
lips flattering with a double heart.

May Adonai close all flattering lips
and tongues speaking the boast that say:
"With our tongues we will triumph,
our lips are our own; who is our master?"

But because of oppression of the weak,
because of groaning of the needy,
now Adonai says, "I will arise and protect them."

Words of Adonai are flawless words,
like silver refined in the furnace of clay,
and being purified seven times over.

You, Adonai, you will keep them safe;
you are our protection to forever.
But doers of the bad will still strut about
when vileness is honored among human beings.

Glory...

Antiphon

PSALM 40:2-14,17-18

Antiphon *I have come to throw fire on the earth*
and how I wish it was ablaze. Lk 12:49

Christmas & Easter Alleluia, alleluia, alleluia.

Waiting, I waited for Adonai,
who turned to me and heard my cry,

who lifted me from the slime pit
and from the muddy mire,
and set my feet on rock,
making firm my standing place,

and put in my mouth a new song,
a hymn of praise to our God.
Many will see and fear and trust Adonai.

Blessed is the one who trusts in Adonai
and looks not to the proud
or those turning to false "gods."

Adonai, my God, many are your deeds of wonder
and your plans cannot be equaled.
Should I speak and tell of them
they would be too many to declare.

Sacrifice and offerings you did not desire,
but my ears you keep open for me.
Burnt offering and sin offering you did not require.
Then I said, "Here, I have come;

in the scroll, in the book, it is written of me.
To do your will, my God, is my desire,
and your law is within my heart."

Your deed I proclaim in the great assembly.
See my lips unsealed; you, Adonai, you know!

I do not hide in my heart what you do;
your faithfulness and your salvation I speak.
I do not conceal your love and your truth
from the great assembly.

Adonai, withhold not your mercies from me,
may your love and your truth protect me always
for countless troubles surround around me.

My sins overtake me and I cannot see.
They are more than the hairs of my head
and my heart fails me.

Be pleased, Adonai, to save me;
Adonai, come quickly to help me!...

May all who seek you rejoice in you and be glad
and may lovers of your salvation say always,
"Let God be exalted."

Yet I am poor and needy.
May the Lord think of me and not delay,
my help and my deliverer, my God.

Glory...

Antiphon

PSALM 82

Antiphon *One is the lawgiver and judge,*
the one able to save and destroy;
who are you
to be judging your neighbor? James 4:12

Christmas & Easter Alleluia, alleluia, alleluia.

God Elohim, presiding in the assembly of El,
gives judgment among little "g" gods:

"Until when will you defend the unjust
and show partiality to the faces of bad doers?
Defend the weak and the orphans!
Maintain justice for the poor and oppressed!
Rescue the weak and the needy!
Deliver them from the hands of doers of the bad!"

They know nothing and they understand nothing.
They walk in darkness
and all the foundations of earth are shaken.

"I said, 'you are gods, all of you,
sons and daughters of Elyon Most High,'
but like all humans you too will die
and like other rulers you too will fall."

Rise up, Elohim, and judge the earth!
For to you belong all the nations!

Glory...

Antiphon

PSALM 120

Antiphon *The Son of Humanity*
did not come to be served
but to serve,
to give his life
in ransom for the many. Mk 10:45

Christmas
& Easter Alleluia, alleluia, alleluia.

In my distress I call on Adonai who answers me.
Adonai, save my self from lips of the lie
and from the deceitful tongue.

What will be done to you and what more
will be done to you, deceiful tongue?
Arrows of war made sharp
with coals of broom trees.

Woe to me, an alien in Meshech,
living among tents of Kedar.

Too long has my self lived
among haters of peace.
I am of peace, but when I speak
they are for war.

Glory…

Antiphon

PSALM 45

Antiphon *Rejoice on that day and leap for joy,*
for great is your reward in heaven. Lk 6:23

Holy Week He had no beauty or majesty
to attract our eyes.

My heart is stirred with a noble theme;
I recite my verses for the ruler;
my tongue is a pen of a skillful scribe.

You were anointed with grace on your lips,
more excellent among children of humanity.
For thus has God blessed you to forever.

Gird your sword upon your side, mighty one,
your splendor and your majesty.
Your majesty, be victorious!
Ride forth on behalf of truth and justice;
let your right hand display awesome deeds.

Your arrows are sharp;
let nations fall beneath you into the heart
of ones who choose enmity with the royal
on God's throne forever and ever.
The scepter of the realm is a scepter of justice.

You love justice
and hate when people do the bad;
for this your God anointed you
above your companions with oil of gladness, - -

with myrrh and aloes and cassia on your robes,
and from ivory palaces strings make you glad.

Children of royalty are honored among you
and the royal spouse stands at your right hand,
honored in gold of Ophir.

Listen, child, and consider!
Give your ear and forget your people
and the house of your parents.
The ruler enthralled for your beauty
is your lord, so give honor!
With the gift of your face, child of Tyre,
wealthy people will seek you.

The all-glorious offspring of the ruler
is in a gown with interweavings of gold,
led to the ruler in embroidered garments
with virgin companions following.
They are led in with joy and gladness;
they enter the royal palace.

In the place of your parents will your children be,
as royals through all the land.
I will make perpetual the memory of your name
through all generations and generation.
For this the nations will praise you
ever and to forever.

Glory…

Antiphon

PSALM 136

Antiphon *My food is that I may do the will*
of the one who sent me. Jn 4:34

Christmas & Easter Whoever is in Christ
is a new creature, alleluia.

Give thanks to Adonai who is good,
loving to forever.
Give thanks to the One who is El of the "els,"
loving to forever.
Give thanks to the One who is Lord of the lords,
loving to forever,

to the One who has alone done great wonders,
loving to forever,
who made the heavens by understanding,
loving to forever,
who spread out the earth upon the waters,
loving to forever,

who made the great lights,
loving to forever,
the sun to govern the day,
loving to forever,
the moon and stars to govern the night,
loving to forever,

who struck down Egypt in their firstborn,
loving to forever, - -

who brought Israel out from among them,
loving to forever,
with mighty hand and outstretched arm,
loving to forever,

who divided the Reed Sea in half,
loving to forever,
and brought Israel through its midst,
loving to forever,
but swept Pharoah and the army into the Reed Sea,
loving to forever,

who then led the people through the desert,
loving to forever,
who struck down great rulers, loving to forever,
and killed mighty rulers, loving to forever,

Sihon, king of the Amorites, loving to forever,
and Og, the king of Bashan, loving to forever,

who gave the land as an inheritance,
loving to forever,
an inheritance to servant Israel,
loving to forever,
who remembered us in our low estate,
loving to forever,

and freed us from enmity, loving to forever,
who gives food to every creature, loving to forever.
Give thanks to El of the heavens,
who indeed is loving to forever!

Glory... Antiphon

EPHESIANS 1:3-10

Antiphon *Come yourselves privately*
to a desert place
and rest a little. Mk 6:31

Advent & Lent God purposed in Christ
a stewardship of the fullness of times,
to head up all things in Christ.

Dec 17-23 Coming to earth,
will the Son of Humanity
find faith in human hearts?

Christmas Jesus grew in wisdom, age, and grace,
and was pleasing to God and humans.

Holy Week God has blessed us in Christ;
through him we have been redeemed.

Easter From the fullness of Christ
we have all received
grace upon grace,
alleluia.

Blessed be the God and Abba
of our Lord Jesus Christ,
who has blessed us in Christ
with every spiritual blessing in the heavens.

God chose us in Christ
before the foundation of the world,
to be holy and free of blemish before him.

In love, God gave us a destiny:
as parents adopt, through Jesus Christ himself,
in accord with the good pleasure of God's will
to the praise of the glory of grace
by which we are favored as God's beloved.

In Christ we have the redemption
through his blood, the forgiveness of sins,
in accord with the riches of his grace
which he made abound to us.

In all wisdom and intelligence
the mystery of God's will is made known to us
in accord with God's good pleasure and purpose:

A stewardship of the fullness of time,
heading up all things in Christ,
the things in the heavens and the things on earth.

Glory...

Antiphon

ORDINARY TIME READING **1 THESSALONIANS 2:13**

And so we give thanks to God unceasingly, that having received the word of God, hearing it from us, you welcomed it not as a word of humans but as it truly is, the word of God, which is at work in you who believe.

RESPONSORY Ps 141:2

When I call, Lord, hear my voice…
…which rises up to you.
Like incense set before you…
…which rises up to you.
Glory to the Father and to the Son and to the Holy Spirit:
…When I call, Lord, hear my voice
which rises up to you.

ADVENT READING **PHILIPPIANS 3:20b-21**

And we await a Savior, the Lord Jesus Christ, who will change the body of our humility, conforming it to the body of his glory, as it is his ability to subject even all things to himself.

RESPONSORY Ps 146:7; 63:3; 67:2

Come and set us free…
…Lord God of power and glory…
Let your face shine upon us
and we will know salvation…
…Lord God of power and glory…
Glory to the Father and to the Son and to the Holy Spirit:
…Come and set us free, Lord God of power and glory.

CHRISTMAS READING **COLOSSIANS 1:13-16**

The Father delivered us out of the authority of darkness, transitioning us into the reign of the beloved Son in whom we have redemption, the forgiveness of our sins. The Son is the image of the invisible God, the firstborn of all creation. In him all things were created, in the heavens and on the earth, the visible and the invisible, whether thrones, lordships, rulers or authorities. All creation has come to be through and for him.

RESPONSORY Jn 1:14

The Word became flesh…
…alleluia, alleluia.
And dwelt among us…
…alleluia, alleluia.
Glory to the Father and to the Son and to the Holy Spirit:
…The Word became flesh and dwelt among us,
alleluia, alleluia.

After Epiphany

All people will be blessed in him…
…in every tribe of the human race.
All nations will acclaim his glory…
…in every tribe of the human race.
Glory to the Father and to the Son and to the Holy Spirit:
…All people will be blessed in him,
in every tribe of the human race.

LENT READING, Weeks 2 & 4 **ROMANS 12:1-2**

I appeal to you, brothers and sisters, through the compassion of God, to present your bodies as a living sacrifice, holy and well-pleasing to God, your worship and reasonable service. Be not conformed to this age, but be transformed by the renewal of your mind, that what you do may prove to be the will of God, the good and well-pleasing and perfect.

RESPONSORY Lk 18:13

To you, O Lord…
…I make my prayer for mercy.
Heal my soul, for I have sinned against you…
…I make my prayer for mercy.
Glory to the Father and to the Son and to the Holy Spirit:
…To you, O Lord, I make my prayer for mercy.

LENT READING, Holy Week **ROMANS 5:6-10**

Us being weak, yet in accord with time on behalf of the impious, Christ died. Hardly will anyone die for a just person, though perhaps someone would dare die for a good person. But God commends God's own love for us in that while we were still sinners Christ died for us. Justified now by his blood, by much more through him shall we be saved from the anger. For if being enemies we were reconciled to God through the death of the Son of God, by much more having been reconciled we shall be saved by his life.

RESPONSORY Rev. 5:9

We worship you, O Christ…
…and we praise you.
By your cross you have redeemed the world…
…and we praise you.
Glory to the Father and to the Son and to the Holy Spirit:
…We worship you, O Christ, and we praise you.

EASTER READING **HEBREWS 8:1b-3a**

We have a high priest, who sat at the right of the throne of the greatness in the heavens, a minister of the holy things and of the true tabernacle, erected by the Lord, not by human beings. Every high priest is appointed to offer both gifts and sacrifices.

RESPONSORY

The disciples rejoiced…
…alleluia, alleluia.
When they saw the risen Lord…
…alleluia, alleluia.
Glory to the Father and to the Son and to the Holy Spirit:
…The disciples rejoiced, alleluia, alleluia.

Gospel Canticle For Evening

Antiphons

Advent Wk 2

See, your Ruler comes;
the master of the earth
will shatter the yoke of slavery.

Advent Wk 4
19th

O Flower of Jesse's stem, raised as
a sign for all peoples, come to our aid.

Christmas

O radiant child! You brought healing
to human life as you came forth from
the womb of Mary, your mother, like
a spouse from the marriage chamber.

After Epiphany

When they saw the star the Magi
they were filled with great joy;
entering the house, they offered
their gifts to the Lord:
gold, frankincense and myrrh.

Lent Wk 2

Do not judge others
and you will not be judged,
for as you have judged them
so God will judge you.

Lent Wk 4

The father realized that it was
at the very hour when Jesus had
told him: your son will live;
he and all his household
became believers.

Antiphons for Gospel Canticle For Evening, continued

Holy Week	As Moses lifted up the serpent in the desert, so is the Son of Humanity to be raised up so that all who believe in him may have eternal life.
Easter Wk 2	What is born of the flesh is flesh; what is born of the spirit is spirit; alleluia.
Easter Wk 4	I have other sheep that are not of this flock; these also I must lead. They will hear my voice, and there will be one fold and one shepherd, alleluia.
Easter Wk 6	The Spirit of truth who proceeds from the Abba will be my witness, and you will bear witness to me, alleluia.
Ordinary Antiphon	*My soul is stretched full* *with praise of the Lord.*

CANTICLE of MARY (The Magnificat)
LUKE 1:46-55

+ **My soul** is stretched full with praise of the Lord,
and my spirit, beyond joy in God, my Savior,
who chose to lay eyes on this humble servant.

Behold, now and forward,
each and every age will call me blessed,
for the Mighty One did great things to me.

Holy is the name and the mercy
to generations and generations,
the ones fearing the One,

Who scattered the haughty of mind and heart,
pulled the powerful off their high place,
and lifted with dignity the humble in need.

The hungering are filled with good things,
the rich are sent away empty,
and servant Israel is given relief

with a memory of mercy to remember,
the promise spoken to our ancestors,
to Abraham and his descendants forever.

Glory...

Antiphon

INTERCESSIONS

- Lord, keep married couples in love...
- Grow our youth in wisdom and grace...
- For respect for the dignity of the human person...
- For all who have died...

- In gratitude for blessings, Abba thank you...
- For the sins of this day, Lord Jesus have mercy...
- With concerns over tomorrow, Holy Spirit help...

RESTLESS HEART *Confessions,* Saint Augustine

To praise you, Lord,
is the desire of the human,
a little piece of your creation.
You stir us to take pleasure in praising you,
for you have made us for yourself,
and our heart is restless until it rests in you.

OUR FATHER...

WEEK II
TUESDAY MORNING

\+ *God, come to my assistance;* Psalm 70:2
Lord, make haste to help me!

Glory...

CHRISTMAS

A-way in a man-ger, no crib for a bed,
The lit-tle Lord Je-sus laid down his sweet head.
The stars in the sky\ looked down where he lay,
The lit-tle Lord Je-sus, a-sleep in the hay.

The cat-tle are low-ing, the Ba-by a-wakes,
But lit-tle Lord Je-sus, no cry-ing he makes;
I love you, Lord Je-sus, look down from the sky
And stay by my cra-dle till morn-ing is nigh.

Be near me, Lord Je-sus, I ask you to stay
Close by me for-ev-er, and love me, I pray;
Bless all the dear chil-dren in your ten-der care,
And fit us for heav-en to live with you there.

18, Text: verses 1-2, Anon.,
Little Children's Book for Schools and Families , ca.1885;
verse 3, John T. McFarland, d. 1913,
Gabriel's *Vineyard Songs*, 1892, altered
Music: 11 11 11 11 MUELLER, attributed
to James R. Murray, d. 1905

ORDINARY TIME

In/ Christ there is no/ East or West,
In him no South\ or/ North;
But/ one com-mu-nion of God's love
Through/-out/ the whole\ wide earth.

In/ Christ shall true hearts/ ev-'ry-where
Their high vo-ca\-tion/ find;
His/ ser-vice is the gold-en cord,
Close/ bind/-ing hu\-man-kind.

Join/ hands, then, mem-bers/ of the faith,
What-e'r your race\ may/ be!
Who/ serves my Fa-ther as his child
Is/ sure/-ly kin\ to me.

In/ Christ now meet both/ East and West,
In him meet South\ and/ North;
All/ souls of Christ are one in him
Through/-out/ the whole\ wide earth.

102, Text: see Galatians 3:8, William A. Dunkerley, 1908,
under the pseudonym of John Oxenham, altered
Music: MCKEE, CM; African American Spiritual,
arranged by Harry T. Burleigh, 1866-1949

ORDINARY TIME

additional verses to
In Christ There Is No East or West

In/ God's eye all are/ black and white,
All shades, pink, yell-ow and/ brown,
For to live, all sis-ters, bro-thers free,
Let our love for each fam-'ly a-stound.

Un-til ev-'ry-bo-dy/ matters to me
As much as my\ own/ tribe,
Un-til all the lives of our one race
Are/ cher-ished with-out\ div-ide,

Whe-ther Jew-ish, Chris-tian/, Mus-lim, Hin-du,
Bud-dhist, Sikh, Ba-hai or None,
Let us yet a-gree that dig-ni-ty
Is the birth-right of ev\-'ry-one.

102, Text: Stephen J. Wolf, 2022
Music: MCKEE, CM; African American Spiritual,
arranged by Harry T. Burleigh, 1866-1949

ADVENT

Proph-ets out/ of an-cient times\ to
Je-sus out of Naz\-a-reth
and his saints by the Ho-ly Spir\-it
tell the truth to peo-ple of wealth:
If we want to live by our Lord's\ Way
we will watch for the mar-gin-al-ized.
Their\ wel-fare\ is our\ best mea/-sure\ of
our o-be-dience to God's de-signs.

Judge with hum-ble and faith-ful jus\-tice
know-ing who is Judge of us all
for your Lord/ a-lone knows ev-'ry thought
in the heart of each of us all.
To each o-ther show kind com-pass\-ion
as to wid-ows and or-phans, the poor,
with\ the res-i-dent strang\-er
liv-ing in your midst;
keep your heart clean of self-ish store.

I was hung/-ry so you fed\ me,
thirst-y and you gave me to drink,
a-lien strang/-er and you wel-comed me,
nak-ed and you gave me to wear,
sick_ so\ you gave me tend-er care,
locked in pris-on, you vis-it-ed there;
when\ my peo-ple were griev-ing you
bur/-ied their dead;
Christ your King is for you pre-pared.

LENT & EASTER

What won-drous love is this,
O my soul, O my soul!
What won-drous love is this, O my soul!
What won-drous love is this
that caused the Lord\ of bliss
To bear the dread-ful curse for my soul, for my soul,
To bear the dread-ful curse for my soul.

To God and to the Lamb, I will sing, I will sing;
To God and to the Lamb, I will sing.
To God and to the Lamb who is the great\ "I Am"
While mil-lions join the theme I will sing, I will sing;
While mil-lions join the theme, I will sing.

And when from death I'm free I'll sing on, I'll sing on
And when from death I'm free, I'll sing on.
And when from death I'm free,
I'll sing and joy\-ful be;
And through e-ter-ni-ty, I'll sing on, I'll sing on;
And through e-ter-ni-ty, I'll sing on.

134, Text: attributed to Alexander Means, first appeared in 1811
Music: 12 9 12 12 9, WONDROUS LOVE; adapt. by William Walker, *The Southern Harmony and Musical Companion*, 1835

113, Text: Zechariah 7:9-10 & Matthew 25, Stephen J. Wolf, 2017, tribute to the priesthood of Michael Johnston
Music: 87 87 D, HYFRYDOL, Rowland H. Prichard, 1811-1887
Popular melody for: *Love Divine All Love Excelling*

PSALM 37

Antiphon *There is nothing entering from outside that can defile a human; rather things that defile come from within.* Mk 7:15

Christmas & Easter The meek will inherit the land
and enjoy peace, alleluia.

Fret not over those who do the bad;
envy not those who do wrong.
For like grass their efforts will soon wither,
and like the green plant they wilt away.

Trust in Adonai and do good!
Dwell in the land and enjoy safe pasture!
Delight in Adonai
who will give the desires of your heart.

Commit your way and your trust
to Adonai who will do it:
making your integrity shine like the dawn
and your justice like the noonday sun.

Be still before Adonai and wait with patience.
Fret not over the ways of the successful,
over schemes carried out by human beings.

Refrain from anger and turn from wrath!
Fret not; it brings only the bad,
for humans doing the bad will be cut off;
those who hope in Adonai will inherit the land.

A little while and bad doings will be no more;
you will look and not find them in their places.
But the meek will inherit the land
and they will enjoy greatness of peace.

Plotters of bad things to do to the just
gnash their teeth at them.
But the Lord laughs at them,
knowing their day is coming.

They draw their sword and bend their bow
to bring down the poor and the needy,
to slay those of the honest way.
Their sword will pierce into their own heart
and their bows will be broken.

Better the little bit of the just
than the wealth of many who do the bad,
for the powers of bad doers will be broken
while Adonai upholds the just.

Adonai knows the days of the blameless
and their inheritance will endure to forever.
They will not wither in times of disaster
and in days of famine they will enjoy plenty.

But bad ways will perish
and those who choose enmity with Adonai
will vanish like the beauty of fields;
like smoke they will vanish.

Psalm 37, continued

A doer of the bad borrows and does not repay,
but the just are generous and giving.
Their blessing is to live in the land;
but the curse of doing the bad is to be cut off.

The steps of human beings are made firm
by Adonai who delights in their way.
Though we stumble, we will not fall
for Adonai upholds us by the hand.

I was young and now I am old,
yet never have I seen the just forsaken
or their children begging bread.
Generous and lending all the day,
their children are a blessing.

Turn from the bad and do the good!
Then live to always!
For Adonai loves justice
and will not forsake the faithful…
The just will inherit the land
and they will dwell in her to forever.

The mouth of the just he utters wisdom
and the tongue she speaks justice.
The law of their God is in their heart
and their feet do not slip.

Bad ways lie in wait for the just,
seeking to kill them;
Adonai will not leave them under this power
nor let them be condemned when on trial.

Wait for Adonai and keep to the way
of the one who will exalt you to possess the land,
and you will see bad ways cut off.

I saw a ruthless human flourishing
like a native green tree,
but passing away is seen no more;
though I looked he was not to be found.

Consider the honest and observe the upright
for the future is for the person of peace.
But sinners sinning will be destroyed together;
the future of bad ways will be cut off.

The salvation of the just is from Adonai,
their stronghold in times of trouble.
Their help and deliverance and salvation,
their deliverance from ways that are bad,
is Adonai in whom they take refuge.

Glory...

Antiphon *There is nothing entering from outside*
that can defile a human;
rather things that defile
come from within. Mk 7:15

Christmas & Easter The meek will inherit the land
and enjoy peace, alleluia.

PSALM 102

Antiphon *Whoever is not against you*
is for you. Lk 9:50

Christmas & Easter Lord, let my cry for help come to you;
hide not your face,
alleluia.

Adonai, hear my prayer
and let my cry for help come to you.
Hide not your faces from me
on the day of my distress.
Turn your ear to me on the day I call!
Quickly! Answer me!

My days vanish like smoke
and my bones burn like a glowing ember.
My heart is blighted like the grass
and so withered that I forget to eat my food.
Because of my loud groaning
my bones cling to my skin.

I am like a desert owl;
like an owl of the ruins lying awake,
I became like a bird alone on the housetop.
Enmity taunts me all the day,
railing against me, cursing by me.

I eat ash as food and mingle my drink with tears
because of your anger and your wrath,
for you took me up and threw me aside.
My days are like the long shadow,
and like the grass I wither away.

But you, Adonai, sit enthroned to forever;
your renown is to generation and generation.
You will arise.
You will have compassion on Zion,
for the time to show favor to her,
the appointed time, has come,
for her stones are dear to your servants
and her dust moves them to pity.

The nations will fear your name, Adonai,
and all the rulers of the earth your glory.
Adonai will rebuild Zion and appear in glory
and respond to the prayers of the destitute
and not despise their plea.

Let this be written for future generations
that people yet to be created may praise Yah.
Adonai looked down
from the high sanctuary place
viewing from heavens to earth,
to hear the groans of prisoners
and release those doomed to death

Psalm 102, continued

Declare in Zion the name of Adonai
and give praise in Jerusalem
when peoples assemble together,
and nations, to give worship.

Adonai broke my strength in mid-course
and cut short my days, and I said, "My El,
take me not away in the midst of my days.
Your years are through generation of generations.

In the beginning you founded the earth
and the heavens, the work of your hands.
They will perish, but you remain;
they will all wear out like a garment;
like clothing you will change them
and they will be discarded.

But you: the same; your years will never end.
Children of your servants will live
and their descendants
will be established before you."

Glory...

Antiphon *Whoever is not against you*
is for you. Lk 9:50

Christmas & Easter Lord, let my cry for help come to you;
hide not your face,
alleluia.

PSALM 43

Antiphon *Blessed are those mourning,*
for they will be comforted. Mt 5:4

Holy Week Lord, rescue me from deceit.

Christmas & Easter You have come to Mount Zion,
the city of the living God, alleluia.

God, vindicate me;
plead my cause against an ungodly nation;
rescue me from humans deceitful doing the bad.

God, my strength, why am I rejected?
Why must I go about mourning,
oppressed by enmity?

Send forth your light and your fidelity;
let them guide me to your dwellings
and bring me to your holy mountain.

Then I will go to the altar of God,
to El, my joy and delight,
and I will praise you with harp, God, my God.

Why are you downcast, my soul?
Why are you disturbed within me?
Put hope in God, whom I will yet praise,
the saving help of my face, my God.

Glory... Antiphon

PSALM 101

Antiphon *A great prophet is risen among us,*
and God has visited the people of God. Lk 7:16

Christmas God has visited the people of God,
alleluia.

Easter Whoever does the will of my Abba
will enter the reign of heaven,
alleluia.

What the prophet
does is not so much predict
the future as to so accurately describe
the present that it becomes clear what is going
to happen unless we change our collective ways.

I will sing of *hesed* love and justice;
to you, Adonai, I will sing praise.
I will take care to act with integrity in life.
When will you come to me?

I will walk with integrity of heart
in the midst of my house.
I hate and will not set before my eyes
vile things that faithless people do;
they will not cling to me.

The corrupt heart will be far from me;
I will know nothing of the bad.
I will silence the secret slandering of a neighbor;
haughty eyes and proud hearts I will not endure.

My eyes are on the faithful of the land,
to dwell with me;
one who walks in a way of integrity
can be in my service.

Anyone practicing deceit
will not dwell in the midst of my house;
nor will one speaking falsehoods
stand before my eyes.

Each morning I will silence bad doers in the land
to cut off doings of bad things
from the city of Adonai.

Glory…

Antiphon

ISAIAH 38:10-14,17b-20

Antiphon *The living alive praise Adonai.*

Holy Week Lord, you defended my cause
and ransomed my life.

Christmas & Easter Lord, you have kept my life
from destruction, alleluia.

I asked, "Must I go in the prime of my days
through the gates of Sheol;
must I be robbed of the rest of my years?"

I said, "I will no longer see Adonai,
Adonai in the land of the living.
As a dweller of the place of cessation
I will look on humanity no longer."

My house was pulled down
and taken from me
like the tent of my shepherd;
I rolled up my life,
as a weaver cuts off from a loom.

From day to night you made an end of me.
I waited till dawn;
all my bones are broken as by a lion.
From day to night you made an end of me.

Like a swift or thrush I cried;
I moaned like the dove.
My eyes to the heavens grew weak.
Lord, troubles are at me; come to my aid…

In your love you have kept my self
out of the pit of destruction;
indeed you put behind your back all my sins.

Sheol cannot praise you
and death cannot sing to you praise,
nor can those going down the pit
hope for your faithfulness.

The living alive praise you, as I do this day.
Fathers and mothers tell the children
all about your faithfulness.

Adonai saves us;
we will play our stringed instruments
and sing in the temple of Adonai
all the days of our lives.

Glory… Antiphon

For the Christian, Easter makes all the difference, and Easter is not just about our earthly death. By the time we get to heaven, we will have let go of everything unhealed about us, mainly through forgiving enemies, family, friends, ourselves, even God. Jesus is inviting us to the extent made possible by grace to live right now today as if all this has happened, to be fully alive right now.

DANIEL 3:26-27,29,34-41b

Antiphon *Lord, do not withhold your mercy.*

Dec. 17-23 Zion is our mighty citadel;
throw open the gates,
for our God is here among us,
alleluia.

Christmas & Easter Let all the nations, O Lord,
know the depths of your mercy,
alleluia.

Blessed be you, Lord, God of our ancestors,
your name worthy of praise and glory forever.

For you are just in all you do;
all your deeds are true and your ways upright,
and all your judgments are true…

We have sinned and broken your law
in turning from you;
in all ways possible we have sinned...

For the sake of your name,
do not give us up to forever
and do not void your covenant.

Do not take your mercy from us
for the sake of Abraham your beloved,
for the sake of Isaac your servant,
and Israel, your holy one,

to whom you promised to multiply
descendants like the stars of heaven
and like the sand on the shore of the sea.

For we, Lord, have become
least of the other nations
and are brought low in the world this day
because of our sins.

We have in our day no ruler, prophet, or leader,
no burnt offering, sacrifice, oblation or incense,
no place to make an offering before you
and so find your favor.

But with a contrite heart and a humble spirit
may we be accepted
as if they were burnt offerings of rams and bulls
or thousands of fat lambs.

As such may our sacrifice be seen by you today
and may we follow you without reserve,
for no shame will come to those who trust you.

And so we follow you with all our heart;
we fear you and seek your face.

Glory... Antiphon

Let nothing trouble. Let nothing frighten.
Everything passes. God never changes. Patience obtains.
Whoever has God wants for nothing. God alone is enough.

Saint Teresa of Avila, d. 1582, written in the margin of her breviary

PSALM 65

Antiphon *And that sown on the good soil*
is the one hearing
and understanding the word,
who indeed bears fruit. Mt 13:23

Holy Week The servant, the Just One,
will justify many.

Christmas & Easter You care for the earth
and water her for a rich abundance,
alleluia.

For you, O God, praise we owe in Zion,
and to you will our vow be fulfilled.

You hear our prayer.
To you all humanity will come.
When my sins overwhelm me
you forgive them.

Blessed are the ones you choose
and bring near to live in your courts.
We are filled with the goodness of your house
and the holiness of your temple.

Deeds awesome and just are your answer,
God of our salvation,
hope of all the ends of the earth
and of the far seas.

You form mountains by your power,
arming yourself with strength.
You still the roar of the seas,
the roar of their waves,
and the turmoil of nations.

Those who live in far away places
fear your wonders;
in dawns of morning and in the evening
you call forth songs of joy.

You care for the land and water her;
with an abundance you enrich her.
God's stream is as you ordain the earth:
filled with waters, providing grain.
You drench its furrows and level its ridges;
you soften her with showers and bless the crops.

You crown the year with your bounty;
paths overflow with your abundance.
The desert grasslands are overflowing
and the hills are clothed with gladness.

The meadows are covered with the flock
and valleys are coated with grain.
They shout for joy; for joy they sing.

Glory… Antiphon

My book, sir philosopher, is the nature of created things,
and it is always at hand when I wish to read the words of God.

Anthony of Egypt, see *Praktikos* (#92) by Evagrius Ponticus

ORDINARY TIME READING **1 THESS 5:1-11**

Concerning the times and the seasons, brothers and sisters, you have no need to be written, for you know correctly that the day of the Lord comes as a thief in the night. Whenever they say, "peace and safety," then sudden destruction comes on them as the birth pang to a pregnant woman, and by no means may they escape. But you, brothers and sisters, are not in the darkness that the day should overtake you as a thief.

For all of you are children of light and children of the day. We are not of the night nor of darkness. And so let us not sleep as the rest, but let us watch and be sober. For those sleeping by night sleep, and those being drunk by night are drunk. But being of the day, let us be sober, putting on a breastplate of faith and of love and a helmet of hope in salvation because God did not appoint us to wrath but to come to salvation through our Lord Jesus Christ, the one who died for us, in order that whether we watch or we sleep, together with him we may live. And so, comfort one another and edify one another, as indeed you do.

RESPONSORY Ps 119:147

Lord, hear my voice,...

...my hope is in your word and promise.

Awake in the watch for dawn I cry for help,...

...my hope is in your word and promise.

Glory to the Father and to the Son and to the Holy Spirit:

...Lord, hear my voice; my hope is in your word and promise.

ADVENT READING **GENESIS 49:8-10**

You, Judah, will your brothers praise; your hand on the neck of enmity, the sons of your father will bow to you. Judah, lion cub, my son, you return from prey crouching, lying like a lion and like a lioness, whom no one would dare rouse. The scepter will not depart from Judah nor the ruling staff from between his feet until when he comes, the one to whom is due the obedience of the peoples.

RESPONSORY

Your light will come, Jerusalem…
…the Lord will dawn on you in radiant beauty.
The glory of the Lord you will see within you…
…the Lord will dawn on you in radiant beauty.
Glory to the Father and to the Son and to the Holy Spirit:
…Your light will come, Jerusalem;
the Lord will dawn on you in radiant beauty.

CHRISTMAS READING **ISAIAH 62:11-12**

"See," Adonai proclaimed to the end of the earth, "Say to the Daughter of Zion, 'See your salvation coming! See his reward with him, his recompense in his company!' " They will be called the Holy People and the Redeemed of Adonai, and you will be called One-Being-Sought and the City-Not-Deserted.

RESPONSORY

The Lord has made known...
...alleluia, alleluia.
The saving power...
...alleluia, alleluia.
Glory to the Father and to the Son and to the Holy Spirit:
...The Lord has made known the saving power, alleluia.

After Epiphany

All the royal powers on earth
...will bow down in worship.
Men and women of every nation...
...will bow down in worship.
Glory to the Father and to the Son and to the Holy Spirit:
...All the royal powers on earth
will bow down in worship.

LENT READING, Weeks 2 & 4 **JOEL 2:12-13**

Even now, declares Adonai, return to me with all your heart and with fasting and weeping and mourning! Rend now your heart, not your garments, and return to your God Adonai, gracious and compassionate, slow of angers and abundant of love and relenting from the calamity.

RESPONSORY Lk 18:13

The Lord God will set me free…
…from the hunter's snare.
From all those who would trap me with lying words,
…and from the hunter's snare.
Glory to the Father and to the Son and to the Holy Spirit:
…The Lord God will set me free from the hunter's snare.

LENT READING, Holy Week **ZECHARIAH 12:10-11a**

I will pour out on the house of David and on the one living in Jerusalem a spirit of grace and supplications and they will look on me whom they pierced and they will mourn as one mourns for an only child and grieve bitterly as one grieves for the firstborn. On that day the weeping in Jerusalem will be great.

RESPONSORY Rev. 5:9

Lord, by your own blood…
…you brought us back to God.
From every tribe and tongue and people and nation...
…you brought us back to God.
Glory to the Father and to the Son and to the Holy Spirit:
…Lord, by your own blood you brought us back to God.

EASTER READING **ACTS 13:30-33**

God raised out of the dead Jesus, who appeared over many days to the ones who came up with him from Galilee to Jerusalem, who are now his witnesses to the people. And we evangelize to you what was promised to our ancestors, that God has fulfilled to their children this promise, raising up Jesus, as also it is written in the second psalm: *You are my Son; today I have begotten you.*

RESPONSORY

The Lord is risen from the tomb…
…alleluia, alleluia.
He hung upon the cross for us…
…alleluia, alleluia.
Glory to the Father and to the Son and to the Holy Spirit:
…The Lord is risen from the tomb, alleluia, alleluia.

Gospel Canticle For Morning

Antiphons

Advent Wk 2 Matt 18:12-14	Rejoice and be glad, O daughter of Zion; I will come and make my dwelling in you, says the Lord.
Advent Wk 4 (see pg 759)	The angel Gabriel was sent to Mary, who was engaged to Joseph.
Christmas (see pg 759)	The Word became flesh, full of grace and truth, and lived among us; from this fullness we have all received gift upon gift of love, alleluia.
After Epiphany Mark 6:34-44	The wise ones offered gifts of gold, frankincense, and myrrh to the Lord, the Son of God and Ruler Most High, alleluia.
Lent Wk 2 Matt 23:1-12	You have one teacher, and he is in heaven: Christ your Lord.
Lent Wk 4 John 5:1-16	The man who cured me told me to pick up my sleeping mat and go in peace.

Antiphons for Gospel Canticle For Morning, continued

Holy Week Jn 13:21-33,36-38	Abba, give me the glory that I had with you before the world was made.
Easter Wk 2 John 3:7b-15	I am the Alpha and the Omega, the first and the last, the beginning and the end; I am the root and offspring of David's race; I am the splendor of the morning star, alleluia.
Easter Wk 4 John 10:22-30	The works that I do in the name of the Abba speak on my behalf, alleluia.
Easter Wk 6 John 16:5-11	In a little while the world will no longer see me but you will see me for I live and you will live, alleluia.

Ordinary
Antiphon *God raised salvation in the house of David.*

Gospel Reading for Tuesday of

Week	**2**	Mark 2:23-28	**14**	Matt 9:32-38	**26**	Luke 9:51-56
	4	Mark 5:21-30	**16**	Matt 12:46-50	**28**	Lk 11:37-41
	6	Mark 8:14-21	**18**	Mt 15:1-2,10-14	**30**	Lk 13:18-21
	8	Mark 10:28-31	**20**	Matt 19:23-30	**32**	Luke 17:7-10
	10	Matt 5:13-16	**22**	Luke 4:31-37	**34**	Luke 21:5-11
	12	Matt 7:6,12-14	**24**	Luke 7:11-17		

CANTICLE of ZECHARIAH (The Benedictus)
LUKE 1:68-79

+ **Blessed be** the Lord the God of Israel
who chose a people to visit with redemption,
and raised salvation in the house of David,
saving strength from God's own servant,

speaking from the age of the prophets
through the mouth of the holy prophet:
Salvation out of enmity,
even out of those who hate us,

to show our ancestors how mercy works, -
and to remember the holy promise of the Lord,
the covenant made for our ancestor Abraham,
calming our fear and making us free
to serve with holy justice before God all our days.

And you also child -
will be called a prophet of the Most High
for you will go before the Lord to prepare his way
and give to people a knowledge of salvation
known in accepting forgiveness of their sins.

From the tender mercy of our God,
the sun rising from the height will visit with light
for those who sit in the dark or shadow of death
and to guide our feet into the way of peace.

Glory...

Antiphon

PETITIONS FOR THE CONSECRATION
OF THE DAY AND ITS WORK

- For the Church and her ministry and apostolates...
- For secular authorities and all serving as stewards...
- For people who are poor or sick or in sorrow...
- For peace and the basic needs of each human being...
- For those who weigh on my heart...

A FRANCISCAN BLESSING

adapted from a blessing
by Sr. Ruth Fox, OSB

Bless us, O Lord, with discontent
at easy answers, half-truths, and superficiality,
that we may live out of the depths of our hearts.
Bless us, O Lord, with anger
at injustice, oppression, and exploitation of people,
that we may work for justice, freedom and peace.
Bless us, O Lord, with tears to shed
for those who suffer from pain, rejection,
starvation, and war,
that we may reach out
hands of Christ that bring comfort.
And bless us, O Lord, with enough foolishness
to believe that your way makes all the difference
so that your desire may be fulfilled.

OUR FATHER...

WEEK II
TUESDAY EVENING

\+ *God, come to my assistance;* Psalm 70:2
Lord, make haste to help me!

Glory...

ORDINARY TIME

How love-ly is_ your dwell-ing place,
O Lord of hosts_! Be-lov-ed\ Lord!
My soul does yearn_ for the liv-ing God.
Bod-y and soul_ cry out, "my God!"

The spar-row finds_ a home to rest,
The swal-low too_ a set-tled\ nest,
The mock-ing-bird_ her\ place to sing:
"My home is with_ my God and King!"

Pass-ing through val_-leys, hills and springs
And pools of wa_-ter for the\ lost;
Hap-py in ref_-uge\ pil-grims bring
Good news of God_, our Lord and King.

99 (first three verses), Text: Psalm 84, by Stephen J. Wolf, 2007,
tribute to Thomas Merton
Music: O WALY WALY, LM; traditional English
Popular melody for: *As The Deer Longs For Flowing Streams*

ADVENT

O Lord of life, to you\ we/ lift
our hearts in\ praise for those,
Your proph-ets who have shown\ your/ gift
of grace that\ ev-er grows,
Of/ mer-cy spread\ from\ shore/ to/ shore,
of wis-dom's wide-ning ray,
Of light that shines forth more\ and/ more
un-to your\ pro-mised day.

Shine forth, O Light, that we\ may/ see,
with hearts made\ un-a-fraid,
The mean-ing and the mys\-te/-ry
of all that\ you have made:
O/ Light of light\! with\-in/ us/ dwell,
through us your ra-diance pour;
Your truth be told in words\ and/ lives
that praise you\ ev-er-more.

118, Text: Washington Gladden, 1897, altered
Music marked: 86 86 86 86 FOREST GREEN,
traditional English melody,
harmony by Ralph Vaughan Williams, 1906
Popular melody used by James Quinn, SJ, in 1969
for Morning Prayer: *Blessed Be The God of Israel*
Alternate music: KINGSFOLD, CMD, trad. English melody,
adapted by Williamsm 1906
Popular melody for: *I Heard The Voice of Jesus Say*

34, Text: Traditional English Carol,
17th C., possibly 13th C.;Music: Irregular

CHRISTMAS

The\ first/ No/-el, the/ an-gel did say,
Was to cer-tain poor s hep-herds in fields as they lay;
In\ fields/ where/ they lay/ keep-ing their sheep,
On a cold win-ter's night/ that was\ so deep.

Refrain **No\-el/, No/-el, No\-el, No-el,**
Born is the King/ of Is\-ra-el.

They\ look/-ed/ up and/ saw\ a star
Shin-ing in\ the east/, be-yond\ them far,
And\ to/ the/ earth it/ gave\ great light,
And/ so it con-tin-ued both day\ and night. *Refrain*

And\ by/ the/ light of/ that\ same star
Three/ ma\-gi came/ from coun\-try far;
To\ s eek/ for a king was/ their\ in-tent,
And to fol-low the star/ wher-ev-er it went. *Refrain*

This\ star/ drew/ nigh to/ the\ north-west,
O'er Beth\-le-hem/ it took\ its rest;
And\ there/ it/ did both/ stop\ and stay,
Right/ o-ver the place/ where Je\-sus lay. *Refrain*

Then\ en/-tered/ in those/ ma\-gi three,
Full/ rev\-'rent-ly/ up-on\ their knee,
And\ off/-ered/ there , in his pres\ \-ence,
Their/ gold\ and myrrh/ and frank\-in-cense. *Refrain*

Then\ let/ us/ all with/ one\ ac-cord
Sing/ prais\-es to/ our heav\-'nly Lord;
Who\ with/ the/ Fa- ther/ we\ a-dore
And/ Spir\-it blest/ for ev\-er more. *Refrain*

LENT & EASTER

Be still, my soul, the Lord is at your side/!
Bear pa-tient-ly the cross of grief or pain;
Leave to your God to or-der and pro-vide/
In ev-'ry change, who faith-ful will re-main.
Be still, my soul, your best, your heav'n-ly friend/
Through thorn-y ways leads to a joy-ful end.

Be still, my soul, your God does un-der-take/
To guide the fu-ture as God has the past;
Your hope, your con-fi-dence let noth-ing shake/
All now mys-te-rious shall be bright at last.
Be still, my soul, the waves and winds still know/
His voice who ruled while dwell-ing here be-low.

Be still, my soul, the hour is has-t'ning on/
When we shall be for-ev-er with the Lord,
When dis-ap-point-ment, grief, and fear are gone/,
Sor-row for-got, love's pur-est joys re-stored.
Be still, my soul, when change and tears are past/,
All safe and bless-ed we shall meet at last.

135, Text: Katherina von Schlegel;
in *Neue Sammlung Geistlicher Lieder*, 1752;
translated by Jane Borthwick, 1813-1897
Music: 10 10 10 10 10 10 FINLANDIA; Jean Sibleius, 1865-1957

PSALM 13

Antiphon *Emmanuel!*
God is with us! Mt 1:23

Advent & Christmas Emmanuel! God is with us!

Lent My heart rejoices, Lord,
in your salvation.

Easter Alleluia, alleluia, alleluia.

Until when, Adonai?
Will you forget me to forever?
Until when will you hide your faces from me?
Until when must I wrestle
with thoughts of my soul
and sorrow in my heart by day?
Until when will enmity triumph?

Look! Answer me, my God Adonai!
Give light to my eyes, or I will sleep the death!
Or enmity will say, "I overcame that one,"
and foes will rejoice when I fall.

But my trust is in your unfailing love;
my heart rejoices in your salvation.
I will sing to Adonai, who is good to me.

Glory…

Antiphon

PSALM 53

Antiphon *Whoever does not receive the reign of God as a child by no means may enter into it.* Mk 10:15

Christmas & Easter Alleluia, alleluia, alleluia.

In the heart of a fool is said, "There is no God."
The bad way is vile and corrupt;
there is no one doing good.

God looks from the heavens
on children of humanity
to see if there is one who understands,
one who is seeking God.

All of them turned away together;
they became corrupt;
there is no one doing good, not even one.

Will the ones doing the bad never learn?
Devouring my people, they eat bread;
they do not call on God.

There they dreaded as dread had not been,
for God scattered the bones of attackers
put to shame in God's rejection.

Who would be brought from Zion
for the salvation of Israel?
When God restores the people of God,
let Jacob rejoice, let Israel be glad.

Glory... Antiphon

PSALM 54:1-6,8-9

Antiphon *The Son of Humanity will be betrayed*
into human hands and they will kill him,
and three days after being killed
he will rise up. Mk 9:31

Advent See! God is helping me;
the Lord sustains my very self.

Christmas
& Easter Alleluia, alleluia, alleluia.

God, save me by your name
and by your might vindicate me.
God, hear my prayer!
Listen to the words of my mouth!

For strangers attack me
and ruthless people seek my life
without regard for God before them.
See, God is helping me!
The Lord sustains my self…

With a freewill offering I will sacrifice to you;
I will praise, Adonai, your good name,
for my eyes have seen enmity
but you delivered me from every trouble.

Glory…

Antiphon

PSALM 49

Antiphon *You cannot serve God and mammon;*
where your treasure is
there also will your heart be. Mt 6:24b,21

Christmas & Easter Seek the things of heaven,
not those of earth, alleluia.

Hear this all peoples! Listen, all alive in the world!
Men and women, all sons and daughters,
rich and poor alike:

My mouth will speak words of wisdom
and my heart utter understanding of things.
I will turn an ear to a proverb;
I will expound my riddle with harp music.

Why should I fear in days of the bad
the deceivers who surround me,
the trusters of wealth,
and the boasters of the greatness of their riches?

No human can redeem redemption of another,
nor for oneself give a ransom to God.
Ransom of a life is costly; no ransom can be enough
for one to live to forever and not see the decay.

For we see that even wise people die;
like the foolish and the senseless they perish,
and leave all their wealth to others.

Their thoughts are of their houses to forever
as their dwelling for generations and generation,
and so they call lands by their own names.

The human, despite riches, does not endure,
but perishes just like the beasts.

This is their fate who trust in themselves
and their followers who give them approval.
Like the sheep they are destined for Sheol,
and death will be their shepherd.

Upright ones will rule over them in the morning
and their form will decay in Sheol, their mansion.
But God will redeem my soul
and take me from the hand of Sheol.

Be not overawed when human beings grow rich,
when they increase the splendor of their houses.
For in death they will take none of it;
with none of their splendor will they descend.

Though during their lives they blessed themselves,
and people do praise you when you prosper,
they will go to the generation of their ancestors
and never see light to forever.

Like the beast that must perish
so is a human with riches
but still poor in understanding.

Glory...

Antiphon

PSALM 137:1-6

Antiphon *God so loved the cosmos,*
and so gave the only begotten Son that
everyone believing in him may not perish
but have eternal life. Jn 3:16

Advent & Lent — If I forget you, Jerusalem,
may my right hand forget its skill.

Dec 17-23 — The Lord will come to save us.

Christmas & Easter — Sing for us a Zion song, alleluia.

By rivers of Babylon, there we sat and wept
as we remembered Zion;
On the poplars in their midst we hung our harps,

for there our captors asked us for words of song,
our tormentors for joy:
"Sing for us from the songs of Zion!"

How can we sing in a foreign land
a song of Adonai?
If I forget you, Jerusalem,
may my right hand forget its skill.

May my tongue cling to the roof of my mouth
if I remember you not,
if I consider any but Jerusalem
as the height of my joy.

Glory... Antiphon

PSALM 138

Antiphon *Put out into the deep*
and let down your nets for a catch. Lk 5:4

Advent & Lent — Before those who would be gods
I will sing praise of You.

Dec 17-23 — Zion is a mighty citadel;
throw open the gates, for our God
is here among us, alleluia.

Christmas & Easter — Though I walk in the midst
of trouble, you keep me alive,
alleluia.

I will praise you, **Adonai**, with all my heart.
Before those so-called "gods"
I will sing my praise of you.
I will bow toward your holy temple
and I will praise your name
for your love and your fidelity.

You are exalted above all,
your name and your word.
On the day I called, then you answered me.
You made me bold and stout in my heart.

May all the rulers of the earth praise you, Adonai,
when they hear the words of your mouth.
May they sing of the ways of Adonai,
for great is the glory of Adonai.

Psalm 138, continued

Though on high, Adonai looks upon the lowly
and knows the proud from afar.
Though I walk in the midst of trouble,
you keep me alive
against the anger of enmity.

You stretch out your hand, your right hand,
and you save me.
Adonai will fulfill me.
Your love, Adonai, is to forever.
Abandon not the works of your hands.

Glory...

Antiphon *Put out into the deep*
and let down your nets for a catch. Lk 5:4

Advent & Lent: Before those who would be gods
I will sing praise of You.

Dec 17-23: Zion is a mighty citadel;
throw open the gates, for our God
is here among us, alleluia.

Christmas & Easter: Though I walk in the midst
of trouble, you keep me alive,
alleluia.

The opposite of war
isn't peace...; it's creation.

Jonathan Larson, d. 1996, composer/playwright

REVELATION 4:8b,11; 5:9,10,12,13b

Antiphon *Holy, Holy, Holy, Lord God Almighty*
who was and is and is to come. Rev 4:8b

Advent & Lent — Worthy is the Lamb.

Christmas & Easter — The Lord has rescued my life
from the powers that be,
alleluia.

Worthy are you, our Lord and our God,
to receive the glory and honor and power,
for you have created all things,
and by your will all things were created and are.

Worthy are you to receive the scroll and unseal it
for you were sacrificed, and by your blood
ransomed for God those from every
tribe and tongue and people and nation.

You made of them for our God
a realm of royals and priests,
and thus will they reign over the earth.

Worthy is the Lamb, sacrificed to receive
the power and riches and wisdom and strength
and honor and glory and blessing.

Glory...

Antiphon

ORDINARY TIME READING **ROMANS 3:21-31**

Now without law a righteousness of God has shown forth, witnessed by the law and the prophets, a righteousness of God through faith in Jesus Christ for all who believe.

There is no difference, for all have sinned and come short of the glory of God, and are justified freely by God's grace through the redemption in Christ Jesus, in whom God set forth an expiation through faith by his blood, for a showing forth of his righteousness because of the passing by of the sins previously committed, in the forebearance of God, for the showing forth of righteousness in the present time, that God should be just and justifying those of faith in Jesus.

And so, where is the boasting? It was shut out. Through what law? Of works? No, but through a law of faith. For we reckon a person to be justified by faith without works of the law. Or is God of Jews only? Not also of nations? Yes, also of nations, since there is one God who will justify circumcision by faith and uncircumcision through the faith. And so, do we destroy law through faith? May it not be. But we support the law.

RESPONSORY Ps 16:11

You will make known to me the path of life,...
...fullness of joy in your presence.
Eternal pleasure at your right hand,...
...fullness of joy in your presence.
Glory to the Father and to the Son and to the Holy Spirit:
...You will make known to me the path of life,
fullness of joy in your presence.

ADVENT READING **1 CORINTHIANS 1:4-9**

I give thanks to God always concerning you, on the grace of God given to you in Christ Jesus, because in everything you were enriched in him, in all speech and all knowledge, as the testimony of Christ was confirmed in you, that you be lacking in no gift, awaiting the revelation of our Lord Jesus Christ, who will also confirm you to the end, blameless in the day of our Lord Jesus Christ.

Faithful is God, through whom you were called to communion with God's Son Jesus Christ our Lord.

RESPONSORY Ps 146:7; 63:3; 67:2

Come and set us free...
...Lord God of power and glory...
Let your face shine upon us
and we will know salvation...
...Lord God of power and glory...
Glory to the Father and to the Son and to the Holy Spirit:
...Come and set us free, Lord God of power and glory...

CHRISTMAS READING **1 JOHN 1:5b-7**

God is light, and in God there is no darkness, none. If we say we have communion with God and we walk in the dark, we lie and are not doing the truth.

But if we walk in the light as God is in the light, we have communion with each other, and the blood of Jesus the Son cleanses us from all sin.

RESPONSORY Jn 1:14

The Word became flesh...
...alleluia, alleluia.
And dwelt among us...
...alleluia, alleluia.
Glory to the Father and to the Son and to the Holy Spirit:
...The Word became flesh and dwelt among us,
alleluia, alleluia.

After Epiphany

All people will be blessed in him...
...in every tribe of the human race.
All nations will acclaim his glory...
...in every tribe of the human race.
Glory to the Father and to the Son and to the Holy Spirit:
...All people will be blessed in him,
in every tribe of the human race.

LENT READING, Weeks 2 & 4 **JAMES 2:14-18**

What is the profit, my brothers and sisters, if anyone claims to have faith but has not works? Can the faith save that one? If a brother or sister is naked and lacks the daily food, and anyone of you says, "Go in peace, be warm and filled," and not give the necessaries of the body, what is the profit? So indeed faith if it has not works is dead by itself. But someone will say, "You have faith and I have works." Show me your faith without the works, and I will show you by my works the faith.

RESPONSORY Lk 18:13

To you, O Lord…
…I make my prayer for mercy.
Heal my soul, for I have sinned against you…
…I make my prayer for mercy.
Glory to the Father and to the Son and to the Holy Spirit:
…To you, O Lord, I make my prayer for mercy.

LENT READING, Holy Week **1 CORINTHIANS 1:27b-30**

God chose the weak things of the world to shame the strong things. God chose the base things of the world and the despised things, the things not being, so that God might abolish the things being, so that no flesh might boast before God, of whom you are in Christ Jesus, who became to us wisdom from God, and justice and holiness and redemption.

RESPONSORY Rev. 5:9

We worship you, O Christ...

...and we praise you.

By your cross you have redeemed the world...

...and we praise you.

Glory to the Father and to the Son and to the Holy Spirit:

...We worship you, O Christ, and we praise you.

EASTER READING **1 PETER 2:4-5**

Approach the Lord, a living stone, rejected by humans, chosen precious by God. And as living stones you are being built, a spiritual house for a holy priesthood, to offer spiritual sacrifices acceptable to God through Jesus Christ.

RESPONSORY

The disciples rejoiced...

...alleluia, alleluia.

When they saw the risen Lord...

...alleluia, alleluia.

Glory to the Father and to the Son and to the Holy Spirit:

...The disciples rejoiced, alleluia, alleluia

Gospel Canticle For Evening

Antiphons

Advent Wk 2

A voice is heard
crying in the wilderness:
prepare the way of the Lord;
make straight the path of our God.

Advent Wk 4
20th

O Key of David, O Royal Power,
come lead your people into freedom.

Christmas

Let us dance with delight in the Lord
and let our hearts
be filled with rejoicing,
for eternal salvation
has appeared on the earth,
alleluia.

After Epiphany

Christ, you are Light from Light;
when you appeared on earth,
the magi offered their gifts to you,
alleluia.

Lent Wk 2

You are all siblings,
children of one Abba in heaven;
do not call anyone on earth
your father;
nor must any of you be called teacher,
for your only teacher is Christ.

Antiphons for Gospel Canticle For Evening, continued

Lent Wk 4	Do you want to be well?
Holy Week	I have power to lay down my life and I have power to take it up again.
Easter Wk 2	Did not our hearts burn within us as Jesus talked to us on the road? Alleluia.
Easter Wk 4	I know my sheep and they follow me; I give them eternal life, alleluia.
Easter Wk 6	You will receive the power of the Holy Spirit and you will be my witnesses to the ends of the earth, alleluia.
Ordinary Antiphon	 *My spirit is beyond joy* *in God, my Savior*

CANTICLE of MARY (The Magnificat)
LUKE 1:46-55

+ **My soul** is stretched full with praise of the Lord,
and my spirit, beyond joy in God, my Savior,
who chose to lay eyes on this humble servant.

Behold, now and forward,
each and every age will call me blessed,
for the Mighty One did great things to me.

Holy is the name and the mercy
to generations and generations,
the ones fearing the One,

Who scattered the haughty of mind and heart,
pulled the powerful off their high place,
and lifted with dignity the humble in need.

The hungering are filled with good things,
the rich are sent away empty,
and servant Israel is given relief

with a memory of mercy to remember,
the promise spoken to our ancestors,
to Abraham and his descendants forever.

Glory…

Antiphon

INTERCESSIONS

- For a culture of vocations all over the world…
- For all who have died…

- In gratitude for blessings…; Abba thank you.
- For the sins of this day…; Lord Jesus have mercy.
- With concerns over tomorrow…; Holy Spirit help.

PRAYER of the CONFIRMED from the Rite of Confirmation

Almighty God,
Abba of our Lord Jesus Christ,
who brought your servants to new birth
by water and the Holy Spirit,
freeing us from sin:
send upon us, O Lord,
the Holy Spirit, the Paraclete;
give us the spirit of wisdom and understanding,
the spirit of counsel and fortitude,
the spirit of knowledge and piety;
fill us with the spirit of the fear of the Lord,
through Christ our Lord.
Amen.

OUR FATHER…

121, Text: from Psalm 103, Henry F. Lyte, 1834, altered
Music: 87 87 87 LAUDA ANIMA, John Goss, 1869

WEEK II
WEDNESDAY MORNING

+ *God, come to my assistance;* Psalm 70:2
Lord, make haste to help me!

Glory…

ORDINARY TIME

Praise, my soul, the King of heav-en;
To these feet your trib-ute bring.
Ran-somed, healed, re-stored, for-giv-en,
Ev-er-more God's prais-es sing:
Al-le-lu-ia! Al-le-lu-ia!
Praise the ev-er-last-ing King.

Praise for grace and fav-or giv-en
In our an-ces-tral dis-tress.
Praise God, still the same as ev-er,
Slow to chide and swift to bless.
Al-le-lu-ia! Al-le-lu-ia!
Glo-rious love and faith-ful-ness.

As a par-ent, tend-ing, spar-ing,
Well our fee-ble frame God knows.
Gent-ly bear-ing and res-cu-ing
Us from all who'd be our foes.
Al-le-lu-ia! Al-le-lu-ia!
Wide-ly yet the mer-cy flows.

ORDINARY TIME & ADVENT

We plow the fields and scat-ter
the good seed on the land,
But it is fed and wa-tered
by God's al-migh-ty hand;
God sends the snow in win-ter,
the warmth to swell the grain,
The breezes and the sun-shine,
and soft refresh-ing rain.

God on-ly is the Ma-ker
of all things near and far;
the Paint-er of the flow-er,
the Ligh-ter of the star;
The winds and waves o-bey-ing,
while all the birds are fed;
Much more as God's own chil-dren
are giv-en dai-ly bread.

We thank you, then, O Fa-ther,
for all things bright and good,
The seed time and the har-vest,
our life, our health, our food;
No gifts have we to offer,
for all your love im-parts,
But that which you de-sire\,
our hum-ble, thank-ful hearts.

CHRISTMAS

While shep-herds kept their watch-ing
O'er si-lent flocks by night
Be-hold through-out the heav-ens
There shone a ho-ly light/.

Refrain **Go, tell it on the moun-tain,**
Over the hills and ev-'ry-where\
Go, tell it on the moun-tain,
That Je-sus Christ\ is born.

The shep-herds feared and trem-bled,
When lo! a-bove the earth,
Rang out the an-gels chor-us
That hailed the Sav-ior's birth/. *Refrain*

Down in a low-ly man-ger
The hum-ble Christ was born
And God sent us sal-va-tion
That bless-ed Christ-mas morn/. *Refrain*

20, Text: John W. Work, Jr., 1872-1925;
Folk Songs of the American Negro, Nashville, 1907
Music: 76 76 with refrain; African American Spiritual

128, Text: Matthias Claudius, 1782,
hearing the words sung by farmers;
translated by Jane M. Campbell, 1861, altered
Music: 76 76 D, AURELIA, Samuel S. Wesley, 1864
Popular melody for: *The Church's One Foundation*

LENT

Spir-it, come and fill all your faith-ful hearts,
Set fire in us your con-firm-ing love,
Send forth your Spir-it Breath to all cre-a/-tion
And/ the face of the earth you\ will re-new.

Give us Wis-dom to seek the face of God,
Com-pre-hen-sion of bap-tis-mal grace,
Good Judg-ment to dis-cern Christ's call
in free/-dom.
Give us the grace\ to know/ our Ab-ba's will.

Give us Cour-age for our vo-ca-tion "yes!",
Know-ledge of what Je-sus teach/-es,
Rev-er-ence for the ways of our good Ab/-ba;
Give/ us Strength\ to do/ the will of God.

Give us fear of the Lord, that joy-ful awe,
Our wit-ness giv'n to the Ris-en Son:
May it be pleas\-ing\ to our Ab/-ba
And help you, Spir-it, re-new/ the face of earth.

Through you, Spir-it , may we hear Je-sus Christ,
And bet-ter know our\ Ab/-ba.
You, Lov-ing Spir-it of the Ab-ba and the Son,
May/ our trust be in you for all time to come.

75, Text: Vs 1-4 from *Easter Prayer for Vocations* by Stephen J. Wolf, 2011, 2017; Vs 5from the Latin by Rabanus Mauras, d. 856, Music: VENI CREATOR SPIRITUS, LM; Mode VIII

EASTER

Come/, Cre\-a-tor\ Spir/-it,
Souls\ of yours, now\ vis/-it:
Fill/ with grace\ be\-yond/ na/-ture
All/ these hearts\ that you have cre-a\-ted.

Your/ name is the Com-fort Par-a-clete,
The high-est gift of our giv-ing God,
Font/ of life and fire and lov-ing char-i-ty,
Font/ of spir-it-u-al a\-noint\-ing.

You/ sev\-en-fold\ ho-ly gift,
Fing-er of the right\ hand of God,
You who were prom-ised du-ly by the Ab/-ba,
En-rich our throats\ to speak words\ you want heard.

Kin-dle light in our minds, your ho-ly light;
Send and in-fuse in-to hearts your love.
Hu-man weak-ness dwell-ing in hu-man bod/-ies
Your pow-er streng-thens in-to per-pet-u-i-ty.

Spir-it, drive a-way ev-'ry en-mit-y
Bring-ing the peace ev-er-last/-ing.
With you, our faith-ful lead-er pro/-ceed/-ing
May we a-void\ all harm/ and e\-vil.

Glo-ry be to our God and Ab/-ba,
And to the Son Res-u-rec/-ted,
And to their Ho-ly Spir-it, Com-fort Par-a-clete,
For gen-er-a-tions and each gen-er-a\-tion. **A**/\-men/.

74, Text: from the Latin by Rabanus Mauras, d. 856,
Veni Creator Spiritus, with assistance from the literal translation

PSALM 103

Antiphon *Forgive each of your siblings*
from your heart. Mt 18:35

Christmas & Easter Praise the Lord, my soul, and forget not
all of the Lord's benefits, alleluia.

My soul, praise Adonai!
All my inmost being, praise the holy Name!
My soul, praise Adonai,
whose benefits are not to be forgotten:

forgiveness of all your sins,
healing of all your diseases,
redemption of your life from the pit,
crowning you with love and compassion,
satisfying your desire with good,
renewing your youths like the eagle,
working vindication
and justice for all who are oppressed.

Adonai's ways are made known to Moses
and the deeds to peoples of Israel.

Compassionate and gracious is Adonai,
slow to anger and abundant in love,
neither accusing to always
nor harboring anger to forever,
neither treating us in accord with our sins
nor repaying us in accord with our iniquities.

As high as the heavens are above the earth
so great is the love for ones who fear Adonai.
As far as the east is from the west
so far from us are our transgressions removed.

As a father has compassion on his children,
so has Adonai compassion on ones fearing,
knowing our form and remembering we are dust.

The days of a human are like the grass
flourishing like flowers of the field,
for wind blows over and it is no more
and the place remembers it no more.

But the love of Adonai for the awestruck
is from everlasting to everlasting,
with favor for children of their children,
of those keeping the covenant
and remembering to obey the precepts.

Adonai established a throne in the heavens,
a reign to rule over all.
Praise Adonai, you angels,
you strong and mighty ones doing the bidding,
obeying the voice of the word.

Praise Adonai, you hosts,
you serving and doing the will.
Praise Adonai, all you works,
in all places of the dominion.
My soul, praise Adonai!

Glory… Antiphon

PSALM 39

Antiphon *You are the salt of the earth;*
you are the light of the cosmos. Mt 5:13a,14a

Christmas & Easter We ourselves groan in ourselves,
eagerly expecting adoption,
the redemption of our body,
alleluia.

I said, "I will watch my ways
of sinning with my tongue;
I will put on my mouth a muzzle
as long as temptation is in my presence."
So in silent stillness I said nothing,
and still my anguish increased.

My heart grew hot inside me;
in my meditation a fire burned.
I spoke with my tongue,
"Show me, Adonai, my end,
what is the number of my days;
let me know how fleeting I am.

See the handbreadths you made!
My days and my span are as nothing before you.
Indeed, each of all humanity stands as a breath.
Indeed, as a phantom the human goes out.
Indeed, vainly bustling about, heaping up wealth
without knowing who will get it."

But what am I looking for now, Lord?
My hope she is in you.
Save me from all my transgressions!
Make me not the scorn of fools.
I was silent and opened not my mouth,
for you, you have done it.

Remove your scourge from me;
from the touch of your hand I am overcome.
With a rebuke for sin you discipline the human
and you consume our wealth like a moth;
indeed we are each but a breath.

Hear my prayer, Adonai, and my cry for help;
listen, El, and be not deaf to my weeping.
For I am with you as a passing guest,
an alien stranger like all my ancestors.
Look away from me that I may rejoice
before I depart and am no more.

Glory...

Antiphon

In years to come when I
look back on my life in these
days, what will I wish had gotten
just a little bit more of my attention?

PSALM 77

Antiphon *Blessed are those who are persecuted for what is right, for theirs is the reign of heaven.* Mt 5:10

Advent & Lent God, in your holiness way, what "god" is as great as God?

Christmas & Easter The waters saw you, O God; you led your people through the sea, alleluia.

I cry aloud for God, indeed I cried for help.
My cry is for God to hear me.

In the day of my distress I sought the Lord,
my hand was stretched in the night without tiring;
my soul refused to be comforted.
I remembered God and I groaned;
I meditated and my spirit grew faint.

You kept open the lids of my eyes;
I was troubled and could not speak.
I thought of former days and of years long ago.
I remembered my song in the night;
my heart mused and searched my spirit,

"Will the Lord reject to forever,
never to show favor again?
Is the unfailing love vanished to forever?
Has the promise failed for all generations?
Has God forgotten mercy
or withheld compassion in anger?"

Then I thought, "My appeal is this,
the years at the right hand of the Most High."
I will remember the deeds of Adonai;
yes, I will remember your long-ago miracles.
I will meditate on all of your works
and ponder your mighty deeds.

God in your holiness way,
what "god" is as great as God?
You are the God who does miracles;
you display among the peoples your power.
With your arm you redeemed your people,
the descendants of Jacob and Joseph.

The waters saw you, God,
the waters saw you and writhed;
indeed the depths were convulsed.
Clouds poured down waters,
thunder resounded in the skies,
and your arrows flashed around.

Your thunder sounded in the whirlwind,
lightnings lit up the world;
the earth trembled and quaked.
Through the sea is your path,
and your way through mighty waters,
though your footprints were not seen.

You led your people like the flock
by the hand of Moses and Aaron.

Glory... Antiphon

PSALM 108

Antiphon *The one doing the truth*
comes to the light. Jn 3:21

Advent & Lent — My heart is ready, O God,
my heart is ready.

Dec. 17-23 — The Lord, the mighty God,
will come forth from Zion
to set the people free.

Christmas — Awake the harp and lyre;
I will wake up the dawn.

Easter — O God, arise above the heavens,
alleluia.

My heart is steadfast, God; I will sing
and even my soul will make music.
Awake the harp and lyre;
I will wake up the dawn!

I will praise you among the nations, Adonai,
and I will sing of you among the peoples,
for greater than above the heavens is your love
and to the skies your fidelity.

Be exalted above the heavens, God,
your glory over all the earth
that your loved ones may be delivered.
Save your right hand, and help me!

God spoke from the sanctuary:
"I will triumph and parcel out Shechem,
and measure the valley of Succoth;
mine are Gilead and Manasseh,

Ephraim my head helmet,
Judah my scepter,
and Moab my washbasin;
On Edom I toss my sandals
and over Philistia I shout in triumph."

Who will bring me to the Fortress City?
Who will lead me into Edom?
Have you, God, not rejected us,
and not gone out, God, with our armies?

Against enmity give to us aid,
for worthless is human help.
In God will we gain victory...

Glory...

Antiphon

All shall be well
and all shall be well and
all manner of things shall be well.

Julian of Norwich, d. 1416

1 SAMUEL 2:1-10

Antiphon *My spirit rejoices in God my Savior.* Lk 1:47

Advent & Lent My heart rejoices in the Lord,
who humbles and raises up.

Christmas God fills the hungry
with good things, alleluia.

Holy Week If we have died with Christ
we believe we will also
live with Christ.

Easter The Lord allows death
and raises to life, alleluia.

My heart rejoices in Adonai,
my horn is lifted high in Adonai.

My mouth boasts over enmity,
for I delight in being delivered.
There is no Holy One like Adonai,
indeed there is no one who compares;
there is no Rock like our God.

Arrogant pride is coming from their mouth.
Do not keep talking so proudly
or proudly let arrogance come from your mouth,
for Adonai is God who knows,
by whom all deeds are weighed.

Bows of warriors are broken
but those stumbling are armed with strength.
The full hire themselves out for more food,
but the hungry ones hunger no more.
She who was barren bore seven sons;
blessed with many, another is pining away.

Adonai allows death and is making alive,
brings down to Sheol and is raising up.
Adonai allows poverty and is sending wealth,
humbling and exalting,
raising the poor from the dust
and the needy from ash-heaps
to sit with royals and inherit thrones of honor.

For Adonai's are the foundations of the earth,
setting the world upon them.
The feet of the saints will be guarded
but doers of the bad will be silenced in darkness.

For not by strength does the human prevail;
Adonai shatters opposition,
thundering from the heavens.
Adonai will judge the ends of the earth,
give strength, and raise the horn
of the one chosen and anointed.

Glory...

Antiphon

ISAIAH 61:10-62:5

Antiphon *My God has clothed me*
in garments of salvation.

Dec. 17-23 I shall not cease
to plead with God for Zion
until the Holy One is sent
in all radiant beauty.

Christmas & Easter The Lord will make
praise and justice to blossom
before all the nations,
alleluia.

To delight, I delight in Adonai,
my soul rejoices in my God,
who clothed me in garments of salvation
and arrayed me in a robe of justice,
as spouses dress their heads like priests
and adorn themselves with jewels,

for as the soil makes the sprout come up
and as a garden makes seeds to grow
so will Sovereign Adonai
make justice spring up
and praise before all the nations.

For the sake of Zion, I will not keep silent;
for the sake of Jerusalem I will not remain quiet,
till vindication comes out like the dawn
and salvation blazes like a torch.

The nations will see your vindication
and all the rulers your glory
and you will be called by a new name
that the mouth of Adonai will bestow.
You will be a crown of splendor
in the hand of Adonai
and a royal diadem in the hand of your God.

No longer will you be called One Being Deserted,
nor will your name be called Desolation,
but you will be called "my delight is in her"
and your land "espoused."
Adonai will delight in you
and your land will be married.

As young folks marry each other,
your Builder will marry you;
and as a newlywed rejoices over a spouse,
so will your God rejoice over you.

Glory...

Antiphon

PSALM 97

Antiphon *Fill the water pots with water;*
now draw and carry some
to the master of the feast. Jn 2:7,8

Advent & Lent The Lord reigns;
let the earth be glad.

Christmas Begotten of God
before the sun first shined
or time began,
the Lord our Savior
has appeared on earth.

Holy Week By Christ Jesus,
we are sanctified and redeemed.

Easter A light has dawned for the just;
joy has come to the honest of heart,
alleluia.

Adonai reigns; let the earth be glad.
Let all the distant shores rejoice.
Clouds and thick darkness surround the throne
founded on justice and right.

Fire goes before,
consuming enmity on every side.
Lightnings light up the world;
the earth sees and trembles.

Mountains melt like wax before Adonai,
before the Lord of all the earth.
The heavens proclaim God's justice
and all peoples see the glory.

Let those who worship idols be shamed,
those boasting in their images.
Worship God, all you "gods."

Zion hears and rejoices
and the villages of Judah are glad
because of your judgments, Adonai.

For you, Adonai,
are Most High over all the earth,
far exalted above all the "gods."

The bad is despised by lovers of Adonai,
who guards the lives of faithful ones
and delivers them from the hands
of doers of the bad.

Light dawns for the just
and joy for the honest of heart.
Rejoice in Adonai, you just,
and praise the holy name.

Glory...

Antiphon

PSALM 146

Antiphon *Blessed are the meek,*
for they will inherit the earth. Mt 5:5

Advent & Lent: I will sing praise to my God
all the days of my life.

Dec 17-23: The Spirit of the Lord rests upon me,
and has sent me to preach
good news to the poor.

Christmas & Easter: The Lord your God will reign forever,
alleluia.

Hallelujah!

Praise Adonai, my soul!
I will praise Adonai during my life;
I will sing praise to my God while I still am.

Trust neither royalty nor human beings
in whom there is no salvation.
Their spirit-breath departs,
and they return to the ground.
On that day their plans come to nothing.

Blessed are they whose help is the God of Jacob,
whose hope and God are Adonai,
the maker of heaven and earth
and the sea and all that is in them.

The one staying faithful to forever
defends justice for the oppressed
and gives food to the hungry.

Adonai sets prisoners free;
Adonai gives sight to the blind;
Adonai lifts those who are bowed down;
Adonai loves the just.

Adonai watches over alien strangers,
and sustains the orphan and the widow,
but frustrates the ways that are bad.
Adonai reigns to forever,
your God, Zion,
from generation to generation.

Hallelujah!

Glory...

Antiphon

ORDINARY TIME READING **ROMANS 8:35,37-39**

Who will separate us from the love of Christ? Affliction? Distress? Persecution? Famine? Nakedness? Peril? The Sword? But in all these things we overconquer through the one who has loved us.

For I am persuaded that not death, nor life, nor angels, nor rulers, nor present things, nor things coming, nor powers, nor height, nor depth, nor any other creature will be able to separate us from the love of God in Christ Jesus, our Lord.

RESPONSORY Ps 34:2

My soul will boast in the Lord…
…and at all times.
Praise always on my lips…
…and at all times.
Glory to the Father and to the Son and to the Holy Spirit:
…My soul will boast in the Lord, and at all times.

Intimacy is a basic human need and
I tend to it or it will find unhealthy ways
to tend to me. It is the grace of being known,
the blessing of being with a friend or a spouse who
knows me so well that I am free to simply be who I am.

See *Being Spouses* by Stephen Joseph Wolf

ADVENT READING **ISAIAH 7:10-15**

Adonai spoke again to Ahaz to say, "Ask for a sign from your God Adonai; ask to dig deep or to go high above." But Ahaz said, "I will not ask, I will not test Adonai." So Isaiah said, "Hear now, house of David! Is it not enough for you to try the patience of humans? Will you also try the patience of my God?

And so the Lord will give to you a sign to see: the virgin with child, bearing a son, and she will call his name Immanuel! He will be eating curds and honey when he knows to reject the bad and choose the good."

RESPONSORY

Your light will come, Jerusalem…
…the Lord will dawn on you in radiant beauty.
The glory of the Lord you will see within you…
…the Lord will dawn on you in radiant beauty.
Glory to the Father and to the Son and to the Holy Spirit:
…Your light will come, Jerusalem;
the Lord will dawn on you in radiant beauty.

CHRISTMAS READING **ISAIAH 45:22-25**

"Turn to me and be saved, all you ends of the earth, for I am God and there is no other. By myself I swore integrity out of my mouth, the word that will not be revoked. Indeed, in front of me every knee will bow, and every tongue will swear, and say, 'In my Adonai alone are justice and strength,' to whom will come and be shamed all who have raged otherwise." In Adonai they will find vindication and all the descendants of Israel will exult.

RESPONSORY

The Lord has made known…
…alleluia, alleluia.
The saving power…
…alleluia, alleluia.
Glory to the Father and to the Son and to the Holy Spirit:
…The Lord has made known the saving power, alleluia.

After Epiphany

All the royal powers on earth
…will bow down in worship.
Men and women of every nation…
…will bow down in worship.
Glory to the Father and to the Son and to the Holy Spirit:
…All the royal powers on earth
will bow down in worship.

LENT READING, until Holy Week **DEUT. 7:6b,8-9**

Your God Adonai chose you to be the people treasured from all the peoples on the faces of the earth. Because of Adonai's love for you and to keep the oath sworn to your ancestors, Adonai brought you out with a mighty hand and redeemed you from the house of slaveries from the hand of Pharaoh, king of Egypt, so you know that your God Adonai is the God, the faithful God keeping the covenant and the love to a thousand generations of those loving God and keeping God's commands.

RESPONSORY Lk 18:13

The Lord God will set me free…
…from the hunter's snare.
From all those who would trap me with lying words,
…and from the hunter's snare.
Glory to the Father and to the Son and to the Holy Spirit:
…The Lord God will set me free from the hunter's snare.

LENT READING, Holy Week **ISAIAH 50:4b-7**

Sovereign Adonai wakens my ear to hear as one taught and opens my ear, and I did not rebel nor draw back. I offered my back to beaters and my cheeks to beard pullers and did not hide my faces from mockings and spittings because Sovereign Adonai helps me. For this I will not be disgraced. For this I set my faces like the flint and I know that I will not be shamed.

RESPONSORY Rev. 5:9

Lord, by your own blood…

…you brought us back to God.

From every tribe and tongue and people and nation…

…you brought us back to God.

Glory to the Father and to the Son and to the Holy Spirit:

…Lord, by your own blood you brought us back to God.

EASTER READING **ROMANS 6:8-11**

If we died with Christ, we believe that we shall also live with him, knowing that Christ raised from the dead dies no more. Death lords it over him no more, for in that he died to sin he died once. But in that he is alive, he is alive to God. So also you reckon yourselves dead indeed to sin, but alive to God in Christ Jesus.

RESPONSORY

The Lord is risen from the tomb…

…alleluia, alleluia.

He hung upon the cross for us…

…alleluia, alleluia.

Glory to the Father and to the Son and to the Holy Spirit:

…The Lord is risen from the tomb, alleluia, alleluia.

Gospel Canticle For Morning

Antiphons

Advent Wk 2
Matt 11:28-30

He will be enthroned in David's place
to reign for ever,
alleluia.

Advent Wk 4
(see pg 759)

Be not afraid;
our Lord will come to us.

Christmas
(see pg 759)

Christ our God, in whom
the fullness of God dwells,
took on our wounded nature
and became the first new human,
alleluia.

After Epiphany
Mark 6:45-52

We have seen the star in the East
and have come with gifts
to worship the Lord.

Ash Wednesday
Matt 6:1-6,16-18

When you fast, do not put on
a gloomy face, like the hypocrites.

Lent Wk 2
Matt 20:17-28

The Son of Humanity did not come
to be served but to serve, to give
his life as a ransom for the many.

Lent Wk 4
John 5:17-30

Whoever hears my words,
says the Lord, and believes in the
One who sent me has eternal life.

Antiphons for Gospel Canticle For Morning, continued

Holy Week Matt 26:14-25	Through the eternal Spirit, Christ offered the self to God as the perfect sacrifice.
Easter Wk 2 John 3:16-21	God so loved the cosmos and so gave the only Son of God to save with eternal life all who believe in him, alleluia.
Easter Wk 4 John 12:44-50	I am the light come into the cosmos that those who believe in me may not remain in the dark, alleluia.
Easter Wk 6 John 16:12-15	I have many more things to tell you but you cannot bear it now; when the Spirit of truth comes that One will guide you to all truth, alleluia.
Ordinary Antiphon	*Show us, Lord, how mercy works,* *and remember your holy covenant.*

Gospel Reading for Wednesday of

Week **2** Mark 3:1-6	**14** Matt 10:1-7	**26** Luke 9:57-62
4 Mark 6:1-6	**16** Matt 13:1-9	**28** Lk 11:42-46
6 Mark 8:22-26	**18** Matt 15:21-28	**30** Lk 13:22-30
8 Mark 10:32-45	**20** Matt 20:1-16	**32** Lk 17:11-19
10 Matt 5:17-19	**22** Luke 4:38-44	**34** Lk 21:12-19
12 Matt 7:15-20	**24** Luke 7:31-35	

CANTICLE of ZECHARIAH (The Benedictus) LUKE 1:68-79

+ **Blessed be** the Lord the God of Israel
who chose a people to visit with redemption,
and raised salvation in the house of David,
saving strength from God's own servant,

speaking from the age of the prophets
through the mouth of the holy prophet:
Salvation out of enmity,
even out of those who hate us,

to show our ancestors how mercy works, -
and to remember the holy promise of the Lord,
the covenant made for our ancestor Abraham,
calming our fear and making us free
to serve with holy justice before God all our days.

And you also child -
will be called a prophet of the Most High
for you will go before the Lord to prepare his way
and give to people a knowledge of salvation
known in accepting forgiveness of their sins.

From the tender mercy of our God,
the sun rising from the height will visit with light
for those who sit in the dark or shadow of death
and to guide our feet into the way of peace.

Glory...

Antiphon

PETITIONS FOR THE CONSECRATION TO GOD
OF THE DAY AND ITS WORK

- For the Church and her ministry and apostolates...
- For secular authorities and all serving as stewards...
- For people who are poor or sick or in sorrow...
- For peace and the basic needs of each human being...

LENTEN PRAYER FOR VOCATIONS

God of compassion,
through honest awareness of sin
and the grace of repentance
you protect us from what could harm us
and lead us to what will save us.
Your Son, Jesus Christ, accepted the cross
and redeemed your sons and daughters.
Through prayer, fasting, and almsgiving
you call us each to a unique vocation
of health, healing and mercy.
May we embrace the paschal mystery
and faithful to the gospel of Christ
become a people who worship you
in spirit and in truth.

OUR FATHER...

Lord, do for me today what I cannot do for myself.

See *The Anonymous Disciple* by Gerard Goggins

WEEK II
WEDNESDAY EVENING

+ *God, come to my assistance;* Psalm 70:2
Lord, make haste to help me!

Glory…

ORDINARY TIME & LENT

Shep-herd of souls, re-fresh and bless
Your cho-sen pil-grim flock
With man-na in the wil-der-ness,
And wa-ter from the rock.

Hung-ry and thirs-ty, mor-tal, weak,
As you would come and go:
Our souls the joys of heav-en seek
Which from your pass-ion flow.

We would not live by bread a-lone,
But by your Word of grace,
In strength of which we trav-el on
To our a-bi-ding place.

Be known to us in break-ing bread,
But do not then de-part;
Sa-vior, a-bide with us and spread
Your ta-ble in our heart.

124, Text: James Mongtomery, 1825, altered
Music: ST. AGNES, CM, John B. Dykes, 1866

ADVENT, CHRISTMAS & EASTER

All crea-tures of our God and King
Lift up your voice and with us sing,
Al-le-lu-ia! Al-le-lu-ia!
You burn-ing sun with gold-en beam,
You sil-ver moon with soft-er gleam!
Al-le-lu-ia! Al-le-lu-ia!
Al-le-lu-ia! Al-le-lu-ia! Al-le-lu_-ia!

You flow-ing wa-ter, pure and clear,
Make mu-sic for your Lord to hear,
Al-le-lu-ia! Al-le-lu-ia!
You fire so mas-ter-ful and bright,
Giv-ing the hu-man warmth and light.
Al-le-lu-ia! Al-le-lu-ia!
Al-le-lu-ia! Al-le-lu-ia! Al-le-lu_-ia!

Dear moth-er earth, who day by day
Un-fold your bless-ings on our way,
Al-le-lu-ia! Al-le-lu-ia!
Flow-ers and fruits, all in you grown,
And God's own glo-ry let be shone.
Al-le-lu-ia! Al-le-lu-ia!
Al-le-lu-ia! Al-le-lu-ia! Al-le-lu_-ia!

You rush-ing winds that are so strong,
You clouds that sail in heav'n a-long,
Al-le-lu-ia! Al-le-lu-ia!
You ri-sing moon, in praise re-joice,
You lights of eve-ning, find a voice!
Al-le-lu-ia! Al-le-lu-ia!
Al-le-lu-ia! Al-le-lu-ia! Al-le-lu_-ia!

And you most kind and gen-tle death,
Wait-ing to hush our la-test breath,
Al-le-lu-ia! Al-le-lu-ia!
You lead to home the child of God,
As Christ our Lord the way has trod.
Al-le-lu-ia! Al-le-lu-ia!
Al-le-lu-ia! Al-le-lu-ia! Al-le-lu_-ia!

Let all things their Cre-a-tor bless,
And wor-ship God in hum-ble-ness,
Al-le-lu-ia! Al-le-lu-ia!
Praise, praise the Fa-ther, praise the Son,
And praise the Spir-it, Three in One!
Al-le-lu-ia! Al-le-lu-ia!
Al-le-lu-ia! Al-le-lu-ia! Al-le-lu_-ia!

78, Text: Francis of Assisi, 1225; translated by William H. Draper, *Public School Hymn Book,* 1919, altered.
Music: LASST UNS ERFREUEN, LM with alleluias; *Geistliche Kirchengesange,* 1623

PSALM 52

Antiphon *Laying his hands*
on each one brought to him,
Jesus healed those ailing with disease. Lk 4:40b

Advent & Lent I trust in God's unfailing love
forever and ever.

Christmas & Easter Alleluia, alleluia, alleluia.

Why, mighty liar, do you boast of the bad
to the disgrace of El all the day?
Your tongue plots destruction
like a sharpened razor, practicing deceit.

You love the bad rather than the good,
lies rather than honest speech.
Your tongue of deceit loves every harmful word.

Surely El will bring you down,
snatch you from your tent,
and uproot you from the land of the living.

Then the just will see and fear,
and they will laugh at you.
See the one who did not see God as the refuge,
but grew strong by destruction
and trusted in great wealth.

But I am like an olive tree
flourishing in the house of God;
I trust in God's unfailing love forever and ever.

I will praise you to forever
for what you have done,
and in the presence of your saints
I will hope in you
for your name is good.

Glory...

Antiphon

PSALM 75

Antiphon* *Let the one of you without sin*
be the first to throw a stone. Jn 8:7

Advent & Lent God is the judge, only God.

Christmas & Easter Alleluia, alleluia, alleluia.

**One adulterer is there, the other is not. A mob of self-appointed judges demands judgment. After the words of the just judge, all the stones drop to the earth, one by one, beginning with the eldest, presumed to be the most wise & just, but now with new understanding.*

We give thanks to you, God;
we give thanks for your name is Near,
and they tell of your wonderful deeds.

You choose and appoint the time
to be the just judge.
The earth quakes, and all its people,
and you hold her pillars firm.

I say to the arrogant, "boast not,"
and to doers of the bad, "lift not your horn;
lift not your horns against the heavens
nor speak with arrogance."

For there is no one from east or from west
and no one from the desert to exalt.
But God is the one judge,
bringing low this one and raising another.

A cup is full in the hand of Adonai,
and wine foams and mixed spice pours out.
Indeed from this they drink to her dregs,
all doers of the bad on the earth.

And I will rejoice to forever,
and sing praise to the God of Jacob.
All the horns of doers of the bad will be cut off,
and the horns of the just will be lifted up.

Glory…

Antiphon

PSALM 94

Antiphon *Jesus touched her hand, the fever left her,*
and rising she began serving them. Mt 8:15

Christmas & Easter Alleluia, alleluia, alleluia.

God of vindication,
Adonai, God of vindication, shine forth!
Rise up, One Judge of the earth!
Pay back desserts to the proud!

Until when, Adonai, will doers of the bad?
Until when will doers of the bad be jubilant?
They pour out and speak arrogance;
all the doers of the bad make boast.

They crush your people, Adonai,
and they oppress your very own.
They slay the widow and alien;
they murder the orphan.

They say Adonai does not see
and the God of Jacob pays no heed.
Take heed, senseless ones among the people;
fools, when will you become wise?

Does the one who shapes the ear not hear?
Does the one who forms the eye not see?
Will the one who disciplines nations not punish?
Will the one who teaches have no knowledge?

Adonai knows the thoughts of humans,
that they are puffs of air.

Blessed is the one you instruct, Adonai,
the one you teach from your law
to grant relief from days of trouble
till a pit is dug for doers of the bad,

for the people of Adonai will not be rejected,
your very own never forsaken.
Judgment will again be just;
all the upright of heart will follow it.

Who will rise up for me against doers of the bad?
Who will take a stand against people doing bad?
Unless Adonai helps me,
I would as soon dwell in the silence of my self.

When I said, "My foot slips,"
your love, Adonai, supported me.
When my anxieties were great inside me
your consolations brought joy to my soul.

Can a throne of corruptions be allied with you,
one that brings misery by decree?
They band together against the life of the just
and condemn the innocent to death.

But Adonai became to me as a fortress,
and my God as a rock of refuge.
A rock of refuge is my God,
who will repay their sin to them
and destroy their bad ways.
Our God, Adonai, will destroy them.

Glory... Antiphon

PSALM 62

Antiphon *Do not worry about tomorrow*
for tomorrow will worry about itself;
sufficient to the day is its own trouble. Mt 6:34

Advent & Lent
Rest, my soul, in God alone;
from God is my salvation.

Holy Week
Humans doing the bad said,
let us make the just human suffer
for opposing our way of life.

Christmas & Easter
Do not let your hearts be troubled;
have faith in me,
alleluia. Jn 14:1

My soul finds rest in God alone,
from whom is my salvation,
alone my salvation and my rock,
my fortress never to be shaken.

Until when will you assault a human being,
will you throw down, all of you,
like a leaning wall or a tottering fence?

They fully intend to topple from the lofty place;
they delight in lies
and bless with their mouth
and curse in their heart.

My soul finds rest in God alone,
from whom is my hope,
alone my salvation and my rock,
my fortress not to be shaken.

From God is my salvation and my honor;
my mighty rock and refuge.
Trust in God at all times, people;
pour out your heart to God our refuge.

Sons and daughters of humanity are but a breath;
the so-called great ones are an illusion.
On balanced scales they both rise;
together they are only a breath.

Trust not in extortion
and take no pride in stolen things;
even when riches increase
do not set your heart on them.

One thing God has spoken,
two things I have heard:
that to God is power
and to you, Lord, is love;
and surely you will reward to each
according to our deeds.

Glory…

Antiphon

PSALM 139:1-18,23-24

Antiphon *To you hearing I say, love your enemies*
and do good to the ones hating you. Lk 6:27

Advent, Lent & Christmas How precious, God, are your designs,
how vast are they, the sums of them.

Easter The night will shine as the day, alleluia.

Adonai, you search me and you know me.
You know my sitting and my rising;
you perceive my thoughts from afar.
You mark my going and my lying down,
and you are familiar with all of my ways.

When a word is not yet on my tongue
you see it, Adonai; you know them all.
Behind and before you hem me in
and rest your hand upon me.
Too wonderful for me is this knowledge,
more lofty than what I can attain.

Where can I hide from your Spirit?
Where could I flee from your presences?
If I go up to the heavens, you are there;
if I make a bed in Sheol, you I see!

If I rise on the wings of dawn,
if I settle on the far side of the sea,
even there your hand will guide me
and your right hand will hold me…

If I say, "Surely darkness will hide me
and the night will light around me,"
even darkness will not be dark to you
and night will shine as the day;
as the darkness, so the light.

For you created my inmost beings;
you knit me together in my mother's womb.
I praise you because I am full of fear and wonder;
my self knows well
how wonderful are your works.

My bones were not hidden from you
when I was made in the secret place,
woven together in the depths of earth.

Your eyes saw my body
and in your book were written and ordained
all the days before the first day was.

How precious to me, El, are your designs,
how vast are they, the sums of them;
if countable they number more than the sand.
Awake and still, I am with you.

Search me, El, and know my heart!
Test me, and know my anxious thoughts!
See if there is in me an offensive way,
then lead me in the way everlasting!

Glory…

Antiphon

PSALM 67

Antiphon *Peace I leave with you;*
my peace I give to you. Jn 14:27a

Advent & Lent May God be gracious to us, bless us,
and shine the holy face upon us.

Holy Week He took on all our sins
and asked that we be forgiven.

Christmas & Easter May the peoples praise you, God,
and rejoice in your salvation, alleluia.

May God be gracious to us and bless us,
may God's faces shine upon us.
How else can your ways be known on the earth
and your salvation among all the nations?

May the peoples praise you, God,
may the peoples praise you, all of them.

May the nations be glad and sing for joy
for you rule the peoples
and guide nations of the earth into justice.

May the peoples praise you, God,
may the peoples praise you, all of them.

The land will yield her harvest, God will bless us,
and all the ends of the earth will revere our God.

Glory... Antiphon

COLOSSIANS 1:12-20

Antiphon *Who follows me will have the light of life.* Jn 8:12c

Give joyful thanks to the Abba who made you fit
for your part of the lot of the saints in light,

who delivered us out of the authority of darkness,
transitioning us into the realm of the beloved Son
in whom we have redemption,
the forgiveness of our sins.

The Son is the image of the invisible God,
the firstborn of all creation.
In him all things were created,
in the heavens and on the earth,
the visible and the invisible,
whether thrones, lordships, rulers or authorities.

All creation has come to be through and for him.
He is before all things,
and in him all things hold together.

He is the head of the body, the church,
and the beginning, the firstborn from the dead,
so that in all things he may hold the first place.

In him all the fullness was well pleased to dwell,
and through him reconciliation to himself
of all things on earth and things in the heavens,
making peace through the blood of his cross.

Glory… Antiphon

ORDINARY TIME READING **1 PETER 5:1-7**

And so to presbyters among you, I exhort as a presbyter myself, a witness of the sufferings of Christ, and a share in the glory to be revealed. Shepherd the flock of God in your midst, not by compulsion but willingly according to God, not from eagerness for profit but eagerly, nor in exercising lordship over others but in being an example for the flock. And when the chief Shepherd appears, you will receive the unfading crown of glory.

Likewise, younger members submit yourselves to the presbyters, and all to one another gird yourselves in humility, because *God resists the arrogant, but gives grace to the humble.*

And so be humble under the mighty hand of God, who may then exalt you in time. Cast all of your anxiety on God, to whom everything about you matters.

RESPONSORY Ps 17:8

Keep us, O Lord…
…as the apple of your eye.
Hide us in the shade of your wings…
…as the apple of your eye.
Glory to the Father and to the Son and to the Holy Spirit:
…Keep us, O Lord as the apple of your eye.

ADVENT READING **1 CORINTHIANS 4:5**

Judge not anything before the time, until the coming of the Lord, who will shed light on our dark and hidden things and will show forth what goes on in human hearts. Then will be the praise to each one from God.

RESPONSORY Ps 146:7; 63:3; 67:2

Come and set us free...
...Lord God of power and glory.
Let your face shine upon us
and we will know salvation...
...Lord God of power and glory.
Glory to the Father and to the Son and to the Holy Spirit:
...Come and set us free, Lord God of power and glory.

I can never really know what goes on
in the heart of another. Indeed I hardly
know what is going on in my own heart,
but God knows. Only God has all the data,
and so the job of judging belongs to God alone.

CHRISTMAS READING **ROMANS 8:1-5**

Now there is no condemnation for the ones in Christ Jesus. For the law of the Spirit of life in Christ Jesus freed you from the law of sin and death. For the thing impossible by the law, weak through the flesh, God did, sending God's own Son in the likeness of sinful flesh condemning sin in the flesh, that the ordering of the law might be fulfilled in us, walking not in accord with the flesh but in accord with the Spirit.

RESPONSORY Jn 1:14

The Word became flesh…
…alleluia, alleluia.
And dwelt among us…
…alleluia, alleluia.
Glory to the Father and to the Son and to the Holy Spirit:
…The Word became flesh and dwelt among us,
alleluia, alleluia.

After Epiphany

All people will be blessed in him…
…in every tribe of the human race.
All nations will acclaim his glory…
…in every tribe of the human race.
Glory to the Father and to the Son and to the Holy Spirit:
…All people will be blessed in him,
in every tribe of the human race.

LENT READING, until Holy Week **PHILIPPIANS 2:12b-16**

My beloved, with fear and trembling you work out your salvation, for God is the one working in you both to will and to work on behalf of God's good will.

Do what you do without murmurings or disputes, blameless and harmless, children of God faultless in the midst of a crooked and perverse generation. Shine as luminaries in the world, holding up a word of life, a boast to me in the day of Christ, that not in vain did I run nor in vain labor.

RESPONSORY Lk 18:13

To you, O Lord…
…I make my prayer for mercy.
Heal my soul, for I have sinned against you…
…I make my prayer for mercy.
Glory to the Father and to the Son and to the Holy Spirit:
…To you, O Lord, I make my prayer for mercy.

LENT READING, Holy Week **EPHESIANS 4:32-5:2**

Be kind to one another, tenderhearted, and forgive yourselves as also God in Christ has forgiven you. Be therefore imitators of God, as beloved children, and walk in love. Christ has loved you and gave up himself on our behalf, an offering and a sacrifice to God for an odor of sweetness.

RESPONSORY Rev. 5:9

We worship you, O Christ...

...and we praise you.

By your cross you have redeemed the world...

...and we praise you.

Glory to the Father and to the Son and to the Holy Spirit:

...We worship you, O Christ, and we praise you.

EASTER READING **HEBREWS 7:24-27**

Jesus, because he remains unto the eons, has the priestly office without end. And so he is able to save entirely those approaching to God through him, always alive to intercede for them. To us indeed was suitable such a high priest, holy, harmless, undefiled, set apart from sinners, becoming higher than the heavens. He does not have the daily need of the high priests to offer up sacrifices first for their own sins and then for the sins of the people. For he did this once for all, offering up his very self.

RESPONSORY

The disciples rejoiced...

...alleluia, alleluia.

When they saw the risen Lord...

...alleluia, alleluia.

Glory to the Father and to the Son and to the Holy Spirit:

...The disciples rejoiced, alleluia, alleluia.

Gospel Canticle For Evening

Antiphons

Advent Wk 2	Zion, you will be renewed, and you will see the Just One who is coming to you.
Advent Wk 4 21st	O Radiant Dawn, sun of justice, come shine on those in the shadows.
Christmas	I have come forth from God into the world; I have not come of myself, but the Abba has sent me.
After Epiphany	Herod questioned the Magi: what is this sign of which you speak, this sign of a newborn ruler? We saw a brilliant star in the heavens; its splendor filled the world.
Ash Wednesday	When you give alms, do not let your left hand know what your right is doing.
Lent Wk 2	The Son of Humanity will be handed over to the gentiles to be mocked, scourged and crucified; and on the third day will rise again.

Antiphons for Gospel Canticle For Evening, continued

Lent Wk 4	By myself, says the Lord, I can do nothing. I judge as I am told and my sentence is just.
Holy Week	The Master says: my hour is close at hand; I and my disciples shall celebrate the Passover in your house.
Easter Wk 2	The child of God welcomes the light that searches deeds done and finds them true, alleluia.
Easter Wk 4	God sent the Son into the world not as judge but as savior, alleluia.
Easter Wk 6	The Spirit will glorify me and proclaim to you all that has been received from me, alleluia.
Ordinary Antiphon	*The Mighty One has done* *great things for me.*

CANTICLE of MARY (The Magnificat)
LUKE 1:46-55

+ **My soul** is stretched full with praise of the Lord,
and my spirit, beyond joy in God, my Savior,
who chose to lay eyes on this humble servant.

Behold, now and forward,
each and every age will call me blessed,
for the Mighty One did great things to me.

Holy is the name and the mercy
to generations and generations,
the ones fearing the One,

Who scattered the haughty of mind and heart,
pulled the powerful off their high place,
and lifted with dignity the humble in need.

The hungering are filled with good things,
the rich are sent away empty,
and servant Israel is given relief

with a memory of mercy to remember,
the promise spoken to our ancestors,
to Abraham and his descendants forever.

Glory…

Antiphon

INTERCESSIONS

- For all who have had a hard day at work…
- For all who have died…
- In gratitude for blessings…; Abba thank you.
- For the sins of this day…; Lord Jesus have mercy.
- With concerns over tomorrow…; Holy Spirit help.

FOR VOCATIONS

Father, you call us to the table of your Son,
renew us by word and sacrament,
and send us to labor in your harvest.
We are a people in need of the witness
of faithful marriages and priests,
generous single people and deacons,
religious sisters, brothers, monks and nuns.
Help each disciple to trust in your call,
make us able and willing to do what you ask,
keep us united in our gifted diversity,
and bring to maturity every seed you sow.
All this we ask through the Good Shepherd:
Jesus Christ, your Son and our Lord.

OUR FATHER…

Seeker, everybody is looking for God.
Disciple, Jesus has more to teach you.
Minister, whose feet are you washing?
Apostle, you are sent out as good news.

See *God's Ones* by Stephen Joseph Wolf

WEEK II
THURSDAY MORNING

\+ *God, come to my assistance;* Psalm 70:2
Lord, make haste to help me!

Glory...

ORDINARY TIME

A **O/ breathe on me, O/ breath of God,**
Fill/ me with life a//-new,
That I may love what you have loved,
And do what you would do.

O/ breathe on me, O/ breath of God,
Un/-til my heart is// pure,
Un-til with you I will one will,
To do and to en-dure.

O/ breathe on me, O/ breath of God,
In/-spire my bu-sy// mind,
Un-til this earth-ly part of me
Glows with your fire div-ine.

O/ breathe on me, O/ breath of God,
My/ soul shall nev-er// die,
But live in your e-ter-nal life,
Your love the rea-son why.

116, Text: Edwin Hatch, 1878, altered
Music: ST. COLUMBA, CM; Gaelic Folk Melody
Popular melody for: *The King Of Love My Shepherd Is*

ORDINARY TIME

B **Je-sus, my Lord\, my God/, my all\;**
How late, my Je-sus, have I sought.
You pour down rich\-es of/ your grace\;
How can I love you as I ought?
Je-sus, our Lord, we you a-dore!
Call us to love you more/ and more\.
Call us to love you more and more.

Je-sus, what could you have found/ in me\
That you have dealt so pa-tient-ly?
How great the joy\ that you/ have brought\,
So far ex-ceed-ing hope or thought!
Je-sus, our Lord, we you a-dore!
Call us to love you more/ and more\.
Call us to love you more and more.

Had I but Ma\-ry's sin/-less heart\
With which to love you, dear-est King;
O! with what bursts\ of fer/-vent praise\
Your good-ness, Je-sus, would I sing.
Sweet Sac-ra-ment, we you a-dore!
Call us to love you more/ and more\.
Call us to love you more and more.

104, Text: Henry A. Collins, 1854, altered;
vs. 3 Frederick W. Faber, d. 1863, altered
Music: SWEET SACRAMENT, LM with refrain,
Romischkatholisches Gesanguchlein , 1826

ADVENT

God, our/ ref\\-uge and strength,
Ev-er/ pres-ent help in stress.
God is with us, so we fear not.
Though the\ earth and moun-tains shake,
Deep of\ wa-ters foam and rage,
Moun-tains tot-ter, wa-ter surg-ing,
God of Ja-cob is our strong-hold, God is with_ us.

Ho-ly/ dwell-ing of our God,
Stream-ing/ riv-er glad-den there
In the cit-y of our ref-uge.
Na-tions\ rage and king-doms fall,
All earth\ trem-bles at the call,
God will help at break of new day,
God of Ja-cob is our strong-hold, God is with_ us.

"**B**e still and know that I am God."
Come and/ see the works of God:
Stop-ping war in ev-'ry na-tion,
Break-ing\ weap-on, break-ing spear,
Burn-ing\ bow and ar-mor shield,
Say-ing, "Be still, know your God now,"
God of Ja-cob is our strong-hold, God is with_ us.

80, Text: Psalm 46, by Stephen J. Wolf, 2003,
tribute to the priesthood of Joseph E. Wesley
Music: LASST UNS ERFREUEN, LM with alleluias;
Geistliche Kirchengesange, 1623
Popular melody for: *All Creatures of Our God and King*

CHRISTMAS

Lo_, how a Rose e'er bloom_-ing_
From_ ten-der_ stem_ hath sprung_!
Of_ Jes-se's lin-eage com_-ing_,
As_ those of_ old_ have s ung_.
It came, a flow-er bright,
A-mid the cold of win_-ter_,
When_ half spent_ was_ the night.

I_-sai-ah 'twas fore-told_ it_,
This_ Rose I_ have_ in mind_,
With_ Ma-ry we be-hold_ it_,
The_ Vir-gin_ Moth_-er kind_.
To show God's love a-right,
She bore to us a Sav_-ior_,
When_ half spent_ was_ the night.

O_ Flow'r, whose fra-grance ten_-der_
With_ sweet-ness_ fills_ the air_,
Dis_-pel in glo-rious spen_-dor_
The_ dark-ness_ ev_-'ry-where;
True man, yet ver-y God,
From sin and death now save_ us_,
And_ share our_ ev_-'ry load.

41, Text: based on Isaiah 11:1; traditional German carol, 15th C.;
translated by Theodore Baker, 1851-1934, altered
Music: 76 76 6 76 ES IST EIN' ROS' ENTSPRUNGEN,
Alte Catholische Geistliche Kirchengesange , Cologne, 1599

LENT

Face to face with all who would be "gods,"
Our God ri-ses to judge-ment give:
"How long will you judge with-out jus-tice?"
Asks the One true God who\ lives,
"How long will you give
To those with pow'r and means
All your fa-vor, judge-ment, and will?"

"**Y**ou who would be "gods," seek-ing pow-er,
Nei-ther know nor un-der\-stand,
Wan-der-ing the land, walk in dark-ness,
Shake the world's foun-da-tion a-round;
'gods' though you would be,
Off-spring of the Most High,
Your lives, mor-tal prin-ces, will end."

If you would be God's judg-ing ser-vant,
Ren-der jus-tice to God's own poor,
Keep-ing safe from all who would harm them,
Or-phan, wid-ow, strang-er at shore.
To the low-ly and peo-ple af-flict\-ed
Give their due of earth's fruit and store.

90, Text: Psalm 82, Stephen J. Wolf, 2007, tribute to the priesthood of James D. Niedergeses, ninth bishop of Nashville
Music: 87 87 87 PICARDY,
Chansons Populaires des Provinces de France, 1860
Popular melody for: *Let All Mortal Flesh Keep Silence*

EASTER

Refrain

Great are the works of the Lord,
we trea-sure them with de-light!
Al-le-lu-ia! Al-le-lu-ia! Praise God our Mak-er!

Praise I give to the Lord, all my heart, with
peo-ple as-semb-led seek-ing good-ness and light.
Refrain

Works of wis-dom, ma-jes-tic de-sign,
en-dur-ing re-nown for-e-ver, won-der-ful deeds.
Refrain

Who gave food, fill-ing up wan-d'ring awe,
re-mem-b'ring the cov-e-nant in mer-cy you made.
Refrain

Peop-le lost wit-ness pow-er-ful deeds,
your chos-en in-her-i-ted the land, prom-ised land.
Refrain

From the works of the hands of the Lord
de-crees made rel-i-a-ble and worth-y of trust.
Refrain

Fear the Lord on-ly: awe-some and wise;
and pru-dent are those who sing out praise,
simp-le praise. *Refrain*

95, Text: from Psalm 111, by Stephen J. Wolf, 2005,
tribute to the priesthood of Patrick Connor
Music: FESTIVAL CANTICLE, Irregular, Richard Hillert, b.1923.
Popular melody for: *This Is The Feast Of Victory For Our God*

PSALM 3

Antiphon *Whoever does and teaches*
these commandments
will be called great in
the reign of heaven. Mt 5:19

How many, Adonai,
are rising against me,
saying of me in enmity,
"No deliverance by God for this self!"

But you, Adonai, shield around me,
my glorious One, you lift my head.
My voice cries to Adonai
who answers me from the holy mountain.

I lie down and I sleep;
and I wake because Adonai sustains me.
I will have no fear of tens of thousands of people
who are drawn up on every side against me.

Arise, Adonai! Deliver me, my God!
You struck the jaw of enmity
and broke the teeth of bad doings.
From Adonai is the deliverance.
May your blessing be on your people.

Glory...

Antiphon

PSALM 6

Antiphon *Young human, I say to you: Arise!* Lk 7:14

Christmas & Easter Be merciful, Lord, and heal me, alleluia.

Adonai, do not rebuke me in your anger
nor discipline me in your wrath.
Be merciful to me, Adonai, for I am weak.
Heal me, Adonai, for my bones are in agony
and my soul is in great anguish.

But you, Adonai, how long?
Turn, Adonai, and deliver my soul!
Save me because of your unfailing love!
Not from death are you remembered.
Who can praise you from Sheol?

I am worn out from my groaning;
through all the night I flood my bed with tears,
I drench my couch.
My eye grows weak with sorrow;
she weakens because of enmity.

Away from me, all doers of the bad,
for Adonai has heard the sound of my weeping.
Adonai has heard my cry for mercy.
Adonai accepts my prayer.
May enmity be ashamed and greatly dismayed,
and turn back in humble confusion.

Glory... Antiphon

PSALM 44

Antiphon *The reign of heaven is like leaven*
a woman mixes into three measures
of flour until the whole is leavened. Mt 13:33

With our ears, God, we have heard,
our ancestors told us the deed you did
in their days, in days long ago.

You drove out nations by your hand
and you planted them;
you crushed peoples so they could flourish.

For they won victory not by their sword and arm,
but by your right hand and arm
and the light of your faces,
for you loved them.

You are my Ruler and my God;
decree the victories of Jacob.
Through you we push back enmity;
through your name we trample opposition.

Indeed I trust not in my bow
and my sword does not bring me victory,
but you give to us victory over enmity
and shame the adversity.
In God we boast all the day
and we will praise your name to forever.

Psalm 44, continued

But you let us be rejected and humbled
and you do not go out with our armies.
You turned us back before enmity
and adversity plundered from us.

You gave us up like sheep devoured;
among the nations you scattered us.
You sold your people for no great price,
gaining nothing from their sale.

You made us a reproach to our neighbors,
scorn and derision to those around us.
You made us a byword among the nations,
a shaking of heads among the peoples.

All the day my disgrace is before me
and shame covers my face
at taunts of reproachers and revilers
because of avenging enmity.

All of this though we did not forget you
and were not false to your covenant.
Our hearts did not turn back
and our feet did not stray from your path,
but you pushed us into haunts of jackals
and you covered us over with deep darkness.

If we forgot the name of our God,
if we spread out our hands to a foreign "god,"
would God not have discovered this,
the One knowing the secrets of the heart?
Yet for you we face death all the day;
we are considered as sheep for slaughter.

Wake up, Lord! Why do you sleep?
Rouse yourself! Do not reject us to forever.
Why do you hide your faces
and forget our misery and oppression?

Indeed our self is brought down to the dust;
our body clings to the ground.
Rise up as our help and redeem us!
because of your unfailing love.

Glory...

Antiphon *The reign of heaven is like leaven*
a woman mixes into three measures
of flour until the whole is leavened. Mt 13:33

A human has the right to act in conscience
and in freedom so as personally to make moral
decisions and 'must not be forced to act contrary to
their conscience. Nor must they be prevented from acting
according to their conscience, especially in religious matters.'

See *Catechism* #1782, Vatican II *Declaration on Religious Freedom*

PSALM 80

Antiphon *The reign of God will be given*
to a people who produce its fruit. Mt 21:43

Advent & Lent Shepherd of Israel, awaken your might.

Holy Week See my suffering, Lord,
and come quickly.

Christmas & Easter I am the vine, you are the branches;
alleluia. Jn 15:5a

Hear us, One Shepherd of Israel,
you who lead Joseph like a flock.
From your throne on the cherubim, shine forth
before Ephraim, Benjamin and Manasseh!
Awaken your might! Come to our salvation!

O God, restore us!
Make your faces shine that we may be saved!

Until when, Adonai, God of Hosts,
will you smolder against
the prayer of your people?
You fed them with bread of tears
and you made them drink tears by the bowlful.
You made us a contention to our neighbors,
and enmity mocks us.

God of Hosts, restore us!
Make your faces shine that we may be saved!

Out from Egypt, you brought a vine;
you drove out the nations and you planted it.
You cleared the ground before her;
her roots took root and she filled the land.

Mountains were covered by her shade
and the mighty cedars by her branches.
She sent out her branches to the Sea,
and her shoots as far as the River.

Why have you broken down her walls?
All who pass by the way pluck her fruit.
The boar from the forest ravages her,
and creatures of the field feed on her.

God of Hosts, return now!
Look down from heaven!
See and watch over this vine,
this root that your right hand planted.
Some would burn it or cut it down;
at the rebuke of your faces may those plans perish.

Let your hand be on the one at your right hand,
the descendant of Adam you raised up for yourself.
Then we will not turn away from you;
you revive us and we will call on your name.

Adonai, God of Hosts, restore us!
Make your faces shine that we may be saved!

Glory…

Antiphon

PSALM 81

Antiphon *The sabbath was made for human beings,*
not human beings for the sabath. Mk 2:27

Holy Week The Lord has fed us
with finest of wheat
and honey from the rock.

Christmas & Easter The Lord feeds us
with finest of wheat,
alleluia.

Sing for joy to God our strength!
Shout to the God of Jacob!

Begin the music! Strike the tambourine,
the melodious harp and the lyre!
Sound the ram horn at the new moon,
the full moon, the day of our feast!

For this is a decree for Israel,
an ordinance of the God of Jacob,
a statute established for Joseph
when time to go out from the land of Egypt.

I hear a tongue I do not know:
"I removed the burden from their shoulders,
their hands were freed from the basket.
In distress you called and I rescued you;

I answered from the thundercloud
and tested you at the waters of Meribah.
Hear, my people, and I will warn you, Israel,
if you will listen to me:

'No foreign "god" shall be among you;
you shall bow to no alien "god."
I am Adonai, your God,
who brought you out of the land of Egypt.
Open wide your mouth and I will fill it!'

But my people did not listen to my voice,
and Israel did not submit to me.
So I gave them to their stubborn heart
and they followed their devices.

If my people were listening to me,
if Israel would walk in my ways,
as quickly would I subdue enmity
and turn a firm hand to adversity.

Anyone hating Adonai would cringe
under punishment lasting to forever.
But I will feed my people with finest of wheat
and satisfy you with honey out of rock."

Glory...

Antiphon

ISAIAH 12:1b-6

Antiphon *The crowds asked John the Baptist,*
what then shall we do? Lk 3:10

Advent & Lent Make known among the nations
the deeds of the Lord.

Christmas & Easter You will rejoice and draw water
from the well of the Savior, alleluia.

I will praise you, Adonai.
Though you were angry with me,
your anger turned away and you comforted me.

Surely God is my salvation!
I will trust and will not be afraid
for Yah is my strength and my song.

Adonai became for me salvation
and you will draw with joy
waters from wells of salvation…

Give thanks to Adonai! Call on the name!
Make the deeds known among the nations!
Proclaim that the name is exalted!

Sing to Adonai, who has done glory!
Let this be known to all the world.

Shout! And sing for joy, dwellers of Zion!
For great in your midst is the Holy One of Israel.

Glory… Antiphon

ISAIAH 66:7-14a

Antiphon *Know this: the reign of God is at hand.*

Lk 10:11b

Christmas Let the prophets be proven true.

Easter I will see you again
and your heart will rejoice, alleluia.

"**Before she goes into labor** she gives birth;
before pain comes upon her, she delivers a son.
Who has heard of such as this?
Who has seen such as these?

Can a country be born in one day
or a nation be brought forth in one moment?
Yet she is in labor,
then Zion gives birth to her children.

Do I bring to the moment of birth
and not give delivery?"
asks your God Adonai;
"Do I bring one to delivery and then close up?

Rejoice with Jerusalem and be glad for her!
All who love her, rejoice with her!
Rejoice, all who mourn over her,

for you will nurse and you will be satisfied
at the breast of her comforts,
for you will drink deeply and you will delight
in the overflow of her abundance."

Isaiah 66, continued

For this says Adonai:
"See, I extend peace to her like a river,
and wealth of nations like a flooding stream,
and you will nurse, being carried at her side,
and you will be playdanced on her knees.

As a child is comforted by a mother,
so will I comfort you
and over Jerusalem you will be comforted.

When you see, your heart will rejoice
and your bones will flourish like the grass."

Glory...

Antiphon *Know this: the reign of God is at hand.* Lk 10:11b

Christmas Let the prophets be proven true.

Easter I will see you again
and your heart will rejoice, alleluia.

PSALM 143:1-11

Antiphon *Go into all the cosmos and*
proclaim the gospel to all creation. Mk 16:15

Adonai, hear my prayer.
Listen in your fidelity to my cries for mercy.
Relieve me in your justice.
Bring not your servant into judgment
for not anyone alive is just before you.

Indeed enmity pursues my self
and crushes my life to the ground
and makes me dwell in dark places
like dead ones of long ago.
My spirit grows faint within me;
within me my heart is dismayed.

I remember days of long ago
and meditate on all of your work
and consider the deeds of your hands.
I stretch out my hands to you;
like land parched my soul thirsts for you.

Be quick! Answer me, Adonai! My spirit faints!
Hide not your faces from me
or I will be like and with ones going down the pit.

Bring in the morning your word of unfailing love,
for in you I trust.
Show me the way I should go
for to you I lift up my soul!

Rescue me, Adonai, from enmity; in you I hide.
Teach me to do your will, for you are my El.
May your good Spirit lead me on level ground.

For the sake of your Name, Adonai,
you keep me alive in your justice;
you bring my self out from trouble.

Glory…

Antiphon

ORDINARY TIME READING **ROMANS 14:13-19**

And so let us no longer judge one another, but rather judge ourselves thus: to put no stumbling block in the way of a brother or sister or any offense. I know and am persuaded by the Lord Jesus that nothing is unclean in itself, except to the one reckoning something unclean to whom it is unclean. For if your brother or sister is grieved because of food, you no longer walk in love. Do not destroy by food one on whose behalf Christ died. Do not let what is good to you be blasphemed.

For the reign of God is not eating and drinking, but justice and peace and joy in the Holy Spirit. Those serving Christ in these are approved and well-pleasing to God and human beings. And so let us pursue the things of peace and the things of building up for one another.

RESPONSORY Ps 63:7,8

On my bed through the watch of night…
…O Lord, I think of you.
You who are my help,...
…O Lord, I think of you.
Glory to the Father and to the Son and to the Holy Spirit:
…On my bed through the watch of night,
O Lord, I think of you.

ADVENT READING **ISAIAH 45:5-8**

I am Adonai and there is no other; apart from me there is no God. I will strengthen you though you do not know me so that they may know there is none besides me, from the rising of the sun to its setting place. I am Adonai and there is no other, forming light and creating darkness, bringing prosperity and allowing disaster; I Adonai am the one doing all of these. Heavens at above, let them rain; and let clouds shower justice; let the earth open and let salvation spring up and with justice; let them grow together, as I Adonai have created.

RESPONSORY

Your light will come, Jerusalem…
…the Lord will dawn on you in radiant beauty.
The glory of the Lord you will see within you…
…the Lord will dawn on you in radiant beauty.
Glory to the Father and to the Son and to the Holy Spirit:
…Your light will come, Jerusalem;
the Lord will dawn on you in radiant beauty.

CHRISTMAS READING **WISDOM 7:26-30**

Lady Wisdom Sophia is the shining of eternal light, a spotless mirror of the working of God, an image of God's goodness. But one, she can do all things; while perduring, she renews all things. From age to age she passes into holy souls and makes of them friends of God and prophets.

God's love is as great for nothing as for the one who lives with wisdom. Her beauty is greater than the sun, and every constellation of the stars. She is superior to light itself, taken over by the night, for the bad cannot prevail against wisdom.

RESPONSORY

The Lord has made known…
…alleluia, alleluia.
The saving power…
…alleluia, alleluia.
Glory to the Father and to the Son and to the Holy Spirit:
…The Lord has made known the saving power, alleluia.

After Epiphany

All the royal powers on earth
…will bow down in worship.
Men and women of every nation…
…will bow down in worship.
Glory to the Father and to the Son and to the Holy Spirit:
…All the royal powers on earth
will bow down in worship.

LENT READING, until Holy Week **1 KINGS 8:51-53a**

For your people and your inheritance whom you brought from Egypt, from the midst of the iron furnace, let your eyes be open to the plea of your servant and to the plea of your people Israel, to listen to them in all their cries to you, for you singled them out from all nations of the earth as an inheritance for you.

RESPONSORY Lk 18:13

The Lord God will set me free…
…from the hunter's snare.
From all those who would trap me with lying words,
…and from the hunter's snare.
Glory to the Father and to the Son and to the Holy Spirit:
…The Lord God will set me free
from the hunter's snare.

READING, Holy Week **HEBREWS 2:9-10**

We see Jesus, who was made for a little while less than the angels for the suffering of death, now crowned with glory and honor, that by the grace of God he might taste of death on behalf of every human.

It was fitting for the One for whom and through whom all things exist, leading many sons and daughters to glory, that the leader of their salvation be perfect through sufferings.

RESPONSORY Rev. 5:9

Lord, by your own blood…
…you brought us back to God.
From every tribe and tongue and people and nation…
…you brought us back to God.
Glory to the Father and to the Son and to the Holy Spirit:
…Lord, by your own blood you brought us back to God.

EASTER READING **ROMANS 8:9-11**

You are not in flesh but in Spirit, since the Spirit of God dwells in you. If anyone does not have the Spirit of Christ, this one is not of him. But if Christ is in you, the body is dead because of sin and the spirit is alive because of vindication.

If the Spirit of the one who raised Jesus from the dead dwells in you, the one who raised Christ Jesus from the dead will also give life to your mortal bodies through the indwelling of the Spirit in you.

RESPONSORY

The Lord is risen from the tomb…
…alleluia, alleluia.
He hung upon the cross for us…
…alleluia, alleluia.
Glory to the Father and to the Son and to the Holy Spirit:
…The Lord is risen from the tomb, alleluia, alleluia.

Gospel Canticle For Morning

Antiphons

Advent Wk 2 Matt 11:11-15	I will help you, says the Lord. I am your Savior, the Holy One of Israel.
Advent Wk 4 (see pg 759)	At the sound of Mary's greeting Elizabeth's child in womb leapt for joy.
Christmas (see pg 759)	The Lord our God has come to the people of God and set us free.
After Epiphany Luke 4:14-22	All peoples, bearing gifts, will come from afar, alleluia.
Thursday after Ash Wednesday Luke 9:22-25	Let anyone who wishes to be my disciple deny their self, take up their cross, and follow me.
Lent Wk 2 Luke 16:19-31	Remember the good things you received in your lifetime and the bad things Lazarus received in his.
Lent Wk 4 John 5:31-47	John gave witness to the truth, and though I need no human witness, says the Lord, I remind you of this for your own salvation.

Antiphons for Gospel Canticle For Morning, continued

Holy Week Luke 4:16-21	I have longed to eat this meal with you before I suffer.
Easter Wk 2 John 3:31-36	God does not ration the gift of the Spirit, alleluia.
Easter Wk 4 John 13:16-20	No disciple is greater than the teacher; be glad to become like your master, alleluia.
Easter Wk 6 John 16:16-20	In a little while you will no longer see me, says the Lord; then a little later you will see me again since I am going to the Abba, alleluia.
Ordinary Antiphon	*Lord, give us knowledge of salvation* *known in the forgiveness of our sins.*

Gospel Reading for Thursday of

Week **2**	Mark 3:7-12	**14**	Matt 10:7-15	**26**	Luke 10:1-12
4	Mark 6:7-13	**16**	Matt 13:10-17	**28**	Lk 11:47-54
6	Mark 8:27-33	**18**	Matt 16:13-23	**30**	Lk 13:31-35
8	Mark 10:46-52	**20**	Matt 22:1-14	**32**	Lk 17:20-25
10	Matt 5:20-26	**22**	Luke 5:1-11	**34**	Lk 21:20-28
12	Matt 7:21-29	**24**	Luke 7:36-50		

CANTICLE of ZECHARIAH (The Benedictus)
LUKE 1:68-79

+ **Blessed be** the Lord the God of Israel
who chose a people to visit with redemption,
and raised salvation in the house of David,
saving strength from God's own servant,

speaking from the age of the prophets
through the mouth of the holy prophet:
Salvation out of enmity,
even out of those who hate us,

to show our ancestors how mercy works, -
and to remember the holy promise of the Lord,
the covenant made for our ancestor Abraham,
calming our fear and making us free
to serve with holy justice before God all our days.

And you also child -
will be called a prophet of the Most High
for you will go before the Lord to prepare his way
and give to people a knowledge of salvation
known in accepting forgiveness of their sins.

From the tender mercy of our God,
the sun rising from the height will visit with light
for those who sit in the dark or shadow of death
and to guide our feet into the way of peace.

Glory...

Antiphon

PETITIONS FOR THE CONSECRATION TO GOD OF THE DAY AND ITS WORK

- For the Church and her ministry and apostolates...
- For secular authorities and all serving as stewards...
- For people who are poor or sick or in sorrow...
- For peace and the basic needs of each human being...
- For a culture of vocations all over the world...

PONDER QUESTIONS for a CULTURE of VOCATIONS

My Lord and my God, help me to know how you have wired me for community, friendship and **love.** What is the form of life into which you are calling me that I may best **love** and be loved? Single? Married? Religious?

Lord, how have you made me in your image? With what gifts, virtues, talents and charisms? How are you calling me to participate in your ongoing **work** of creation?

Lord, for whom might you call me to place my life on the line? For what value, **truth**, reality, idea or person are you preparing me to give my life? How should I begin to live fully alive for this?

Lord, you know and love me even better than I know and love myself; how are you calling me to **be alone** with you in prayer? How are you calling me to participate in the redemptive, forgiving, healing mission of your Son, my Lord, Jesus Christ?

OUR FATHER...

WEEK II
THURSDAY EVENING

\+ *God, come to my assistance;* Psalm 70:2
Lord, make haste to help me!

Glory...

LENT

Sing, my tongue, the Sa-vior's glo-ry,
Of his flesh the mys-t'ry sing,
Of the blood, all price ex-ceed-ing,
Shed by our im-mort-al King,
Des-tined, for the world's re-demp-tion,
From a no-ble womb to spring.

On the night of that Last Sup-per,
Seat-ed with his cho-sen band,
He, the pas-chal vic-tim eat-ing,
First ful-fills the law's com-mand;
Then as food to all his sib-lings
Gives him-self with his own hand.

To the ev-er-last-ing Fa-ther,
And the Son who made us free,
And the Spir-it, God pro-ceed-ing,
From them each e-ter-nal-ly,
Be sal-va-tion, hon-or, bless-ing,
Might and end-less maj-es-ty.

53, Text: Thomas Aquinas, *Pange lingua gloriosi*, d. 1274,
translated by Edward Caswell, 1849, altered
Music: 87 87 87 ST. THOMAS (TANTUM ERGO) JohnF.Wade,d.1786
Popular melody for: *Down In Adoration Falling*

ORDINARY TIME & EASTER

Lord, when at your
Last Sup-per you did pray
That all your Church
might be for-ev-er one.
Grant us at ev'-ry
Eu-cha-rist to say
With long-ing heart and soul,
"Your will be done."
O may we all
one bread, one bod-y be,
Through this blest
Sac-ra-ment of U-ni-ty.

For all your Church,
O Lord, we in-ter-cede;
Make all our sad
div-is-ions soon to cease;
Draw us the near-er each,
to each we plead,
By draw-ing all to you,
O Prince of Peace;
Thus may we all
one bread, one bod-y be,
Through this blest
Sac-ra-ment of U-ni-ty.

We pray for all
who wan-der from your fold;
O bring them home,
Good Shep-herd of the sheep,
Back to the faith which
saints be-lieved of old,
Back to the Church which
still the faith does keep;
Soon may we all
one bread, one bod-y be,
Through this blest
Sac-ra-ment of U-ni-ty.

So, Lord, at length
when sac-ra-ments shall cease,
May we be one with
all your Church a-bove,
One with your saints
in one un-bro-ken peace,
One with your saints
in one un-bound-ed love;
More bless-ed still
in peace and love to be
One with the Trin-i-ty
in U-ni-ty.

106, Text: William H. Turton, 1859-1938, altered
Music: 10 10 10 10 10 10 UNDE ET MEMORES,
William H. Monk, 1823-1899

ADVENT & CHRISTMAS

I\ heard the voice of Je-sus say,
"Come/ un-to me\ and rest;
Lay\ down, you wea-ry one, lay down
Your/ head up-on\ my breast."
I/ came to Je\-sus as I was,
So/ wea-ry\, worn and sad;
I\ found in him a rest-ing place,
And/ he has made\ me glad.

I\ heard the voice of Je-sus say,
"Be/-hold, I free\-ly give
The\ liv-ing wa-ter; thirs-ty one,
Stoop/ down, and drink\ and live."
I/ came to Je\-sus, and I drank
Of/ that life\-giv-ing stream.
My\ thirst was quenched, my soul re-vived,
And/ now I live\ in him.

I\ heard the voice of Je-sus say,
"I/ am this dark\ world's light;
Look\ un-to me, your morn shall rise
And/ all your day\ be bright."
I/ looked to Je\-sus, and I found
In/ him my\ star, my sun;
And\ in that light of life I'll walk,
Till/ trav'l-ing days\ are done.

100, Text: Horatius Bonar, *Hymns Original and Selected*, 1846, altered
Music: KINGSFOLD, CMD, trad. English melody,
adapted by Ralph Vaughan Williams, 1906

PSALM 56:2-7,9-14

Antiphon *The word of God is the seed.* Lk 8:11b

Advent & Lent In God I trust, I will not be afraid;
what can humanity do to me?

Christmas & Easter Alleluia, alleluia, alleluia.

Be merciful to me, my God!
Human beings pursue me all the day,
attacking with oppression
and with slander all the day.

Indeed in their pride do the many attack me.
On the day I am afraid, in you I trust.
My praise is of God's word, in God I trust.
I will not be afraid; what can a mortal do to me?

All the day they twist my words against me;
all their plots are for harm.
They conspire, they lurk, they watch my steps;
they are eager for my life...

Record my lament, put my tears in your wineskin;
are they not in your record?
Enmity will turn back on the day I call;

I will know that God is for me.
In God whose word I praise,
in Adonai whose word I praise, in God I trust.
I will not be afraid; what can a human do to me?

Psalm 56, continued

Upon me, God, are my vows to you;
I will present thank offerings to you
for you delivered my soul from death
and my feet from stumbling,
to walk in God's presence
in the light of the living.

Glory…

Antiphon *The seed is the word of God.* Lk 8:11b

Advent & Lent In God I trust, I will not be afraid;
what can humanity do to me?

Christmas & Easter Alleluia, alleluia, alleluia.

PSALM 60:3-14a

Antiphon *Do not judge, lest you be judged.* Mt 7:1

Holy Thursday Jesus Christ,
the firstborn from the dead
and Ruler of the rulers of the earth,
has made us a royal people
to serve our God and Abba.

Christmas & Easter Alleluia, alleluia, alleluia.

God you rejected us,
breaking our defenses;
you were angry, now restore us.

You shook the land and tore her open;
mend her fractures, for she quakes!
You showed your people a desperate time;
you made us drink wine to staggering.

For those who fear you, you raised a banner
to be unfurled against the bow,
that your beloved ones may be delivered.
Help us with your right hand and save us!

God spoke from the sanctuary:
"I will triumph and parcel out Shechem,
and measure out the valley of Succoth;
mine are Gilead and Manasseh,

Ephraim my head helmet,
Judah my scepter,
and Moab my washbasin;
On Edom I toss my sandal
and over Philistia I shout in triumph"

Who will bring me to the Fortress City?
Who will lead me to Edom?
Have you, God, not rejected us,
and not gone out, God, with our armies?

Against enmity give to us aid,
for worthless is human help.
In God will we gain the victory…

Glory…

Antiphon

PSALM 128

Antiphon *Everyone having will be given more*
and to abundance; but the one not having,
even that will be taken. Mt 25:29

Advent & Lent May the Lord bless you from Zion
and see to the prosperity of Jerusalem
all the days of your life.

Christmas & Easter Alleluia, alleluia, alleluia.

Blessed are all who fear Adonai
and walk in the way.

Indeed you will eat from the labor of your hands.
To you will be blessings and prosperity,
and your spouse like a fruitful vine
inside and outside your house,
sons and daughters around your table
like shoots of the olives.

See: one who fears Adonai is blessed;
may Adonai bless you from Zion.
See and enjoy the prosperity of Jerusalem
all the days of your life,
and the joy of the children of your children.

Peace be upon Israel.

Glory...

Antiphon

PSALM 129

Antiphon *I am the bread of life; who comes to me*
does not hunger and who believes in me
will never thirst. Jn 6:35

Advent & Lent The Lord gains victory over me.

Christmas & Easter Alleluia, alleluia, alleluia.

"**From my youths** they oppressed me greatly,"
let Israel now say.
"From my youths they oppressed me greatly,
but gained no victory over me.

On my back the plowers plowed;
long are the furrows they made.
Adonai the Just
cut free the cords of bad doings."

May all haters of Zion
be shamed and turned back;
May they be like grass on housetops
which withers before it grows,

which cannot fill one hand of the reaper
nor an arm of the gatherer,
and passers-by will not say,
"Blessing of Adonai upon you!
We bless you in the name of Adonai!"

Glory... Antiphon

PSALM 72

Antiphon *Out of you, Bethlehem, will come forth a ruler*
who will shepherd my people Israel. Mt 2:6;
Micah 5:2

Lent I will make you a covenant of the
people, a light for the Gentiles. Is 42:6b

Easter God has appointed him to judge
the living and the dead, alleluia.

God, endow your justice to King Solomon
and your judgment to the royal heir,
to judge your people with integrity
and your afflicted with justice.

Mountains will bring prosperity to the people,
the hills too in abundance.
He is to defend people afflicted,
save the children of the needy,
and crush the oppressor.

They will fear you as long as the sun,
as long as the moon,
from generation to generations.
He is to be like rain falling on a mown field,
like showers watering the earth.

In his days the just are to flourish
in prosperous abundance til the moon is no more.
He will rule from sea to sea
and from the River to the ends of the earth.

Desert tribes will bow;
the royals of Tarshish and the distant shores
will bring tribute and present gifts
with royals of Sheba and Seba.
They will bow down to him;
the royals of all the nations will thus serve.

For he is to deliver the needy one crying out
and the afflicted one when no one is helping,
to take pity on the weak and the needy
and save the lives of the poor;

to rescue their lives
from oppression and violence,
for their lifeblood will be precious in his eyes.

May he live and be given gold of Sheba;
may all ever pray that he be blessed all the day.

May grain be abundant throughout the land,
on tops of hills, swaying like the fruit of Lebanon,
and people flourish and thrive like grass in a field.

May his name endure to forever
and continue as long as the sun;
being thus blessed, may the nations bless him.

Blessed be God, Adonai, God of Israel,
alone doing marvelous deeds.
Blessed be the glory of the name to forever;
may the earth be filled with the glory of God.
Amen and amen.

Glory... Antiphon

PSALM 144

Antiphon *Zaccheus, come down quickly,*
for this day it is fitting
for me to stay at your house. Lk 19:5

Advent & Lent
Lord who am I that you care for me?
Human heir that you think of me?

Dec. 17-23
To you, O Lord, I lift up my soul;
come and rescue me,
my refuge and my strength.

Christmas & Easter
The Lord is my stronghold
and my savior, alleluia.

Praised be Adonai, my Rock,
who trains my hands for war, my fingers for battle,

my love and fortress, my stronghold and deliverer,
my shield in whom I take refuge,
who subdues peoples under me.

What, Adonai, is a human, that you care for us?
Children of humanity, that you think of them?
Like a breath is the human,
whose days are like a shadow passing.

Adonai, part your heavens and come down!
Touch the mountains so they smoke!
You send lightning lit to scatter enmity!
Shoot your arrows and you rout them!

Reach your hands from on high!
Deliver me! Rescue me from the mighty waters,
from the hand of foreign peoples speaking lies
whose right hands are the right hand of deceit.

I will sing a new song to you, God,
and on the lyre of ten make music to you,
the One giving victory to the rulers,
the One delivering your servant David
from the deadly sword.

Deliver me! Rescue me from foreign hands,
whose mouths speak the lie,
whose right hands are the right hand of deceit.

Our children in their youth
are like well nurtured plants,
like carved pillars adorning a palace,

our barns filled with provisions of every kind,
our sheep becoming thousands
and tens of thousands in our fields,
and our oxen drawing loads,

no break in the walls and no exile
nor a cry of distress in the streets:
Blessed are the people of whom all this is true;
blessed are the people whose God is Adonai.

Glory…

Antiphon

REVELATION 11:17-18, 12:10-12a

Antiphon *Now have come*
the salvation, the power,
and the reign of our God.

Dec 17-23 Turn to us, O Lord;
make haste to help your people.

Christmas Our God, who is and who was,
has taken great power to reign.

Holy Thursday The saints won their victory over
death through the blood of the Lamb
and the truth to which
they bore witness.

Easter Christ yesterday, today,
and the same forever, alleluia.

We thank you, Lord God Almighty,
the One who is and who was;
you have taken your great power and reign.

The nations raged and your anger came,
and the time to judge the dead
and to reward your servants and prophets,
the saints, and those fearing your name,
the small and the great...

Now have come the salvation and power
and reign of our God
and the authority of Christ.
The accuser of our brothers and sisters was cast,
accusing them before our God day and night.

Their victory was because of the blood of the Lamb
and by the word of their witness.
They loved their life into their death,
and so be glad, you heavens,
and all you dwelling in them.

Glory...

Antiphon

ORDINARY TIME READING **1 PETER 1:22-25**

Your souls now purified by obedience to the truth of unfeigned love for brothers and sisters, love one another earnestly from the heart, having been regenerated not by corruptible seeds but incorruptible through the living and abiding word of God.

All flesh is as grass, and all its glory as a flower of grass; the grass dried up and the flower fell out, but the word of the Lord remains unto the age. This is the gospel word preached to you.

RESPONSORY Ps 23:1

The Lord is my shepherd…
...nothing shall I lack.
My Lord lays me down in green pastures…
...nothing shall I lack.
Glory to the Father and to the Son and to the Holy Spirit:
...The Lord is my shepherd; nothing shall I lack.

ADVENT READING **JAMES 5:7-11**

And so be patient, brothers and sisters, until the parousia of the Lord. Behold, the farmer awaits the precious fruit of the earth, being patient over it until receiving early and late rains. You also be patient and build up your hearts, because the parousia of the Lord has drawn near. Do not murmur, brothers and sisters, about one another lest you be judged. Behold, the judge stands before the doors.

Brothers and sisters, take as an example of suffering and patience the prophets, who spoke in the name of the Lord. Behold we count blessed the ones enduring. You have heard of the endurance of Job, and you have seen the purpose of the Lord, that the Lord is full of compassion and mercy.

RESPONSORY Ps 146:7; 63:3; 67:2

Come and set us free...
...Lord God of power and glory...
Let your face shine upon us
and we will know salvation...
...Lord God of power and glory...
Glory to the Father and to the Son and to the Holy Spirit:
...Come and set us free, Lord God of power and glory...

CHRISTMAS READING **1 JOHN 5:20**

We know that the Son of God has come and has given to us discernment that we might know the true One. And we are in the true One in God's Son Jesus Christ. This is the true God and eternal life.

RESPONSORY Jn 1:14

The Word became flesh…
…alleluia, alleluia.
And dwelt among us…
…alleluia, alleluia.
Glory to the Father and to the Son and to the Holy Spirit:
…The Word became flesh and dwelt among us,
alleluia, alleluia.

After Epiphany

All people will be blessed in him…
…in every tribe of the human race.
All nations will acclaim his glory…
…in every tribe of the human race.
Glory to the Father and to the Son and to the Holy Spirit:
…All people will be blessed in him,
in every tribe of the human race.

LENT READING, Weeks 2 & 4 **JAMES 4:7-10**

Be subject to God, but oppose the diabolo who will flee from you. Draw near to God, who will draw near to you. Cleanse your hands, sinners; and purify your hearts, you two-souled. Be distressed and mourn and weep; let your laughter be turned to mourning and your joy to dejection. Be humbled before the Lord, who will exalt you.

RESPONSORY Lk 18:13

To you, O Lord...
...I make my prayer for mercy.
Heal my soul, for I have sinned against you...
...I make my prayer for mercy.
Glory to the Father and to the Son and to the Holy Spirit:
...To you, O Lord, I make my prayer for mercy.

LENT READING, Holy Thursday **HEBREWS 13:11-15**

Of the blood of animals concerning sins brought into the holies through the high priest, the bodies are burned outside the camp. Indeed that he might sanctify the people through his own blood, Jesus suffered outside the gate. So let us go forth outside the camp to him bearing his reproach, for we have here no continuing city, but seek the one coming. And so through him let us offer up always a sacrifice of praise to God. This is the fruit of lips confessing his name.

RESPONSORY Rev. 5:9

We worship you, O Christ...
...and we praise you.
By your cross you have redeemed the world...
...and we praise you.
Glory to the Father and to the Son and to the Holy Spirit:
...We worship you, O Christ, and we praise you.

EASTER READING **1 PETER 3:18,21b-22**

Christ died once for sins, a just human for the unjust, put to death in the flesh and made alive in the spirit, that he might bring you to God. Jesus Christ, at the right hand of God, having gone into heaven, subject to him are angels and authorities and powers.

RESPONSORY

The disciples rejoiced...
...alleluia, alleluia.
When they saw the risen Lord...
...alleluia, alleluia.
Glory to the Father and to the Son and to the Holy Spirit:
...The disciples rejoiced, alleluia, alleluia.

Gospel Canticle For Evening

Antiphons

Advent Wk 2

The one who is coming after me
existed before me;
I am not worthy to untie his sandals.

Advent Wk 4
22nd

O Ruler of all the nations,
authentic joy of every human heart,
O Keystone of the arc of humanity,
save the creature you fashioned
from the dust.

Christmas

We have found Jesus of Nazareth,
the son of Joseph,
the one of whom
Moses and the prophets wrote.

After Epiphany

The people of Seba shall come
bringing gold, frankincense
and myrrh, alleluia.

Thursday after
Ash Wednesday

Whoever gives up their life for
my sake in this world will find it
again forever in the next,
says the Lord.

Lent Wk 2

The rich human, who had refused
Lazarus a crust of bread,
pleaded for a drop of water.

Antiphons for Gospel Canticle For Evening, continued

Lent Wk 4
The works that I do witness
on my behalf, says the Lord,
proving that the Abba has sent me.

Holy Thursday
While they were at supper,
Jesus took bread,
said the blessing,
broke the bread,
and gave it to the disciples.

Easter Wk 2
Whoever believes in the Son
possesses eternal life,
alleluia.

Easter Wk 4
I am the shepherd of my sheep;
I have come that they may have life
and have it more abundantly,
alleluia.

Easter Wk 6
Your sorrow will be turned into joy
that no one can take from you,
alleluia.

Antiphon
God has exalted with dignity
the humble in need.

CANTICLE of MARY (The Magnificat)
LUKE 1:46-55

+ **My soul** is stretched full with praise of the Lord,
and my spirit, beyond joy in God, my Savior,
who chose to lay eyes on this humble servant.

Behold, now and forward,
each and every age will call me blessed,
for the Mighty One did great things to me.

Holy is the name and the mercy
to generations and generations,
the ones fearing the One,

Who scattered the haughty of mind and heart,
pulled the powerful off their high place,
and lifted with dignity the humble in need.

The hungering are filled with good things,
the rich are sent away empty,
and servant Israel is given relief

with a memory of mercy to remember,
the promise spoken to our ancestors,
to Abraham and his descendants forever.

Glory...

Antiphon

INTERCESSIONS

- For ever deeper understanding of what Jesus taught when he washed the feet of his disciples…
- For the courage to wash feet…
- For all who have died…

- In gratitude for blessings…; Abba thank you.
- For the sins of this day…; Lord Jesus have mercy.
- With concerns over tomorrow…; Holy Spirit help.

AN ACT OF CONTRITION

My God,
I am heartily sorry for having offended you
and I detest all my sins
because of your just judgment
but especially that they offend you
who are all-mighty, all-good,
and deserving of all my love.
I firmly intend with the help of your grace
to do the good,
avoid situations that lead to sin,
and in penance amend my life.

OUR FATHER…

91, Text: *Liturgy of St. James,* 5th Century;
translated from Greek by Gerard Moultrie, 1864
Music: 87 87 87 PICARDY, *Chansons Populaires des Provinces de France,* 1860

WEEK II
FRIDAY MORNING

+ *God, come to my assistance;* Psalm 70:2
Lord, make haste to help me!

Glory...

ORDINARY TIME

Let all mor-tal flesh keep\ si-lence,
And with fear and tremb-ling\ stand;
Pon-der noth-ing earth-ly\ mind-ed,
For with bless-ing in his\ hand,
Christ our God to earth de-scend//\-eth,
Our full hom-age to de/-mand.

King of kings, yet born of\ Ma-ry,
As of old on earth he\ stood,
Lord of lords, in hu-man\ ves-ture,
In the bo-dy and the\ blood;
He will give to all the faith//\-ful
His own self for heav-en-ly food.

Rank on rank the host of\ heav-en
Spreads its van-guard on the\ Way,
As the Light of light de\-scend-eth
From the realms of end-less\ day,
That the pow'rs of hell may van//\-ish
As the dark-ness clears a/-way.

ADVENT

Of your sing-u-lar jus-tice we sing,
God, our trust, our hope\ from youth.
In your jus-tice res-cue us.
Fill our lungs with cause
to sing your prais-es dai-ly.

Do not cast_ a-side in old age
those of fail-ing strength\ or mind.
Be our ref-uge strong, sec-ure,
shame us not and show
fi-del-i-ty for all eyes.

God, you teach us from days\ of youth.
We pro-claim, 'til old\ and gray.
Won-der, mer-cy, jus-tice, might,
To new gen-er-a-tions yet
to know your stor-y.

We de-pend_ on you from our birth.
From af-flict-ion, wat-er-y deep,
raise us up, re-vive, re-store,
help our harp and voice
sing jus-tice, joy and won-der.

129, Text: from Psalm 71, by Stephen J. Wolf, 2003
Music: THE CALL, 7777, Ralph Vaughan Williams, 1872-1958
Popular melody for: *Come My Way My Truth My Life*

38, Text: Christopher Wordsworth, 1862, altered
Music: 77 77 D, SALZBURG; Jakob Hintze, 1678

CHRISTMAS

Songs of thank-ful-ness and praise,
Jesus, Lord, to you we raise,
Man-i-fest-ed by the star
To the ma-gi from a-far;
Branch of roy/-al Da-vid's stem
In your birth at Beth-le-hem;
Prais-es be to you ad-dressed,
God in flesh made man-i-fest.

Man-i-fest at Jor-dan's stream,
Pro-phet, Priest and King su-preme;
And as Ca-na's wed-ding guest,
In your God-head man-i-fest;
Man-i-fest/ in pow'r div-ine,
Chang-ing wa-ter in-to wine;
Prais-es be to you ad-dressed,
God in flesh made man-i-fest.

Grant us grace to see you, Lord,
Mir-rored in your ho-ly Word;
May our im-i-ta-tion show,
In your like-ness may we go;
Pure and ho/-ly may we be
At your great E-pi-pha-ny;
May we praise you, ev-er blest,
God in flesh made man-i-fest.

LENT

O Sa-cred Head, sur-round-ed
By crown of pierc\-ing thorn.
O Bleed-ing Head, so wound-ed,
Re-viled and put\ to scorn.
Our sins\ have marred the glo-ry
Of your most ho-ly Face,
Yet an/-gel hosts a-dor-ing
And trem-ble as they gaze.

I see your strength and vig-or
All fa-ding in\ the strife,
And death with cru-el rigor,
Be-reav-ing you\ of life;
O ag\-o-ny and dy-ing!
O love to sin-ner's free!
Je-sus/, all grace sup-ply-ing,
O turn your face on me.

In this, your bit-ter pass-ion,
Good Shep-herd, think\ of me
With your most sweet com-pass-ion,
un-wor-thy though\ I be:
Be-neath\ your cross a-bi-ding
For ev-er would I rest,
In your/ dear love con-fi-ding,
And in your pres-ence blest.

EASTER

The/ Head that once was/ crowned with thorns
Is crowned in glo\-ry/ now;
A/ roy-al di-a-dem a-dorns
The/ migh/-ty vic\-tor's brow.

The/ high-est place that/ heav'n af-fords
Be-longs to him\ by/ right;
The/ King of kings and Lord of lords
and/ heav'ns/ e-ter\-nal Light.

The/ joy of all who/ dwell a-bove,
The joy of all\ be/-low,
To/ whom he man-i-fests his love
And/ grants/ his Name\ to know.

To/ them the cross with/ all its shame,
With all its grace\, is/ giv'n;
Their/ name an ev-er-last-ing name,
Their/ joy/ the joy\ of heav'n.

71, Text: Thomas Kelly,
Hymns on Various Passages of Scripture, 1820, altered
Music: MCKEE, CM; African American Spiritual,
arr.by Harry T. Burleigh, d.1949
Popular melody for: *In Christ There Is No East Or West*

51, Text: Ascribed to Bernard of Clairvaux, 1091-1153;
translated by Henry Baker, 1821-77
Music: 76 76 D, PASSION CHORALE; Hans Leo Hassler, 1601

PSALM 38

Antiphon *If a house be divided against itself,*
that house will be unabe to stand. Mk 3:25

Christmas & Easter I confess my iniquity; do not forsake me,
Lord my Savior, alleluia.

Adonai, **rebuke me not** in your anger
nor discipline me in your wrath,
for your arrows have pierced into me
and your hand has come down upon me.

There is no health in my body
because of your anger;
my bones ache because of my sin.
Indeed my guilts overwhelm my head
like a heavy burden, too heavy for me.

I loathe them and they fester my wounds
because of my foolishness.
I am bowed down and brought very low;
all the day I go about mourning.

Indeed my backside is filled with searing
and there is no health in my body.
Numb and utterly crushed,
my heart groans in anguish.

Lord, before you is all of my longing;
my sighing is not hidden from you.
My heart pounds, my strength fails me,
and my eyes are without their light.

My friends and companions from the past
avoid being present to my woundedness,
and my neighbors stay far away.
People seeking my life set traps;
wanting to harm me, they talk of ruins
and plot deceptions all the day.

I am like the deaf and cannot hear,
like a mute unable to open my mouth.
I became like one who does not hear,
like one whose mouth gives no reply.

Indeed, I wait for you, Adonai;
you will answer, Lord my God.
For I said, "let them not gloat over me
nor puff themselves up when my foot does slip."

For my fall is near; my pain is ever with me.
Indeed I confess my iniquity
and am troubled by my sin.

Vigorous ones seek enmity;
many and numerous hate me for no reason.
When I seek the good they slander me,
repaying the good with the bad.

Forsake me not, Adonai;
my God, be not far from me.
Come quickly to help, my Lord, my salvation.

Glory…

Antiphon

PSALM 55:2-15,17-24

Antiphon *Whoever receives me*
receives the One who sent me. Mk 9:37b

Christmas & Easter Cast your cares on the Lord,
who will sustain you, alleluia.

Listen, Elohim, to my prayer!
Ignore not my plea, but hear me and answer me,
as I am troubled by my thoughts
and groan at the voice of enmity,
at the stares of the faces of doers of the bad,
for they bring suffering down upon me
and revile me in anger.

My heart is in anguish within me
and the terrors of death assail me.
Fear and trembling harass me
and horror has overwhelmed me.

And I said, "If I had wings like the dove;
I would fly away and find rest.
See! I would flee far and stay in the desert.
I would hurry to my place of shelter
from the storm of the raging wind."

Confuse them, Lord; confound their scheming,
for I see violence and strife in the city.
By day and by night they prowl on her walls;
within her are malice and abuse.

Destructive forces are within her
and threats and lies never leave her streets. - -

It is not insults of enmity rising against me;
from that I could hide and endure.

But it is you, my other self, my companion,
my friend with whom together
we shared close companionship
walking with the throng at the house of Elohim…

To Elohim I call and am saved by Adonai
who hears my voice when I cry out in distress
at dusk, dawn and noon,
who ransoms my whole self from battle
though many oppose me.

El enthroned forever will hear and let be afflicted
those who never allow themselves to change,
who have no fear of God,
who stretch hands against friends,
and violate covenants.

This one's mouth is smooth as butter,
yet war is in the heart,
speaking words more soothing than oil
that are yet drawn swords.

Cast your cares on Adonai, who will sustain you
and to forever let not the just fall.

But you, God, will bring bloody deceit
into the pit of corruption,
not living half their days;
And I will trust in you.

Glory… Antiphon

PSALM 51

Antiphon *One who loves one's life loses it.* Jn 12:25

Advent & Lent — Create in me a clean heart, O God;
renew inside me a spirit to be steadfast.

Dec 17-23 — Our Ruler will come; the Lord,
God-is-with-us, is his mighty name.

Christmas & Easter — Have courage;
your sins are forgiven, alleluia. Mt 9:2b

Have mercy on me, God,
in accord with your unfailing love;
in accord with your great compassion
blot out my transgressions.

Wash me of my many iniquities
and cleanse me from my sin,
for I know my transgressions
and my sin is before me always.

Against you yourself I sinned;
what I did is bad in your eyes.
You are proven right when you speak
and justified when you judge.
Surely we are sinners from birth,
from conception in a mother's womb.

Surely you desire truth in our inner parts;
in my inmost place you teach me wisdom.
You cleanse me with hyssop and I will be clean;
you wash me and I will be whiter than snow…

You let me hear joy and gladness;
let the bones you let be crushed now rejoice.
Hide your faces from my sins
and blot out all my iniquities.

A clean heart create in me, God!
Renew inside me a spirit to be steadfast.
Do not cast me from your presences,
nor take from me your Holy Spirit.

Restore to me the joy of your salvation
and sustain in me a willing spirit.
I will teach transgressors your ways
and sinners will turn back to you.

Save me from bloodguilt, God,
God of my salvation;
my tongue will sing of your justice.
Lord, open my lips
and my mouth will proclaim your praise.

Sacrifices give you no delight;
I could bring a burnt offering,
but it would give you no pleasure.
The sacrifices, God, you will not despise
are a broken spirit and a contrite heart.

Make Zion prosper in your pleasure,
and build up the walls of Jerusalem.
Then you will delight in the sacrifice of the just,
burnt offerings and whole offerings,
bulls offered on your altar.

Glory... Antiphon

HABAKKUK 3:2-4,13a,15-19

Antiphon *Looking round on them with anger,*
Jesus grieved
at their hardness of heart. Mk 3:5

Advent & Lent: Even in wrath you remember
mercy and compassion.

Christmas & Easter: You go forth to save your people,
to save your anointed one,
alleluia.

Adonai, I heard your fame;
I stand in awe of your deeds, Adonai.
Now, in the midst of years, renew them!
In the midst of years, make them known!
Even in wrath you remember compassion.

Eloah came from Teman,
the Holy One from the Mount of Paran.
The heavens are covered with glory
and the earth is filled with praise

like the splendor of the rays of the sunrise
or the hand from a hiding place of power...
You came out to deliver your people,
to deliver your anointed one...

You trample on the sea,
your horses churning up the great waters.
My heart heard and she trembled,
at the sound my lips quivered;

decay crept into my bones
and my legs trembled.
Yet, I will wait patiently for the day,
calamity to come on the nation invading.

Though the fig tree does not bud
and there is no grape on the vine,
the crops of the olive fail
and fields produce no food,

the sheep cut themselves off from the pen
and there are no cattle in the stalls,
yet will I rejoice in Adonai
and be joyful in the God of my salvation.

Sovereign Adonai, my strength,
makes my feet like that of the deer,
makes me go to the heights.

Glory…

Antiphon

When I am angry, perhaps something unhealed in
the other is hooked into something unhealed in me. Is that why
Jesus asks us to pray for 'enemies,' to receive the healing to forgive?

See *Anger the Jesus Way* (reflections on Mark 3:1-6, the only time the gospels specify the word *anger* for Jesus) by Stephen Joseph Wolf

TOBIT 13:8-11,13-15

Antiphon *One of the seven angels showed me*
the holy city of Jerusalem
shining with the glory of God. Rev 21:10,11

Advent & Lent
Rejoice and exult, Jerusalem;
be gathered together
and bless the Lord of the ages.

Dec. 17-23
Wait for the Lord
who will come with saving power.

Christmas & Easter
Jerusalem, city of God,
you will shine as a bright light,
alleluia.

Acknowledge the Lord in Jerusalem.

You Jerusalem, Holy City, will be scourged
for what your children have done.
The Lord will again have mercy
on the children of the just.

Acknowledge the Lord as is deserving
and bless the Ruler of the ages,
that your sanctuary will be built in you again
with joy and cheer by all who were exiles,
and love for all generations
those who were distressed.

A bright light will shine
to all the ends of the earth;
many nations will come from far away.

Those living in the most remote parts of earth
will come to your holy Name,
bearing in their hands
gifts for the Ruler of Heaven.

Generation to generation will give joyful praise
and the name of the Lord will be great forever...

Then, children of the just, rejoice and exult;
be gathered together
and bless the Lord of the ages.

Happy are those who love you,
and happy will be those
who rejoice in prosperity.

Happy also are all
who grieve over your afflictions
for they will rejoice with you
and give witness to your joy forever.

My soul, praise the Lord,
the mega Ruler.

Glory...

Antiphon

PSALM 147:1-11

Antiphon *Let me preach also in nearby villages.* Mk 1:38

Hallelujah!
How good it is to sing praise to our God!
How pleasant and fitting to give praise!

Adonai rebuilds Jerusalem, gathers Israel's exiles,
heals broken hearts and binds up wounds,
determines the number of the stars,
and calls to each of them by name.

Great and mighty in power is our Lord,
with unlimited understanding.
Adonai sustains the humble
and throws doers of the bad to the dust.
Sing to Adonai with thanksgiving!

Make music on the harp to our God,
who covers the skies with clouds
and supplies rain to the earth,
making grass to grow on the mountains,
providing food for cattle
and young ravens when they call.

Adonai finds pleasure
not in the strength of the horse
nor delight in the legs of the human,
but is delighting in those who fear Adonai
who hope in this unfailing love.

Glory... Antiphon

PSALM 147:12-20

Antiphon *I am the living bread from heaven;*
anyone who eats of this bread
will live to the eon. Jn 6:51a

Christmas & Easter I saw the new Jerusalem,
coming down from heaven, alleluia.

Glorify Adonai, Jerusalem!
Zion, now give praise!

Your God strengthens the bars of your gates,
blesses your peoples within you,
brings peace to your border,
and satisfies you with finest of wheat.

Your God sends a command to the earth,
and swiftly runs a word,
spreading snow like the wool
and scattering frost like the ash.

Hail is hurled like pebbles;
who can stand before the icy blast?
The word of the Lord is sent, and they melt;
wind stirs up and the waters flow.

The word of the Lord is revealed to Jacob,
decrees and laws of the Lord to Israel.
Not for another nation did the Lord do this;
they do not know these laws.
Hallelujah!

Glory... Antiphon

ORDINARY TIME READING **EPHESIANS 2:11-22**

And so remember that when you were the nations in the flesh, called "uncircumcision" by those who were called "circumcision" in the flesh by the hand, that you were at that time without Christ, alienated from the commonwealth of Israel and strangers to the covenants of the promise, without hope and godless in the world. But now in Christ Jesus you who were then afar became near by the blood of Christ.

For he is our peace, the one who made both one, breaking the partition wall of enmity, abolishing in his flesh the law of commandments in decrees, that he might create in himself the two into one new human making peace, and might reconcile both in one body to God through the cross, ending in himself the enmity. And coming he preached peace to those afar and peace to those near, because through him we have access both by one Spirit and to the Father.

And so you are no longer strangers and aliens, but you are equal citizens with the saints and members of the family of God, having been built on the foundation of the apostles and prophets, with the very self of Christ Jesus as the cornerstone, in whom the whole building fits together and grows into a holy temple in the Lord, in whom you also are being built together into a dwelling place of God in the spirit.

RESPONSORY Tobit 1:13

The Most High has kept me in favor…
…with all my heart I will keep God in mind.
May the Most High rescue me from captivity…
…with all my heart I will keep God in mind.
Glory to the Father and to the Son and to the Holy Spirit:
…The Most High has kept me in favor;
with all my heart I will keep God in mind.

ADVENT READING **JEREMIAH 30:21,22**

This Adonai says: "Their leader will be from them and will arise from among them, and I will bring their ruler near, who will come close to me.

...So you will be my people, and I will be your God."

RESPONSORY

Your light will come, Jerusalem…
…the Lord will dawn on you in radiant beauty.
The glory of the Lord you will see within you…
…the Lord will dawn on you in radiant beauty.
Glory to the Father and to the Son and to the Holy Spirit:
…Your light will come, Jerusalem,
the Lord will dawn on you in radiant beauty.

CHRISTMAS READING **ISAIAH 61:1-2a,10-11**

The Spirit of Sovereign Adonai is on me, because Adonai anointed me to preach good news to poor ones and sent me to bind up ones broken of heart, to proclaim freedom for ones being captive, and release for ones being imprisoned, to proclaim a year of favor of Adonai… To delight, I delight in Adonai, my soul rejoices in my God, who clothed me in garments of salvation and arrayed me in a robe of justice, as a bridegroom dresses his head like a priest and a bride adorns herself with her jewels, for as the soil makes the sprout to come up and as a garden makes seeds to grow so will Sovereign Adonai make justice spring up and praise before all the nations.

RESPONSORY

The Lord has made known…
…alleluia, alleluia.
The saving power…
…alleluia, alleluia.
Glory to the Father and to the Son and to the Holy Spirit:
…The Lord has made known the saving power, alleluia.

After Epiphany

All the royal powers on earth
…will bow down in worship.
Men and women of every nation…
…will bow down in worship.

Glory to the Father and to the Son and to the Holy Spirit:
...All the royal powers on earth
will bow down in worship.

LENT READING, until Holy Week **ISAIAH 53:11b-12**

After the suffering of the soul my servant will justify the many and bear their iniquities. And so I will give him a portion among the many and a division of the spoil among the numerous because he poured out his life to the death, was numbered with the transgressors, bore the sins of the many, and interceded for the transgressors.

RESPONSORY Lk 18:13

The Lord God will set me free...
...from the hunter's snare.
From all those who would trap me with lying words,
...from the hunter's snare.
Glory to the Father and to the Son and to the Holy Spirit:
...The Lord God will set me free from the hunter's snare.

GOOD FRIDAY READING **ISAIAH 52:13-15**

See, my servant will act wisely and be raised and lifted up and highly exalted!

Just as many were appalled at him, so disfigured beyond human appearance and his form beyond that of a human being, so will he startle many nations.

Because of him rulers will shut their mouth, for what was not told to them they will see, and what they did not hear they will understand.

RESPONSORY

For our sake Christ was obedient,
accepting even death.

EASTER READING **ACTS 5:30-32**

The God of our ancestors raised Jesus, whom you killed by hanging on a tree. This one is exalted to the right hand of God as ruler and savior to bring conversion to Israel and forgiveness of sins.

Of these things, we are witnesses with the Holy Spirit given by God to the obedient.

RESPONSORY

The Lord is risen from the tomb…
…alleluia, alleluia.
He hung upon the cross for us…
…alleluia, alleluia.
Glory to the Father and to the Son and to the Holy Spirit:
…The Lord is risen from the tomb, alleluia, alleluia.

Gospel Canticle For Morning

Antiphons

Advent Wk 2 Matt 11:16-19	Say to the fainthearted: take courage! The Lord our God is coming to save us.
Advent Wk 4 (see pg 759)	All that God promised Mary through the angel has been accomplished.
Christmas (see pg 759)	He came through blood and water, Jesus Christ our Lord.
After Epiphany Luke 5:12-16	All who once reviled you will come and bow down in worship before your very footprints.
Friday after Ash Wednesday ` Mt 9:14-15	When you meet those who are in need of clothing, do not turn away from them, for they are your siblings; then your light shall break forth like the dawn, and your good deeds shall go before you. Is 58
Lent Wk 2 Mt 21:33-43,45-46	The owner will bring those doers of the bad to an end, and entrust the vineyard to other tenants who will give the harvest at the proper season.

Antiphons for Gospel Canticle For Morning, continued

Lent Wk 4 Jn 7:1-2,10,25-30	Indeed you know me, says the Lord, and you know from where I come; yet I have not come of my own accord; it was my Abba who sent me.
Good Friday	Over his head they hung their accusation: Jesus of Nazareth, King of the Jews.
Easter Wk 2 John 6:1-15	Jesus took bread, and when he had given thanks, he gave it to those at table with him, alleluia.
Easter Wk 4 John 14:1-6	I go now to prepare a place for you but I shall return to take you with me so that where I am you also may be, alleluia.
Easter Wk 6 John 16:20-23	Having suffered death, we see Jesus crowned with glory and honor, alleluia.
Ordinary Antiphon	*God chose to visit God's people* *and brought redemption.*

Gospel Reading for Friday of

Week **2**	Mark 3:13-19	**14**	Matt 10:16-23	**26**	Lk 10:13-16
4	Mark 6:14-29	**16**	Matt 13:18-23	**28**	Luke 12:1-7
6	Mark 8:34 - 9:1	**18**	Matt 16:24-28	**30**	Luke 14:1-6
8	Mark 11:11-26	**20**	Matt 22:34-40	**32**	Lk 17:26-37
10	Matt 5:27-32	**22**	Luke 5:33-39	**34**	Lk 21:29-33
12	Matt 8:1-4	**24**	Luke 8:1-3		

CANTICLE of ZECHARIAH (The Benedictus) LUKE 1:68-79

+ **Blessed be** the Lord the God of Israel
who chose a people to visit with redemption,
and raised salvation in the house of David,
saving strength from God's own servant,

speaking from the age of the prophets
through the mouth of the holy prophet:
Salvation out of enmity,
even out of those who hate us,

to show our ancestors how mercy works, -
and to remember the holy promise of the Lord,
the covenant made for our ancestor Abraham,
calming our fear and making us free
to serve with holy justice before God all our days.

And you also child -
will be called a prophet of the Most High
for you will go before the Lord to prepare his way
and give to people a knowledge of salvation
known in accepting forgiveness of their sins.

From the tender mercy of our God,
the sun rising from the height will visit with light
for those who sit in the dark or shadow of death
and to guide our feet into the way of peace.

Glory...

Antiphon

PETITIONS FOR THE CONSECRATION TO GOD
OF THE DAY AND ITS WORK

- For the Church and her ministry and apostolates...
- For secular authorities and all serving as stewards...
- For people who are poor or sick or in sorrow...
- For peace and the basic needs of each human being...
- For guardian angel intercession for those considering use of violence...
- For any elders or children who feel abandoned...
- In gratitude for blessings and grace...

ANGELUS

The Angel of the Lord declared unto Mary.
And she conceived of the Holy Spirit.

> *Hail Mary full of grace, the Lord is with thee; Blessed art thou among women, and blessed is the fruit of thy womb, Jesus. Holy Mary, Mother of God, pray for us sinners, now and at the hour of our death. Amen.*

Behold the handmaid of the Lord.
Be it done unto me according to your word.
Hail Mary . . .

And the Word became flesh.
And dwelt among us. Hail Mary . . .

Pray for us, O Holy Mother of God;
That we may be made worthy of the promises of Christ.

OUR FATHER...

WEEK II
FRIDAY EVENING

\+ *God, come to my assistance;* Psalm 70:2
Lord, make haste to help me!

Glory...

LENT

Crown him with ma-ny crowns
The Lamb up-on his throne;
Hark how the heav'n-ly an-them\ drowns
All mu-sic but its own.
A-wake, my soul, and sing
Of him who died for thee
And hail him as your King of kings
Through all e-ter-ni-ty.

Crown him the Lord of Love.
Be-hold his hands and side,
Rich wounds, yet vis-ib-le a\-bove,
In beau-ty glo-ri-fied.
No an-gel in the sky
Can ful-ly bear that sight,
But down-ward bends his wond'-ring eye
At mys-te-ry so bright!

46, Text: from Revevelation 19:12;
Verses by Matthew Bridges, 1851, altered
Music: DIADEMATA, George J. Elvey, 1868

ORDINARY TIME, ADVENT & CHRISTMAS

Crown him with ma-ny crowns
The Lamb up-on his throne;
Hark how the heav'n-ly an-them\ drowns
All mu-sic but its own.
A-wake, my soul, and sing
Of him who died for thee
And hail him as your King of kings
Through all e-ter-ni-ty.

Crown him the Vir-gin's Son,
The God in-car-nate born,
Whose arm those crim-son tro-phies\ won
Which now his brow a-dorn;
Fruit of the mys-tic rose,
As of that rose the stem;
The root whence mer-cy ev-er flows,
The Babe of Beth-le-hem.

Crown him the Lord of Heav'n,
En-throned in worlds a-bove,
Crown him the King to whom is\ giv'n
The won-drous name of Love.
Crown him with ma-ny crowns
As thrones be-fore him fall;
Crown him, you kings, with ma-ny crowns
For he is King of all.

89, Text: from Rev. 19:12; Verses by Matthew Bridges, 1851, altered
Music: DIADEMATA, George J. Elvey, 1868

EASTER

Crown him with ma-ny crowns
The Lamb up-on his throne;
Hark how the heav'n-ly an-them\ drowns
All mu-sic but its own.
A-wake, my soul, and sing
Of him who died for thee
And hail him as your King of kings
Through all e-ter-ni-ty.

Crown him the Lord of Love.
Be-hold his hands and side,
Rich wounds, yet vis-ib-le a\-bove,
In beau-ty glo-ri-fied.
No an-gel in the sky
Can ful-ly bear that sight,
But down-ward bends his wond'-ring eye
At mys-te-ry so bright!

Crown him the Lord of Heav'n,
En-throned in worlds a-bove,
Crown him the King to whom is\ giv'n
The won-drous name of Love.
Crown him with ma-ny crowns
As thrones be-fore him fall;
Crown him, you kings, with ma-ny crowns
For he is King of all.

62, Text: from Rev. 19:12; Verses by Matthew Bridges, 1851, altered
Music: DIADEMATA, George J. Elvey, 1868

PSALM 59:2-5,10-11a,17-18

Antiphon *The reign of heaven is like*
a merchant who seeking fine pearls
finds one precious pearl and going away
sells everything and buys it. Mt 13:45,46

Advent & Lent You protect me, my God.

Christmas & Easter Alleluia, alleluia, alleluia.

Deliver me from enmity; protect me, God,
from those who rise up against me.
Deliver me from doers of the bad
and save me from bloody ways.

See, they lie in wait for my self;
fierce people conspire against me
for no offense of me nor sin, Adonai.
For no wrong they make ready to attack;
arise to help me and look!...

For you, my Strength, I watch,
for you God, my fortress,
you God are my love.

I will sing of your strength
and I will sing at dawn of your love,
for you are my fortress
and my refuge in times of trouble.

To you, my Strength, I sing praise
for you God, my fortress,
you God are my love.

Glory… Antiphon

PSALM 133

Antiphon *The multitude of believers*
was heart and soul one. Acts 4:32a

Christmas & Easter Alleluia, alleluia, alleluia.

See how good and how pleasant it is
to live as siblings
dwelling in unity.

Like the precious oil
running down on the head
and on the beard of Aaron,
running down on his collar and robes,

as if the dew of Hermon
was falling on Mount Zion,
there Adonai bestows
the blessing of life to forever.

Glory…

Antiphon

God saw all that God made
and found it very good. Genesis 1:31a

PSALM 140:1-9,13-14

Antiphon *Blessed are you when they disrespect*
and persecute and tell all the lies
against you for my sake;
rejoice and be glad,
for great is your reward
in the heavens. Mt 5:11

Christmas & Easter Alleluia, alleluia, alleluia.

Rescue me, Adonai,
from humans doing bad things;
protect me from humans of violence
who devise the bad in their hearts
and stir up conflict every day.
They make their tongues sharp as a serpent;
viper poison is on their lips.

Keep me, Adonai, from their hands;
protect me from humans of violence
who plan to trip up my feet.
Arrogance has hidden a snare for me,
spread a net of cords,
and set a trap for me beside the path.

I say to Adonai, "You are my God!"
Hear, Adonai, the cry of my cries for mercy!
Lord Adonai, my strength, my deliverance,
you shield my head on the day of battle.
Grant not, Adonai, their desires;
let not their plans to do the bad succeed…

I know that Adonai secures justice for the poor
and the cause of the needy.
Surely the just will praise your Name;
the upright will live before your faces.

Glory…

Antiphon

PSALM 116:1-9

Antiphon *It is fitting for the Son of Humanity*
to suffer much and be rejected
and be killed, and rise after three days. Mk 8:31

Christmas & Easter The Lord has rescued my self
that I may walk in the land of the living.

I love Adonai who heard my voice
and my cries for mercy, and turned an ear to me,
so all during my days I will call.

Cords of death entangled me
and worries over Sheol came upon me;
trouble and sorrow came over me.
Then I called on the name of Adonai:
"Oh, Adonai, save my self!"

Adonai is gracious and just,
our God the compassionate one.
Adonai protects the simple hearted;
I was in need and then I was saved.

Return, my soul, to your rest,
for good to you has been Adonai,
who freed my soul from death,
my eyes from tears, and my feet from stumbling,

that I may walk before Adonai
in the land of the living.

Glory... Antiphon

PSALM 121

Antiphon *When coming, will the Son of Humanity find faith on earth?* Lk 18:8

Advent & Lent My help is from the Lord,
the Maker of heavens and earth.

Christmas & Easter The Lord watches over the people of God
as the apple of God's eye, alleluia.

I lift up my eyes to the mountains.
From where does my help come?
My help comes from Adonai,
Maker of heavens and earth,

who will not let your foot slip
nor slumber when guarding you.
Indeed the guardian of Israel
will not slumber and will not sleep.

Adonai is your guardian,
the Most High at your right hand.
By day the sun will not harm you,
nor the moon by the night.

Adonai will keep you from all harm
and guard your life.
Adonai will guard your going and coming
from now and to forevermore.

Glory...

Antiphon

PSALM 145

Antiphon *The Son of Humanity came*
to seek and to save the lost. Lk 19:10

I will exalt you, my God the Ruler,
and I will praise your Name to forever.

In every day I will praise you
and I will bless your Name to forever.
Great is Adonai, and greatly being praised,
an unfathomable greatness.

Generation to generation commend your works
and tell of your mighty acts
and the glorious splendor of your majesty,
and I will meditate on your wonderful deeds.

They will tell of your awesome works
and I will proclaim your great deeds.
They will celebrate and remember
the abundance of your goodness
and they will sing of your justice.

Gracious and compassionate is Adonai,
slow to anger, rich in love, and good to all.
Adonai's compassion is on every creature.

All your works will praise you, Adonai,
and your saints will bless you.
They will tell of the glory of your reign
and speak your might to make known

to sons and daughters of humanity your acts
and the glorious splendor of your reign,
the realm of all the ages,
and your dominion through all
generation and generation.

Adonai is faithful to all the promises
and loving to all who are made.
Adonai upholds all who are falling
and lifts up all who are bowed down.

The eyes of all look to you
and you give them their food in due season,
opening your hand and satisfying the desire
of every living thing.

Just is Adonai in all ways,
and loving to all who are made.
Near is Adonai to all who call,
to all who call in truth.

Fulfilled is the desire
of all who fear and love Adonai,
who hears their cry and saves them
and watches over them.
But bad ways will be destroyed.

My mouth will speak praise of Adonai.
Let every creature praise the holy Name
to forever and ever.

Glory... Antiphon

REVELATION 15:3b-4

Antiphon *They sang the song*
of Moses the servant of God
and the song of the Lamb. Rev 15:3a

Advent & Lent Ruler of all nations,
just and true are your ways.

Dec. 17-23 Eagerly I watch for the Lord;
I wait in joyful hope
for the coming of God my Savior.

Christmas & Easter The Lord my strength
has become to me salvation,
alleluia.

Great and wonderful are your works,
Lord God Almighty.
Just and true are your ways,
Ruler of the nations.

Who will not fear, O Lord,
or glorify your name?

Only you are holy.
All the nations will come
and worship before you;
your ordinances are shown to all.

Glory…

Antiphon

ORDINARY TIME READING **1 CORINTHIANS 2:1-16**

Coming to you, brothers and sisters, I came not with excellence of speech or of wisdom announcing to you the testimony of God. For I decided to know nothing among you except Jesus Christ, and this one having been crucified. And I was with you in weakness and fear and much trembling. My speech and proclamation (*kerygma*) was not persuasive words of wisdom, but a demonstration of spirit and power, that your faith may be not in human wisdom but in the power of God.

We speak wisdom among the mature, but wisdom not of this age, nor of the leaders of this age being brought to naught. But we speak of God, a wisdom in mystery, hidden, which God foreordained before the ages for our glory, which none of the leaders of this age has known. For if they knew, they would not have crucified the Lord of glory. But as it has been written, *things which eye has not seen and ear has not heard and have not come upon the human heart, how many are prepared for those loving God,* it is revealed to us by God through the Spirit.

For the Spirit searches all things, even the deep things of God. Who of human beings knows the things of a human except the spirit in that human? So also no one has known the things of God except the Spirit of God. We have not received the spirit of the world but the Spirit from God, that we may know the things freely given to us by God, which we also speak not in teaching of human words of wisdom, but in teaching of the Spirit, comparing spiritual things with spiritual things.

A natural human does not receive the things of the Spirit of God, for they are folly to one who cannot know what is discerned spiritually. But the spiritual human discerns on one hand all things; on the other the Spirit is discerned by no one: *For who has known the mind of the Lord and so who will instruct?* But we have the mind of Christ.

RESPONSORY 1 Cor 15:3; Rom 5:8; 1 Ptr 3:18

Christ died for our sins…
…while we were still sinners.
Put to death, he rose to life in the Spirit…
…while we were still sinners.
Glory to the Father and to the Son and to the Holy Spirit:
…Christ died for our sins while we were still sinners.

The world is making a discovery that there is and always has been a regularly occurring non-pathological minority variant in the human condition known in our time as being lesbian, gay, bi-sexual, transgender, queer, intersex, asexual, +. So what will we do with this discovery?

See writings of James Alison, Theologian

ADVENT READING **2 PETER 3:8b-10**

One day with the Lord is as a thousand years and a thousand years as day one. The Lord is not slow on the promise, as some deem slowness, but is patient with you, not for the purpose that any perish but that all people might come to repentance.

But the day of the Lord will come as a thief, in which the heavens will pass away with rushing sound and the elements burning will be dissolved and the earth and its works will be uncovered.

RESPONSORY Ps 146:7; 63:3; 67:2

Come and set us free…
…Lord God of power and glory…
Let your face shine upon us
and we will know salvation…
…Lord God of power and glory…
Glory to the Father and to the Son and to the Holy Spirit:
…Come and set us free, Lord God of power and glory…

CHRISTMAS READING **ACTS 10:36-39b**

Peter said, "You know the thing having become throughout all Judea, beginning from Galilee after the baptism which John proclaimed: Jesus the one from Nazareth, how God anointed him with the Holy Spirit and power. He went about doing good and curing all those oppressed by the diabolo. God was with him. And we are witnesses of all things he did, both in the country of the Judeans and in Jerusalem..."

RESPONSORY Jn 1:14

The Word became flesh…
…alleluia, alleluia.
And dwelt among us…
…alleluia, alleluia.
Glory to the Father and to the Son and to the Holy Spirit:
…The Word became flesh and dwelt among us,
alleluia, alleluia.

After Epiphany

All people will be blessed in him…
…in every tribe of the human race.
All nations will acclaim his glory…
…in every tribe of the human race.
Glory to the Father and to the Son and to the Holy Spirit:
…All people will be blessed in him,
in every tribe of the human race.

LENT READING, until Holy Week **JAMES 5:16,19-20**

And so confess your sins to one another, and pray on behalf of one another, that you may be healed. A prayer of a just person made effective is very strong. Brothers and sisters, if one among you errs from the truth and is turned by someone, know that the one turning a sinner out of an error way will save that soul out of death and will cover a multitude of sins.

RESPONSORY Lk 18:13

To you, O Lord…
…I make my prayer for mercy.
Heal my soul, for I have sinned against you…
…I make my prayer for mercy.
Glory to the Father and to the Son and to the Holy Spirit:
…To you, O Lord, I make my prayer for mercy.

GOOD FRIDAY READING **1 PETER 2:21-24**

To this you were called, because indeed Christ suffered on your behalf, leaving you an example to follow in the steps of him who was found neither in sin nor with guile in his mouth, who being reviled reviled not in return, who in suffering threatened not, but delivered himself to the one judging justly and carried up our sins in his body onto the tree, that dying to sins we might live to genuine justice, by whose wounds you are healed.

RESPONSORY Rev. 5:9

We worship you, O Christ…
…and we praise you.
By your cross you have redeemed the world…
…and we praise you.
Glory to the Father and to the Son and to the Holy Spirit:
…We worship you, O Christ, and we praise you.

EASTER READING **HEBREWS 5:8-10**

Though being a Son, he learned obedience from things he suffered, and being perfected he became the source of eternal salvation to all those obeying him, designated by God a high priest in the order of Melchizedek.

RESPONSORY

The disciples rejoiced…
…alleluia, alleluia.
When they saw the risen Lord…
…alleluia, alleluia.
Glory to the Father and to the Son and to the Holy Spirit:
…The disciples rejoiced, alleluia, alleluia.

Gospel Canticle For Evening

Antiphons

Advent Wk 2	Rejoicing you shall draw water from the wellsprings of the Savior.
Advent Wk 4 23rd	O Emmanuel, Desire of the nations and Savior of all people, come and set us free.
Christmas	The voice proclaimed from heaven: you are my Son, my beloved, in whom I take delight.
After Epiphany	An angel warned the magi in a dream to return to their country by a different route.
Friday after Ash Wednesday	When the newlywed is taken away from them, then will be the time for the wedding guests to fast.
Lent Wk 2	They would have arrested Jesus but they feared the people who regarded him as a prophet.
Lent Wk 4	No one could lay a hand on Jesus, because his time had not yet come.

Antiphons for Gospel Canticle For Evening, continued

Good Friday
While we were still sinners,
God reconciled us to God's self
by the death of the Son of God.

Easter Wk 2
To destroy the power of hell
Christ died upon the cross;
on the third day
clothed in strength and glory,
he triumphed over death;
alleluia.

Easter Wk 4
The Good Shepherd
laid down his life for the sheep,
alleluia.

Easter Wk 6
To those who ask,
the Abba will send the Holy Spirit,
alleluia.

Ordinary
Antiphon
God has given relief to servant Israel
with a memory of mercy to remember.

CANTICLE of MARY (The Magnificat)
LUKE 1:46-55

+ **My soul** is stretched full with praise of the Lord,
and my spirit, beyond joy in God, my Savior,
who chose to lay eyes on this humble servant.

Behold, now and forward,
each and every age will call me blessed,
for the Mighty One did great things to me.

Holy is the name and the mercy
to generations and generations,
the ones fearing the One,

Who scattered the haughty of mind and heart,
pulled the powerful off their high place,
and lifted with dignity the humble in need.

The hungering are filled with good things,
the rich are sent away empty,
and servant Israel is given relief

with a memory of mercy to remember,
the promise spoken to our ancestors,
to Abraham and his descendants forever.

Glory...

Antiphon

INTERCESSIONS

adapted from Intercessions
of Good Friday

- Give unity to your Church.
- Protect N. our Pope and all our Bishops.
- Sanctify your faithful people by your Spirit.
- Increase the faith and understanding of seekers.
- Gather all Christians in unity.
- Be faithful to the Jewish people of the covenant.
- Hear the praise of all who worship the One God, including Muslims and so many indigenous peoples.
- Show the marks of your love in creation to those who do not yet see them.
- Guide the minds and hearts of those who govern us.
- Console all who are troubled.
- Have mercy on all who have died.

- In gratitude for blessings…; Abba thank you.
- For the sins of this day…; Lord Jesus have mercy.
- With concerns over tomorrow…; Holy Spirit help.

A LATIN AMERICAN PRAYER

Lord, to those who have hunger,
give bread;
and to those who have bread,
give hunger for justice.

OUR FATHER...

WEEK II
SATURDAY MORNING

+ *God, come to my assistance;* Psalm 70:2
Lord, make haste to help me!

Glory...

ORDINARY TIME & CHRISTMAS

Refrain

On\ this day, O beau-ti-ful Mo-ther,
On\ this day we give you our love.
Near you, Ma-don-na, fond-ly we hov-er,
Trust-ing your gen-tle care/ to prove.

Verse 1 **O**n this day we ask to share,
Dear-est Mo-ther, your sweet care;
Help us 'lest our feet\ a-stray\,
Wand-'ring from your guid-ing way.

Refrain

Verse 2 **Q**ueen of an-gels, deign to hear
Lisp-ing chil-dren's hum-ble pray'r;
Young hearts gain, O Vir\-gin pure\
Sweet-ly to your-self al-lure.

Refrain

139, Text: Louis Lambillotte, SJ, 1796-1855, altered
Music: 77 77, BEAUTIFUL MOTHER,
Rohr's *Favorite Catholic Melodies*, 1857

ADVENT

Ho-ly\ Ma-ry/, grace-ful Mo-ther,
Hear your\ sons and/ daugh-ters say,
Mo-ther\, Bless-ed/ a-mong wo-men,
for your\ sons and/ daugh-ters, pray.
May the\ grace of Christ our\ Sa-vior
And the\ Fa-ther's bound-less\ love
With the\ Ho-ly/ Spir-it's fa-vor
Rest up\-on us/ from a-bove.

Thus may\ we a/-bide in u-nion
With each\ oth-er/ and the Lord,
And pos\-sess, in/ sweet com-mu-nion,
Joys which\ earth can/-not af-ford.
May the\ grace of Christ our\ Sa-vior
And the\ Fa-ther's bound-less\ love
With the\ Ho-ly/ Spir-it's fa-vor
Rest up\-on us/ from a-bove.

136, Text: Verse 1a by Stephen J. Wolf, 2018;
Verses 1b & 2 by John Newton, *Olney Hymns,* 1779
Music: 87 87 D, PLEADING SAVIOR,
Joshua Leavitt, Christian Lyre, 1830
Popular melody for: *Sing of Mary, Pure and Lowly*

122, Text: Stan. 1,2, Foundling Hospital Collection, 1801;
Stan. 3, Edward Osler, 1836, altered
Music: 87 87 D, PLEADING SAVIOR,
Joshua Leavitt, Christian Lyre, 1830
Popular melody for: *Sing of Mary, Pure and Lowly*

LENT

Praise the\ Lord, you/ heav'ns, a-dore\;
Praise you\ an-gels/ in the height;
Sun and\ Moon, re/-joice be-fore\;
Shine your\ praise, you/ stars of light.
Give praise\, for the Lord has\ spo-ken;
Might-y\ voice the worlds o\-beyed;
Laws which\ nev-er/ shall be bro-ken,
Guid-ance\ that the/ Lord has made.

Praise the\ Lord, the/ Lord is glo-rious,
Prom-is\-es that/ do not fail;
God has\ made the/ saints vic-tor-ious,
Sin and\ death shall/ not pre-vail.
Praise the\ God of our sal\-va-tion;
Hosts on\ high the pow'r pro\-claim;
Heav-en and earth and/ all cre-a-tion,
Praise and\ mag-ni/-fy the name.

Wor-ship\, hon-or/, glo-ry, bles-sing,
Lord, we\ off-er/ un-to thee;
Young and\ old, your/ praise ex-pres-sing,
In glad\ hom-age/ bend the knee.
All the\ saints in heav-en a-dore you,
We would\ bow be-fore your\ throne;
As your\ an-gels/ serve be-fore you,
So on\ earth your/ will be done.

EASTER

Lord God/, Sab-a-oth, El, A-do-nai,
Proph-et E-ze-kiel's song we lift high:
Spir-it and heart\, re-newed you pro-vide,
You are our God.

Refrain ***You* are our God\,**
your peo-ple are we, Al-le-lu-ia!

Take us out-side of our pride that div-ides,
Gath-er us in from all na\-tions wide,
Bring us back in-to your land at your side,
You are our God. *Refrain*

Sprink-le on-to us your wa\-ters clean,
From our im-pur-i-ties help us to wean,
Clean from i-dol-a-try let us be seen,
You are our God. *Refrain*

Take from our flesh\ these hearts\ of stone,
Make in us new hearts of flesh, not of bone,
In-side our be-ing your Spir-it be shown,
You are our God. *Refrain*

Praise to you Fa-ther, and praise to you Son,
Praise to you Spir-it, three prais-es in One.
Jus-tice and Mer-cy un-til days are done,
You are our God. *Refrain*

142, Text: Ezekiel 36:24-28, Stephen J. Wolf, 2016
Music: 888, O FILII ET FILIAE; Chant Mode II,
Airs sur les hymnes sacrez, odes et noels, 1623
Popular melody for: *Ye Sons And Daughters*

(Lent & Easter)

PSALM 78

Antiphon *The bread of God*
comes down from heaven
and gives life to the world. Jn 6:33

Give ear, **my people**, to my teaching.
Turn your ear to words of my mouth.
I will open my mouth in a parable;
I will utter things hidden from of old.

Our ancestors told us things we heard and know;
these we will not hide from their descendants
but tell to the next generation
the power and deeds of Adonai worthy of praise.

Statutes decreed for Jacob and laws for Israel
command our ancestors to teach their children
so the next generation will come to know;
children born will grow to tell their children.

In God will they put their trust, remembering
the deeds of El and keeping God's commands,
unlike the stubborn generation of their ancestors,
a generation of divided hearts and rebellion
and in spirit unfaithful to God.

Children of Ephraim, armed to shoot the bow,
retreated on the day of battle,
refusing to keep and live by God's covenant.

PSALM 78, continued

They forgot the deeds of wonder done
shown in the sight of their ancestors,
miracles in the land of Egypt, the plain of Zoan,

dividing the sea and leading them through it,
making the waters stand like a wall,
guiding them with a cloud by day
and all the night by light of fire,

splitting the rock in the desert,
giving water as abundant as the deep sea,
bringing streams from the rocky crag,
and making waters flow down like rivers.

But they kept on with the sin
rebellious in the desert against Sabaoth.
They tested God by their will
demanding the food of their craving.

Against God they questioned,
"can a table be spread in the desert by God,
whom yes we saw strike a rock
from where waters gushed and streams flowed,
and too for the people of God give meat?"

Adonai heard and was then angry
for they did not believe in God
nor trust in the deliverance.

And yet God did command the skies above
and opened doors of the heavens
and rained down for them manna to eat.

The humans ate the bread of angels in abundance.
And God set the east wind free from the heavens
and led by power the south wind
and rained down meat on them like dust.

Birds of flight like sand on the seashore
fell around their tents in the middle of their camp
and they ate to more than enough,
being given all of their cravings.

They did not turn from their cravings
and while their food was still in their mouths
the anger of God rose to slay their sturdy
and cut down the strong young of Israel.

Still with all this they sinned
and did not believe in the deeds of wonder done.
So their days vanished in futility
and their years in sudden death.

When God slew them they would repent
and seek and be eager for God
and remember that God is their Rock
and God Sabaoth their Redeemer.

They would flatter with their mouths
and lie to God with their tongues;
their hearts were divided
and they were unfaithful to the covenant.

PSALM 78, continued

But God was merciful and forgiving
and did not wipe them out,
refraining from wrath and restraining anger,
remembering that they were but flesh,
a passing breath that does not return.

How often they rebelled in the desert,
giving God grief in the wasteland.
Again and again they tested God,
vexing the Holy One of Israel.

They did not remember the power of God
nor the day of their redemption from adversity,
God's miracle signs in Egypt
and wonders in the plain of Zoan.

God turned those rivers to blood
and their streams were undrinkable.
Swarms of insects were sent and devoured,
and frogs for devastation.

Their crops were given to the grasshopper
and their produce to the locust.
With hail their vines were destroyed
and their sycamore figs with sleet.

Their cattle were given over to the hail
and their livestock to the lightning bolts.

God unleashed blazing anger against them,
wrath and indignation and hostility,
a band of angel destruction.

They were not spared from death
and the animals were given over to the plague.
All the firstborn of Egypt were struck,
the strong young firstfruits in the tents of Ham.

But the people of God were brought out as a flock
and led like sheep through the desert
guided in safety to be not afraid
while the sea engulfed enmity.

Thus were they brought to the holy land,
the mountain won by the right hand of God
who drove out nations from before them
and allotted from their lands an inheritance
and settled in their tents the tribes of Israel.

But they tested and rebelled against God Sabaoth
whose statutes they did not keep.
They were divided and faithless like the ancestors
and as unreliable as a bent bow.

With their high-place shrines they angered God
who was jealous because of their idols,
who heard them and became angry
and rejected Israel completely
and abandoned the shrine at Shiloh,
the very tent God set up among humans.

God gave the ark into captivity,
the glorious ark into the hands of enmity,
and the people to the sword.

PSALM 78, continued

Their young people were consumed in fire
and heard no wedding songs;
their priests fell by the sword
and their widows could not weep.

Then the Lord woke up as from sleep
as a big strong human in a stupor from wine,
and beat back enmity to everlasting shame.

The Lord rejected the tent of Joseph
and chose not the tribe of Ephraim
but chose the tribe of Judah,
loving the Mount of Zion.

The Lord built the shrine like the heights
and like the earth established her to forever
and chose the servant David
and took him from the sheepfolds,

and brought him instead to shepherd the people,
Jacob called Israel, the heritage.
He tended them with integrity of heart
and with skillful hands he led them.

Glory…

Antiphon *The bread of God*
comes down from heaven
and gives life to the world. Jn 6:33

(Lent & Easter continue on page 741.)

(Ordinary Time & Advent & Christmas)

PSALM 106:1-16,19-48

Antiphon *Whose sins you forgive, they are forgiven;*
whose sins you hold, they are held. Jn 20:23

Advent & Christmas The Lord remembered
the covenant for them
and relented, alleluia.

Hallelujah!
Give thanks to Adonai who is good,
whose love is to forever.

Who can proclaim the mighty acts of Adonai?
Who can tell the fullness of praise?
Blessed are they who maintain justice,
doing just deeds at all times.

Remember me, Adonai, as you favor your people!
In your salvation, come with your aid for me
to enjoy the prosperity of your chosen ones,
to have joy in the joy of your nation,
and to give praise with your inheritance.

We have sinned as did our ancestors;
we have done wrong with bad deeds.
Our ancestors when in Egypt
gave no thought to your miracle deeds,
did not remember your many kindnesses,
and rebelled by *Yam Suf,* the Sea of Reeds.

Psalm 106, continued

Still you saved them for the sake of your name,
to make known your power.
You rebuked the Sea of Reeds; it dried up.
You led them through the depths as the desert.

And you saved them from the hands of hostility
and redeemed them from the power of enmity.

The waters covered the adversity;
not one of them survived.
Then they believed in the promises made,
and sang out praise.

But soon did they forget those deeds
and would not wait for good counsel.
They craved cravings in the desert
and in the wasteland they tested their El,
who gave them their request
but sent a wasting disease on their life.

They envied Moses in the camp
and Aaron, the consecrated of Adonai…
They made a calf at Horeb
and gave their worship to a cast idol.
They exchanged their Glory
for an image of a grass-eating bull.

They forgot El who had saved them,
doing great things in Egypt,
miracle deeds in the land of Ham
and awesome deeds by the Sea of Reeds.

By a word spoken they were to be destroyed,
except that Moses the chosen stood in the breach.
Then they despised the beautiful land
and did not believe the promise made.

They grumbled in their tents
and did not obey the voice of Adonai,
who lifted a hand to let them fall in the desert
and their descendants fall among the nations;
they were scattered through the lands.

They yoked themselves to Baal of Peor
and they ate of sacrifices to lifeless ones.
They provoked anger by their deeds
and a plague broke out among them.

Phinehas stood up and intervened
and the plague was checked;
this was credited to him as a just and good deed
for generation and generations to forever.

They angered by the waters of Meribah,
the cause of trouble for Moses,
who spoke rashly with his lips
when they made his spirit bitter.

They did not defeat the peoples as commanded,
but mingled with the nations
and adopted their customs.
They worshiped their idols
which became to them as a snare.

Psalm 106, continued

They sacrificed their sons and daughters.
They shed the innocent blood
of their own sons and daughters
whom they sacrificed to idols of Canaan,
desecrating the land by this blood.

They defiled themselves by their deeds
and prostituted themselves in their doings.
Against the people grew the anger of Adonai,
abhorring the promised inheritance.

Into the hands of nations they were given,
ruled by adversity, oppressed by enmity,
and made subject to their power.
Many times were they delivered,
but they rebelled in their decisions
and wasted away in their guilt.

And yet on hearing their cry
the Lord took note of their distress
and remembered for them the covenant
and relented in abundant love
bringing to them compassion
from even their captors.

Save us, Adonai our God!
Gather us from the nations
to give thanks to your holy name
and glory in your praise.

Blessed be Adonai, God of Israel
from everlasting to everlasting
and let all the people say, "Amen!"
Hallelujah!

Glory...

Antiphon *Whose sins you forgive, they are forgiven;*
whose sins you hold, they are held. Jn 20:23

Advent & Christmas The Lord remembered
the covenant for them
and relented,
alleluia.

PSALM 50

Antiphon *I desire mercy and not sacrifice,*
knowledge of God
rather than burnt offerings. Mt 9:13a; 12:7; Hosea 6:6

Christmas & Easter Our God will be shown
and not in silence,
alleluia.

El Elohim Adonai
speaks and summons earth
from the rising of the sun to its setting.
From Zion, perfect of beauty, God shines forth.

Our God comes and will not be silent,
before whom a fire devours,
around whom a storm is fierce.
The heavens at above are summoned,
and the earth to judge the people:

"Gather the ones faithful to me,
the ones making my covenant by sacrifice."
The heavens proclaim the justice of God,
the One who is judge.

"Hear, my people, and I will speak, Israel,
and I will testify against you;
God, your God, am I.

Not for your sacrifices do I rebuke you,
or your burnt offerings ever before me.
I do not need a bull from your stall
or goats from your pen,

for every animal of the forest is mine,
cattle on the mountains, the thousands.
I know every bird in the air,
and every creature of fields is mine.

Were I hungry, I would not tell it to you,
for the world is mine and all in her.
Do I eat the flesh of bulls?
Drink the blood of goats?

Offer thanksgiving as your sacrifice to God!
And fulfill your vows to the Most High!
Call upon me in the day of trouble;
I will deliver you and you will honor me."

But God says to those who do the bad,
"What to you to recite my laws
or to take my covenant on your lips?
You hate instruction,
and cast my words behind you.

When you see a thief, you join in,
and cast your lot with doers of adultery.
You use your mouth for the bad
and harness your tongue to deceit.

You sit and speak against your brother and sister
and slander your mother's children.
You did these, and I kept silent;
you thought me to be like you?

...Consider now this: ...there is no one to rescue
...those who insist on forgetting God.
One offering thanksgiving offered as a sacrifice,
I will show that one to the salvation of God."

Glory...

Antiphon *I desire mercy and not sacrifice,*
knowledge of God rather than burnt offerings.
Mt 9:13a; 12:7; Hosea 6:6

Christmas & Easter Our God will be shown
and not in silence, alleluia.

PSALM 92:1-9,11,13-16

Antiphon *The reign of God is as when*
a human might throw seed on the earth
and sleep and rise night and day
and the seed sprouts and grows
without the human knowing how. Mk 4:26,27

Advent & Lent
It is good to proclaim
your love in the morning
and your fidelity at night.

Dec. 17-23
Bethlehem in Judah's land,
how glorious your future!
The ruler who will rule my people
comes from you.

Christmas & Easter
You fill me with gladness, O Lord,
alleluia.

It is good to praise Adonai,
to make music to your name, Most High,
to proclaim your love in the morning
and your fidelity at night
on the ten-string and on the lyre,
and the melody of the harp.

For you make me glad by your deeds, Adonai;
at the works of your hands I sing for joy.
How great are your works, Adonai;
very profound are your thoughts.
The senseless human does not know
and the fool does not understand.

Though the bad springs up like grass
and doers of the bad seem to flourish,
their ways will be destroyed to forever.
But you, Adonai, are on high to forever…

You gave me strength like a wild ox
and I was anointed with fresh oil…
The just will flourish like the palm tree,
and grow like a cedar of Lebanon.

Planted in the house of Adonai,
in the courts of our God they will flourish.
In old age they will still bear fruit,
ever full of sap and still green,
to proclaim, "Adonai is just,
in my Rock there is no wrong."

Glory…

Antiphon

The psalms …express accurately the pain and hope,
the unhappiness and trust, of people of every age and country…
See *Introduction to the Liturgy of the Hours*, 107

DEUTERONOMY 32:1-12

Antiphon *Praise the greatness of our God.*

Christmas & Easter It is I who allow death
and I who give life;
I allow injury
and I bring healing,
alleluia.

Listen, heavens, and I will speak:
Hear, earth, the words of my mouth.
Let my teaching fall like the rain,
let my word descend like the dew,
like showers on grass,
like abundant rains on plants.

The name of Adonai I will proclaim,
and praise the greatness of our God.
The work of the Rock is perfect indeed;
all the ways of our faithful God are just
and without wrong, upright and just.

The children acted corruptly with no shame,
a generation warped and crooked.
Foolish and unwise people,
you repay Adonai in this way?
Did not your Father create you
and make you and form you?

Remember the days of old!
Consider the years of generation and generation!
Ask your parents and they will tell you!
Ask your elders and they will explain to you

how the Most High gave inheritance to nations,
dividing sons and daughters of humanity
and setting up boundaries of peoples
by numbers of sons and daughters of Israel.

For the portion of Adonai is the people,
Jacob the allotment of inheritance,
found in desert land,
a barren and howling waste,
shielded with care,
guarded as the apple of the eye,

like an eagle stirring up the nest
and hovering over the young ones,
spreading wings to catch them
and carrying them on its flight feathers.

Led by Adonai alone,
no foreign "god" was with them.

Glory...

Antiphon

All repressed emotions are stored in the
body... The deep rest of contemplative prayer reduces
the defenses that hold these oppressive feelings in the unconscious.

See *Divine Therapy & Addiction* by Thomas Keating, Trappist monk

EZEKIEL 36:24-28

Antiphon *Let any who thirst*
come to me and drink. Jn 7:37

Advent & Lent: I will give you a new heart
and put inside you a new spirit.

Christmas & Easter: I will pour onto you clean water,
alleluia.

I will take you out of the nations
and I will gather you from all the countries,
and I will bring you back into your land.

I will sprinkle on you clean waters,
and you will be clean from all your impurities,
and from all your idols I will cleanse you.

I will give you a new heart
and I will put inside you a new spirit,
and I will remove the stone-heart from your flesh
and I will give you a flesh-heart,

and I will put inside you my Spirit
and I will move you to follow in my decrees
and my laws you will be careful to keep,

and you will live in the land I gave your ancestors,
and you will be my people
and I will be your God.

Glory... Antiphon

PSALM 8

Antiphon *I have much more to tell you,*
but you cannot bear it yet. Jn 16:12

Advent & Lent From lips of children and infants
your glory is set above the heavens!

Adonai, our Lord!
How majestic is your name in all the earth!

Your glory is set above the heavens!
From lips of children and infants
you ordained strength to bring to silence
enmity, adversity and vengeance.

When I consider your heavens,
the works of your fingers,
the moon and stars which you set in place,
what is a human that you would be mindful,
a child of Adam and Eve that you would care?

And you made us little lower than a "god"
crowning us with glory and honor,
making us to rule over works of your hands,
putting everything under our feet,

all the flocks and herds and beasts of the field,
birds of the air and fishes of the sea,
all that swims through the paths of the seas.

Adonai, our Lord!
How majestic is your name in all the earth!

Glory... Antiphon

ORDINARY TIME READING **ROMANS 12:9-21**

Let love be unassumed. Shrinking from the bad, cleave to the good. Love one another warmly in filial love, giving preference in honor of one another, unslothful in zeal, burning in spirit, serving the Lord, rejoicing in hope, enduring in affliction, steadfast in prayer, imparting to the needs of the saints, and pursuing hospitality.

Bless your persecutors; bless and do not curse them. Rejoice with those rejoicing; weep with those weeping. Be of the same mind toward one another, not attentive to the high things, but being present to the humble. Do not become wise in your own mind.

Instead of returning evil for evil, don't. Provide for good things before all people. If possible, as far as it rests on you, seek peace with all human beings.

Do not avenge yourselves, beloved, but leave room for the wrath, for it has been written, *Vengeance is mine; I will repay, says the Lord.*

But if your enemy is hungry, feed him or her; or if they are thirsty, give them drink. In doing this you will heap on their heads coals of fire. Be not conquered by the evil, but conquer the evil (*kakon*) by the good.

RESPONSORY Ps 92:4,2

Made glad, Lord, by your deeds...

...I make music to your name.

At the works of your hands I sing for joy;...

...I make music to your name.

Glory to the Father and to the Son and to the Holy Spirit:
...Made glad, Lord, by your deeds,
I make music to your name.

ADVENT READING **ISAIAH 11:1-5**

A shoot will sprout from the stump of Jesse, and a branch from the roots will bear fruit. The Spirit of Adonai she will rest on him, the Spirit of wisdom and understanding, the Spirit of counsel and power, the Spirit of knowledge and fear of Adonai, and for delight the fear of Adonai.

He will judge, not by seeing with eyes nor by hearing with ears, but he will judge the needy with integrity and decide with justice for poor ones of the earth, and strike the earth with the rod of his mouth and stop bad doings with the breath of his lips.

RESPONSORY

Your light will come, Jerusalem...
...the Lord will dawn on you in radiant beauty.
The glory of the Lord you will see within you...
...the Lord will dawn on you in radiant beauty.
Glory to the Father and to the Son and to the Holy Spirit:
...Your light will come, Jerusalem,
the Lord will dawn on you in radiant beauty.

CHRISTMAS READING **ISAIAH 9:1a,5-6**

The people walking in the dark have seen a great light... For a child is born to us, a son is given to us, and the ruling will be on his shoulders. And his name will be Wonder Counselor, God Hero, Father Everlasting, Prince of Peace.

No end to the expanse of ruling and of peace, the throne of David is established over the realm to be upheld with judgment and justice from now and to forever. The zeal of Adonai Sabaoth will do this.

RESPONSORY

The Lord has made known...
...alleluia, alleluia.
The saving power...
...alleluia, alleluia.
Glory to the Father and to the Son and to the Holy Spirit:
...The Lord has made known the saving power, alleluia.

After Epiphany

All the royal powers on earth
...will bow down in worship.
Men and women of every nation...
...will bow down in worship.
Glory to the Father and to the Son and to the Holy Spirit:
...All the royal powers on earth
will bow down in worship.

LENT READING, until Holy Week **ISAIAH 1:16-18**

Wash! Make yourselves clean! Take your bad deeds from before my eyes! Stop doing wrong! Learn to do right! Seek justice! Encourage the oppressed! Defend orphans! Plead the case for the widow!

Come! Let us come to an understanding, says Adonai. Though your sins are like the scarlets they shall be white as the snow; though they are red as the crimson they shall be like the wool.

RESPONSORY Lk 18:13

The Lord God will set me free…
…from the hunter's snare.
From all those who would trap me with lying words,
…and from the hunter's snare.
Glory to the Father and to the Son and to the Holy Spirit:
…The Lord God will set me free from the hunter's snare.

HOLY SATURDAY READING **HOSEA 6:1-6**

Come and let us return to Adonai, who let us be torn up but will heal us, who let us be injured but will bind our wounds, who will revive us after two days and restore us on the third day that we may live in the presence. So let us know, let us press on to know Adonai, who will appear coming as the sun rises, who will come to us like the winter rain, watering the earth like spring rain.

Hosea 6:1-6, continued

What can I do with you Ephraim? What can I do with you Judah? Your love indeed is like morning mist, and like the early dew that disappears. For this I cut to pieces with the prophets and have slain with words of my mouth and judgments of lightning flashes: For it is mercy that I desire and not sacrifice, knowledge of God rather than burnt offerings.

RESPONSORY

For our sake Christ was obedient,
accepting even death, death on a cross.
Therefore God raised him on high and
gave him the name above all other names.

EASTER READING **ROMANS 14:7-9**

None of us lives to the self, and no one dies for the self. While alive, we live to the Lord; if we die, we die to the Lord. And so whether we live or we die, we are of the Lord. For this Christ died and lived again, that of both the dead and of the living he might be Lord.

RESPONSORY

The Lord is risen from the tomb…
…alleluia, alleluia.
He hung upon the cross for us…
…alleluia, alleluia.
Glory to the Father and to the Son and to the Holy Spirit:
…The Lord is risen from the tomb, alleluia, alleluia.

Gospel Canticle For Morning

Antiphons

Advent Wk 2 Mt 17:9a,10-13	The Lord will set up the standard in the sight of all the nations, and gather the dispersed of Israel.
Advent Wk 4 (see pg 759)	The time has come for Mary to give birth to her firstborn Son.
Christmas (see pg 759)	This is the one of whom it has been written: Christ is born in Israel; this reign will last forever.
After Epiphany John 3:22-30	At Cana in Galilee Jesus worked the first of the signs showing his glory.
Saturday after Ash Wednesday Luke 5:27-32	Store up for yourselves treasures in heaven where neither moth nor rust can destroy.
Lent Wk 2 Lk 15:1-3,11-32	Father, I have sinned against heaven and against you; I no longer deserve to be called your son; treat me as one of your servants.
Lent Wk 4 John 7:40-53	Never has a human spoken in this way.

Holy Saturday	Save us, Savior of the world; on the cross you redeemed us by the shedding of your blood; we cry out for your help, O God.
Easter Wk 2 John 6:16-21	Peace be with you; it is I, alleluia; do not be afraid, alleluia.
Easter Wk 4 John 14:7-14	And you will do greater things than these, for I am going to the Abba, alleluia.
Easter Wk 6 John 21:20-25	Know that I am with you always, even to the end of the world, alleluia.

Ordinary
Antiphon *Lord, shine on those hidden in the shadows.*

Gospel Reading for Saturday of

Week **2**	Mark 3:20-21	**14**	Matt 10:24-33	**26**	Lk 10:17-24
4	Mark 6:30-34	**16**	Matt 13:24-30	**28**	Luke 12:8-12
6	Mark 9:2-13	**18**	Matt 17:14-20	**30**	Lk 14:1,7-11
8	Mark 11:27-33	**20**	Matt 23:1-12	**32**	Luke 18:1-8
10	Matt 5:33-37	**22**	Luke 6:1-5	**34**	Lk 21:34-36
12	Matt 8:5-17	**24**	Luke 8:4-15		

CANTICLE of ZECHARIAH (The Benedictus)
LUKE 1:68-79

+ **Blessed be** the Lord the God of Israel
who chose a people to visit with redemption,
and raised salvation in the house of David,
saving strength from God's own servant,

speaking from the age of the prophets
through the mouth of the holy prophet:
Salvation out of enmity,
even out of those who hate us,

to show our ancestors how mercy works, -
and to remember the holy promise of the Lord,
the covenant made for our ancestor Abraham,
calming our fear and making us free
to serve with holy justice before God all our days.

And you also child -
will be called a prophet of the Most High
for you will go before the Lord to prepare his way
and give to people a knowledge of salvation
known in accepting forgiveness of their sins.

From the tender mercy of our God,
the sun rising from the height will visit with light
for those who sit in the dark or shadow of death
and to guide our feet into the way of peace.

Glory...

Antiphon

PETITIONS FOR THE CONSECRATION TO GOD OF THE DAY AND ITS WORK

- For the Church and her ministry and apostolates…
- For secular authorities and all serving as stewards…
- For people who are poor or sick or in sorrow…
- For the basic needs of each human being…
- For awareness of being created in the image of God…
- For discovery and discernment of our charisms…
- For consensus on both rights and responsibilities…
- For loving respect for folks who think differently…
- For God's healing of the core wounds of enemies…
- For the world peace that only God can give…
- For elders who feel abandoned…
- For just treatment of migrant workers and refugees…
- For the starving child awakening our conscience…
- For those suffering physical and mental torture…
- For people living in subhuman conditions…
- For human beings enslaved or unjustly imprisoned…
- For workers in degrading or unsafe conditions…
- For laborers where treated as mere tools for profit…
- For rejection of judging the inner guilt of others…
- For a culture of vocations all over the world…
- For those who have asked for my prayer…
- For those for whom I have promised to pray…
- For those who weigh on my heart…

OUR FATHER...

ADDITIONAL GOSPEL READINGS

Proximate Days of Advent

December 17	Matthew 1:1-17	*O Wisdom, O holy Word*
December 18	Matthew 1:18-25	*O Lord of ancient Israel*
December 19	Luke 1:5-25	*O Flower of Jesse's stem*
December 20	Luke 1:26-38	*O Key of David*
December 21	Luke 1:39-45	*O Radiant Dawn*
December 22	Luke 1:46-56	*O King of all the nations*
December 23	Luke 1:57-66	*O Emmanuel*
December 24	Luke 1:67-79	O Come O Come, pg 388

Weekdays in the Octave of Christmas

Week I

December 26	Mon	Matthew 10:17-22	St. Stephen, Martyr
December 27	Tue	John 20:1a,2-8	St. John, Evangelist
December 28	Wed	Matthew 2:13-18	The Holy Innocents
December 29	Thu	Luke 2:22-35	St. Thomas Becket
December 30	Fri	Luke 2:36-40	6th Day, Christmas Octave
December 31	Sat	John 1:1-18	St. Sylvester

January Weekdays in Christmas Season before Epiphany

Week II

January 2	John 1:19-28	January 5	John 1:43-51
January 3	John 1:29-34	January 6	Mark 1:7-11
January 4	John 1:35-42	January 7	John 2:1-11

Solemnities in Ordinary Time

Friday after Corpus Christi **Sacred Heart of Jesus**

A Matthew 11:25-30 B John 19:31-37 C Luke 15:3-7

June 24	**Birth of John the Baptist**	Luke 1:57-66,80
June 29	**Peter and Paul, Apostles**	Matthew 16:13-19
August 15	**Assumption of Mary**	Luke 1:39-56
November 1	**All Saints**	Matthew 5:1-12a

ACKNOWLEDGEMENTS, SOURCES & CHOICES MADE in this MEDITATION RENDERING

The official translation approved by the Catholic Church for the *Liturgy of the Hours* is a beautiful translation for chanting in monasteries and seminaries. As a parish priest for twenty-two years and now in retirement, almost all of my time with the Psalter is with the church universal but alone with God, whether in my room, in a chapel, or in the woods. Praying in *Lectio Divina,* trying to listen to the Lord, I have found much prayerful fruit in several translations.

I used the regular four-week cycle of the Liturgy of the Hours for a long time before switching to a two-week cycle. After a brief experiment with "all in one week," I went back to these two weeks.

This meditation rendering follows consciously these choices:

1. For the name *YHVH,* or *Yahweh,* the Hebrew word ***Adonai*** (ah-duh-nigh') meaning *My Lord,* is used. In several places the words *El* or *Elyon* or *Elohim* are retrieved, as is *Sabaoth* instead of *Mighty* or *Hosts.*

2. Following the Christian understanding of one God in the three persons of the Trinity, masculine pronouns for God are avoided (I really don't know why women tolerate them), except when God is referred to as Father, or specific references to Jesus. I do this as an openly gay cis-gender male.

3. Except in the traditional Lord's Prayer and doxology, rather than the Greek ***Father*** (*pater*) the more intimate Aramaic ***Abba*** is used (think Dad, Daddy, Papa) as in Mark 14:36. Among my family and friends, no one addresses their Daddy as Father. See also Saint Paul's use of *Abba* in Romans 8:15 and Galatians 4:6 (see pgs 23, 140).

4. In an admittedly imperfect effort to pray the gospel as well as the psalms, the word *enemy* is most often rendered as *enmity* and *foes* as *adversity.*

5. Where people are referred to as *evil,* the emphasis is shifted to those who *do* the bad, or *ways* that are bad.

6. Since *race* is a human construct, and we are all members of the one human race, words such as *tribe* and *family* are used.

There are problems with all of these choices. Still, in my judgment, the benefits overwhelm the problems.

Any errors in this rendering are entirely my own. Let us be grateful for all those who do the real work of translating sacred scripture.

Most of the Antiphons for Ordinary Time are **Sayings of Jesus** drawn from Sunday Gospel readings: In the Sunday Lectionary, the Old Testament readings have connections with the Gospel reading, and the Responsorial Psalm is a response to the Old Testament reading. This means that on any given Sunday there is a relationship between the Gospel reading and the Psalm. The antiphons were chosen based on this relationship.

Some of the **intercessions and petitions** are drawn from *Guadium et Spes*, "Pastoral Constitution on the Church in the Modern World," Vatican II, 1965, paragraph 27.

SOURCES

The primary source for this work is the grace of three decades with the psalms, canticles and readings from many translations, including:

The Liturgy of the Hours (Four Volumes), Copyright © 1974 ICEL International Committee on English in the Liturgy, Inc.

New American Bible with Revised New Testament, (1986) ***and Revised Psalms*** (1991) Copyright © 1991, 1986, 1970 Confraternity of Christian Doctrine, Inc. Washington, D.C. All rights reserved. (*This is my favorite translation of the Psalms.*)

New American Bible Revised Edition (NABRE), Copyright © 2010, 1986 Confraternity of Christian Doctrine, Washington, D.C. All rights reserved. (*This is the current Catholic translation.*)

New Revised Standard Version Bible: Catholic Edition, Copyright © 1993 and 1989 by the Division of Christian Education of the National Council of the Churches of Christ in the U.S.A.

The New Jerusalem Bible, Copyright © 1985 by Darton, Longman & Todd, Ltd. & Doubleday, a division of Bantam Doubleday Dell Publishing Group, Inc.

The Jewish Study Bible, Copyright © 1985, 1999 by the Jewish Publication Society

Acknowledgments & Sources, continued

The Interlinear NIV Hebrew-English Old Testament, by John R. Kohlenberger III, Copyright © 1979, 1980, 1982, 1985, 1987 by the Zondervan Corporation

The NRSV-NIV Parallel New Testament in Greek and English, by Alfred Marshall, Copyright © 1990 by the Zondervan Corporation

The New Greek-English Interlinear New Testament, translators Robert K. Brown & Philip W. Comfort, Copyright © 1990 by Tyndale House Publishers

I am especially grateful for these three, and to all those who worked on the *New American Bible* Psalms of 1991.

These works were also very helpful:

The New Jerome Biblical Commentary, edited by Raymond E. Brown, S.S., Joseph A. Fitzmyer, S.J., and Roland E. Murphy, O.Carm., Copyright © 1990, 1968 by Prentice-Hall, Inc.

The following volumes from the **Anchor Bible**:

Psalms I (1-50); Psalms II (51-100); Psalms III (101-150), The Anchor Bible, Volumes 16, 17, and 17A, by Mitchell Dahood, S.J., Copyright © 1965,1966, © 1968, © 1970, Doubleday

The Wisdom of Ben Sira; The Anchor Bible, Vol. 39, by Patrick W. Skehan, Copyright © 1987, Doubleday & Company, Inc.

Tobit; The Anchor Bible, Vol. 40A, by Carey A. Moore, Copyright © 1996, Doubleday

The Wisdom of Solomon; The Anchor Bible, Vol. 43, by David Winston, Copyright © 1979, Doubleday & Company, Inc.

Daniel, Esher and Jeremiah, the Additions; The Anchor Bible, Vol.44, by Carey A. Moore, Copyright © 1977, Doubleday & Company, Inc.

The summary of ***Lectio Divina*** on page 775 comes from many guides, all of whom have my deep gratitude, expecially Rev. Paul Wachdorf of Mundelein Seminary, north of Chicago.

And a stack of dictionaries.

Stephen Joseph Wolf Nashville, Tennessee **www.idjc.org**

INDEX of PSALMS

"Sunday Vigil" is Saturday Evening Psalms 58, 83, & 109 omitted as in *Liturgy of the Hours*

PSALTER COMPARISON

PSALMS of the FOUR-WEEK PSALTER

	Office of Readings				*Morning Prayer*			
	I	II	III	IV	I	II	III	IV
SUN	1	104	145	24	63	118	93	118
	2 3			66	149	150	148	150
MON	6	31	50	73	5	42	84	90
	9A				29	19A	96	135
TUE	10	37	68	102	24	43	85	101
	12				33	65	67	144
WED	18A	39	89A	103	36	77	86	108
		52			47	97	98	146
THU	18B	44	89B	44	57	80	87	143
			90		48	81	99	147A
FRI	35	38	69	55	51	51	51	51
					100	147B	100	147B
SAT	132	136	107	50	119-19	92	119-14	92
					117	8	117	8

DAWN & DUSK WEEK ONE

	Morning Prayer	*Evening Prayer*
VIGIL		*4 61* 113 116 141 142
SUN	*1 2* 63 93 148 149	*64 91* 110 111 114
MON	*5 9* 29 84 96	*7 71* 11 15 123 124
TUE	*10 68* 24 33 67 85	*14 74* 20 21 125 131
WED	*18A 89A* 36 47 98	*17 28 70* 27 126 127
THU	*18B 89B* 48 57 87 99	*25 79* 30 32 86 132
FRI	*35 69* 51 95 100	*22 26 88* 41 46 135
SAT	*105 107* 117 119	

PSALTER COMPARISON

PSALMS of the FOUR-WEEK PSALTER

	Daytime Prayer				*Evening Prayer*				*Night*
	I	II	III	IV	I	II	III	IV	
SUN	118	23	118	23	110	110	110	110	91
		76		76	114	115	111	112	
MON	19B	119-6	119-12	119-17	11	45	123	136	86
	7	40	71	82 120	15		124		
TUE	119-1	119-7	119-13	119-18	20	49	125	137	143
	13 14	53 54	74	88	21		131	138	
WED	119-2	119-8	119-14	119-19	27	62	126	139	31
	17	55	70 75	94		67	127		130
THU	119-3	119-9	119-15	119-20	30	72	132	144	16
	25	56 57	79 80	128 129	32				
FRI	119-4	119-10	22	119-21	41	116A	135	145	88
	26 28	59 60		133 140	46	121			
SAT	119-5	119-11	119-10	119-22	119-14	113	122	141	4
	34	61 64	34	45	16	116B	130	142	134

DAWN & DUSK WEEK TWO

	Morning Prayer	*Evening Prayer*
VIGIL		*34 134* 16 119 122 130
SUN	*66 104* 118 150	*23 76* 110 112 115
MON	*31 73* 19 42 90	*12 40 82 120* 45 136
TUE	*37 102* 43 65 101	*13 53 54* 49 137 138
WED	*39 103* 77 97 108 146	*52 75 94* 62 67 139
THU	*3 6 44* 80 81 143	*56 60 128 129* 72 144
FRI	*38 55* 51 147	*59 133 140* 116 121 145
SAT	*50* 78 *106* 8 92	

CANTICLES & READINGS

OLD TESTAMENT CANTICLES

NEW TESTAMENT CANTICLES

OLD TESTAMENT READINGS

NEW TESTAMENT READINGS

NEW TESTAMENT READINGS, continued

PRAYERS

INDEX of SAYINGS & RESPONSORY VERSES

CORNER NOTES & QUOTES

IMAGES

SONGS

SONGS, continued

SONGS, continued

The number given with each song is the page number of ***Fr Steve's Three-Finger-Chord Ukulele Hymns***. www.idjc.org/ukulele. Most of the songs have been altered, and some are marked for an alternate melody. Original texts for most of these and music tunes are available on www.nethymnal.org. Most of these songs were previously published in *Hinge Hour Singer* and are thought by the publisher to be in the public domain.

Stephen Joseph Wolf is retired, a former parish priest (22 lents & holy weeks), spiritual director and retreat leader, and former certified public accountant (14 tax seasons), and before that worked as a landscaper, desk clerk, laundry worker, janitor, paper boy, and student, growing up the second of eight sons of a parish secretary and Nashville's best television repairman. He continues to write for faith-sharing groups and retreats, paint folk art icons, sing baritone for the LGBTQ+ chorus Nashville in Harmony, play the ukulele with Music for Seniors and others, volunteer as bookkeeper for two non-profits, serve on the board of PFLAG Nashville, and live in Nashville with his husband Billy.

One Chapter-A-Day, the Whole Bible takes 44 months.

One plan: Begin with the shortest Book (2nd John with 13 Verses) and read through to the longest (Isaiah with 66 chapters). Don't skip the footnotes!

PENTATEUCH

50 Genesis
40 Exodus
27 Leviticus
36 Numbers
34 Deuteronomy

HISTORICAL

24 Joshua
21 Judges
4 Ruth
31 1st Samuel
24 2nd Samuel
22 1st Kings
25 2nd Kings
29 1st Chronicles
36 2ndChronicles
10 Ezra
13 Nehemiah
14 Tobit
16 Judith
10 Esther
16 1st Maccabees
15 2nd Maccabees

WISDOM BOOKS

42 Job
41 Psalms 1-41
31 Psalms 42-72
17 Psalms 73-89
17 Psalms 90-106
44 Psalms 107-150
31 Proverbs
12 Ecclesiastes
8 Song of Songs
19 Wisdom
51 Sirach

THE PROPHETS

66 Isaiah
52 Jeremiah
5 Lamentations
6 Baruch
48 Ezekiel
14 Daniel
14 Hosea
4 Joel
9 Amos
21vs. Obadiah
4 Jonah
7 Micah
3 Nahum
3 Habakkuk
3 Zephaniah
2 Haggai
14 Zechariah
3 Malachi

THE GOSPELS

28 Matthew
16 Mark
24 Luke
21 John
28 Acts

PAULINE LETTERS

16 Romans
16 1st Corin.
13 2nd Corin.
6 Galatians
6 Ephesians
4 Philippians
4 Colossians
5 1st Thess.
3 2nd Thess.
6 1st Timothy
4 2nd Timothy
3 Titus
23vs.Philemon
13 Hebrews

CATHOLIC LETTERS

5 James
5 1st Peter
3 2nd Peter
5 1st John
13vs. 2nd John
15vs. 3rd John
25vs. Jude
22 Revelation

LECTIO DIVINA

lek'-see-oh div-ee'-nuh

1. ***Lectio*** – Read the passage of the word of God with attention, silently, aloud, or in a whisper. If drawn to a word or phrase or image, stop.

2. ***Meditatio*** – Breathe. Repeat the word or phrase or image over and over as you breathe. Let it sink into your mind, heart, soul and strength. Savor the word. Ask just one question: *Why this? What do you wish to say, Lord?*

3. ***Oratio*** – Be not afraid to enter into a spontaneous and loving dialogue with God. Talk to God as you would talk to your closest most intimate friend. Be totally honest about what you are thinking and feeling. Are any memories provoked? What do you want to say to God who loves you just the way you are? You may be drawn to praise, thanksgiving, contrition, petition, desires, decisions, resolutions, commitments, dedications… God is interested in everything you have to say and will not judge you. You get to decide whether you will integrate this Word of God into your heart, life and work, or whether you will reject it or dismiss it as of no worth or value to you.

4. ***Contemplatio*** – For the remainder of the time you have set aside, go back to the word, phrase or image. Breathe. Relax. Simply repeat the word, phrase or image over and over. When distracting thoughts or feelings enter your mind (they will), go back to your word. There is nothing to accomplish; just give this time to the God who loves you. Sitting in God's presence in this silence, you are making an act of faith that God is working in you in God's own time and way. When your time is up, offer a prayer of gratitude. Many people who do *Lectio Divina* find regular journaling helpful.

9 781937 081744

Printed by Libri Plureos GmbH in Hamburg,
Germany